The Powers of the Union

The Powers of the Union develops and tests a new theory of centralization and bureaucratization in the European Union. Using original data spanning five decades and a multi-method approach, Franchino argues that most EU laws rely extensively on national administrations for policy implementation and provide for ample national discretionary authority, while limiting tightly the involvement of the European Commission. However, when Council ministers do not share the same policy objectives, some have the incentive to limit national executive discretion and to rely more on the Commission. Majority voting facilitates this outcome, but the limited policy expertise of supranational bureaucrats and their biased views impede extensive supranational delegation. Finally, the European Parliament systematically attempts to limit national discretion, especially when its views differ from ministerial opinions, and tries to increase the Commission's policy autonomy. The book contributes to understanding political–bureaucratic relations and evaluates the implications for EU democracy and subsidiarity.

FABIO FRANCHINO is Lecturer in Political Science in the Department of Political Science at University College London and Director of the MSc in European Public Policy at the UCL School of Public Policy. He has published in the *British Journal of Political Science, European Union Politics*, the *Journal of European Public Policy*, the *Journal of Legislative Studies*, the *Journal of Theoretical Politics* and *West European Politics*.

The Powers of the Union

Delegation in the EU

Fabio Franchino

Department of Political Science
University College London

CAMBRIDGE
UNIVERSITY PRESS

JE
225
. F73
2007

CAMBRIDGE UNIVERSITY PRESS
Cambridge, New York, Melbourne, Madrid, Cape Town, Singapore, São Paulo

Cambridge University Press
The Edinburgh Building, Cambridge CB2 8RU, UK

Published in the United States of America by Cambridge University Press, New York

www.cambridge.org
Information on this title: www.cambridge.org/9780521689328

© F. Franchino 2007

First published 2007

Printed in the United Kingdom at the University Press, Cambridge

A catalog record for this publication is available from the British Library

ISBN 978-0-521-86642-2 hardback
ISBN 978-0-521-68932-8 paperback

316698976

To Eliana for making this book possible
and
to Mathias and Thomas for making it (almost) impossible

Contents

Figures

Tables

Preface

I care about the European Union (EU) and I care to understand it, possibly without too many preconceptions. The desire to comprehend, explain or, at least, minimally grasp its complexities is what motivates this work and probably also, as a European, my innate eagerness to be part of it.

Most of my adult life, first as a student and then as an academic, has been inexorably shaped by EU policies. I had the chance to study, work and travel abroad, opportunities that my parents would have not even dreamt of. As a result, my horizons broadened and my desire for critical understanding deepened.

This book is therefore the result of a long journey of research. It would have not seen the light of day without the support and encouragement of many institutions, colleagues and friends. Early on, in 1994, the Brighton Business School provided me with much needed financial backing, and its staff with much appreciated encouragement, even before I commenced my academic career. They were my springboard and I thank them dearly. The foundations of this work were laid down between 1995 and 2000 during my Ph.D. at the London School of Economics where I encountered a challenging and stimulating research environment. I am profoundly indebted to Cheryl Schonhardt-Bailey, a tough – and thus excellent – supervisor, and to Simon Hix, a friend and an inspiring colleague with contagious enthusiasm about Europe and our discipline. When I was lecturing at the LSE, Alessandro Volcic provided invaluable research assistance to my project.

Over the past few years, parts of the book have been presented at many workshops, seminars and conferences. There are too many to mention, though I would like to thank the organizers, especially Christophe Crombez (Stanford University), Daniela Giannetti (University of Bologna), Sara Hagemann and Bjørn Høyland (EURATE discussion group), Joseph Jupille (Florida International University), Hussein Kassim (London EU group and ESRC workshops), and Paolo Martelli and Francesco Zucchini (University of Milan). Participants have supplied much valued comments which have considerably improved the manuscript. I thank especially Giacomo Benedetto, Clifford Carrubba, Patrick Dunleavy, Hae-Won Jun, Mathias Koenig-Archibugi, Amie Kreppel, Jeffrey Lewis, David Marshall, Berthold Rittberger, Andreas Warntjen and, for his extraordinarily thorough analysis of Chapter 7, Marco Giuliani.

At various stages of the work, I have received informative and challenging comments from many colleagues. I am grateful to Dietmar Braun, Fabrizio Gilardi, Jonathan Golub, Daniel Kelemen, Mark Pollack, Claudio Radaelli, Mark Thatcher, Eiko Thielemann, George Tsebelis, Diego Varela and Craig Volden. Sections of the book that have been published in article format have benefited greatly from reviews and editorial comments. I thank the anonymous reviewers and the editors: Keith Dowding, Klaus Goetz, Nicholas Miller, Jeremy Richardson, Gerald Schneider and Albert Weale.

Since 2002, I have had the privilege of working at the Department of Political Science (School of Public Policy) of the University College London with colleagues whose professionalism and collegiality I admire. Their appreciation of academic work has eased the burden of the final writing stages. I would like to thank David Coen, Tony Draper and Wolf Hassdorf for advice on parts of the manuscript. I am especially grateful to Jennifer Van Heerde who has read most of it and has incessantly (and, for me, frustratingly) demanded amelioration. This book would have not been as good without her remarks. I also would like to thank the people whose behind-the-scenes work makes our life much easier and our job possible but which is, unjustly, rarely acknowledged. Hence my gratitude goes to the administrative staff of the department: Sally Welham, Michelle Bishop and Helen Holt.

Finally, I am grateful to John Haslam, the political science editor of Cambridge University Press, who has guided me through the process of publishing my first book with great professionalism. I was impressed by the rigorousness and punctiliousness of the two reviewers of the manuscript. Their comments have radically improved my work.

I am writing these last few comments peering through my office window that overlooks Tavistock Square. It is hard to avoid thinking of the suicide attack that took place two weeks ago on the street opposite the department. This message of death, hatred and intolerance is at the opposite pole of what, if anything, the European project stands for: peace, integration and tolerance. The sadness and, perhaps, disillusionment that we feel in these circumstances should not overshadow our successes. Even in the face of setbacks, past achievements should comfort us into realizing that integration and tolerance permeate most of today's societies and, when challenged, these values have prevailed over time.

The final, and most important, acknowledgment goes to the love and support of my family. The encouragement and assistance I have received from my parents, Paolina Lazzarini and Sergio Franchino, are of inestimable proportions. My sons, Mathias and Thomas, have made the journey full of joy and laughter, while my wife, Eliana Colla, deserves an equal share of any credit that this work may receive, for her strength, tenacity and tolerance of the idiosyncrasies of academic life. I dedicate this book to them.

London, July 2005

1 Introduction

"The European Union: centralised, bureaucratic, unaccountable and corrupt, eroding our independence and dictating policies that we would never vote for in an election."[1] The charge is serious and the response is too frequently a laconic nod of compassionate understanding. Some academics share these concerns. According to Alesina and Wacziarg (1999), Europe has gone too far beyond an optimal degree of centralization on most issues. Its policy makers, regardless as to whether they are ministers, parliamentarians or commissioners, have a strong vested interest in this outcome (see Vaubel, 1994). For Siedentop (2000: 216–7), "the élites of Europe have fallen victims to the tyranny of economic language at the expense of political values such as the dispersal of power and democratic accountability." European liberal democracy has become hostage to economic thinking and, since the mid 1980s, Europe has been inexorably propelled towards a model of unitary state with concentrated power and authority, betraying the intrinsic values of federalism and precipitating a crisis of democracy. While, curiously, for Gillingham (2003), the ill-fated, and failed, centralizing campaigns of the abhorred European bureaucrats, and their national supporters, are instead the product of a deep misunderstanding, and mistrust, of the market mechanism.

Some of these works are speculative, broad-brush analyses that fall well short of systematic empirical investigation. Others are comprehensive, but essentially atheoretical and, therefore, nonanalytical, fact-listing stories. None is value neutral, or attempts to separate, at least somewhat, the positive from the normative.

This book investigates the central tenets of these arguments by explaining the distribution of powers to implement the policies of the European Union (EU)[2] across supranational institutions and levels of governance.

---

[1] Extract from the June 2001 General Election manifesto of the UK Independence Party.
[2] Although this study is centered on the European Community pillar of the Treaty on European Union, I will use the terms European Union and EU throughout the whole book.

It analyzes why, and the extent to which, EU law constrains national governments and administrations. Why do our political leaders delegate powers to, presumably unaccountable, supranational bureaucrats? Why do they decide to adopt EU laws that limit their own policy autonomy and room for maneuver? What are the underlying trade-offs that our politicians face when they choose to shift powers to the supranational level and to constrain their own national authorities?

We need to answer these questions if we want to understand much of what the EU is today, how it operates and "who does what and why." And we need to concentrate our analysis on how EU law is designed because it is via this legislation that national governments establish policy criteria and impose limits on each other and on their own national bureaucracies. It is via these measures that EU legislators confer powers upon supranational institutions and set the conditions under which those powers must be exercised.

More broadly, these issues go to the core of the study of legislative–bureaucratic relations in modern democracies. Indeed, they are linked to important normative considerations about the quality of European democracy at both national and EU level. As the argument for representative democracy goes, periodic and competitive elections give citizens the opportunity to depose politicians who have not delivered on their policy commitments. When in office, policy makers therefore have the incentives to make good on their electoral pledges, carry through their policy proposals and ensure that bureaucrats comply with their policy prescriptions.

Member states are still the predominant sources of democratic legitimacy in the EU, and we should recognize that the EU political system severs this national chain of accountability because a change in a single government is rarely a sufficient condition for the reform of EU policies. Any new government is constrained in implementing its agenda, because some policy options may be proscribed under EU law and some policy tools may be delegated to supranational institutions. But excessive delegation to supranational bureaucrats could be troublesome even from the perspective of EU-level democracy since the actions of these officials is notoriously hard to sanction by EU legislators. These issues raise normative questions: is the EU too centralized? Are EU laws and policies overly prescriptive and bureaucratic? Although we cannot provide value-free answers, we can assess the extent of centralization and bureaucratization in the EU and unveil the imperatives and trade-off facing our politicians when taking these decisions.

This book provides the first systematic application of the theory of delegation to the day-to-day operation of a supranational political system and frames this contribution within the comparative literature on delegation. It explicitly models the choice between a national and a supranational path of policy implementation – a choice between administrators and levels of governance – that EU legislators have to confront on a routine basis. It unveils how key factors, such as bargaining conflict and decision rules, shape this choice. In doing so, the book provides a more complete understanding of the patterns of delegation in the EU and their interaction with variables such as conflict among member states and legislative procedures. It also challenges and qualifies some of the expectations about the causes and consequences of bureaucratic autonomy in democratic systems.

Centralization and bureaucratization

This study explains centralization and bureaucratization in the EU. Centralization refers to the administration of a policy by a central authority. For my purposes, it implies extensive reliance for policy implementation on the European Commission, the EU supranational executive and bureaucracy.[3] In popular parlance, the adjective "bureaucratic" has the negative connotation of overly detailed, constraining or prescriptive. The choice of the administrator that will be in charge of implementation and the degree of prescription guiding policy execution are decisions that are taken frequently by politicians of representative democracies and are openly stipulated in legislative statutes. Consider the following provisions extracted from EU laws.

Where a worker has been subject to the legislation of a Member State and where he satisfies its conditions for entitlement to benefits [. . .] the competent institution of that Member State shall [. . .] determine the amount of benefit corresponding to the total length of the insurance periods to be taken into account in pursuance of such legislation.[4]

A Member State shall approve all vehicle types which satisfy the following conditions: (a) the vehicle type must conform to the particulars in the information document; (b) the vehicle type must satisfy the checks listed in the model, referred to in Article 2 (b), of the type approval certificate.[5]

Where short-term capital movements of exceptional magnitude impose severe strains on foreign-exchange markets and lead to serious disturbances in the conduct of a Member State's monetary and exchange rate policies [. . .] the Commission may, after consulting the Monetary Committee and the Committee

---

[3] In the EU context, centralization may also mean the shift of law-making powers from national legislatures and governments to the Council of Ministers and the European Parliament, but this book studies only the centralization of executive powers.
[4] Article 46.1 of Regulation 1408/71 on the application of social security schemes to employed persons and their families.
[5] Article 4.1 of Directive 70/156/EEC on the approximation of the laws relating to the type-approval of motor vehicles.

of Governors of the Central Banks, authorize that Member State to take [. . .] protective measures the conditions and details of which the Commission shall determine.[6]

Where preliminary examination of the matter shows that there is dumping and there is sufficient evidence of injury and the interests of the Community call for immediate intervention, the Commission, acting at the request of a Member State or on its own initiative, shall: having due regard to the provisions of Article 19(3), fix an amount to be secured by way of provisional anti-dumping duty.[7]

The first two provisions specify that the award of social security benefits and the approval of vehicle types are measures to be taken by national authorities. They also stipulate the conditions which national administrations should abide by. The third provision indicates that member states can suspend the free movement of capital, but only upon approval and under the conditions set by the Commission. The last provision confers upon the Commission the power to set anti-dumping duties and the principles that it should follow. These clauses illustrate increasing degrees of centralization of power and different levels of prescription in the exercise of those powers. This study introduces and tests a theory that explains the relative reliance on national administrations and on the Commission (centralization) and the degree of formal autonomy, discretion or room for maneuver (one could say bureaucratization), that these actors enjoy in the implementation of EU policies.

The argument of this study

This study argues that the choices of delegation and the degree of discretion that EU legislators confer upon administrators in secondary legislation are affected by: the availability and characteristics of two types of administrators (the Commission and national administrations), the decision rules, the complexity of the policy, the severity of conflict between the Commission and the Council, and between the Commission and Parliament, the bargaining environment (or conflict) within the Council and between the Council and Parliament, and the availability of nonstatutory control mechanisms.

I show that ministers of the Council have a strong bias in favor of national implementation, ample discretion, and limited or no involvement of the Commission. They prefer to be in control of implementation, at least within their own country, and to rely on the extensive expertise that

---

[6] Article 3.1 of Directive 88/361/EEC for the implementation of Article 67 of the Treaty.
[7] Article 15.1(a) of Regulation 459/68 on protection against dumping or the granting of bounties or subsidies.

resides in national bureaucracies. These administrations play the predominant part in EU policy implementation. However, conflict within the Council is likely to generate concerns about the correct national implementation of the relevant measures and some ministers will prefer more detailed laws, limiting national room for maneuver, and greater reliance on the Commission. Qualified majority voting in the Council facilitates these outcomes because these objectives are likely to be shared by the Commission, which proposes new laws, and by the pivotal member state in the Council, whose support is necessary to adopt a proposal. Additionally, in majority voting, more constrained national implementation and greater delegation to the Commission occur as conflict in the Council intensifies because greater divergence increases the cost of national relative to supranational implementation for the decisive member states of the Council.

Two factors operate against excessive reliance on the Commission, however. Conflict between this institution and the Council is likely to narrow the executive discretion of the supranational bureaucracy. Additionally, highly complex policy measures require technical expertise that is more easily available in national bureaucracies than in the Commission. This institution is likely to be used only for measures requiring generalist and managerial skills at the supranational level.

Two important changes occur when the Parliament is involved in the adoption of a measure (in the codecision procedure). In the case of national implementation, members of the Parliament are likely to prefer lower national executive discretion because they face higher costs of ongoing control than Council ministers. This situation is heightened when the Council and the Parliament do not share similar views. In the case of Commission implementation, the Parliament would prefer greater discretionary authority of this institution than the Council, to the extent that the Parliament and the Commission have more similar preferences.

In the next two sections, I review the growing comparative and EU literature that studies processes of delegation, highlighting gaps and biases. I provide only a concise overview of the state of the discipline. Where necessary, works will be analyzed in greater depth in the substantive chapters. I conclude outlining of the structure of the book.

The study of delegation: distant origins and the modern agenda

In a stimulating review, Huber and Shipan (2002) illustrate how issues of centralization and bureaucratization were the concern of illustrious scholars. They trace the uneasiness about these processes, which the

UK Independence Party so clearly and powerfully articulates, back to Montesquieu's *The Spirit of the Laws* and Tocqueville's *Democracy in America*.

Indeed, most of the classical thinkers had a problem with despotism but, perhaps surprisingly, these worries were also aired in the most unlikely quarters. In *The Prince*, Machiavelli exhorts the aspiring leader to base his power on the people rather than on the elite (*grandi*).[8] In the *Discourses*, he investigates, sometimes freely interprets but clearly admires, the popular mechanisms used in the Roman republic for controlling elites, such as elite selection, public accusations and popular appeals.[9] The centerpiece to his analysis is how the republic managed to distribute power between the people and elites to ensure control and accountability (but not complete subjugation) of the latter. These concerns arise from Machiavelli's deep distrust of elites, because of their appetite for domination, power and aggrandizement, and his appreciation for the people whose only desire is to avoid oppression.

If we take a modern read of elites as entrenched bureaucrats and government officials, we realize how strikingly familiar these themes are. Euroskepticism originates from strong resentment and misgivings about the motivations and objectives of European elites. It advocates greater control over the bureaucratic excesses and centralizing tendencies of the (EU) government and more freedom for its citizens. This thread emerges in many writings of successive political thinkers, but the modern agenda of bureaucratic–political relations is clearly set by Weber. In his essay on *Bureaucracy*, Weber recognizes both the tension between an expert bureaucracy and a politician who lacks in-depth understanding of the administration and the immense opportunities that control of the machinery of government generates for political leaders. The contemporary literature hence predominantly concentrates on the rationales for relying on the bureaucracy, the risks that this delegation entails and the mechanisms of control used by politicians to ensure that bureaucrats implement policies faithfully and correctly.[10] Since Huber and Shipan

---

[8] "Therefore, one who becomes a prince through the favor of the people ought to keep them friendly, and this he can easily do seeing they only ask not to be oppressed by him. But one who, in opposition to the people, becomes a prince by the favor of the nobles (*grandi*), ought, above everything, to seek to win the people over to himself, and this he may easily do if he takes them under his protection." Chapter IX.5 On Civil Principality.

[9] See the acute analyses of Skinner (1981, 1993) and McCormick (2001).

[10] Similar problems of delegation, asymmetric information, incentive compatibility and control have been intensively investigated in relation to many economic activities. Analyses date back to illustrious scholars such as Adam Smith and Chester Barnard, see Laffont and Martimort (2002: 7–27) for a recent excursus into the study of incentives in economic thought (see also Laffont, 2003).

(2002) have written the most comprehensive review to date, hereafter I will follow their analysis. To avoid unnecessary repetition, I will summarize this scholarship and highlight gaps and biases.

A common concern of the early literature was the dominance of bureaucrats and the administrative state in policy making. Complex, modern societies were seen to be generating increasing demand for governmental services and the administrative state emerged from the need to rely on the technical expertise of public administrators, to reduce workload and to enhance efficient decision-making (e.g. Crozier, Huntington and Watanuk, 1975; King, 1975; Putman, 1975). Related studies have emphasized alternative strategic reasons for delegation. The work of Fiorina (1977, 1982), for instance, represents a break from the earlier literature. In his view, the US Congress delegates to the executive in order to shift blame for unpopular policies and to reap the credit for making things right when problems arise. Contemporaneously, Kydland and Prescott (1977) have published a highly influential work that shows how electoral imperatives could prejudice a politician's commitment to some policy objectives. One implication is that the delegation of powers to an independent bureaucracy secures credibility to such a commitment.

Scholars have disagreed about the consequences of the administrative state. Some, especially students working in the fields of public policy, administration and management, have emphasized its benign implications. Extensive reliance on a "neutral" bureaucracy was seen as an efficient method to achieve the best outcomes with minimal mistakes (e.g. Kaufman, 1956; LaPalombara, 1958; Heclo, 1974; Mashaw, 1985). Others were far more critical. They expressed concern about the lack of accountability and the elitist and conservative bias of the public administration (e.g. Strauss, 1961; Offe, 1972; Wright, 1978; Hall, 1983). Along similar lines, later scholars assume that bureaucrats have specific policy, budgetary or work-related preferences which may not coincide with those of politicians (Niskanen, 1971; Dunleavy, 1985; Bendor, Taylor and Van Gaalen, 1987; Horn, 1995). This dissonance is the key source of bureaucratic drift, a mismatch between politicians' intent and policy outcomes that is biased toward bureaucratic objectives.

However, the all-encompassing view of an administrative state has been challenged on both methodological and empirical grounds. In a groundbreaking article, Weingast and Moran (1983) assert that the key empirical observation used to support the bureaucratic dominance view, the lack of oversight activities, is also equivalent to a view of political dominance whereby bureaucrats are perfect agents of their political superiors. This crucial remark has led to a series of studies that has tried to establish the extent to which policy outputs and bureaucratic actions reflect politicians' objectives. Most of them have found a degree of responsiveness both in presidential (e.g. Weingast and Moran, 1983; Moe, 1985; Wood, 1988; Wood and Waterman, 1991; Shipan, 2004) and in parliamentary systems (e.g. Budge, Hofferbert and Klingemann, 1994; Bawn, 1999; Tsebelis, 1999; Swank, 2003).

The end result is a more refined understanding of politico-bureaucratic relations. The all-or-nothing view that underpinned the debate on bureaucratic dominance has been gradually replaced by an assessment of the circumstances under which bureaucrats and politicians shape policy outcomes, the varying degrees of control that politicians exercise on bureaucratic actions, and politicians' choice of institutional mechanisms for bureaucratic control. Scholars have studied appointment and promotion power, ombudsman offices, budgetary incentives and sanctions, and departmental and jurisdictional reorganization.[11] More relevant for our purposes, the literature on American politics has recognized early on the central role that laws play in influencing bureaucratic actions. McCubbins and Schwartz (1984) argue that, instead of centralized, direct, resource-intensive hearings (police-patrol oversight), the US Congress can opt for decentralized, reactive and indirect forms of control of the bureaucracy (fire-alarm oversight). These are procedures inserted into statutes that facilitate control by interest groups close to Congress. In one of the most influential works on this topic, McCubbins, Noll and Weingast (1987, 1989) show how a bureaucracy, once it has been delegated powers, could exploit conflict among politicians to shift a policy closer to its position.[12] In these circumstances, *ex-post* monitoring and sanctions seldom are credible strategies to redress bureaucratic excesses. It is for these reasons that politicians are likely to resort to administrative procedures[13] which reveal politically important information prior to bureaucratic decisions, stack the deck in favor of groups benefiting from the policy and ensure durability even when the policy environment has changed. Along similar lines, Moe (1989, 1990a, 1990b) and Horn and Shepsle (1989) argue that overly cumbersome agency structures could be the result of politicians' desire to preserve policy objectives beyond their tenure in office, by making these agencies hard to reform.

These works have spurred an impressive array of sophisticated theoretical analyses followed by systematic empirical tests. With regard to theory, Tsebelis (1995, 2002: 2–5, 236) has generalized the insight of

---

[11] For an extensive review of these works see Huber and Shipan (2002: 26–38).

[12] This point was originally made, less comprehensively, by Hammond, Hill and Miller (1986).

[13] Examples of administrative procedures are public disclosure requirements, evidentiary standards and appeal procedures.

McCubbins, Noll and Weingast (see also Hammond and Knott, 1996; Steunenberg, 1996). He argues that an increase in policy stability gives more discretion to bureaucrats. In a political system, high policy stability results from the presence of many legislative veto players that have heterogeneous preferences and, if collective, are internally cohesive. More relevant for us, Epstein and O'Halloran (1994, 1999a, 1999b), have developed a model where the legislator's choice variable is agency discretion, intended as a segment of a one-dimensional policy space. They show that discretion increases with uncertainty and decreases with conflict between the legislature and the agency.[14] Volden (2002b: 124) generalizes this model and shows that conflict between an agenda-setting legislature and an executive with veto power results in greater discretion of an independent agency. Finally, Huber and Shipan (2002) develop a model that is applicable to both parliamentary and separation of powers systems. They argue that, during times of divided government, the discretion of the executive is likely to be greater if the two legislative chambers do not share the same preferences.[15] These works do not analyze how different decision rules operating within the same legislature could affect discretion. Equally, they disregard the fact that legislators may have the opportunity to rely on different agencies for policy implementation. The features of these agencies could shape the choices of delegation.

As far as empirical analysis is concerned, some tests have reported mixed results (e.g. Balla, 1998; Spence, 1999a, 1999b; Balla and Wright, 2001) but two important works stand out as the most comprehensive and systematic investigations of the theory of delegation. Epstein and

---

[14] In an earlier formal work, McCubbins (1985) covers a similar topic but his article, very advanced for his period, is not based on what later became standard modeling principles. Calvert, McCubbins and Weingast (1989) assess the conditions under which an agency enjoys discretion. Discretion, however, is not a choice variable. Banks and Weingast (1992) analyze the conditions under which agencies are likely to be created. Their model, however, assumes budget maximization as the agency's objective function. Finally, the works of Gilligan and Krehbiel (1989, 1990) on the organization of the US Congress could also be construed as models of delegation.

    The roots of these works also rest on the principal-agent model in economics, as they investigate information problems of adverse selection, moral hazard and nonverifiability. Classic economic contributions are Spence and Zeckhauser (1971), Ross (1973) and Jensen and Meckling (1976). See Laffont and Martimort (2002) for the latest treatment of the literature.

[15] In a related literature, models evaluate the effectiveness of and the circumstances under which a legislature relies on police-patrol and fire-alarm oversight (Lupia and McCubbins, 1994a, 1994b; Bawn, 1995, 1997; Epstein and O'Halloran, 1995; Hopenhayn and Lohmann, 1996; de Figueiredo, Spiller and Urbiztondo, 1999). The most recent formal works on delegation are by Huber and Lupia (2001), Huber and McCarty (2004, 2006), Bendor and Meirowitz (2004) and Epstein and O'Halloran (2006).

O'Halloran (1999b) have coded a large data set of important post-war US legislation with regard to the amount of discretion that these acts have conferred upon agencies. Discretion is measured as the share of legal provisions delegating powers, net of the procedural constraints placed on agencies. Epstein and O'Halloran demonstrate how Congress delegates more policy authority during times of unified rather than divided government and in informationally intense, or complex, issue areas. They also show, in common with Volden (2002a), that independent agencies enjoy greater discretion under divided government. In testing their comparative theory of delegation, Huber and Shipan (2002) concentrate more on policy rather than procedural details inserted into legislation as means to influence bureaucratic autonomy. They study the design of Medicaid laws in US states and of labor legislation in European parliamentary democracies.[16] In line with the existing literature, they find systematically lower discretion during divided government in separation of powers systems. Additionally, they show that, during times of divided government, the discretion of the executive is likely to be greater if there is bicameral conflict in the legislature. For parliamentary systems, Huber and Shipan illustrate how coalition and minority governments tend to adopt more constraining laws than single-party majority governments. They also reveal how discretion decreases when nonstatutory control mechanisms, such an *ex-post* legislative veto and corporatism, are unavailable. Along similar lines, Bawn (1997) shows that legislators who are not members of the relevant congressional committees, face higher costs of ongoing nonstatutory oversight and are likely to prefer more restrictive provisions to be inserted in the relevant statutes.

The majority of these studies have been confined to the American political system. Scholars have only recently started to apply the theory of delegation to parliamentary systems and, as I will argue below, studies of the EU are also rather sparse. However, there is no reason to expect that factors such as conflict, policy complexity, nonstatutory control tools and bargaining environment should not play an important role in shaping the distribution of powers in the EU. Moreover, its institutional framework shows strong similarities with a separation of powers system and the law plays an important role in determining the distribution of policy competencies among EU institutions and levels of governance. The EU appears to be an ideal candidate for testing the robustness of the theory of delegation. Additionally, EU institutional peculiarities, such as the possibility of

---

[16] Discretion is operationalized as the number of new words inserted in an existing statute in the case of the US and as a standardized measure of page length for parliamentary systems.

relying upon different administrators and levels of governance for policy implementation and the different decision rules under which the legislature operates, requires a careful reformulation of the existing propositions and the production of new hypotheses. These institutional features have received almost no attention in previous studies[17] and they are likely to reveal systematic differences in delegation and to generate new insights for the comparative literature.

The study of delegation in the European Union

The study of bureaucracy and delegation in the EU has run parallel with the general literature on the subject. Themes and concepts used by scholars of bureaucratic politics have frequently appeared in contemporaneous analyses on bureaucracy in the EU. Ground-breaking seminal works on bureaucracy have been the precursors of highly original studies on the EU.

Hence, it should not come as a surprise that the earlier works consider expertise as the key rationale for relying on a bureaucracy. Functionalist and late neofunctionalist writings on European integration underscored the benefit of relying on technically oriented international organizations and their expert officials. Mitrany (1966) prescribed technical cooperation at international level as a way to produce a working peace system. Haas (1964) and Lindberg (1963) shared with Jean Monnet the view that a supranational expert bureaucracy was crucial for the promotion of European integration and for developing and upgrading a common European interest. Centralized technical expertise was a prerequisite for the management of modern economic and political systems.

These authors, however, did not share similar normative views about European integration. As thoughtfully argued by Cram (1997: 9–18), Mitrany's opposition to territorially circumscribed organizations and a dislike of political spill-over made him critical of European integration and set him apart from the more supportive neofunctionalist scholars. Echoing criticisms toward the administrative state, the federalist Spinelli (1966, 1986) strongly disapproved of the lack of accountability which resulted from what he considered excessive centralization of policy-making powers in the Commission and the Council of Ministers.

The first studies of the Commission recognized early on the typical Weberian tension between its political leadership, the commissioners

---

[17] An exception is the work of Kelemen (2004) on comparative federalism. It is discussed in the next section.

and the administrators (Scheinmann, 1966; Coombes, 1970).[18] Yondorf (1965) emphasized the importance of supranational entrepreneurship in shaping political outcomes, even before the establishment of the Commission. Others were much more skeptical (e.g. Hoffmann, 1966). Finally, Noel (1973) underscored the Commission's important power of legislative initiation.

Spurred by important developments such as the signing of the Single European Act in 1986 and the Maastricht Treaty in 1992, we have seen a burgeoning of scholarly studies on the EU over the past fifteen years. For the sake of clarity, I will review this literature selectively and divide it up into three groups. The first group studies EU constitutional politics, namely the negotiations of Treaty amendments (but its insights can be applied to cases where the Council decides by unanimity). One of its most prominent themes has been the assessment of the circumstances under which the Commission and member states shape Treaty negotiations and outcomes.[19] The second group of works examines EU legislative politics. Here, an important area of research has been the assessment of the circumstances under which the Council, the Commission and the European Parliament shape EU law. With regard to the Commission for instance, formal scholars investigate its ability to use its monopoly of legislative initiation to exploit conflict within the Council, especially in the case of qualified majority voting (Steunenberg, 1994; Crombez, 1996; Garrett and Tsebelis, 1996).[20] As far as the Parliament is concerned, a large body of work assesses whether and why parliamentary amendments are incorporated into EU statutes (see Chapter 7 for a more extensive review).

The last important group, central to our interest, includes studies of executive politics and delegation. These works have been heavily influenced by the principal-agent framework from economics and its applications to US politics. Following the American literature, EU scholars have

---

[18] Others debated whether the Commission could be conceived as any other international secretariats (Siotis, 1964; Sidjanski, 1965). Over the years, the relation between the political leadership and the bureaucracy within the Commission has been extensively investigated (Donnelly, 1993; Edwards and Spence, 1994; Page and Wouters, 1994; Ross, 1995b; Christiansen, 1996, 1997; Cini, 1996; Nugent, 1995, 2000, 2001; Hooghe, 2001; Peterson and Shackleton, 2001; Stevens and Stevens, 2001).

[19] Some authors argue that the Commission can independently shape outcomes (Sandholtz and Zysman, 1989; Cameron, 1992; Sandholtz, 1993a). Others are much more skeptical (Moravcsik, 1991, 1998, 1999).

[20] On this issue the empirical literature abounds more with case studies than with large-N systematic analyses. Although some works are geared toward theory testing, many are mostly interpretive (e.g. Hall, 1992; Cram, 1993, 1994; Sandholtz, 1993b; Bulmer, 1994; Fuchs, 1994; Kelemen, 1995; Mazey, 1995; Esser and Noppe, 1996; Schmidt, 1996, 1998, 2000; Smith, 1996, 1998; Eichener, 1997; Guay, 1997; Nugent, 2000; Wendon, 1998; Thatcher, 2001).

recognized immediately the centrality of law in controlling bureaucratic behavior.[21] In a seminal article, Pollack (1997b) reviews the rationales for delegating powers to supranational institutions and the mechanisms of member state control. Subsequently, a large literature has focused on one of these mechanisms, namely a set of administrative procedures, termed under the general rubric of *comitology*, that are inserted into EU law to oversee the Commission's executive powers. Scholars have assessed the discretion of the Commission under these procedures and a debate has developed with regard to the relative importance of their control and coordination–informational functions.[22]

Only a few of these works however, have, been framed using agency and delegation theory (i.e. those following Pollack's (1997b) characterization of comitology as police-patrol oversight[23]). Note, moreover, that these procedures are one of many possible constraints that can be inserted into EU law. For instance, exempting an industry from the reach of the Commission's measures could be another important limitation imposed on the powers of this institution. Additionally, there are other procedures that are normally used when national administrations are in charge of implementing EU policies. And, finally, as argued by Huber and Shipan (2002), policy rather than procedural details can be used to influence bureaucratic autonomy.

Before we proceed with this review, it is useful to clarify that there are two processes of delegation in the EU. They differ with regard to the procedures and actors involved in the delegation decisions and the legal documents that confer powers. In the first process, *Treaty delegation*, member states delegate powers to supranational institutions. They hold intergovernmental conferences where they unanimously agree amendments to the Treaty, which need subsequently to be ratified by national parliaments. Member states act as principals while the Commission, the Parliament and other supranational institutions are the beneficiaries of

---

[21] Most likely because the EU has institutional features that are similar to a separation of powers system, see Lenaerts (1991), Bignami (1999), Ballmann, Epstein and O'Halloran (2002) and Hix (2005: 27–110). Other control mechanisms are moderately researched: on Commission appointment see Hix and Lord (1995), Crombez (1997b), Hix and Gabel (2002), on parliamentary scrutiny see Raunio (1996) and on budgetary control see Jun (2003a).

[22] One of the many descriptions of these procedures is available in Hix (2005). On the control-information debate see Docksey and Williams (1994), Pedler and Schaefer (1996), Dogan (1997), Joerges and Neyer (1997a, 1997b), Vos (1997, 1999), Wessels (1998), Christiansen and Kirchner (2000), Franchino (2000b), Dehousse (2003) and Pollack (2003a, 2003b).

[23] Pollack's characterization was justified on the basis of the resource intensive nature of these procedures. Note, however, that McCubbins and Schwartz (1984) considered administrative procedures as indirect and decentralized fire-alarm oversight.

delegation and are subject to control. The second process is *executive delegation*. EU legislators (ministers of the Council and, where involved, members of the Parliament – MEPs) confer powers upon bureaucrats via secondary legislation according to the EU legislative procedures. The beneficiaries are the Commission, other EU-level agencies and national administrations. Control mechanisms are also set up in these circumstances to ensure faithful implementation.

Two works stand out as the most explicit, direct and systematic tests of the theory of delegation in the EU. Moravcsik's (1998) well-known contribution is based on a three-stage approach to analyzing the outcome of negotiations at the EU level. A process of formation of preferences on substantive policies and institutional design underpins the negotiating stance of each member state in the supranational arena. Factors such as the best alternative to the negotiated agreement, the possibility of unilateral action and coalitional alternatives shape the pattern of mutual concessions and compromises at the negotiating table. Finally, the need to bolster the credibility of policy commitments is the strongest determinant of institutional choices such as pooling of sovereignty (i.e. a shift from unanimity to qualified majority voting in the Council) and the delegation of powers to supranational institutions.

Moravcsik argues that the inability to write complete contracts and incentives for defection create problems of time consistency. Pooling and delegation should thus facilitate commitment to policy objectives. Shifts to majority voting enhance credibility especially where there is a perceived risk of *ex-post* obstruction to the adoption of implementing measures of an agreed policy. Delegation performs a similar function where there are concerns about state compliance to policy objectives.[24] In five case studies spanning over almost forty years of European integration, Moravcsik finds strong evidence in support of this proposition.

Pollack's (2003b) book is the most systematic attempt yet at applying agency theory to the EU. His work is an extended application of the arguments in his seminal article (Pollack, 1997b). Pollack uses the literature on international regimes (Keohane, 1984) and on legislative organization to predict the functions that are likely to be delegated to supranational institutions: monitoring compliance, filling incomplete contracts, providing expert and credible regulation, and setting the formal legislative agenda. He then reviews the various types of mechanisms adopted by the principals to control agency behavior (e.g. appointment and removal powers, administrative procedures and judicial review) and how their

---

[24] This argument was originally made by Gatsios and Seabright (1989: 49–50) and Majone (1992, 1994, 1996: 61–79).

establishment is motivated by policy conflict and by underlying demands for expertise and credibility. He argues that the discretion that agents enjoy in the exercise of those delegated functions should vary with different degrees of informational and distributive pressures. Pollack reviews cross-policy and issue-specific powers and control mechanisms of the Commission, the Court of Justice and the Parliament that are primarily specified in Treaty provisions. He finds that the expectations are strongly corroborated especially with regard to the first two supranational institutions.[25]

These works present specific biases and share features with the broader literature on delegation. They predominantly focus on Treaty delegation to supranational institutions and, hence, they neglect the fact that many delegating decisions take place via secondary legislation, under different decision rules, and with national administrators as key players involved in policy implementation. A result of this bias is the emphasis on credibility as the key rationale for delegating powers. Some factors such as policy complexity and conflict are of secondary importance. Others, such as the decision rules, the bargaining environment and the availability of nonstatutory control tools, are mostly ignored.

These scholars recognize only indirectly how the need to rely on the expertise of national bureaucracies shapes delegation decisions (and Pollack (2003b: 153) acknowledges a secondary informational function of the Commission).[26] They do not systematically test if conflict between the authors and the implementers of statutes limits discretion, although they both show how control mechanisms are carefully designed to minimize agency loss. They suggest, without testing, that the Commission's discretion should decrease with more intense conflict within the Council (Moravcsik, 1998: 75; Pollack, 2003b: 26–34), while Pollack (2003b: 136–45) analyses and reviews the attempts made by the Parliament to change the comitology procedures.

Some recent studies are redressing these biases. Hug (2003: 60–5) shows that, during the Amsterdam Intergovernmental Conference, the member states opposing delegation to the Commission on the third pillar, employment and foreign policies, were generally those more distant from

---

[25] In the second part of the book, Pollack introduces and tests propositions about the preferences of supranational actors and the conditions under which they are more likely to achieve their objectives.

[26] This is not to say that the problem of commitment is irrelevant of course. Chapter 5 shows how this rationale is substantively important, but it is not easy to operationalize. In Franchino (2002), I suggest a method to distinguish information- and credibility-based delegating provisions. This is only an *ex-post* legal analysis however, it is not a measurement of the severity of the problem. Nevertheless, Majone (2001, 2002) warns against dismissing this logic.

the Commission's policy positions. Jun (2003a) illustrates the importance of ideology to explain MEPs' positions on granting budgetary discharge to the Commission. In the most extensive analysis of this topic
to date, she also shows how the Parliament attempts to constrain the
Commission as conflict between these two institutions intensifies (Jun,
2003b). On a similar theme, Kelemen (2002) illustrates how conflict
between the Parliament, Council and Commission is an important factor in explaining the establishment and design of EU agencies, while
Hix (2000) provides a theoretically based analysis of the attempts of
the Parliament to reform the comitology procedures. Finally, Meunier
(2000: 119) introduces an interesting argument for our purposes. She
contends that Commission autonomy in commercial policy negotiations
is related to the rules used to adopt negotiating mandates. In the case of
unanimity, the Commission is kept under tighter control.[27]

As far as national implementation is concerned, the EU literature
abounds with studies trying to explain the variance in the timing and
the quality of national implementation.[28] Héritier (1995, 1996, 1997,
1999) has probably done the most in explaining how EU law is designed
in view of national execution (see also Eising, 2002). Tallberg (2002b,
2003) has recently used the international relations literature on compliance and McCubbins and Schwartz's control typology to review the
mechanisms used by EU institutions to oversee national execution (primarily, the infringement and the preliminary reference procedures).[29]
But EU law has rarely been conceptualized as a mechanism for delegating powers to and exercising control on national administrations. An
exception is Kelemen's (2004) comparative study of environmental regulation in the EU and four federal polities (United States, Germany,
Australia and Canada). He shows how the fragmentation of powers at
the EU and US federal level produces lower executive discretion for the
component states in these polities than in federal parliamentary systems
such as Australia and Canada (see also Kelemen, 2003). Kelemen's work,
however, concentrates on institutional variations across rather than within
federal systems.

---

[27] See also Egan (1998), Meunier and Nicolaïdis (1999) and Stetter (2000) for other
policy-specific case studies. In a related work, König (2001) illustrates how the duration
of the EU legislative process is a positive function of the divergence of member states'
preferences and, interestingly, of the bias of the Commissioner proposing the measure.
[28] See, for example, Siedentopf and Ziller (1988), Mendrinou (1996), Knill and Lenschow
(1998), Lampinen and Uusikylä (1998), Börzel (2000, 2001), Haverland (2000), Knill
(2001), Mbaye (2001), Bursens (2002), Giuliani (2003) and Mastenbroek (2003).
[29] The international relations literature on delegation and compliance will not be covered
by this review. The concluding chapter of the book however, will illustrate how my results
can also be relevant for these works.

On the theoretical front, the EU literature has made less progress.[30] Some formal works have assessed the types of comitology procedures that are likely to be preferred by the Council and Parliament (Steunenberg, Koboldt and Schmidtchen, 1996a; Franchino, 2000a). Others have analyzed the different degrees of discretion that the Commission enjoys under these procedures (Steunenberg, Koboldt and Schmidtchen, 1996b; Ballmann, Epstein and O'Halloran, 2002). More relevant for our purposes, Bednar, Ferejohn and Garrett (1996) and Tsebelis and Garrett (2001) have taken the lead from McCubbins, Noll and Weingast (1987, 1989) and argued that the discretion of the Commission is a function of the decision rules required to override its measures. Finally, Dimitrova and Steunenberg (2000) develop a model to explain the granting of exemptions to some member states in EU legislation. As I will discuss in greater detail in Chapter 2, the first two models ignore the role that national administrations play on EU policy implementation, while the last one ignores the Commission. Moreover, the choice variable is not agency discretion as in the most advanced models of delegation (e.g. Epstein and O'Halloran, 1999b; Huber and Shipan, 2002).

In summary, the EU delegation literature has progressed a long way over the last ten years. But, it has been biased toward Treaty delegation, it has failed to consider seriously the choice between the Commission and national administrators that is available to EU legislators and it has ignored, or has just acknowledged without testing, factors that are now considered important in the general delegation literature. Finally, its formal models have failed to take into account advancements in modeling strategies of delegation. This book aims to redress these shortcomings.

A note on the "grand theories" of European integration

The preceding review has analyzed the EU literature through the lenses of bureaucratic politics, delegation and control. But many of the cited works frame their contributions within the "grand theories" of European integration. Here I provide, a necessarily concise, snapshot of these approaches. Their *explanandum* – integration – is very broadly conceived. It encompasses almost anything, from the adoption of common policies, the establishment of rules and institutions, to the development of a supranational polity. But their systematic differences rely on the emphasis they put on key explanatory factors. On the one hand, intergovernmentalism

---

[30] Some scholars simply review the promises and problems of applying the theory of delegation to the EU, see Doleys (2000), Pollack (2002), Tallberg (2002a) and Kassim and Menon (2003).

views national governments as the primary actors and what we see as integration is the result of a process of national preference formation and inter-state bargaining (e.g. Hoffmann, 1966; Taylor, 1983; Moravcsik, 1998). On the other hand, neofunctionalism and the modern heir, "supranational governance", emphasize the independent influence of supranational actors in shaping political outcomes in the EU (e.g. Lindberg, 1963; Haas, 1964; Sandholtz and Stone Sweet, 1998; Kohler-Koch and Eising, 1999; Hooghe and Marks, 2000; Stone Sweet, Fligstein and Sandholtz, 2001). Finally, a third set of contributions, which originate from the rationalist strand of institutional analysis, attempts to identify the circumstances under which outcomes reflect the views of member states or supranational actors (e.g. Schneider and Cederman, 1994; Crombez, 1996; Garrett and Tsebelis, 1996; Tsebelis and Garrett, 2001; Pollack, 2003b; Jupille, 2004).[31]

Whether this categorization of the literature is meaningful could be a matter of debate. Each scholar decodes the *explanandum* in his or her own way and many doubt the usefulness of encompassing theories. In effect, over the last ten years, grand-theorizing has been gradually replaced by middle-range studies with narrowly focused objects of analysis. This has produced, maybe counterintuitively, more powerful theories.

My study follows this trend. It limits its interest to the design of EU laws and, specifically, to the delegation of executive powers. Nevertheless, as will clearly emerge, this work follows the premises of institutional analysis closely. It moves beyond the extant intergovernmentalist literature on delegation but it also challenges some conclusions put forward by the institutionalist scholarship (especially, Tsebelis and Garrett, 2001). In the concluding chapter, results will be interpreted in view of these main theoretical constructs.

The plan of the book

My main objective is to develop and test a theory of delegation in the EU, one that is specifically focused on the daily workings of this political system and that takes seriously into account its institutional peculiarities. The following chapters elaborate my argument in greater detail. Chapter 2 introduces a formal model of the politics of delegation in the EU. It generalizes my earlier work (Franchino, 2000a)[32] and adapts the

---

[31] This is a broad-brushed review which intentionally neglects substantial differences within each approach and similarities across them. Here, I shadow Hix's (2005: 14–18) succinct categorization of the literature. For recent and more comprehensive surveys see Puchala (1999), Aspinwall and Schneider (2000) and Pollack (2001).

[32] See Franchino (2005) for a variant of the more general model.

most advanced models of delegation to incorporate the institutional features of the EU. The model produces eleven propositions that are translated into thirteen testable hypotheses in subsequent chapters. Chapter 3 introduces the data set used for quantitative testing of the first eight hypotheses. It outlines the procedure employed for the selection of 158 major laws that form the sample for the statistical analysis in Chapter 5. The chapter proceeds to outline the steps I took to produce the measures of discretion for the Commission and national authorities, the core dependent variables for the first eight hypotheses. The chapter makes ample use of descriptive statistics and longitudinal analysis to provide broad impressions of patterns and trends in EU delegation.[33] Chapter 4 explains the procedure for the operationalization of the key variables: decision rules, preferences of Council ministers and commissioners, and policy complexity. Preferences are measured along the three most important dimensions of EU politics. Chapter 5 reformulates the first eight propositions of the model in testable hypotheses. These hypotheses are then tested using the dependent and independent variables developed in Chapters 3 and 4 respectively. The chapter also considers the problem of commitment as an alternative explanation to my theory and briefly compares patterns of delegation in the EU with those in the US. An earlier version of this chapter has been published in Franchino (2004).[34] Chapter 6 provides detailed qualitative evidence of the processes of delegation across four policy areas as a way to complement and further support the results of Chapter 5. Chapter 7 reformulates the three remaining propositions of the model in five testable hypotheses concerning the revealed preferences of the Parliament with regard to national and Commission discretion. It explains the operationalization of discretion and of parliamentary preferences and tests the hypotheses using both statistical and content analysis of the amendments proposed by the Parliament in the codecision procedure. The concluding chapter reviews the main empirical findings and distinguishing features of this study in light of the EU and comparative literature on delegation and implementation, and of the nascent international relations literature on delegation and compliance. It illustrates how these results complement, revisit and, in some cases, challenge existing works. The chapter also evaluates the normative implications with regard to EU democracy, centralization of powers, the principle of subsidiarity, bureaucratization, bureaucratic capacity and enlargement. The chapter concludes with suggestions for future research.

---

[33] The chapter is partially based on Franchino (2001, 2002).
[34] See also Franchino (2000c, 2002) for related, but not overlapping, works.

2 A formal model of delegation in the European Union

Legislation and implementation are heavily intertwined in any political system. Legislators enact policies keeping in mind the structure and preferences of bureaucracies. Administrators implement policies within the boundaries set by the legislature, but also with a view to achieving their own objectives. European policy makers face similar challenges. When they design EU statutes, the legislators delegate powers to the administrators in order to rely on their expert execution but, at the same time, they need to make sure that the policies are implemented faithfully. Administrators may have their own policy objectives, but these are constrained by the requirements set by EU law.

This chapter introduces a formal model of the politics of delegation in the EU. The model produces eleven propositions that will be grouped and reformulated into thirteen testable hypotheses in Chapters 5–7. Hereafter, I introduce the model informally. The following sections will present it in more technical terms. The reader who is less interested in technicalities can skip to the conclusion and Table 2.1 which maps the propositions onto the hypotheses and lists the chapters where they are tested.

As the excerpts from EU law listed in Chapter 1 clearly illustrate, the model starts with the premise that EU legislators can rely on two paths for policy implementation: the Commission and national administrations. This choice is not often put in stark terms. Frequently, it is a matter of relative reliance on these two types of bureaucratic actors. Nevertheless, as I will amply illustrate in Chapter 3, there are clear tendencies to prefer one of the two implementation paths.

The model aims to explain centralization and bureaucratization or, in other words, choices of delegation (i.e. of path) and of degree of discretion of the executive actors. It assesses how well-known factors such as *policy complexity, legislative–bureaucratic conflict, bargaining environment* and *availability of nonstatutory control tools*, and less established ones, such as *decision rules*, affect these choices.

Let me start by considering only the Council of Ministers in its legislative function. The national route has a strong appeal for ministers because, as heads of their home departments, they are in charge of implementation and they will make sure that the relevant measures are executed as they wish. Additionally, national authorities are the repository of extensive policy expertise on which ministers would want to rely upon in complex policy areas.

This route presents risks though. Fifteen (now, twenty-five) national departments may have fifteen different views of how a measure should be implemented. National execution could lead to such a disparate set of national policies that they could defy the purpose of adopting an EU measure in the first place and could even generate serious cross-country distributional costs. Consider, for instance, the case whereby national trade departments use fifteen different definitions of injury to justify the imposition of anti-dumping duties. In other words, a minister cares about how a policy is implemented across the whole of the EU and will have to balance the attractiveness of relying on national administrations with the risk of producing divergent policy outcomes. The model shows that, as this risk increases, ministers holding moderate policy positions are likely to prefer more prescriptive legislation (i.e. lower national executive discretion) and/or delegation to the Commission. But ministers with extreme positions could be better off by broader national discretion, or even by no measure at all, and would be most reluctant to delegate powers to the Commission.

The Commission path of implementation is the alternative to the national one, but it has its own risks too. This supranational executive has preferences and goals and, to the extent that they diverge from those of the Council, it could bias implementation. Delegation to this institution is less likely and its discretion would be lower when there is disagreement between the Council and the Commission. Moreover, the Commission is a small bureaucracy staffed with generalists which can undertake some implementing measures, mostly of managerial nature, but certainly cannot compete with the wealth of expertise available at the national level. Only in policies that require these skills are we likely to see greater reliance on the Commission.

Thus, some expectations of the model are standard. Greater *policy complexity* leads to more discretion, though, in this case, the expertise-related features of bureaucratic actors will further guide the legislators' choice of implementation path. More intense *conflict between the Council and the Commission* leads to less discretion for the supranational executive. However, because of an EU peculiarity whereby ministers are both legislators and key actors in charge of national execution, a third variable, *conflict within the Council*, behaves somewhat differently. It has a dual role. It could be conceived as standard principal-agent conflict because ministers are the authors of EU statutes and national authorities are the implementers, and it is reasonable to assume that ministers share their own departments' preferences. However, conflict within the Council is also a feature of its bargaining environment and, as such, traditional expectations need to be modified.

In order to do so, the model introduces institutional features that are distinct to the EU. First, the EU legislative process must always start with a proposal from the Commission.[1] This institution is likely to use this monopoly of legislative initiation to pursue its own preferences and goals. Unsurprisingly, I will show that the Commission prefers being in charge of policy execution and having ample discretionary authority. If the only option available is national implementation, it prefers to adopt more prescriptive legislation when the preferences of national authorities differ from its own. Second, the *decision-making rules* of the Council vary across policy areas as specified in the Treaty. In some circumstances, the Council can adopt a measure only by unanimity. The power of the Commission is rendered ineffective under this rule and the minister most likely to exercise their veto power is likely to be the one that prefers ample national discretion and a minimal role for the Commission. Moreover, the impact of increased conflict within the Council is ambiguous as some ministers could prefer more national discretion and others less.

Matters change considerably when a qualified majority in the Council is sufficient to adopt the measure at hand. All other things being equal, the Commission can take advantage of different preferences in the Council in these circumstances and make winning proposals that delegate more powers to the supranational executive and restrain further national administrative autonomy. In addition, pivotal ministers in majority voting are likely to have more moderate preferences and, as argued above, they are also likely to prefer lower national executive discretion and/or delegation to the Commission as *conflict within the Council* increases. If this increased conflict is also detrimental to the Commission, this institution is also likely to make similar winning proposals (i.e. with supranational powers and more restrained national authorities) as conflict within the Council becomes more intense.

Finally, the model concludes by analyzing the impact of the Parliament on the politics of EU delegation. The Parliament is introduced within

---

[1] This applies to the European Community pillar of the Treaty on the European Union which is arguably the most important one and is the analytical core of this study.

the context of a third legislative procedure, called codecision, where the Council and the Parliament must agree on the same text to adopt an EU law. I do not analyze the final outcome of codecision. This would be the focus of a study on legislative bargaining as this outcome is the result of mutual concessions between the two institutions. My model instead evaluates how and when the delegation preferences of the Parliament vary systematically from those of the Council. Three factors are at work: *legislative–bureaucratic conflict*, the *availability of nonstatutory control tools* and the *bargaining environment*. First, the Parliament is likely to prefer greater executive discretion for the Commission, at least to the extent that it is more likely to share the same preferences as the supranational executive rather than the Council. Second, in the case of national execution, it is likely to prefer lower national executive discretion because it faces higher costs of ongoing control than the Council. Finally, this preference is reinforced as conflict between the Parliament and the Council becomes more intense because this implies more severe differences between the authors (the Parliament) and the implementers (national authorities) of policies.

I now proceed with the formal treatment of the model. In the next section, I review the existing formal works on EU delegation and I place my model within the general literature on delegation. The following section describes the structure and the assumptions of the model. Next, I analyze the delegation preferences of the actors. Then, I derive and compare the equilibria under unanimity and qualified majority voting. I summarize the results in eight propositions in the next section. A further three propositions are then introduced from the analysis of the preferences of the Parliament in codecision. I then relax some assumptions of the model to see whether the propositions also hold in other circumstances.

The literature modeling the politics of delegation in the European Union

My model of the politics of EU delegation shares a core set of assumptions with the formal work on delegation by Epstein and O'Halloran (1994, 1999b; see also the extension of Volden, 2002b). These consist of quadratic utility, unidimentional policy space, additive and homogeneous random shocks to policy, and discretion measured as a segment of the policy space.[2] But it also differs in two crucial aspects. First, there is only one bureaucratic agent in Epstein and O'Halloran. I instead consider the choice between a supranational and a national implementation path and the incentives of legislators and administrators that originate

---

[2] See Bendor and Meirowitz (2004) for a critical assessment of these assumptions.

from this peculiar setting. Incidentally, this choice is not uncommon in many federal polities where similar decisions are made about which level of government should implement which policies (e.g. Kelemen, 2004). Second, Epstein and O'Halloran develop their theory within a single institutional context (the US federal system). Consequently, institutional arrangements play no role in their explanation because they are fixed. Instead, since different institutions (i.e. decision-making rules) are used on different pieces of legislation in the EU, my model investigates how institutional changes within the same polity influence delegation strategies.

Recently, Huber and Shipan (2002; see also Huber and McCarty, 2004) have developed a model of delegation that is applicable across political systems. Their framework has technical features that are similar to those used by Epstein and O'Halloran, such as, for instance, unidimentionality, additivity of random shocks and the definition of discretion. Huber and Shipan, however, treat differences in institutions as an important explanatory variable and study how these differences shape delegation on the same issue across states. On the one hand, my model has similar features because it analyzes the impact on delegation outcomes of different decision rules operating within the legislature. Of course, differently from Huber and Shipan, the model fully includes the central, and unique, institutional characteristics of EU decision-making processes. On the other hand, the choice of level of government, which is central to my study, is instead disregarded by Huber and Shipan.

Although the formal literature on EU legislative procedures is extensive (e.g. Steunenberg, 1994; Garrett, 1995; Crombez, 1996, 2001; Garrett and Tsebelis, 1996; Tsebelis and Garrett, 2000), there are only three formal studies that analyze the processes of delegation. Taking the lead from McCubbins, Noll and Weingast (1987, 1989), Tsebelis and Garrett (2001; see also Bednar, Ferejohn and Garrett, 1996: 284) develop a spatial analysis of EU legislative procedures and derive propositions on the executive discretion of the Commission based on the core of each procedure, namely the set of policies that cannot be overruled by applying a specific procedure. The larger the core is, the greater executive discretion the administrator enjoys.[3]

Their work focuses only on one implementation path, the supranational one. It disregards the fact that most European policies are executed

---

[3] According to Tsebelis and Garrett (2001: 383), the executive discretion of the Commission is greater when new acts are adopted in the Council under unanimity rather than under qualified majority voting. Consequently, the move to majority voting reduces the discretionary authority of the Commission. The validity of this assertion will be comprehensively assessed in the concluding Chapter 8.

by national administrations. The opportunity of national implementation generates specific incentives for EU legislators, especially for the members of the Council since they control their own national authorities usually. Therefore, the policy authority enjoyed by the Commission is dependent upon the attractiveness of national delegation. Furthermore, their model derives propositions on the level of discretion only from the rules of legislative override, disregarding the fact that legislators are likely to anticipate bureaucratic behavior and will establish *ex ante* in the statutes the formal boundaries of the Commission's implementation.

Dimitrova and Steunenberg (2000) propose a spatial model to explain the granting of exemptions to some member states in EU legislation. They start by assuming that member states face a different status quo that may not coincide with their ideal policies. If the intersection of the preferred sets[4] of the member states is an empty set, the Council cannot agree on a uniform common policy and will adopt legislative provisions that allow for greater national executive discretion. The choice variable in Dimitrova and Steunenberg's model is dichotomous, that is, the outcome is legislation either with or without exemptions. My model treats national executive discretion as a continuous variable. This is a more accurate depiction of the reality of legislative design. Moreover, Dimitrova and Steunenberg disregard entirely the role of the Commission, both its power to initiate the legislative process and its role in the implementation of common policies. They also neglect the potential impact that different decision rules have on the granting of exemptions.

Finally, the model proposed here generalizes an earlier work of mine (Franchino, 2000a). This previous study integrates the canonical assumptions of delegation models employed by Epstein and O'Halloran (1994, 1999b) with formal works on EU legislative politics (notably Steunenberg, 1994; Crombez, 1996). The analysis, however, is limited only to the delegation of powers to the Commission. It generates propositions on how decision rules, policy preferences, uncertainty and the status quo affect the degree of executive discretion that is conferred upon this institution, but it ignores the crucial fact that the authority of the supranational executive is dependent upon the attractiveness of the national implementation path.

The model proposed here fully takes into account the choice between the two implementation paths and the different decision rules under which the Council and the Parliament operate. It produces propositions on the circumstances under which EU legislators rely on either national

---

[4] For Dimitrova and Steunenberg, the preferred set includes the policies that an actor prefers to the status quo.

authorities or the Commission for the execution of common policies. It considers the effects of legislative procedures, preferences and complexity on the choices of delegation.

The model of delegation in the European Union: players and core assumptions

My goal is to develop a straightforward model of the politics of EU delegation that captures its essential institutional features in a simple and tractable way. At the core of every process of modeling is a trade-off between accuracy and tractability, which requires a well-thought-out choice between those details that are included and those that are abstracted away.

The model incorporates four key aspects that are specific to the EU and set it apart from existing formal works on delegation. First, EU legislators can choose between the Commission and national administrations for the implementation of a common policy. In the case of national implementation, legislators care about the measures taken by each national administration, otherwise there would be no reason for adopting an EU law in the first place. Hence, this model incorporates each of these measures into the utility functions of the players. Second, members of the Council of Ministers act as legislators when they adopt EU laws but they can also be in charge of the national execution of these policies. The model assumes that ministers and their home administrations share similar preferences. Third, the Commission has both a legislative and an executive role. It has the monopoly of legislative initiation, though it does not have the power of gatekeeping, and it can be the administrator of common policies. Finally, the EU adopts legislation using a variety of decision rules. I consider fully two legislative procedures: when the Council acts alone and decides by either unanimous or qualified majority[5] voting. I also investigate the discretion preference of the Parliament when it adopts laws in codecision with the Council, but I will not produce an equilibrium for this procedure.[6]

Players and assumptions

The relevant players in the model consist of two governments, the Commission and the Parliament. The Commission and the Parliament

---

[5] In this procedure, the votes of the member states are weighted. The approval of a measure requires approximately five-sevenths of these votes.
[6] The equilibrium outcomes of codecision are reported in Franchino (2005).

are identified as C and PR respectively, while the two governments are labeled M and U. Collectively, the governments form the Council of Ministers. While both have veto power when the Council decides by unanimity, M is the pivotal government under qualified majority voting. This set up greatly simplifies a Council of fifteen (now, twenty-five) members holding different voting weights under majority voting. However, it is clear and tractable and does not come at the expense of generality (see the penultimate section of the chapter). We also know in practice that ministers negotiate EU laws in the Council while, if decided so, national departments are in charge of policy execution. This distinction should be kept in mind as the game is played out because national administrators have policy expertise which ministers may lack.[7] The latter are legislators in the EU context and the former execute policies. However, I assume that national authorities share the same preferences as their members of the Council, hence there is no need to consider them as distinct players. Almost always, this assumption is innocuous because ministers are heads of their national departments and play an important role within national cabinets and legislatures in transposing and executing EU legislation. Moreover, the preference would be the same if ministers appoint the top ranks of their departments, as is the case in some European bureaucracies.

The next three features are standard assumptions in the literature (see Epstein and O'Halloran, 1994, 1999b; Volden, 2002b). First, the policy space is one-dimensional, $X = \Re^1$. In this space, each actor has a most-preferred policy, or ideal point, x_i for $i = $ m, u, c or pr. Without loss of generality, I assume that the governments' ideal policies $x_m = 0$ and $x_u \geq 0$. Actors may have different positions along the left–right spectrum, the pro–anti-European integration dimension or with regard to substantive policy positions (e.g. regulation–deregulation). However, for simplicity, I refer hereafter to actors with positive (negative) ideal points as holding national (supranational) preferences because this is the oldest recognized cleavage in the study of EU politics, though, not necessarily the most important.[8]

Second, the functional form of the players' utility is quadratic. If a player has an ideal point x_i and the final policy outcome is x, then the actor's utility equals $- (x - x_i)^2$. This quadratic loss function captures the

---

[7] Hence, I use the terms *governments, member states, national administrations, departments, authorities* or *ministries* interchangeably, but I refer to *ministers* or *members* of the Council when I want to differentiate them from their national administrations.

[8] I will review the literature analyzing the EU policy space in Chapter 4. Scholars identify at least three dimensions: European integration, policy-specific and left–right dimensions. Supranational and national labels could then be substituted with left and right ones or with others related to substantive policy positions. The empirical analysis will consider three cleavages.

distributive component as actors' utility increases when outcomes are closer to their ideal points. It also considers the informational element as players are willing to accept some policy bias in return of a more certain outcome (Epstein and O'Halloran, 1999b: 54). As shown shortly below, this formulation is also adapted to the case of national implementation where the final outcome is a combination of national measures.

Finally, I assume that, at the executive stage, the Commission and national administrators are better informed than EU legislators about the consequences of particular policy decisions. For instance, national ministries of the environment are in a better position to take the most cost-effective measures to increase waste recycling. In order to capture the fact that bureaucracies have expertise that legislators lack, I assume that legislators act under uncertainty. As with previous models, I design this information asymmetry with an additive and homogeneous random shock to policy that legislators cannot observe (Epstein and O'Halloran, 1999b: 54; Volden, 2002b: 112). In other words, the final outcome x reflects both the final policy p that is adopted and a random component ω representing unforeseen contingencies that may have an impact on the outcome, so $x = p + \omega$. Legislators hold a prior probabilistic belief that ω is distributed uniformly in the $-R$ and R range. As the game unfolds, actors in charge of execution will have the expertise to know the exact value of ω and to take informed policy measures.

Structure and sequence of moves

Figure 2.1 illustrates compactly the structure of the model and the sequence of moves. Here, the two-member Council is labeled CM. The moves unfold in three stages. A game for each legislative procedure is played out at the legislative stage. Each game then proceeds on to a similar executive stage and produces a final policy outcome.

Legislative stage. At the legislative stage, the games are similar to some models of EU decision-making (see, especially, Steunenberg, 1994; Garrett, 1995; Crombez, 1996). The Commission makes a proposal and the Council and, where involved, the Parliament adopt the legislation according to the different procedures of the EU. The Commission's proposal is strategically important because, as we shall see below, in one procedure, it is easier to adopt than to amend. But a key difference from prior models is that this proposal consists of three elements: a baseline policy, an implementation path and a degree of discretion. For instance, a proposed measure on environmental policy would contain details on the stringency of environmental protection, on the actors in charge of

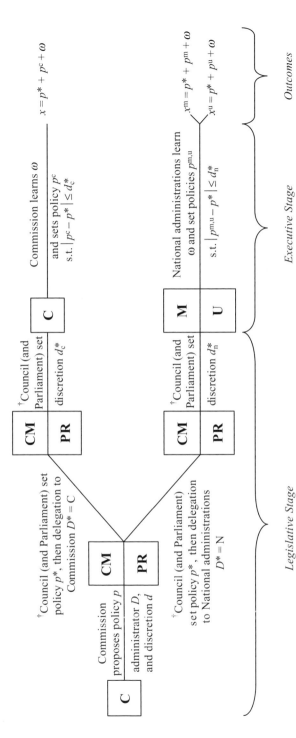

Figure 2.1 *Moves of the games. Note:* The Council of Ministers is labeled CM. The figure compacts three games matching the three EU legislative procedures. At the choice nodes flagged with †, the Council sets $[p^*, D^*, d^*]$ by unanimity, qualified majority voting or in codecision with the Parliament. Each game then proceeds on to similar choice nodes at the executive stage.

taking executive decisions and their latitude in exercising those powers. As with previous models of delegation (e.g. Epstein and O'Halloran, 1999b; Volden, 2002b), the proposed baseline policy p is simply a point on the policy space and the degree of discretion d, bounded between zero and R, is a segment of the policy line which sets the limits of implementation after the legislators have adopted the policy and the contingency is revealed. It measures the latitude enjoyed by the executive actor(s) in the implementation of such a policy. For the implementation path, I use an indicator variable $D \in \{C, N\}$ that takes the letter C if the Council and, where involved, the Parliament delegate policy authority to the Commission and N if they rely on national administrations for execution.[9]

The legislative stage ends with EU legislators adopting first a baseline policy p^*, then choosing an executive actor D^* and a level of discretion d^* (where d_c^* indicates discretion of the Commission and d_n^* indicates discretion of national authorities). For instance, they could establish a certain level of environmental standards to be implemented by national authorities under specific conditions. Importantly, to become law, this composite measure must be preferred to the status quo which, I assume, comprises of national implementation with maximal discretion.

Executive stage. At the executive stage, actors in charge of execution learn the precise value of ω and take fully informed policy measures.[10] This stage consists of two alternative paths of implementation. Depending on the value of D^*, the Commission or the national administrations adopt executive measures on the basis of the equilibrium baseline policy p^* and discretion d^* set by the legislators. For instance, national departments issue new environmental standards under the conditions established in the new law and with the benefit of better information about their cost implications. Importantly, administrators cannot adopt a measure

---

[9] In reality, EU legislators can rely on both paths in a single measure. This could have been taken into account by transforming D from a nominal indicator into a discrete variable measuring the proportion of reliance on the two paths. Though more realistic, this modification would have unnecessarily complicated the model and I doubt that it would have yielded new and substantively interesting insights.

[10] I do not argue, of course, that bureaucrats have perfect knowledge about policy outcomes, they are only more informed than legislators. Moreover, the plausibility of the assumption that the Commission has expertise at the executive stage that it lacks at the legislative stage could be questioned. A fully informed Commission could have been considered but the crucial aspect here is that legislators have *lower* expertise than bureaucrats and decide knowing that they can rely on an expert Commission at the executive stage (such expertise could be acquired along the way). In parliamentary systems, where models of delegation have been developed using a similar design (Huber and Shipan, 2002), most legislation is first drafted by bureaucrats inside ministries, proposed by the government and then adopted by the (less expert) members of parliament, namely in a not too dissimilar way from the EU.

beyond the discretionary limits. In other words, they cannot modify the policy in ways that are substantially different from the legislators' intent. If the Commission does so, the European Court of Justice can overturn its actions by declaring them *ultra vires*. Or, if national administrations do so, their actions will be subject to the infringement procedure and, eventually, a Court's judgement of failure to comply with Treaty obligations and a penalty payment.

Final outcomes and payoffs. In the last stage of the game, after the law has been adopted and implementing decisions issued, policy outcomes result from this combination of measures and actors realize their payoffs. As illustrated in Figure 2.1, the final policy outcome in the case of Commission execution is the sum of the equilibrium baseline policy, the measure p^c adopted by the Commission within the set discretionary limit and the revealed state of Nature, so $x = p^* + p^c + \omega$. In the case of national execution, national administrations adopt their own measures, $p^{m,u}$, subject to the common discretionary boundary d_n^*. For instance, the national authority of government M issues its implementing decision, p^m, which, combined with the equilibrium baseline policy and the true state of Nature, generates a country-specific policy outcome, $x^m = p^* + p^m + \omega$. This design accounts for the divergence in national implementation of EU law that we often witness. The Spanish and Greek environmental ministries are likely to implement a new EU law somewhat differently, subject to common constraints.

As explained above, players' utility or payoff is a quadratic loss function in the final outcome. In the case of Commission implementation, it takes the simple formula $U_i(x) = -(x - x_i)^2$. In the case of national implementation, an important feature of the model is that actors' utility must incorporate the implementation measure of each national administration. There would be no reason for adopting an EU law if legislators did not care about these national decisions collectively. Therefore, I consider the payoff in the case of national implementation as the sum of the utilities arising from the decisions of each national administration divided by the number of states – two in our case. Formally,

$$U_i(x) = -\frac{1}{2}[(x^m - x_i)^2 + (x^u - x_i)^2].   \tag{2.1}$$

The utility to each player is one-half the sum of the utility from each member state's policy. For the governments, this formulation captures the incentives of the members of the Council to rely on their national administrations, which are under their control and, hence, with which they share the preference profile. However, part of each government's utility is also a function of the policy choices taken by the national administration of the other government. The incentives for relying on the expertise of their domestic bureaucrats are counterbalanced by the risk of distributive losses originating from biased implementation in other states. For the Commission and the Parliament, this utility function gauges the supranational nature of these players.[11]

Finally, the division by the number of states allows a comparison with the formulation of utility in the case of Commission implementation. When governments have the same preferences, we have $x^m = x^u$ and the formulas are the same. However, it also implies that ministers weight equally outcomes in their own country and in other states. This assumption could be questioned and arguments about ministers valuing other states' measures less (or more) than their own country's could be advanced. But we lack clear evidence on this issue, I have therefore opted for equal weighting.

Having described the core assumptions and the structure of the model, the ensuing three sections explain its logic and results. As usual, I solve the game proceeding by backward induction, starting from the end and working back to generate equilibrium predictions. In the next section, I introduce the strategies of the actors at the executive stage. Next, I set the stage for legislative policy making by deriving each player's ideal baseline policy, administrator(s) and discretion level for varying preferences of executive actors and by determining the set of proposals that makes each player at least indifferent to a specific status quo, that is, when a new EU law is adopted. I then introduce the rules for amendment and adoption of a Commission's proposal and determine the equilibrium actions and outcomes under the legislative procedures. These outcomes are then summarized in propositions. Appendix 2.1 presents a more formal treatment of the model.

Policy making at the executive stage

Consider the executive actors' decisions when they have to make policy. Legislators have set a baseline policy, they have decided that the Commission will be in charge of implementation and they have conferred upon it a degree of executive autonomy. The Commission now acquires expertise, gathers information and discovers the true value of the state of Nature ω. The final policy outcome will be $p^* + p^c + \omega$, so the Commission will

---

[11] A similar approach has been used by Lohmann and O'Halloran (1994). These scholars formulate trade policy preferences of the US President as the sum of the preferences of legislators in Congress.

adopt the measure p^c that shifts this outcome closest to its ideal point x_c. However, this executive has only a certain amount of power, it can only shift the policy up to a maximum amount represented by the level of discretion d_c^*. Hence, depending on the specific value that Nature takes, the Commission will either be able to implement its ideal policy or will shift the policy towards its ideal point by the full amount of discretion. The final outcome is either x_c, $\omega + p^* + d_c^*$ or $\omega + p^* - d_c^*$. For instance, a liberally minded Commission would be inclined to reject applications for the imposition of anti-dumping duties, but it would not be able to decline, at the risk of being sanctioned by the Court, those solidly based on the letter and spirit of EU law.

The same type of reasoning applies if legislators have decided to rely on national authorities. Depending on the value of ω, national administrators will either be able to implement their most preferred policies or will shift the policy towards its ideal point by the full amount of discretion. We have two sets of three possible outcomes, one for each government. Their occurrence varies as a function of the realization of ω.

Setting the ground for policy making at the legislative stage

Step 1: ideal policy, discretion and delegation preferences

Working backward, in order to determine legislators' best responses to executive decisions, we need to establish, for each player, the ideal baseline policy, administrator(s) and level of discretion. Each player expects a certain utility or payoff from each implementation path. Actors will formulate their best responses at the legislative stage based on calculations of this payoff. This expected utility is a function of the player's own preferences, of the range of values that ω can take (i.e. the complexity of the measure) and of the decisions taken by the Commission and national authorities at the executive stage.

Unsurprisingly, the expected utility of any actor is maximized when the baseline policy equals its ideal point. Regardless of the implementation path and the degree of discretion, any legislator would ideally prefer that decisions were taken from a baseline policy that coincides with its own position.

The mathematical formula for the level of discretion that maximizes an actor's utility varies depending on the implementation path. In the case of execution by the Commission, it is $d_c^{\bullet} = R - \sqrt{x_c^2 - p^{*2} - 2x_i(x_c - p^*)}$. In the case of national implementation,

$d_n^{\bullet} = R - [\sqrt{x_u^2 - 2p^{*2} - 2x_i(x_u - 2p^*)}]/\sqrt{2}$ for $i =$ m, u, c or pr. Nevertheless, they tell a similar story. First, they are both a positive function of R, the range of values that ω can take. Second, in general, for given preferences of the executive actors, a legislator would like to delegate to them more (less) discretionary authority as the baseline policy moves away from (towards) the legislator's ideal point. The setting of the baseline policy and of the level of discretion are substitutes. An actor may be willing to make policy concessions in exchange for granting greater discretion to the administrator. She may otherwise agree to give more discretion to the administrator in exchange for defining more on her own terms the policy baseline on which such administrator must act (see also Volden, 2002b: 124).

On the basis of this information (i.e. each actor's ideal baseline policy and ideal discretion for the two implementation paths), we can now compute the ideal implementation path and discretion for each player. These preferences are not a function of the baseline policy but they vary as a result of the policy positions of the executive actors.

The European Commission. The Commission's ideal choice is delegation to itself with maximal discretion. When the legislator objects to delegation to the Commission, the choice confronting the Commission is a matter of how much the national administrations should be constrained. The Commission's ideal level of national discretion diminishes as the policy conflict between the Commission and government U increases (see the $d_n^{\bullet}$ formula for $x_i = x_c$).

The governments. Figure 2.2 shows the delegation preferences of governments in Cartesian planes. The vertical axis represents government U's ideal points, which take only positive values. Policy conflict within the Council, measured by the distance between x_u and x_m, increases as we move upwards. The horizontal axis represents the ideal points of the Commission. A supranational Commission has negative values, namely its preferences are closer to government M than to government U. A national Commission has instead positive ideal points and may have preferences closer to government U. The Commission has the same preferences of government U along the dashed 45-degree line extending from the origin.

The areas where the governments prefer to rely on either the Commission or national administrations for policy execution are coded accordingly. Section a shows the structure of the delegation preferences of government M. It is symmetric across the vertical axis. This state prefers delegation to the Commission when $x_u > |x_c|/\sqrt{2}$. Three considerations

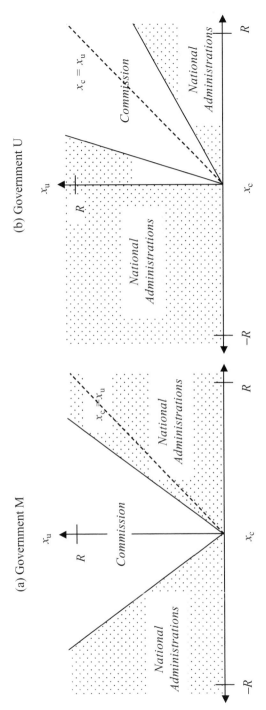

Figure 2.2 *Delegation preferences of governments.*

are in order. First, there is a relatively strong bias in favor of delegation to national administrations. The area where this is the ideal implementation path is 40 percent larger than the area where delegation to the Commission is preferred. The government prefers to confer greater discretion to national authorities than to the Commission for any given baseline policy and similar preferences of executive actors. National execution is generally preferred because one of the two implementing measures is taken by government M's national authorities with a view to maximizing its utility. Second, government M is more likely to prefer delegation to the Commission as policy conflict within the Council increases. Instead, it prefers relying on national authorities as conflict with the Commission increases. The cost of relying on one implementation path increases with the administrator's bias and, consequently, the alternative path becomes more attractive. However, since one implementing measure is taken by government M's authorities the policy bias in the case of national execution should be at least 40 percent greater than the bias in the case of Commission implementation to justify delegation to the EU executive. Third, as we move towards the top left- and right-hand corners, administrators' views increasingly diverge from those of government M and implementation measures will increasingly shift the outcome away from this state's ideal point. Therefore, the discretion conferred by this government upon the executive actors diminishes (ideal levels of discretion are not illustrated in Figure 2.2, the results are provided in Appendix 2.1). Government M prefers to take most of the implementing decisions within the Council when for execution it cannot trust both the Commission and the national administrations.

Section *b* of Figure 2.2 shows the delegation preferences of government U. Since the states' utility functions are similar, the structure resembles that for government M, with three notable differences. First, government U objects entirely to delegation to a supranational Commission as it is an excessively costly implementation path. Therefore, the bias in favor of national execution is stronger. The area of national delegation is more than three times as large as that of Commission execution. Second, as policy conflict within the Council increases from low levels, government U is likely to prefer delegation to a national Commission. However, it prefers national delegation at higher level of Council conflict. Third (not shown in Figure 2.2), ideal national discretion diminishes as Council conflict increases from low levels, but it increases at high levels of intensity of Council conflict (i.e. for $x_u > 2p$). Note the difference between a centrally located government M that prefers lower national discretion as Council conflict becomes very intense and a remotely located government U that is better off with broader national discretion in these circumstances.

The latter two dissimilarities result from the fact that, as government U's preferences become more extreme, the distribution of states of Nature ω is increasingly detrimental to this state. National execution guarantees that at least one measure will be taken for its benefit. And this is preferred even to implementation by a national Commission. This also explains why, in these circumstances, government U wants to assure ample discretion for itself.

The European Parliament. The rationale for the delegation preferences of the Parliament is similar to the previous cases, but, since we also have to take into account the policy preference of the Parliament, planes, instead of lines, separate the areas of delegation. The delegation preferences are motivated by the policy distance between the Parliament's ideal point and, on the one side, the ideal policy of the Commission, on the other side, that of the governments.

Obviously, the Parliament has the same delegation preferences as government M when $x_{pr} = 0$. There are two other scenarios to analyze. The first one is when the Parliament and the Commission both have either national or supranational preferences. In these circumstances, the Parliament has a strong bias in favor of the Commission's execution because implementation by a single institution generates lower distributive losses than execution by two national authorities with different preferences. The second scenario is when the preferences of the Commission and the Parliament are on the opposite side of the policy spectrum. In most circumstances, a supranational (national) Parliament objects to delegation to a national (supranational) Commission.

Needless to say, the Parliament is more likely to prefer delegation to the Commission as policy differences with the governments increase. It is more likely to prefer national delegation as policy conflict with the Commission increases. Similarly, the Parliament prefers lower discretion as the Commission's and governments' preferences diverge from its ideal policy.

Step 2: preferred-to-status-quo proposals and preferences in the case of a new EU law

We now know the ideal baseline policy, implementation path and level of discretion of each player and how these preferences vary as a function of the policy positions of executive actors. We need one additional step before moving on to legislative decision-making. At the legislative stage, actors vote for a proposal only if they prefer it to the status quo or, as a minimum, if they are indifferent between the proposal and the status quo. It is therefore necessary to establish each player's preferred-to-status-quo set of proposals and the ranking within this set. In other words, what are the combinations of implementation path and level of discretion that give, to each player, at least the same utility as the status quo?

Obviously, these combinations depend on which status quo we choose, as each provides a different amount of utility to each player. The analysis on this section is confined to the status quo when a new EU law is adopted. This situation is common in many significant EU statutes and provides an important positional advantage to the states. The restriction will be relaxed later. This status quo comprises the existing national laws (i.e. national implementation path) and maximal discretion for the governments (i.e. national discretion equals R). From these premises, the determination of the status quo utility is straightforward and the set of preferred-to-status-quo proposals is derived by identifying the circumstances under which a player's expected utility from each implementation path is equal to or greater than the status quo utility. In other words, we can determine the conditions under which an actor prefers to change the status quo, namely to restrict national executive discretion or to delegate powers to the Commission. We can also compute the range of values of Commission discretion that each actor would approve of. This is the focus of this section.[12]

The European Commission. The Commission prefers delegation to itself rather than the status quo for a large majority of combinations of x_u and x_c, if its discretion d is not too low. It is willing to accept even lower discretion as conflict between the Commission and government U increases. The second best option is restriction of national discretion, but the preferences of a supranational and a national Commission differ considerably. In the former case, the Commission supports constraining national authority in the large majority of cases and for most values of discretion. In the case of a national Commission, the status quo is preferred if x_c is relatively close to x_u. Nevertheless, when the Commission wants a new law, it prefers executing the policy rather than relying on member states for any given combination of x_u, x_c and d.

The governments. The governments' status quo utility is a negative function of the intensity of conflict within the Council. Two

---

[12] The analysis focuses predominantly on two components of a typical proposal (i.e. the implementation path and the level of discretion), while the baseline policy is considered as given. We know already that the baseline policy and the level of discretion are substitutes. The last section of the chapter considers in greater detail the (few) implications of this restriction in the analysis.

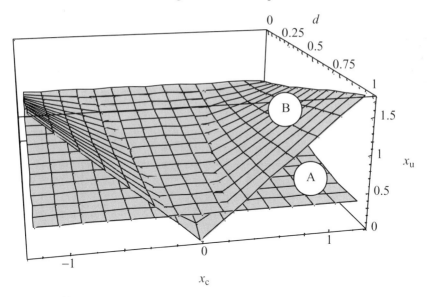

Figure 2.3 *Delegation preferences of government M in the case of a new law.*
Note: We assume $R = 1$ and $p = 0.25$.

indifference planes, illustrated in Figure 2.3, allow us to identify government M's preferred-to-status-quo set of proposals for combinations of x_u, x_c and d, given $R = 1$ and $p = 0.25$. Plane A maps the combinations of x_u, x_c and d where government M is indifferent between the status quo and a proposal with lower national discretion. For instance, for $x_u = 0.8$ and $x_c = -0.8$, this government is indifferent between the status quo and a proposal of national execution with $d = 0.12$. In other words, any proposal that decreases national discretion to any value higher than 0.12 is preferred to the status quo (the ideal national discretion is $d_n^\bullet = 0.49$). Plane B maps the combinations of x_u, x_c and d where government M is indifferent between the status quo and a proposal of Commission execution. At $x_u = 0.8$ and $x_c = -0.6$ for instance, the status quo and a proposal of Commission execution with either $d = 0.13$ or $d = 0.86$ generate the same utility. Any proposal with Commission discretion between 0.13 and 0.86 yields higher utility than the status quo (the ideal Commission discretion is $d_c^\bullet = 0.45$).

The combination of planes A and B produces four areas with distinctly different delegation preferences for government M. First, government M prefers the status quo in the area below the indifference planes where conflict within the Council is limited both in absolute terms and relative to that between government M and the Commission. The status quo generates limited distributive losses here and there is no need to either restrict national discretion or rely on the Commission. Second, the area above plane A and below plane B shows the combinations of x_u and x_c where government M is *only* willing to restrict national administrations and the range of discretion levels that it is willing to accept (here, since conflict in the Council is more intense, limiting national discretion provides benefits to government M, while, because of the Commission's bias, relying on this institution still remains too costly). The lower boundary of this discretion range is determined only by plane A when conflict within the Council is lower or marginally higher than that between M and the Commission. For instance, a line traced in Figure 2.3 along the discretion axis and at $x_u = -x_c = 0.6$ intersects only plane A at $d = 0.41$, the lower boundary where M is indifferent to the status quo. As conflict within the Council intensifies (i.e. x_u increases), the range first increases because government M supports even more restriction of national authority, but then it shrinks because there are also levels of Commission discretion that makes this state at least as well off as the status quo. If, say, x_u shifts to 0.8, a line traced along the discretion axis will intersect plane B at $d = 0.86$ and $d = 0.13$ and plane A at $d = 0.12$. Government M is *only* willing to restrict national administrations for $1 > d > 0.86$ or $0.13 > d > 0.12$.

Third, the area above the two planes shows the combination of x_u, x_c and the range of d levels for which government M would *also* delegate powers to the Commission as its preferences are not too extreme, relative to Council conflict. For example, we have seen that, at $x_u = 0.8$ and $x_c = -0.6$, this government prefers either Commission execution or restriction of national discretion to the status quo when d ranges between 0.86 and 0.13 (although, from the analysis carried out in step 1 above, we can determine that the latter option is the preferred choice). The range widens as $|x_c|$ decreases and the government's ideal choice may become Commission implementation. Finally, in the triangular area below plane A and above plane B, government M and the Commission have similar policy preferences. Therefore, although the state objects to any restriction of national discretion, it prefers delegation to the Commission to the status quo, as long as its discretion is not too small.

The delegation preferences of government U differ from those of government M in three important aspects. First, government U prefers the status quo to any executive role of a supranational Commission. If both the Commission and the baseline policy are supranational, it also objects to any restriction of national discretion. Second, government U supports the constraining of national authorities, up to some values of d, only if there is moderate conflict within the Council and the baseline policy is positive. For example, for $R = 1$ and $p = 0.25$, this government supports less than maximal national discretion only if $0.15 < x_u < 0.85$. Notably, the status quo is preferred if policy conflict in the Council is *either* very low *or* very high. Finally, this state would delegate powers only to a Commission with national preferences that are relatively close to x_u and as long as d is not too low.

The European Parliament. The Parliament accepts restraining national administrations under the same conditions as the Commission does. It prefers delegation to the Commission in circumstances that are similar to those analyzed in the previous section on the ideal delegation preferences. The only difference is that those conditions are less stringent here because the term of comparison is not the Parliament's ideal level of national discretion but the status quo.

Policy making at the legislative stage

Before I proceed onto the analysis of the results of the model, I briefly summarize the rationale of the steps we have taken so far. Models are usually solved starting from the end and moving backward so that we can figure out the actors' best responses to the actions taken down the line in the game. Consequently, we have first analyzed the measures taken by the actors at the executive stage. Here, an administrator is in charge of policy execution on the basis of a baseline policy and enjoys a degree of discretion. She develops expertise (she becomes aware of the shock to the policy) and takes an implementation measure that maximizes her utility. This actor, however, can shift the result of the baseline policy and shock only by a maximum amount, namely her degree of discretion. This behavior generates three possible final outcomes that are a function of the policy shock.

We have then proceeded in two steps to set the stage for legislative decision-making. First, we have formulated the expected utility for each actor on the basis of these final outcomes. This utility is a function of a player's own preferences, the range of shock values and implementation decisions. It allows us to determine the ideal baseline policy, implementation path and level of discretion for each player. Second, we have introduced a status quo (i.e. national implementation with maximum discretion), determined the utility that this status quo generates and established the set of proposals (combinations of implementation path and level of discretion) that each player prefers to this status quo. This latter step is necessary because a legislator votes for a proposal only if it generates at least the same utility as the status quo does.

We can move on now to legislative policy making. This stage is solved following the same logic as existing models of EU legislative politics (Steunenberg, 1994; Garrett, 1995; Crombez, 1996). Recall that the legislative stage terminates with legislators adopting first a baseline policy p^*, then choosing an executive actor D^* and a level of discretion d^*. In order for this composite measure to be adopted and become equilibrium under a specific legislative procedure, three conditions must be satisfied.

- First, the equilibrium measure *cannot be amended*. Each procedure has amendment rules, so there should not be other proposals that amend this measure and make the veto player(s) of the relevant procedure better off.
- Second, the equilibrium measure must *make the veto player(s) at least indifferent to the status quo*, otherwise it could not have been adopted.
- Third, recall that the Commission enjoys the monopoly of legislative initiation under each procedure. The implication is that the Commission will use this power strategically. It will choose the proposal that satisfies the previous two conditions and *maximizes its expected utility*.

Below I introduce the specific rules required for amendment and adoption of a Commission's proposal under unanimity and qualified majority voting. These rules, together with the actors' policy preferences, are the main features driving the results of the model. Recall that I assume that decisions at the legislative stage are taken sequentially. The setting of the policy precedes the conferral of discretionary authority to an administrator. Equilibria are then presented for a given baseline policy p^*. The limited implications of this assumption are assessed in the penultimate section of the chapter. I proceed below by describing the rules of each legislative procedure, the actors' best responses to the actions of others and the process of identification of equilibrium outcomes. I then illustrate with diagrams how key variables affect the choice of administrator(s) and their discretion.

Unanimity

Rules, equilibrium actions and outcomes. Under this procedure, the proposal of the Commission and amendments to its proposal must be approved by all the governments. Any member state can introduce amendments.

Each government's best response to a Commission's proposal consists of two steps. First, it tables amendments to the proposal that both governments support. Second, once these amendments are exhausted, a state votes for the resulting proposal only if such a proposal makes the government at least indifferent to the status quo. Anticipating this behavior, the Commission introduces a proposal *that cannot be amended unanimously by the governments, makes both governments at least indifferent to the status quo and maximizes its utility.*

Identifying this optimum proposal is not too complicated. Before I proceed however, I introduce an assumption that applies to both unanimity and qualified majority voting. I assume that the proposals of a supranational Commission belong to the core of unanimity and, hence, cannot be amended.[13] This assumption is introduced in order to approximate the reality of EU decision-making as much as possible. Most formal models limit the analysis to key states within the Council (e.g. Steunenberg, 1994; Garrett, 1995; Crombez, 1996), instead of considering all the fifteen (now twenty-five) governments. In unanimity, the two important states are those with the most national and the most supranational preferences because their positions determine the unanimity core, to which a Commission's proposal must belong to become law. For simplicity and tractability, I have considered only government U, with the most national preference, and government M with an intermediate position, and disregarded the most supranational government.

This arrangement, however, is objectionable and generates an asymmetry that incorrectly characterizes EU legislative politics. In the current setting, a national Commission can rely on the support from government U to avoid amendments to its proposal, while a supranational Commission has no one to count on as – implausibly – no government shares its (supranational) views. Proposals from a supranational Commission are therefore easier to amend that those from a national Commission. There is no reason why this should be the case, both proposals should have a priori similar chances of amendment. Additionally, the current arrangement neutralizes the effects of unanimity for amending a proposal, as these are mostly felt when the Commission wants to shift the status quo further away; namely, when it holds supranational preferences. The assumption is equivalent to the introduction of a supranational state that shares the Commission's preferences and would veto amendments to its proposals.

The equilibrium measures are determined as follows. In the case of a supranational Commission, the Commission's proposals cannot be amended, so we simply identify the two governments' preferred-to-status-quo sets of proposals that we analyzed above in step 2. The equilibrium is the proposal that belongs to both of these sets and maximizes the Commission's utility. The analysis of the Commission's ideal delegation preferences in step 1 above helps us to determine precisely this

---

[13] The core of a procedure is the set of measures than cannot be amended following such a procedure. An alternative description of this assumption could be the following: if $x_c < x_m$, any Commission proposal cannot be amended because there exists a (unmodeled) member of the Council with preferences close to x_c who would veto such amendments.

equilibrium proposal. We follow the same procedure in the case of a national Commission, with the only difference being that the set of proposals from which the Commission can choose should exclude measures that governments can successfully amend jointly. We use the analysis of the governments' ideal delegation preferences in step 1 above to exclude these measures.

Equilibrium delegation diagram. We are now in a position to illustrate the key results of the model. We are interested in two questions: when EU legislators decide to delegate executive powers to either the Commission or national administrations (i.e. the equilibrium implementation path D^*) and what determines their discretionary authority (i.e. the equilibrium level of discretion d^*). Three variables will affect these decisions: x_c, the ideal policy of the Commission; x_u, the ideal policy of government U, which is a measure of the intensity of conflict within the Council; and R, the degree of policy uncertainty.

Figure 2.4 illustrates the equilibrium outcomes for the first question and for different combinations of x_u and x_c and a given equilibrium baseline policy (i.e. $p^* = R/4$). Before I proceed, it must be noted that using a given p^* restricts our analysis to only a subset of values of x_u. A baseline policy cannot be in equilibrium if it is greater than x_u because both governments would prefer a more supranational policy in this circumstance.[14] In Figure 2.4, this applies for the area where $x_u < R/4$, which I have labeled *no equilibrium*.

The remaining areas are labeled *status quo* if there is no new EU legislation, *national administrations* if a new EU has restricted the discretion of national authorities and *Commission* if a new EU has delegated powers to this institution. I analyze the figure moving from left to right. The left-hand half depicts the equilibrium with a supranational Commission. Recall that, in these circumstances, this institution prefers predominantly delegation to itself and, as a second best, limitation of national discretion. But it has to persuade government U, the state whose preferences differ the most from its own. This state objects to any delegation to this Commission. Therefore, the only viable option is to propose a restriction of national authority that is acceptable to this government. Consequently, as the preferences of this state instruct, national discretion is maximal and the status quo is preserved at either high or low conflict within the Council. A limitation of discretion is accepted by both governments only at an intermediate level of conflict.

---

[14] Government U would reject any change of the status quo in the case of a supranational baseline policy.

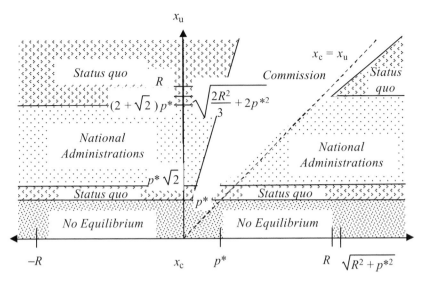

Figure 2.4 *Delegation equilibria with unanimity and a new law.*
Note: Delegation equilibria with $D^0 = N$ and $d^0 = R$, assuming $p^* = R/4$.

Moving further to the right beyond the vertical axis, the figure illustrates the equilibrium with a national Commission. When the preferences of this institution are in between those of the states (i.e. to the left of the dashed line), the left-hand equilibria are initially carried through for low values of x_c, but then both governments agree to confer powers to the Commission. Execution by a Commission with moderate national preferences outperforms the implementation bias of the status quo and it is beneficial to both states.[15] However, as preferences increase (i.e. moving to the right of the dashed line), the cost of Commission implementation rises for government M. This state starts objecting to Commission delegation for any value of discretion and the only option for the Commission is to propose a level restriction of national authority that is acceptable to this government. The state prefers the status quo for low conflict in the Council, while it agrees with government U to reduce national discretionary authority at higher conflict. Finally, in the top right-hand corner of Figure 2.4, there are some values of the Commission's discretion that government M prefers to the status quo. However, the Commission and

---

[15] Note that the area of Commission delegation is likely to shrink further if we consider that a state with supranational preferences may object to delegation to a Commission with strongly national preferences.

government U prefer the status quo to execution by the Commission with limited discretion. Hence, there is no new legislation.

In conclusion, a new law restricting national authority is adopted only if there is an intermediate level of conflict within the Council because only in these circumstances can the Commission obtain approval from both states. The Commission is delegated powers if its preferences are in between those of the governments as, only here, can it better the implementation bias of the status quo.

Equilibrium discretion diagram.   We move now on to the second question of what determines the discretionary authority of the executive actor(s) (d^*). We begin with the equilibrium national discretion. Recall the conditions we set earlier. In the case of a supranational Commission, the exact level of this discretion is the one that is most preferred by the Commission and makes both states at least indifferent to the status quo discretion. In the case of a national Commission, this value should also be one that cannot be altered by the states. Differing from most results in the literature on delegation, an increase in policy conflict between legislators and administrators may lead to a higher level of discretion. This result is illustrated in Figure 2.5 for both a national and a supranational Commission. The equilibrium level of national discretion first decreases and then increases as policy conflict within the Council increases. The difference between the two curves is due to the Commission's proposal power. This outcome originates from the executive–legislative role of the members of the Council, this specific status quo and, more importantly, the unanimity rule. At a moderate level of Council conflict, the two states agree, with the Commission, to reduce national discretion. But, as Council conflict increases above a certain level, the peripherally located government U prefers greater national room for maneuver and, ultimately, the status quo.

When legislators instead decide to rely on the Commission, the equilibrium discretion of this institution is the highest value that cannot be reduced by a unanimous Council. For our purposes, it important to point out that, as conflict between the Commission and the governments decreases (i.e. the preference of the Commission x_c moves from either the left or the right end of Figure 2.4 towards the dashed line), the likelihood of delegation to the Commission increases and, consequently, its discretion will be greater than zero.

Qualified majority voting

Rules, equilibrium actions and outcomes.   In this procedure, the proposal of the Commission must be approved by the pivotal government

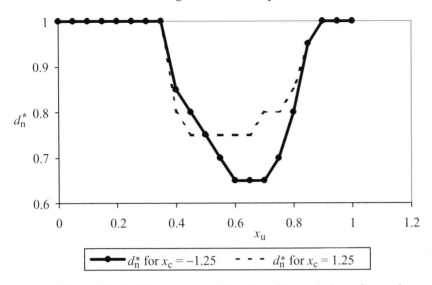

Figure 2.5 *Equilibrium national discretion with unanimity and a new law.*
Note: Discretion equilibria with $D^0 = N$ and $d^0 = R$, assuming $R = 1$
and $p^* = 0.25$.

under qualified majority voting. I consider government M to be such a
pivotal state. Amendments to the Commission's proposal can be tabled
by any state but require unanimity in the Council for approval.

As in unanimity, the governments' best response to a Commission's
proposal consists of two steps. First, any government tables amendments
to the proposal that both states support. Second, once these amendments
are exhausted, government M votes for the resulting proposal only if
such a proposal makes this state at least indifferent to the status quo. In
anticipation of this process, the Commission introduces a proposal *that
cannot be amended unanimously by the governments, makes government M at
least indifferent to the status quo and maximizes its utility.* The second is the
only condition that differs from the unanimity case and is the factor that
drives the differences in results across procedures.

The identification of the optimum proposal is also relatively straightforward. In the case of a supranational Commission, we can identify government M's preferred-to-status-quo set of proposals as determined above
in step 2. The equilibrium is the proposal that belongs to this set and
maximizes the Commission's utility. Again, the procedure in the case of
a national Commission is similar, with the only difference being that the
set of proposals from which the Commission can choose should exclude
measures that governments can unanimously amend. The analysis of

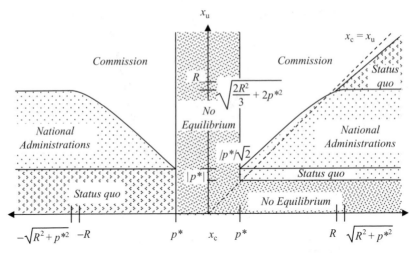

Figure 2.6 *Delegation equilibria with majority voting and a new law.* Note: Delegation equilibria with $D^0 = N$ and $d^0 = R$, and assuming $p^* = -R/4$ for $x_c < 0$, $p^* = R/4$ for $x_c > 0$.

governments' ideal delegation preferences carried out above in step 1 guides us in the exclusion of these measures.

Equilibrium delegation diagram. Recall the two key questions we are interested in: what determines the choice of administrator(s) and their discretionary authority. The variables affecting these decisions are the same as those for unanimity voting: the ideal policy of the Commission, the ideal policy of government U and the degree of policy uncertainty.

For the first question, Figure 2.6 illustrates the delegation equilibrium under this procedure. The labels have the same meaning as those in Figure 2.4. In addition to the case of $x_u < p$, there is another set of circumstances of *no equilibrium*. This is when the baseline policy does not lie in between the preferences of the Commission and of government M (i.e. for $p < [>]0$ and $p < [>]x_c$). This policy cannot be an equilibrium in majority voting because a shift toward zero would be beneficial to both the Commission and government M. Figure 2.6 therefore depicts the delegation outcomes with a given negative baseline policy (i.e. $p^* = -R/4$) for a supranational Commission and the outcomes with a given positive baseline policy (i.e. $p^* = R/4$) for a national Commission.

The most interesting results are in the left-hand half of the figure where the Commission has supranational preferences. For low values of x_u, namely for limited conflict within the Council, both governments are happy with the status quo. As conflict increases, government M prefers to restrain national administrations to limit the distributive losses originating from national execution. Initially, however, this state prefers the status quo rather than delegating powers to the Commission, for any level of discretion. Therefore, the Commission successfully proposes national implementation with less than maximal discretion. With further increases in conflict within the Council, there are levels of Commission discretion that government M prefers to the status quo. The Commission will then propose itself as the administrator. The results in the case of a national Commission in the right-hand half of Figure 2.6 resemble the outcomes from unanimity in Figure 2.4. Hence, I will not elaborate on them further.

In conclusion, a distinguishing feature of qualified majority voting is the greater likelihood of delegation to the Commission than to national administrations. In other words, majority voting allows the Commission to sidestep the opposition from the state with the most dissonant views and to pursue its objectives more successfully.

Equilibrium discretion diagrams. Moving on to the second question, we first assess the determinants of national discretion. In the case of a supranational Commission, the Commission's ideal level of national discretion is lower than that of government M for any equilibrium policy and preference configuration. The Commission successfully proposes a (less-than-maximal) level of discretion that is closest to its ideal and that makes government M at least indifferent to the status quo. This level decreases as conflict within the Council intensifies. In the case of a national Commission, the process and equilibrium levels of national discretion do not differ between unanimity and qualified majority voting (hence, the dashed line in Figure 2.5 also applies to majority voting). The Commission proposes its most preferred level which is preferred to the status quo and cannot be amended by the Council.

Figure 2.7 superimposes the equilibrium levels of national discretion in the case of qualified majority voting and a supranational Commission onto the equilibrium values in the case of unanimity which are shown in Figure 2.5.[16] The latter values form the U-shaped line which applies for any supranational Commission, that is for any negative value of x_c. The

---

[16] The equilibrium baseline policy p^* in Figure 2.7 differs between the two decision rules because negative values of the policy are not in equilibrium in unanimity voting while positive values are not in equilibrium in majority voting. I took two values that are symmetric across zero. Note that this does not violate the *ceteris paribus* conclusions of this analysis. If we consider any out-of-equilibrium negative value of p^* in unanimity, the equilibrium level of national discretion would take the maximal amount R. For any out-of-equilibrium positive value of p^* in majority voting, the equilibrium level of national discretion would be equal to or lower than the case of unanimity.

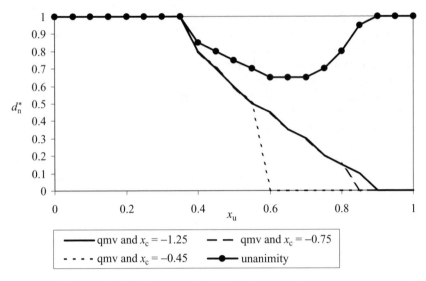

Figure 2.7 *Equilibrium national discretion, a new law and a supranational commission.*
Note: Discretion equilibria with $D^0 = N$ and $d^0 = R$; assuming $R = 1$, $p^* = 0.25$ for unanimity, $p^* = -0.25$ for qualified majority and $x_c < 0$.

other lines depict the equilibrium national discretion in the case of qualified majority voting and for an increasingly supranational Commission (i.e. decreasing values of x_c).

Two important conclusions can be derived from this analysis. First, the equilibrium levels of national discretion in qualified majority voting are likely to be equal to or smaller than those produced with unanimity. They are the same in the case of a national Commission and they are likely to be smaller with a supranational Commission, which succeeds in proposing lower discretion. Second, the downward sloping lines in Figure 2.7 suggest that, in the case of qualified majority voting and any supranational Commission, national equilibrium discretion decreases as conflict in the Council intensifies (i.e. x_u increases).

Finally, what are the determinants of the equilibrium levels of Commission discretion? As conflict within the Council intensifies, there are levels of Commission discretion that government M prefers to the status quo. The Commission then successfully proposes the highest of these values that makes state M at least indifferent to the status quo and, in the case of a national Commission, that cannot be amended unanimously by the Council.

Figure 2.8 illustrates how the Commission equilibrium discretion varies as a function of the preferences of the Commission and of the intensity of conflict with the Council (i.e. the preferences of government U).[17] Two important results must be highlighted. First, the downward sloping lines imply that the Commission equilibrium discretion increases as the preferences of this institution converge towards those of government M (recall that $x_m = 0$). Second, this discretion also increases as conflict within the Council increases. For a given ideal Commission policy, say $x_c = -0.6$, this institution has no discretion at a low level of conflict in the Council ($d_c^* = 0$ for $x_u = 0.5$), some discretion at moderate conflict ($d_c^* = 0.7$ for $x_u = 0.75$) and maximal discretion at high conflict ($d_c^* = 1$ for $x_u > 0.85$).[18]

Does the Commission equilibrium discretion differ systematically under the two decision-making rules? A supranational Commission is not delegated powers under unanimity while it may have an executive role in the case of qualified majority voting (this can be easily seen by comparing the left-hand sides of Figures 2.4 and 2.6). Therefore, while the discretion of a supranational Commission is zero under unanimity, it may take positive values under majority voting. When the preferences of a national Commission are in between those of the governments, the equilibrium level of discretion in unanimity cannot exceed and may be lower than the level in the case of majority voting. This is because as the Commission's preferences converge towards those of government M, the Commission can rely, in majority voting, on the support from a (converging) government M to enjoy greater discretion, while, in unanimity, the support from a (diverging) government U is still needed. When the Commission and government U have similar preferences, the equilibrium level is the same across the two procedures. This is because government M prefers less discretion than government U but the approval of this state is still necessary in both procedures. In conclusion, the equilibrium levels of Commission discretion in unanimity are likely to be equal to or smaller than those produced from qualified majority voting, essentially because the Commission needs support from the most distant state in the former procedure.

---

[17] Results are shown for given equilibrium baseline policies on the two sides of the policy dimension. As argued above, these policies must lie in between government M's and the Commission's ideal policies. Hence, the area labeled *no equilibrium* represents for circumstances where this is not the case.

[18] This result is not too dissimilar from Proposition 2 in Volden (2002b). In a separation of power system, a moderate independent agency may enjoy greater discretion as conflict between an agenda-setting legislature and an executive with veto power increases.

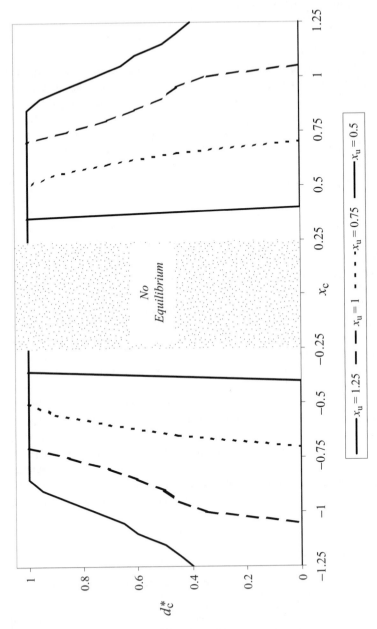

Figure 2.8 *Equilibrium discretion of the Commission, a new law, Council conflict and majority voting.*
Note: Discretion equilibria with $D^0 = N$ and $d^0 = R$; assuming $R = 1$, $p^* = -0.25$ for $x_c < 0$, $p^* = 0.25$ for $x_c > 0$.

$x_u = 1.25$ $x_u = 1$ $x_u = 0.75$ $x_u = 0.5$

Before summarizing these results for general propositions, we have left out an important variable affecting both national and Commission equilibrium discretion: the degree of policy uncertainty R. The equilibrium levels of both national and Commission discretion increase with policy uncertainty. The formal results in Appendix 2.1 clearly illustrate this relation. An equilibrium diagram is unnecessary as this is a standard outcome of the literature on delegation, but I elaborate further on this issue below.

Summing up: propositions

The findings of the model can be reorganized and summarized in a set of propositions (the proofs are given in Appendix 2.1). Our four variables of interest (delegation to and discretion of national administrations and the Commission) are affected by four factors: decision rules, conflict within the Council, conflict between the Commission and the pivotal government under a specific procedure, and policy complexity. I will demonstrate in the last section of the chapter that these conclusions also hold if we relax some assumptions of the model.

National administrations: delegation and discretion

The first proposition is on decision rules and the general pattern of delegation.

Proposition 2.1 *Delegation to national administrations is more likely under unanimity than qualified majority voting.*

This outcome originates from the possibility of the Commission eliciting support for its proposal from only government M, rather than both states, in the case of majority voting. This opportunity is of no use if a national Commission has delegation preferences that are more similar to those of government U than of government M. Therefore, outcomes do not differ between the two procedures. Majority voting instead gives a supranational Commission, which shares its preference profile more with government M than with government U, a better chance of achieving its objective. And what does this Commission want? Something that government U would not approve of: the transfer of powers from national administrations to the Commission. *Ceteris paribus*, majority voting makes this outcome more likely and delegation to national administrations less likely. At a glance, this result can be illustrated by comparing Figure 2.4 with Figure 2.6. The area of delegation to national administrations is larger in the former figure.

The impact of decision rules on national discretion can be summarized as follows.

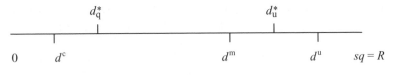

National discretion

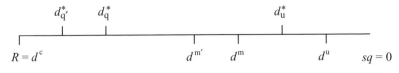

Commission discretion

Figure 2.9 *An example of equilibrium national and Commission discretion.* Note: d^i ideal discretion for actor $i = $ u, m, c, d_u^* equilibrium under unanimity, d_q^* equilibrium under QMV.

Proposition 2.2   *The level of discretion of national administrations under unanimity voting is equal to or greater than the level of discretion under qualified majority voting.*

The logic behind this proposition is similar. The result is shown in its entirety in Figure 2.7, while the upper part of Figure 2.9 provides a more intuitive illustration of the dynamics. It shows the players' ideal levels of discretion and the equilibria under the two procedures along a one-dimensional space of national discretion.[19]

A national Commission sharing the preferences of government U would still need the support from both governments. Therefore, national discretion does not differ between unanimity and qualified majority voting. As shown in Figure 2.9, a supranational Commission instead prefers lower national discretion than the governments. In initiating its proposal, this institution exploits the fact that, as conflict in the Council increases, government M prefers less discretion that government U. Hence, discretion is likely to be lower in majority voting as it requires the support of only government M.

The next proposition recapitulates how conflict within the Council affects national discretion.

---

[19] Figure 2.9 simplifies matters considerably because it disregards the fact that actors can choose between implementation paths and related discretion. Moreover, states' ideal national discretion levels are interlocked, complicating a comparative statics analysis. Nevertheless, discretion preferences are single-peaked.

Proposition 2.3 *In the case of qualified majority voting and a supranational Commission, the level of discretion of national administrations decreases as conflict within the Council increases.*

Figure 2.7 also displays this relation. The proposition is generated from the fact that both government M's and this Commission's ideal levels of national discretion decrease as Council conflict increases (in Figure 2.9, they would both shift to the left). These actors want to limit the distributional losses originating from implementation by a government U with increasingly extreme preferences. Why is this proposition limited to two circumstances? A centrally located government M always prefers to limit national discretion to minimize the losses produced by the other increasingly extreme state. Instead, above a certain point of Council conflict, these losses for the peripherally located government U decrease by *increasing* national room for maneuver. The need for this government's approval in unanimity severs the negative relation between discretion and policy conflict. The same happens in the case of qualified majority voting and a national Commission, as this Commission is likely to share government U's discretion preferences. Figure 2.5 shows these results (recall that the dashed line also applies to majority voting and a national Commission).

European Commission: delegation and discretion

The first result with regard to delegation to the Commission is a mirror image of Proposition 2.1.

Proposition 2.4 *Delegation to the Commission is more likely under qualified majority than unanimity voting.*

Its logic is explained in the previous section. The area of delegation to the Commission is larger in Figure 2.6 than in Figure 2.4.

Decision rules affect the Commission's discretion as follows.

Proposition 2.5 *The level of discretion of the Commission under unanimity voting is equal to or smaller than the level of discretion under qualified majority voting.*

The lower part of Figure 2.9 illustrates this outcome in a simplified manner. When delegated powers, the Commission always prefer more to less discretion. In unanimity, it needs the support from the government with the lowest ideal discretion. In majority voting, it needs only the support from government M, which could prefer higher Commission discretion than government U (as in Figure 2.9). This is a similar proposition to the one I presented in an earlier model where I considered only delegation of powers to the Commission (Franchino, 2000a: 164).

The next proposition was also introduced in this earlier work (Franchino, 2000a: 165). Whichever government the Commission has to persuade, the ideal discretion of this actor increases as the Commission's preferences move towards its ideal policy. As the risk of distributive losses subsides, states prefer delegating greater authority to deal with policy shocks (in Figure 2.9 this is illustrated with the shift of government M's ideal discretion from d^m to $d^{m'}$). The Commission seizes this opportunity by successfully proposing higher discretion.

Proposition 2.6   *The level of discretion of the Commission increases as the preferences of the Commission and those of the pivotal government converge.*

Figure 2.4 shows that the discretion of this institution is likely to become greater than zero in unanimity as the Commission's preferences move from extreme to moderate values. Figure 2.8 illustrates instead how, in majority voting, discretion increases as these preferences approach those of government M. This is a common expectation of the delegation literature. The discretion of an agency increases if policy conflict with the legislative principals recedes.

An additional opportunity of conferring more powers to the Commission presents itself as conflict within the Council exacerbates. In these circumstances, government M's distributive cost of relying on national administrations increases, for any level of discretion, *relative to* the cost of relying on the Commission (keeping this actor's ideal policy constant). Importantly, as conflict (and national implementation costs) increase, the range of discretion values at which this government prefers delegation to the Commission to the status quo widens and its upper boundary increases. Or, in other words, government M is willing to delegate more discretionary authority to the Commission because more Council conflict has reduced the utility from the status quo. Plane B in Figure 2.3 illustrates this dynamics. The Commission takes advantages of this situation and successfully secures higher discretion. Figure 2.8 shows how these variables covary. The relation can be summarized as follows.

Proposition 2.7   *In the case of qualified majority voting, the level of discretion of the Commission increases as conflict within the Council increases.*

In unanimity, this proposition does not hold because the procedure requires government U's approval. And, depending on whether government U's preference diverges from that of government M at low or high values, state U's cost of relying on national administrations may increase or decrease relative to the cost of Commission delegation (*ceteris paribus*). Therefore, Commission discretion may also increase or decrease.

Complexity of issue areas

Recall that the actors' utility also captures an informational component and that the ideal discretion for any actor and implementation path is a positive function of R, which measures this informational dimension. The last proposition of this section is the standard relation known in the literature between information intensity or policy complexity and discretion. *Ceteris paribus*, actors are willing to delegate more authority and accept greater bias as outcomes become more uncertain. Appendix 2.1 show how all ideal and equilibrium levels of discretion are positively related to policy uncertainty.

Proposition 2.8 *The level of discretion of the administrators increases as the complexity of the issue area increases.*

The model, however, does not produce a proposition that allows us to predict how EU legislators choose between national administrations and the Commission on the basis of complexity of the policy. In other words, if we assume that the pivotal government is indifferent between national and Commission delegation because the distributive losses are the same, which other features, informational or actor-related, are likely to influence the EU legislators choice of administrator? I argue that differences between these two agents are likely to guide this decision. Subsequent chapters will elaborate on this point and introduce testable hypotheses derived from this proposition.

The discretion preferences of the European Parliament in codecision

Rules and equilibrium actions. Since November 1993, the Parliament can influence the EU legislative outcomes through the codecision procedure. This procedure will be described at length in Chapter 7 where the propositions developed in this section are tested. For our purposes, suffice it to say here that, in codecision, the Parliament, together with any government, can put forward amendments to a legislative proposal and that such a proposal requires the approval of both a qualified majority in the Council and the Parliament to become law.

I will not produce equilibrium outcomes for this procedure and will only focus on the comparison between the discretion preferences of the Parliament and those of government M, the pivotal actor in the Council. Nevertheless, since these preferences are analyzed for given equilibrium baseline policies, it is necessary to briefly introduce the actors' equilibrium actions in codecision.

There is some disagreement among formal scholars on the role exercised by the Commission in this procedure, although recent empirical studies are shedding some light on this debate.[20] Anyway, to simplify the procedure to its bare bones, I suggest that the Parliament's and government M's best response to a Commission's proposal consists of first tabling amendments to the proposal that both actors support. Once amendments are exhausted, they vote for the resulting proposal only if it makes them at least indifferent to the status quo. The Commission's best response consists of introducing a proposal *that cannot be amended jointly by the Parliament and government M, makes both the Parliament and government M at least indifferent to the status quo, and maximizes its utility.*

Given these strategies, a baseline policy can be an equilibrium only if it is situated in between the policy preferences of the Parliament and of government M. If that were not the case, these actors would both approve a shift towards their policy positions as their utility would increase from such a move. With this condition in mind, we can now evaluate what determines differences in discretion preferences between the Parliament and government M.

---

[20] The codecision procedure was introduced in the Maastricht Treaty (codecision I) and modified in the Amsterdam Treaty (codecision II). For codecision I, Steunenberg (1994) and Crombez (1997a) assert that the Commission can choose its most preferred measure that belongs to the codecision I winset *and* to its core (the winset is the set of policies formed by the intersection of the preferred-to-status-quo sets of the Parliament and of the pivotal government). Garrett and Tsebelis (1996; see also Garrett, 1995; Tsebelis and Garrett, 2000) instead argue that, since the Council can repropose its common position at the end of the procedure, the agenda-setting power has been transferred from the Commission to the Council's pivotal member which can make a take-it-or-leave-it offer to the Parliament and obtain its best policy within the Parliament's preferred-to-status-quo set. For codecision II, Crombez (2001) claims that the Commission has entirely lost its legislative role. Tsebelis and Garrett (2000: footnote 7) instead contend that this institution could still have some leeway in choosing a proposal which belongs to the codecision II winset *and* to its core. Interestingly, this is the same prediction as Steunenberg (1994) and Crombez (1997a) for codecision I. Along similar lines, Corbett (in Crombez, Steunenberg and Corbett, 2000) and Hix (2002a) argue that the Parliament inserted in its Rules of Procedure the threat of rejecting any proposal reintroduced by the Council, making codecision I operating de facto as codecision II. Kasack (2004) finds empirical support for this assertion, but also a weakened role of the Commission in the second reading of codecision II. In a related work, Selck and Steunenberg (2004) show that the best model characterizing codecision is one whereby the Parliament submits a proposal to the Council.

Ideal discretion preferences and propositions. There are three questions that interest us: how the Parliament's ideal level of national discretion differs from that of government M, how this difference varies as a function of these actors' preferences and how the difference between the ideal Commission discretion of the Parliament and of government M varies as a function of their preferences.

As far as the first question is concerned, a comparison between the ideal levels of national discretion of the Parliament and of government M reveals that any Parliament with supranational preferences prefers less national discretion than government M. If the equilibrium baseline policy is relatively close to government U's ideal policy, also a national Parliament prefers less national discretion than government M. In other words, the Parliament prefers less discretion because, as it is not in charge of execution, it would benefit more than this state from limiting the dispersion of national measures.

The frequency of occurrence of these circumstances is an empirical matter. But an additional factor could make this situation very common, regardless of the actors' policy preferences. As I will elaborate in greater detail in Chapter 7, members of the Parliament have a systematic disadvantage vis-à-vis ministers of the Council with regard to the ability to exert ongoing control of national policy implementation because they do not head national bureaucracies. Since they face higher costs of nonstatutory oversight, they should prefer less statutory discretion for national administrations. This argument can be formalized by considering asymmetric changes of the R range that are systematically biased against the Parliament. As we have reported above in Proposition 2.8, discretion increases with policy complexity, that is with increases by the same amount of the low and the high boundaries of R. Epstein and O'Halloran (1994: 711) also show that, above a threshold of legislative–bureaucratic conflict, ideal discretion does *not* increase as the boundary of the R range that is closer to the agency increases. This situation could depict the Parliament's unfavorable position in the case of national implementation, namely a situation whereby the distribution of states of Nature is biased against the Parliament and in favor of governments, given the former's relative difficulty in exerting ongoing control. Therefore, we can plausibly produce the following proposition.

Proposition 2.9 *In most circumstances, the Parliament's ideal level of discretion of national administrations is lower that the ideal level of the pivotal government.*

Moving on to the second question, the identification of how the difference between the ideal national discretion of the Parliament and of government

M varies as a function of conflict between these two actors leads to the following relatively uncontroversial proposition.

Proposition 2.10   *The Parliament's ideal level of discretion of national administrations, relative to the pivotal government's ideal level, decreases as conflict between this government and the Parliament increases.*

This result can be conceived as the well-known impact of conflict between a legislative principal (the Parliament) and an agency (government M) on the former's discretion preferences. Lower discretion is preferred with greater risk of implementation bias.

The last question evaluates how the difference between the ideal Commission discretion of the Parliament and of government M vary as a function of their preferences (an argument about a systematic difference is less plausible because the Parliament is not disadvantaged, compared to the Council, in the exercise of ongoing Commission oversight). Let us start with a Commission that is located somewhere in between the ideal preferences of the Parliament and of government M, say $x_c = p^*$, where the ideal level of Commission discretion reaches its maximum for both actors. As the Commission moves away from the baseline policy and towards the Parliament's ideal policy, government M's ideal level of Commission discretion decreases while the Parliament's level is unchanged. If the Commission moves in the opposite direction, the Parliament's ideal discretion decreases while government M's ideal level remains the same. The proposition that can be derived from this analysis is the following.

Proposition 2.11   *The Parliament's ideal level of discretion for the Commission, relative to the pivotal government's ideal level, increases as conflict between the Parliament and the Commission decreases relative to the conflict between the pivotal government and the Commission.*

This proposition also results from the impact of legislator–agency conflict on discretion. As this conflict recedes for one legislator, the risk of implementation bias subsides and, *ceteris paribus*, this legislator's ideal level of discretion increases relative to that of other legislators.

Relaxing the assumptions

In this section I consider whether the key results of the model hold if (i) the Council is composed of more than two governments, (ii) the status quo differs and (iii) discretion and policy decisions are taken simultaneously.

Number of governments

The utility of relying on national administrations *relative to* Commission delegation and the ideal level of national discretion vary as a function of the interaction between the number of states and the preferences of each additional state. For instance, an actor's utility from national delegation and its ideal national discretion increase in the case of enlargement to a state that shares this actor's policy preferences. If this actor is pivotal in a procedure, enlargement changes the threshold of Council conflict at which national discretion is restricted and powers are delegated to the Commission. Importantly, however, the number of member states has an effect on the delegation decisions *via* the preferences of the new state rather than independently of them. Changes in policy conflict still have the same consequences with the new government and the propositions are unaffected. Whether this result is empirically plausible is another matter however. Other modeling choices could have led to the conclusion that the number of states has an independent and unambiguous impact on the relative reliance on the Commission or national administrations for policy implementation. Further research is needed.

Amending legislation

How do the choices of executive actors and levels of discretion vary in the case of a different status quo? Consider the case of unanimity and when states have agreed to restrict their own national authorities. The possibility of amendments differs depending on whether there is moderate ($x_u < 2p^*$) or high ($x_u > 2p^*$) conflict within the Council. In the former case, governments reduce (increase) national executive authority as conflict within the Council increases (decreases). Beyond this threshold, states disagree on the direction of the shift in national discretion and there is no amendment. The transfer of powers from national administrations to the Commission is possible only when the preferences of the Commission are in between those of the governments (see Figure 2.4). As long as its preferences remain within this range, its discretion is not reduced[21] and can be increased. A reduction in Commission discretion or, even, a transfer of its powers back to national administrations can occur in the case of a considerable leftward or rightward shift of its policy preferences.

---

[21] This is because at least one of the two states prefers maximal discretion for the Commission (government M for $x_c < p^*$ and government U for $x_u > x_c > p^*$). The Commission relies on this state to avoid any restriction of authority.

In the case of majority voting and a national Commission, changes to national and Commission discretion take place mostly under the same conditions as in the case of unanimity. For a supranational Commission, further reductions in national authority or delegation of powers to the Commission are likely to occur if policy conflict in the Council increases. Both government M and the Commission approve these changes. When the Commission is in charge of execution, it can gain discretion as x_c and x_m converge. Importantly, however, policy convergence in the Council leads to increases in national discretion or transfer of powers from the Commission back to national administrations only if the Council acts unanimously because these amendments are not supported by the Commission. Unanimity is also needed for decreases in Commission discretion when the preferences of this institution become more supranational.

Majority voting facilitates certain types of amendment, so it generates a dynamics in the amendment process that is clearly different from unanimity. It facilitates the adoption of amending legislation that restrains national authority further (as Proposition 2.3 suggests), shifts powers from national administrations to a supranational Commission and increases the discretion of a supranational Commission (see Propositions 2.1, 2.2, 2.4, 2.5 and 2.7). Unanimity will be required to extend national authority, transfer powers back to national administrations and to reduce the Commission's discretion. The causal relations proposed in the previous sections will be stronger in one direction but they would still apply in amending legislation (see also Franchino, 2005). Take, for instance, Proposition 2.3. Assume that the status quo is a certain degree of national discretion lower than R. As conflict increases, a new act may further constrain national administration. If conflict decreases, a new act may increase national discretion, though it is unlikely to be adopted because it will require a unanimous Council. The same line of reasoning applies for Propositions 2.6–2.8, while the remaining ones are unaffected. Nevertheless, only a small percentage of the acts analyzed in the empirical chapters amend previous legislation. Hence, the study of how choices of delegation occur in amending legislation is left to further research.

Simultaneous decisions of baseline policy and discretion

The model assumes that the setting of the baseline policy precedes the conferral of discretionary authority to an administrator and results are reported for a given equilibrium baseline policy. What happens to the equilibrium outcomes if we fully consider the role of the baseline policy or, in other words, if discretion and policy decisions were taken simultaneously? Following Volden's (2002b) application to the US, the main import from simultaneous decisions is related to the location of the status quo baseline policy. A veto player, such as a pivotal government, can secure a discretion level closer to its ideal if the status quo baseline policy is proximal to its ideal policy. An agenda setter, such as the Commission, can secure a discretion level closer to its ideal in other circumstances. As such, the overall findings of the model are not expected to change. However, as with the previous assumption, this discussion underscores the need for further research to consider and, crucially, measure the location of the status quo policy.[22]

Conclusion

This chapter has developed a model of the politics of delegation in the EU which builds on existing applications to the US separation of power system and on formal EU works on legislative procedures and delegation, and incorporates a set of EU-specific institutional features. The primary objectives of the model have been to evaluate when EU legislators decide to delegate executive powers to either the Commission or national administrations, what determines their discretionary authority and the differences between the Parliament and the Council with regard to both national and Commission discretion.

The propositions derived from the model will be grouped and reformulated as testable hypotheses in the following chapters. Table 2.1 provides a map for the rest of the book. It lists the dependent variables, the testable hypotheses, the propositions from which hypotheses originate and the chapters where hypotheses are introduced and tested. The expectations on policy complexity will be adapted to take into consideration differences between executive agents. Additional predictions will be developed concerning relative Commission–national discretion and from Propositions 2.9 and 2.11. Only a variant of Proposition 2.11 will be examined. Before performing these empirical tests however, we need to develop appropriate measures of the dependent and the independent variables. This is the subject of the next two chapters.

[22] For instance, the introduction of a dummy variable for a new law would not solve this measurement problem because it would be based on another, not necessarily plausible, assumption, namely that the status quo policy is closer to that of the pivotal government in new EU laws. Works testing Volden's finding have not been produced as yet.

Table 2.1 *The hypotheses.*

Dependent variable	Hypotheses	Propositions Chapters
Delegation to national administrations	H5.1: Delegation to national administrations is more likely under unanimity than qualified majority voting.	P2.1 Ch. 5 and 6
Discretion of national administrations	H5.2: The discretion of national administrations increases under unanimity and in issue areas that require specialized and technical knowledge.	P2.2 and P2.8[a] Ch. 5 and 6
	H5.3: In the case of qualified majority voting and a Commission more in favor of the underlying shift of the measure than the Council pivotal member, the discretion of national administrations decreases as conflict within the Council increases.	P2.3 Ch. 5 and 6
Delegation to the Commission	H5.4: Delegation to the Commission is more likely under qualified majority than unanimity voting.	P2.4 Ch. 5 and 6
Discretion of the Commission	H5.5: The discretion of the Commission increases under qualified majority voting, as the preferences of the Commission and those of the pivotal government converge and in issue areas that require general and managerial skills at the supranational level.	P2.5, P2.6 and P2.8[a] Ch. 5 and 6
	H5.6: In the case of qualified majority voting, the discretion of the Commission increases as conflict within the Council increases.	P2.7 Ch. 5 and 6
Relative discretion	H5.7: Relative discretion decreases under qualified majority voting.	P2.3 and P2.7 Ch. 5 and 6
	H5.8: In the case of qualified majority voting and a Commission more in favor of the underlying shift of the measure than the Council pivotal member, relative discretion decreases as conflict within the Council increases.	P2.2 and P2.5 Ch. 5 and 6
Parliament vs. Council preferences with regard to:		
Discretion of national administrations	H7.1: The Parliament prefers less discretion for national administrations than the Council.	P2.9 Ch. 7
	H7.4: In the case of national implementation, the Parliament prefers a broader scope, fewer or stricter exemptions and derogations, more or stricter consultation requirements, reporting requirements and appeal procedures and more or shorter time limits. The Parliament prefers greater influence in the appointment of EU-level bodies and in the comitology procedures.	P2.9 Ch. 7

Table 2.1 (*cont.*)

Dependent variable	Hypotheses	Propositions Chapters
	H7.2: The Parliament prefers less discretion for national administrations than the Council as conflict between the Parliament and the Council increases.	P2.10 Ch. 7
Discretion of the Commission	H7.3: The Parliament prefers more discretion for the Commission than the Council.	P2.11[b] Ch. 7
	H7.5: In the case of supranational implementation, the Parliament prefers deleting or loosening consultation and reporting requirements, relaxing spending limits, inserting or strengthening inspection powers, expanding policy-specific powers and loosening the comitology procedures.	P2.11[b] Ch. 7

Note: [a] Hypothesis adapted from this proposition. [b] Hypothesis is a variant of this proposition.

Appendix 2.1 The formal model of delegation in the European Union

I assume four players: two governments (M and U) forming the Council, the Commission (C) and the Parliament (PR). They have single-peaked preferences represented by ideal points x_i for $i = $ m, u, c or pr, in a unidimensional policy space $X = \Re^1$. Without loss of generality, I set $x_m = 0$ and $x_u \geq 0$. Players have quadratic preferences over the final policy outcome $x : U_i(x) = -(x - x_i)^2$. Outcomes depend on the final adopted policy p and an additive and homogeneous random shock ω to policy. Legislators treat ω as unknown when adopting new measures, but they have a prior probabilistic belief that ω is distributed uniformly in the $-R$ to R range. Formally, outcomes $x = p + \omega$, where $f(\omega) \sim U [-R, R]$.

The game starts with the Commission making a proposal $v(p, D, d)$ composed of a baseline policy, an executive actor and a level of discretion. EU legislators adopt the law (p^*, D^*, d^*) following the relevant procedure. Nature then randomly selects the value ω from the distribution $f(\omega)$ and the actor(s) in charge of execution take the implementing decision(s) p^j subject to $|p^j - p^*| \leq d_k^*$, where $j = $ c, m, u and $k = $ c, n (Commission and national discretion), and on the basis of the true value of ω. When the Commission is in charge of implementation, the final policy outcome is $x = p^* + p^c + \omega$. When the national authorities execute the policy, outcomes are country-specific: $x^m = p^* + p^u + \omega$ and $x^u = p^* + p^u + \omega$. In this latter circumstance, the players' utility takes the following formulation: $U_i(x) = -\frac{1}{2}[(x^m - x_i)^2 + (x^u - x_i)^2]$.

Policy making at the executive stage

At the executive stage, actor(s) implement the policy p^j that maximizes their utility U_i, given the baseline equilibrium policy p^*, the degree of equilibrium discretion d_k^* and the state of Nature ω. Formally, let the set of available policies to implement Y determine the function $\delta(p^*, d_k^*, \omega) = \{Y \in R^1\}$ such that $|Y + p^* - \omega| \leq d_k^*$, the condition becomes

$$p^j(p^*, d_k^*, \omega) \in \text{argmax}^j_{p \in \delta(p^*, dk^*, \omega)} U_i(p^* + p^j + \omega).$$

In the case of delegation to the Commission $(D^* = C)$, the outcomes depend on the realization of ω as follows.

Range of ω	Outcome x
$-R \leq \omega \leq x_c - p^* - d_c^*$	$\omega + p^* + d_c^*$
$x_c - p^* - d_c^* \leq \omega \leq x_c - p^* + d_c^*$	x_c
$x_c - p^* + d_c^* \leq \omega \leq R$	$\omega + p^* - d_c^*$

When national administrations are in charge of execution $(D^* = N)$, the outcomes of the executive stage are as follows.

Implementation by government M		Implementation by government U	
Range of ω	Outcome x^m	Range of ω	Outcome x^u
$-R \leq \omega \leq -p^* - d_n^*$	$\omega + p^* + d_n^*$	$-R \leq \omega \leq x_u - p^* - d_n^*$	$\omega + p^* + d_n^*$
$-p^* - d_n^* \leq \omega \leq -p^* + d_n^*$	0	$x_u - p^* - d_n^* \leq \omega \leq x_u - p^* + d_n^*$	x_u
$-p^* + d_n^* \leq \omega \leq R$	$\omega + p^* - d_n^*$	$x_u - p^* + d_n^* \leq \omega \leq R$	$\omega + p^* - d_n^*$

Setting the ground for policy making at the legislative stage

Lemma 2.1   Ideal baseline policy $p^\bullet$, implementation path $D^\bullet$, discretion of national administrations $d_n^\bullet$ and of the Commission $d_c^\bullet$ of each actor are as follows.

$p^{\bullet} = x_i$ for $\forall i$.

Commission: $D^{\bullet} = C$ and $d_c^{\bullet} = R$ for $\forall x_c$ and x_u.

Government M: $D^{\bullet} = N$ and $d_n^{\bullet} = R - (\sqrt{x_u^2 - 2p^{*2}})/\sqrt{2}$ for $x_u < |x_c|\sqrt{2}$, $D^{\bullet} = C$ and $d_c^{\bullet} = R - \sqrt{x_c^2 - p^{*2}}$ otherwise.

Government U: $D^{\bullet} = N$ and $d_n^{\bullet} = R - (\sqrt{4x_u p^* - x_u^2 - 2p^{*2}})/\sqrt{2}$ for $x_c < x_u - x_u/\sqrt{2}$ or $x_c > x_u + x_u/\sqrt{2}$, $D^{\bullet} = C$ and $d_c^{\bullet} = R - \sqrt{x_c^2 - p^{*2} - 2x_u(x_c - p^*)}$ otherwise.[23]

Parliament: $D^{\bullet} = N$ and
$d_n^{\bullet} = R - [\sqrt{x_u^2 - 2p^{*2} - 2x_{pr}(x_u - 2p^*)}]/\sqrt{2}$
for $x_{pr} < (2x_c^2 - x_u^2)/(4x_c - 2x_u)$ if $x_u < 2x_c$
or $x_{pr} > (2x_c^2) - x_u^2/(4x_c - 2x_u)$ if $x_u > 2x_c$, $D^{\bullet} = C$
and $d_c^{\bullet} = R - \sqrt{x_c^2 - p^{*2} - 2x_{pr}(x_c - p^*)}$ otherwise.

Proof On the basis of the decisions taken by actors at the executive stage, we can compute the expected utility of each player from each implementation path (this expected utility will be the basis on which actors at the legislative stage will formulate their best responses to executive decisions). These formulas are long and complicated. For the sake of clarity, I delete the asterisks for the variables p and d. The expected utility in the case of Commission execution is

$$\text{EU}_i = \int_{-R}^{x_c - p - d_c} (\omega + p + d_c - x_i)^2 \frac{1}{2R}\, d\omega - \int_{x_c - p - d_c}^{x_c - p + d_c} (x_c - x_i)^2 \frac{1}{2R}\, d\omega$$

$$- \int_{x_c - p - d_c}^{R} (\omega + p - d_c - x_i)^2 \frac{1}{2R}$$

$$d\omega = \frac{(d_c - R)^3 - 3R(x_i - p)^2 + 3d_c(p^2 - x_c^2 - 2x_i p + 2x_i x_c)}{3R}$$

$$\text{for } i = m, u, c, pr \tag{2.1A}$$

where d_c is the Commission's discretion.

[23] Note that, for $x_u < 2p^*$, $d_n^{\bullet}$ decreases as x_u increases but it increases for $x_u > 2p^*$. Ideal national discretion is a convex function of Council conflict. This explains the U-curves in Figures 2.5 and 2.7.

In the case of national implementation, the actors' expected utility becomes

$$\text{EU}_i = -\frac{1}{2}\int_{-R}^{-p-d_n}(\omega + p + d_n - x_i)^2\frac{1}{2R}\,d\omega - \frac{1}{2}\int_{-p-d_n}^{-p+d_n}(-x_i)^2\frac{1}{2R}\,d\omega$$

$$-\frac{1}{2}\int_{-p+d_n}^{R}(\omega + p - d_n - x_i)^2\frac{1}{2R}\,d\omega$$

$$-\frac{1}{2}\int_{-R}^{x_u-p-d_n}(\omega + p + d_n - x_i)^2\frac{1}{2R}\,d\omega$$

$$-\frac{1}{2}\int_{x_u-p-d_n}^{x_u-p+d_n}(x_u - x_i)^2\frac{1}{2R}\,d\omega$$

$$-\frac{1}{2}\int_{x_u-p+d_n}^{R}(\omega + p - d_n - x_i)^2$$

$$\frac{1}{2R}\,d\omega = [2(d_n - R)^3 - 3R(2x_i^2 + p^2 - 2x_i p) + 3d_n x_u(2x_i - x_u)$$

$$+3p(p - 2x_i)(2d_n - R)]/6R \qquad (2.2A)$$

where d_n is national discretion.

The ideal baseline policy $p^\bullet$ can be calculated by taking the derivative of EU_i with respect to p and setting it equal to zero. For both implementation paths, we have $\partial \text{EU}_i/\partial p = 0 \Leftrightarrow p^\bullet = x_i$.

A similar exercise can be conducted with the ideal level of discretion $d^\bullet$. However, the formulas differ with regard to the implementation paths. In the case of Commission execution, we have

$$\frac{\partial \text{EU}_i}{\partial d_c} = \frac{(d_c - R)^2 - x_c^2 + p^2 + 2x_i(x_c - p)}{R} = 0$$

$$\Leftrightarrow d_c^\bullet = R - \sqrt{x_c^2 - p^2 - 2x_i(x_c - p)}.$$

In the case of national implementation, the derivative leads to the following result:

$$\frac{\partial \text{EU}_i}{\partial d_n} = \frac{2d_n^2 - 4Rd_n + 2R^2 + 2p^2 - 4px_i - x_u^2 + 2x_i x_u}{2R} = 0$$

$$\Leftrightarrow d_n^\bullet = R - \frac{\sqrt{x_u^2 - 2p^2 - 2x_i(x_u - 2p)}}{\sqrt{2}}.$$

For each player, the ideal delegation preferences, or ideal implementation path, are derived by inserting these ideal levels of discretion into the expected utility functions (2.1A) and (2.2A) and determining the circumstances under which one path generates higher utility than the other. Delegation preferences vary as a function of the preferences of executive actors. Note that changes in the equilibrium baseline policy p^* lead to changes in the ideal discretion d^* because the two variables are substitutes. However, the choice of the ideal administrator D^* is unaffected. QED

Legislative decision-making is based on pairwise comparisons. A legislator votes for a proposal if and only if her utility is at least the same as the amount she gains from the status quo. Formally, let $v(p, D, d)$ be a proposal, a vote in favor of this proposal occurs if and only if (iff) $EU_i(v) \geq EU_i^0$, where EU_i^0 is the expected utility from the status quo for player i.

It is therefore necessary to establish each player's preferred-to-status-quo set of proposals. I use as a reference status quo the situation whereby a new EU law is adopted. In this circumstance, the status quo comprises the existing national laws and maximal discretion for the governments. Formally, this means $D^0 = N$, $d_n^0 = R$.

Lemma 2.2 Actors prefer to change a status quo comprising $D^0 = N$, $d_n^0 = R$ under the following conditions.

Commission: the Commission prefers to change the status quo and delegate powers to itself if

$$x_u \geq x_c + \sqrt{\frac{12x_c p(d_c - R) + 3x_c^2(R - 2d_c) - 2(d_c - R)(d_c^2 + 3p^2 - 2d_c R + R^2)}{3R}}$$

or

$$x_u \leq x_c - \sqrt{\frac{12x_c p(d_c - R) + 3x_c^2(R - 2d_c) - 2(d_c - R)(d_c^2 + 3p^2 - 2d_c R + R^2)}{3R}}.$$

It prefers restricting national administrations' discretion if

$$x_u \geq x_c + \frac{\sqrt{3[3x_c^2 - 12x_c p + 2(d_n^2 + 3p^2 - 2d_n R + R^2)]}}{3}$$

or

$$x_u \leq x_c - \frac{\sqrt{3[3x_c^2 - 12x_c p + 2(d_n^2 + 3p^2 - 2d_n R + R^2)]}}{3}.$$

Government M: government M is willing to confer powers to the Commission if

$$x_u \geq \sqrt{\frac{6Rp^2 - 2(d_c - R)^3 - 6d_c(p^2 - x_c^2)}{3R}}.$$

It is willing to restrict the executive discretion of national administrations if

$$x_u \geq \sqrt{\frac{2(d_n^2 + 3p^2 - 2d_n R + R^2)}{3}}.$$

Government U: government U is willing to confer powers to the Commission if

$$\frac{1}{3R}\left\{ 6x_c d_c - 6p(d_c - R) - \frac{}{\sqrt{\begin{array}{c}36(x_c d_c - d_c p + pR)^2 \\ -6R\left[3x_c^2 d_c - (d_c - R)\left(d_c^2 + 3p^2 - 2d_c R + R^2\right)\right]\end{array}}} \right\} \leq x_u$$

$$\leq \frac{1}{3R}\left\{ 6x_c d_c - 6p(d_c - R) + \frac{}{\sqrt{\begin{array}{c}36(x_c d_c - d_c p + pR)^2 \\ -6R\left[3x_c^2 d_c - (d_c - R)\left(d_c^2 + 3p^2 - 2d_c R + R^2\right)\right]\end{array}}} \right\}.$$

The government accepts restraining national administrations if

$$2p - \sqrt{\frac{2\left(3p^2 - d_n^2 + 2d_n R - R^2\right)}{3}} \leq x_u \leq 2p$$

$$+ \sqrt{\frac{2\left(3p^2 - d_n^2 + 2d_n R - R^2\right)}{3}}.$$

Parliament: the Parliament is willing to delegate powers to the Commission if

$$x_u \geq x_{pr} + (3R)^{-1/2}\left\{3Rx_{pr}^2 - 12x_{pr}[x_c d_c + p(R - d_c)] \right.$$
$$\left. +2\left[3x_c^2 d_c - (d_c - R)(d_c^2 + 3p^2 - 2d_c R + R^2)\right]\right\}^{1/2}$$

or

$$x_u \leq x_{pr} - (3R)^{-1/2}\left\{3Rx_{pr}^2 - 12x_{pr}[x_c d_c + p(R - d_c)] \right.$$
$$\left. +2\left[3x_c^2 d_c - (d_c - R)(d_c^2 + 3p^2 - 2d_c R + R^2)\right]\right\}^{1/2}.$$

It accepts restraining national administrations under the same conditions as the Commission does, of course, with the caveat of substituting x_{pr} for x_c.

Proof With $D^0 = \mathrm{N}$, $d_n^0 = R$ players' expected utility from the status quo can be derived by inserting d_n^0 in equation (2.2A), producing[24]

$$\mathrm{EU}_i^0 = -\frac{x_u^2 + 2x_i^2 - 2x_u x_i}{2} \qquad \text{for } i = \mathrm{m, u, c, pr.} \qquad (2.3\mathrm{A})$$

Note that the status quo utility for the governments is a negative function of the intensity of conflict within the Council $\left(\mathrm{EU}_{mu}^0 = -x_u^2/2\right)$. For each player, the set of preferred-to-status-quo proposals is derived by identifying the circumstances under which a player's expected utility of equations (2.1A) and (2.2A) is greater than the status quo utility of equation (2.3A) For instance, the circumstances under which government M prefers to delegate powers to the Commission can be established by solving the following equation:

$$\frac{(d_c - R)^3 - 3Rp^2 + 3d_c\left(p^2 - x_c^2\right)}{3R} \geq -\frac{x_u^2}{2}.$$

The circumstances under which it prefers to restrict national executive discretion are determined by solving

$$\frac{2(d_n - R)^3 - 3Rp^2 - 3d_n x_u^2 + 3p^2(2d_n - R)}{6R} \geq -\frac{x_u^2}{2}. \qquad \text{QED}$$

Policy making at the legislative stage

Definitions and assumptions. Legislative policy making terminates with the adoption of a composite equilibrium measure (p^*, D^*, d^*), consisting of an equilibrium baseline policy, an implementation path, and a level of discretion. The equilibrium under each decision-making mechanism is the proposal that *cannot be amended, makes the veto player(s) at least indifferent to the status quo and maximizes the Commission's expected utility.* The latter condition is related to the Commission's monopoly power of legislative initiation.

The Commission makes a proposal that maximizes its expected utility and is approved under the relevant procedure. I assume that decisions are taken sequentially. The setting of the policy precedes the conferral of discretionary authority to an administrator.

Let $v(p, D, d)$ be the proposal of the Commission and Z be the set of proposals that are strictly preferred to the Commission's proposal by both

---

[24] The baseline policy p^* disappears from equation (2.3A) because, with maximal discretion, the states can shift any realization of the state of Nature. The utility is a function of only the preference bias of national administrations.

governments M and U. A proposal s belongs to Z iff $EU_m(s) > EU_m(v)$ and $EU_u(s) > EU_u(v)$. I assume that $Z = \emptyset$ for $x_c < 0$.

Strategies and equilibria. In the unanimity procedure, the proposal of the Commission and amendments to this proposal must be approved by all the governments. Any member state can introduce amendments. Equilibria can be summarized in the following proposition.

Proposition A   *Delegation and discretion equilibria in unanimity are:*[25]

$D^* = N$ and

$d^* = d_n^0 = R$ if $p^* < 0$

if $x_c < p^*$, $x_u > (2 + \sqrt{2})x_c$ and $[x_u < \sqrt{2}p^*$ or $x_u > (2 + \sqrt{2})p^*]$
if $x_c < p^*$ and $x_u < \sqrt{2}x_c$
if $x_c > p^*$, $x_u < \sqrt{2}p^*$ or $x_u > (2 + \sqrt{2})x_c$
or $[x_u > \sqrt{\frac{2}{3}R^2 + 2p^{*2}}$ and $x_c > g(\bullet)]$

$$d^* = d_n = \left[R - \frac{\sqrt{x_u^2 - 2p^{*2}}}{\sqrt{2}}, \; R - \frac{\sqrt{4x_u p^* - x_u^2 - 2p^{*2}}}{\sqrt{2}} \right]$$

if $x_c < p^*$, $\sqrt{2}p^* < x_u < (2 + \sqrt{2})p^*$ and $x_u > (2 + \sqrt{2})x_c$
if $x_c > p^*$, $\sqrt{2}p^* < x_u < \sqrt{2x_c^2 - \frac{4(x_c^2 - p^{*2})^{3/2}}{3R}}$ and $x_c < \sqrt{R^2 + p^{*2}}$
if $x_c > p^*$, $\sqrt{2}p^* < x_u < \sqrt{\frac{2}{3}R^2 + 2p^{*2}}$ and $x_c > \sqrt{R^2 + p^{*2}}$

$D* = C$ and $d^* = d_c = [R - \sqrt{x_c^2 - p^{*2}}$,
$R - \sqrt{x_c^2 - p^{*2} - 2x_u(x_c - p^*)}]$ otherwise.

Proof In unanimity, a proposal $v(p, D, d)$ of the Commission is adopted if (i) it makes both governments at least indifferent to the status quo and (ii) there are no other proposals that both governments strictly prefer to the Commission's suggestion. Technically, the first condition implies that the proposal must belong to the intersection of the preferred-to-status-quo sets of proposals of the two governments. For the second condition, consider that each state has a set of proposals that are preferred to the Commission's measure (let us call it the preferred-to-Commission-proposal set). The second condition means that the intersection of these sets of the two states should be an empty set. If these conditions are not satisfied, the Council adopts any proposal that is preferred by the two states to both the status quo and the Commission's proposal. Formally,

---

[25] Although these equilibria are sufficiently characterized, this is a concise exposition because it provides ranges for d^* rather than specific values. More detailed equilibria can be developed but they do not add any substantive value to the results. In unanimity, the case of $x_u < p$ is disregarded because p is not an equilibrium; $g(\bullet)$ is a very long expression, available on request.

adoption of a Commission proposal v occurs iff

$$\text{EU}_i(v) \geq \text{EU}_i^0 \quad \text{for } i = \text{u, m and } Z = \emptyset,$$

otherwise the Council adopts any proposal w whereby

$$\text{EU}_i(w) \geq \text{EU}_i^0 \quad \text{and} \quad \text{EU}_i(w) > \text{EU}_i(v) \quad \text{for } i = \text{u, m}$$

Moving back to the first move of the game, we can now determine the equilibrium results. The Commission responds to the governments' strategies by proposing a winning measure that satisfies the two conditions listed above and, in addition, maximizes the expected utility of the Commission. Formally, the Commission introduces a proposal such that

$$v(p, D, d) \in \text{argmax} \, \text{EU}_c(p, D, d),$$
$$\text{EU}_i(v) \geq \text{EU}_i^0 \quad \text{for } i = \text{u, m}$$
$$Z = \emptyset.$$

The identification of the equilibria is an easy, though somewhat laborious, process. I will not explain in detail all the steps taken, only their logic. In the case of a supranational Commission, the equilibrium measure maximizes the Commission's utility and belongs to the intersection of the preferred-to-status-quo sets of proposals of the two governments. Delegation preferences and preferred-to-status-quo sets are listed in Lemmas 2.1 and 2.2 respectively. In the case of a national Commission, the equilibrium measure has the same features but, in addition, the intersection of the two states' preferred-to-Commission-proposal sets of proposals should be an empty set (i.e. $Z = \emptyset$). These sets are derived from each state's delegation preferences listed in Lemma 2.1. QED

In the qualified majority voting procedure, the proposal of the Commission must be approved by government M. Any member state can introduce amendments but they must be approved by both governments to be adopted. The results are as follows.

Proposition B *Delegation and discretion equilibria in qualified majority voting are:*[26]

$$D^* = \text{N} \quad \text{and}$$
$$d^* = d_n^0 = R \quad \text{if } x_u < \sqrt{2} \, |p^*|,$$
$$\text{if } p^* > 0, x_u > \sqrt{\frac{2R^2}{3} + 2p^{*2}} \text{ and } x_c > g(\bullet)$$
$$d^* = d_n = \left[R - \frac{\sqrt{x_u^2 - 2p^{*2}}}{\sqrt{2}}, \ R - \frac{\sqrt{4x_u p^* - x_u^2 - 2p^{*2}}}{\sqrt{2}} \right]$$

[26] Here, the cases for either (i) $p < [>]0$ and $p < [>]x_c$ or (ii) $x_u < p$ are disregarded because p is not an equilibrium.

$$\text{if } \sqrt{2}\left|p^*\right| < x_u < \sqrt{2x_c^2 - \frac{4\left(x_c^2 - p^{*2}\right)^{3/2}}{3R}} \text{ and}$$

$$-\sqrt{R^2 + p^{*2}} < x_c < \sqrt{R^2 + p^{*2}}$$

$$\text{if } \sqrt{2}\left|p^*\right| < x_u < \sqrt{\frac{2R^2}{3} + 2p^{*2}} \text{ and}$$

$$[x_c < -\sqrt{R^2 + p^{*2}} \text{ or } x_c > \sqrt{R^2 + p^{*2}}]$$

$$D^* = C \text{ and } d^* = R - \frac{36\left(p^{*2} - x_c^2\right) + f(\bullet)^2}{6f(\bullet)} \text{ otherwise,}$$

$$\text{where } f(\bullet) = \left[\frac{162R\left(2x_c^2 - x_u^2\right)}{2} + \frac{\sqrt{4\left(36p^{*2} - 36x_c^2\right)^3 + \left(648Rx_c^2 - 324Rx_u^2\right)^2}}{2}\right]^{1/3}.$$

Proof A proposal $v(p, D, d)$ from the Commission is adopted in majority voting if (i) it makes government M at least indifferent to the status quo and (ii) there are no other proposals that both governments strictly prefer to the Commission's measure. Technically, the first condition means that the proposal must belong to the preferred-to-status-quo set of proposals of government M. As in the unanimity case, the second condition implies that the intersection of the preferred-to-Commission-proposal sets of the two states should be an empty set. If either condition is not satisfied, the Council adopts any proposal that is preferred by the two states to both the status quo and the Commission's proposal. Formally, adoption of a Commission's proposal v occurs iff

$$\mathrm{EU_m}(v) \geq \mathrm{EU_m^0} \quad \text{and} \quad Z = \emptyset,$$

otherwise the Council adopts any proposal w whereby

$$\mathrm{EU}_i(w) \geq \mathrm{EU}_i^0 \quad \text{and} \quad \mathrm{EU}_i(w) > EU_i(v) \quad \text{for } i = u, m.$$

Back to the first move of the game, the Commission anticipates governments' strategies by proposing a winning measure that satisfies these two conditions and maximizes the expected utility of the Commission. Formally, the Commission introduces a proposal such that

$$v(p, D, d) \in \operatorname{argmax} \mathrm{EU_c}(p, D, d),$$
$$\mathrm{EU_m}(v) \geq \mathrm{EU_m^0}$$
$$Z = \emptyset.$$

Equilibria are identified as follows. In the case of a supranational Commission, the equilibrium measure maximizes the Commission's utility and belongs to the preferred-to-status-quo set of proposals of government M. In the case of a national Commission, the equilibrium measure has the same features. Additionally, as in the case of unanimity, the intersection of the preferred-to-Commission-proposal sets of proposals of the two states should be an empty set. Delegation preferences and preferred sets are derived from Lemmas 2.1 and 2.2.   QED

Proofs of propositions and comparative statics

Using the two lemmas and propositions developed above, we can now illustrate the proofs for the propositions introduced in the text.

Propositions 2.1 and 2.4. Outcomes differ between unanimity and qualified majority voting only when the Commission has preferences closer to those of government M than of government U. From Propositions A and B, we see that the circumstances under which $D^* \in \{C, N\}$ are similar for $x_c < x_u/2$ (i.e. a strongly national Commission). For $x_c < x_u/2$ (i.e. a moderately national Commission), in majority voting we have $D^* = C$ for all x_u so $D^* = N$ never occurs. In unanimity, $D^* = C$ is realized only for $x_u > (2 + \sqrt{2})x_c$, while $D^* = N$ for $x_u > (2 + \sqrt{2})x_c$. For $x_c < 0$, $D^* = C$ never occurs in the case of unanimity (only $D^* = N$ does), while it is realized for $x_u < \sqrt{\frac{2}{3}R^2 + 2p^{*2}}$ or $x_u > \sqrt{2x_c^2 - [4(x_c^2 - p^{*2})^{3/2}]/3R}$ in majority voting ($D^* = N$ when these conditions are not satisfied).   QED

Proposition 2.2. For similar reasons, for $x_c > x_u/2$, d_n^* is the same under the two procedures when $D^* = N$. For $0 < x_c < x_u/2$, $d_n^* = R$ in unanimity when $D^* = N$, while there is no reliance on national administrations in majority voting ($d_n^* = 0$). Here, the Commission obtains powers thanks to the support of government M (support which is denied by government U). Finally, for $x_c < 0$, d_n^* is lower in majority voting than in unanimity because, as Council conflict increases, government M prefers lower discretion than government U, and the Commission, preferring less discretion than both states, exploits this in initiating its proposal. This preference comparison can be easily drawn from the formulas of ideal national discretion listed in Lemma 2.1.   QED

Proposition 2.3. The ideal level of national discretion of both a supranational Commission and government M decreases as Council conflict increases. This can be shown by taking the derivative of their ideal discretion with respect to x_u. Let d_n^m be government M's ideal national discretion and d_n^c be the Commission's ideal discretion from Lemma 2.1.

We have

$$\frac{\partial d_n^m}{\partial x_u} = \frac{-x_u}{\sqrt{2x_u^2 - 4p^{*2}}},$$

which is always negative because $x_u > 0$, and

$$\frac{\partial d_n^c}{\partial x_u} = \frac{x_c - x_u}{\sqrt{2x_u^2 - 4p^{*2} - 4x_c(x_u - 2p^*)}}$$

which is negative when $x_u > x_c$. This condition always applies with a supranational Commission. Therefore, in majority voting, equilibrium national discretion decreases as Council conflict increases.   QED

Proposition 2.5. Following a similar rationale to Propositions 2.1, 2.2 and 2.4, for $x_c > x_u/2$, d_c^* is the same under the two procedures when $D^* = C$. For $0 < x_c < x_u/2$, the Commission is not delegated powers in unanimity when $x_u > (2 + \sqrt{2})x_c$ (hence its discretion is zero), while it is delegated powers (hence its discretion is greater than zero) for all x_u in majority voting. The same applies for $x_c < 0$: no delegation in the case of unanimity, while the Commission's discretion is greater that zero for $x_u > \sqrt{\frac{2}{3}R^2 + 2p^{*2}}$ or $x_u > \sqrt{2x_c^2 - [4(x_c^2 - p^{*2})^{3/2}]/3R}$ in majority voting.   QED

Proposition 2.6. For any government, the ideal level of Commission discretion increases as the preferences of the Commission and of this state converge. The derivative of the ideal Commission discretion with respect to x_c is

$$\frac{\partial d_c^\bullet}{\partial x_c} = \frac{x_i - x_c}{\sqrt{x_c^2 - p^{*2} - 2x_i(x_c - p^*)}} <> 0 \quad \text{for } x_i <> x_c.$$

The derivative is positive (ideal discretion increases) as x_c increases approaching x_i (conflict diminishes) and it is negative as x_c increases diverging from x_i.   QED

Proposition 2.7. Let d_n^m be government M's ideal national discretion and d_c^m be its ideal Commission discretion as listed in Lemma 2.1. The derivative of the difference between these two values with respect to Council conflict is

$$\frac{\partial(d_c^m - d_n^m)}{\partial x_u} = \frac{x_u}{\sqrt{2x_u^2 - 4p^2}},$$

which is always positive for $x_u > 0$. Government M is willing to delegate more discretionary authority to the Commission relative to national discretion as Council conflict intensifies. Hence, for a given x_c, the utility of the status quo relative to Commission implementation diminishes as conflict deepens, and government M is willing to accept greater Commission discretion. The Commission takes advantage of this situation and successfully secures higher discretion. QED

Proposition 2.8. From Propositions A and B (and Lemma 2.1), the ideal level of discretion for any actor and implementation path is a positive function of R. QED

The last three propositions refer to the Parliament's preferences in the codecision procedure. I will not describe in detail this procedure and the equilibrium actions. The only element to recall is that a measure must receive support from the Parliament and government M to be adopted. Hence, a equilibrium baseline policy must lie in between these actors' preferences, formally $|x_{pr}| > |p^*|$.

Proposition 2.9. From Lemma 2.1, we can compute that the ideal level of national discretion of government M exceeds that of the Parliament for (i) $x_{pr} < 0$ and $x_u > 2p^*$ or (ii) $x_{pr} > 0$ and $x_u < 2p^*$. Note that the condition $x_u > 2p^*$ is always satisfied because $p^* < 0$ for $x_{pr} < 0$ and, by assumption, $x_u > 0$. QED

Proposition 2.10. Let d_n^m be government M's ideal national discretion and d_n^{pr} be Parliament's ideal discretion from Lemma 2.1. The derivative of the difference between these values with respect to the Parliament's policy position x_{pr}, which, since $x_m = 0$, measures the conflict between the two actors, is

$$\frac{\partial(d_n^m - d_n^{pr})}{\partial x_{pr}} = \frac{2p^* - x_u}{\sqrt{2x_u^2 - 4p^{*2} - 4x_{pr}(x_u - 2p^*)}}.$$

In the case of a supranational Parliament (i.e. $x_{pr} < p^* < 0$), the derivative takes negative values. As x_{pr} decreases moving away from zero (i.e. Parliament–government M conflict intensifies), d_n^{pr} lowers and the difference between d_n^m and d_n^{pr} increases. In the case of a national Parliament (i.e. $x_{pr} > p^* > 0$) and moderate Council conflict ($x_u < 2p^*$), the derivative has a positive sign instead, and this difference augments as x_{pr} rises. Finally, with a national Parliament and high Council conflict ($x_u > 2p^*$), the derivative has a negative sign again but $d_n^m < d_n^{pr}$. The difference between the two levels of ideal discretion is negative but it increases in absolute terms as x_{pr} moves away from zero. QED

Proposition 2.11. Starting with $x_c = p^*$, the ideal levels of Commission discretion for government M and the Parliament are $d_c^m = d_c^{pr} = R$ (from Lemma 2.1). As x_c approaches x_{pr}, we have $d_c^{pr} = R > d_c^m$ and $\partial d_c^m / \partial x_c = -x_c / \sqrt{x_c^2 - p^{*2}} <> 0$ for $x_c >< 0$ (d_c^m diminishes as x_c moves away from zero). As x_c approaches x_m, we have $d_c^m = R > d_c^{pr}$ and $\partial d_c^{pr} / \partial x_c = (x_{pr} - x_c) / \sqrt{x_c^2 - p^{*2} - 2x_{pr}(x_c - p^*)} <> 0$ for $x_c >< x_{pr}$. Note that if $x_{pr} = x_c, d_c^{pr} = R \geq d_c^m = R - \sqrt{x_{pr}^2 - p^{*2}}$. This is the basis for Hypotheses 7.3 and 7.5.   QED

3   Data and longitudinal analysis

The eleven propositions laid out in the previous chapter necessitate a number of data sets for empirical testing. In this chapter, I explain how I have produced a data set of major EU laws[1] and derived measures of discretion for the Commission and national authorities. These will be the core dependent variables for testing the first eight hypotheses.

In the first two sections, this chapter outlines the procedure employed for the selection of major laws and the sample of laws that has been used for the empirical analysis. It then proceeds to explain the steps that I took to produce the measures of discretion. I make ample use of descriptive statistics and longitudinal analysis to provide broad impressions of the data set and to assess the validity of existing claims on the historical development of the EU.

The selection of major EU laws

The procedure for selecting major EU laws should be systematic and minimize bias. It should also employ a neutral method to separate significant from trivial legislation. In compiling a list of important post-war US legislation, Mayhew (1991) wanted to capture both retrospective and contemporary judgements on law production. He used references in scholarly books and year-end roundups of both the *New York Times* and *Washington Post*. To my knowledge, there are no lists available of major EU laws, yearly commentaries or publications that are selective enough and can be used systematically from 1958 onwards. I have chosen an approach that mimics Mayhew's methodology and tries to avoid serious selection biases.

The procedure consists of three stages. First, I have collected all the books on EU law published between 1958 and 1999 and available from the British Library of Political and Economic Science of the London

---

[1] Please note that, even if I refer to EU laws, the data set includes only legislation of the EC pillar of the Treaty.

School of Economics and Political Science. This exercise has produced a list of fifty-eight books. It includes three Italian texts, two German, French and Dutch publications, respectively, one Irish text and one official EU publication. The remainder are British books. Three books were published in the 1960s, five in the 1970s, sixteen in the 1980s and the remainder in the 1990s. There are eleven handbooks with abstracts on EU law, four textbooks on EU-national law, two books on substantive EU law and the remaining are textbooks on EU law only.[2]

The second stage is the creation of a database listing (i) the Council directives and regulations[3] cited by these books and (ii) the number of books citing each law. For this exercise, I have considered only the book sections on EU policies, on the budget and on general secondary legislation.[4] The database includes 2835 directives and regulations that can be sorted by the number of citations. For instance, only seven acts have been cited by forty or more books while forty-three acts have been cited by at least twenty books.

The last stage is the selection of the major laws. The initial data set included the 169 directives and regulations that have at least ten citations. However, I had to eliminate eleven acts. Five regulations and four directives have been removed because law books normally refer to legislation in force at the time of publication, so minor amendments of major laws are dragged into the sample by the significance of the parent legislation.[5] Regulation 2001/83 on social security has been removed because it consolidates, with minor amendments, two major laws adopted only two years earlier. Finally, Directive 90/366 on the right of residence

---

[2] Different editions of the same book have been included because they are a sign of the success of the book and, therefore, of the saliency of the referred legislation. I have excluded dictionaries and encyclopaedias because they are not selective enough, while books on a single EU policy are excluded because they are too specific. Legal texts that focus almost solely on legal debates, constitutional matters or on the impact on national law are also excluded.

[3] I have disregarded decisions because of their addressee-related nature, opinions and recommendations because they are not legally binding, and Commission directives and regulations because it is tertiary legislation.

[4] Chapters on EU institutions, jurisprudence, legal technicalities and constitutional matters have not been considered because citations of secondary legislation in these sections are not a sign of saliency. Laws are cited either as examples of, say, Council–Commission relations or because disputes about such laws have led to important case law precedents. For instance, Regulation 2647/72, an otherwise not very significant law, is frequently cited because it has led to the case law principle of legitimate expectations. Regulation 3600/85, another insignificant law, is used as an example of an act struck down by the European Court of Justice because it lacked a legal basis.

[5] These are Regulations 59/62, 118/63, 2822/71, 2864/72 and 312/76, and Directives 72/194, 75/35, 81/1057 and 87/164.

for students has been annulled by the European Court of Justice for procedural reasons. The Council adopted the correct version three years later (Directive 93/96). Only the second directive has been included in the sample. Regulation 2001/83 and Directive 90/366 have been frequently cited by law books for reasons of completeness, but they have been removed because they repeat, in almost identical terms, other major laws adopted in the same period. This brings the final number of acts in the data set down to 158. It implies an analysis of more than 7000 major legal provisions.

It should be acknowledged that there might be two biases built into this selection mechanism. The first is a national bias as the large majority of the sampled books are British. I do not consider this to be too problematic. EU law emerged in the founding member states as a legal subfield only in the late 1960s/early 1970s, hence during the first enlargement. Many books are authored or co-authored by non-British lawyers. Moreover, directives and regulations are rarely country-specific – none of those included in the sample is. Their relevance is likely to be European-wide. Second, the mechanism can be biased towards older legislation as new important acts make their way into books only after a few years. Indeed, the latest acts in the sample were adopted in 1993. However, the fact that almost 60 percent of the books were published in the 1990s and 28 percent in the 1980s might redress this bias, although by no means perfectly.

So far, this process can be compared with the second "sweep" of the procedure used by Mayhew (1991) for selecting important legislation enacted by the US Congress. Books on EU law tend to refer to those acts that the academic community studying the EU considers to be of major legal and political significance. Using Mayhew's words, they can be regarded as retrospective judgements on the EU's legislative output. In his data set, Mayhew also includes a first "sweep" of legislation that captures the contemporary judgements about the productivity of the US government. I have used the *General Report on the Activities of the European Union*, published annually, for a similar purpose. All the laws in the data set have been mentioned by at least a paragraph in the sections of the Report on EU activities.

The data sample and trends in EU law making

Figure 3.1 shows the distribution of the sampled laws across broad categories of issue areas, following the general structure of the Treaty. Interestingly, the area with the greater number of acts is movement of persons,

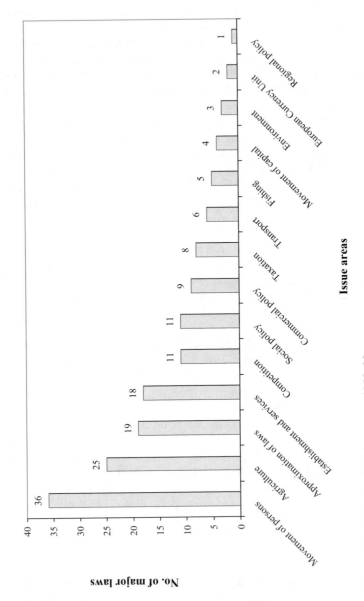

Figure 3.1 *Major laws per issue area, 1958–93.*

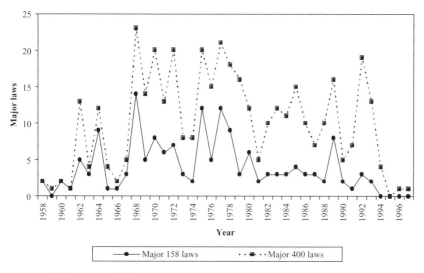

Figure 3.2 *Major laws per year, 1958–97.*

followed by agriculture and then legislation related to the free movement of goods and services. There are also a relatively large number of acts related to social policy, probably more than one would have expected, given the main historical objectives of the EU.

Figure 3.2 shows the number of major laws adopted in the 1958–97 period. It is beyond the scope of this chapter to analyze the EU legislative output but it is worth briefly comparing these results with the more extensive work of Golub (1999). Contrary to conventional wisdom, Golub notes that the most dramatic improvement in decision-making speed of the EU has actually taken place during the "Eurosclerosis" years of 1974–78. He adds that the period 1979–83 shows instead a significant decline in legislative output and detects an increasing inefficiency from 1987 onward (Golub, 1999: 739–43).[6]

Here, his conclusions are confirmed and two potential criticisms are dealt with. Figure 3.2 illustrates the year of adoption for the major 158 and 400 laws. In the sample of 158 laws, the 1974–78 period shows the highest average number of major laws adopted (eight), compared not only with the post-Single European Act period but also with the highly

---

[6] Golub's data set includes all the directives adopted between 1974 and 1995 which he extends in Golub (2000). See also Page and Dimitrakopoulos (1997). Pollack (1994, 2000) reaches different conclusions, though using a much smaller data set. Schulz and König (2000) provides a more theoretically solid work explaining decision-making efficiency in the EU, however they limit their analysis to the 1984–94 period.

productive decade of 1964–73 (less than six). Further, with the exception of 1980 and 1989, the fifteen-year period since 1979 shows a rate of adoption of approximately only three major laws per year. This picture is confirmed if we extend the analysis to the 400 major laws that have been cited at least five times. In this case, there has been an average of sixteen major laws adopted during 1974–78 compared with averages of fifteen in 1969–73, nine in 1964–68 and eleven in the fifteen years after 1978. However, if we include all the 2835 laws cited at least once, the 1984–93 period appears considerably more productive. The average number of laws during 1969–73 (82) and in the decade 1984–93 (108) has been higher than during 1974–78 (80). This means that we should exercise caution because my selection method could be biased in favor of older legislation. However, a larger data set includes many minor acts, so it is less selective.

The two criticisms leveled against Golub's findings concern the lack of control for the significance of the legislation and the disregard of regulations. They remain unsubstantiated as I include regulations in my data set and control for saliency.

Analysis of the major laws: the methodology

I have followed, broadly, the guidelines of Epstein and O'Halloran (1999b: 275–84) in the development of a measure of discretion. Here, I describe its main components and the procedure of operationalization. Appendix 3.1 provides a more detailed explanation of how I have adapted Epstein and O'Halloran's methodology for EU legislation.

The measure of executive discretion is derived from reading EU statutes. There are two steps. The first one consists in identifying the number of major provisions for each act in the sample. Each provision has then been coded as to whether or not it delegates powers. Delegation is the granting of substantive policy discretion to the Commission, member states or their national administrations. It gives these institutions the authority to move the policy away from the status quo. The first component of the discretion variable is the delegation ratio, that is the proportion of major provisions, in a legislative act, delegating policy authority. Second, I have identified twelve possible categories of procedural constraints that EU legislators can impose on the Commission or on national administrations while they exercise their delegated powers. I have then recorded, for each law, which constraint appears at least once and developed the second component of the discretion variable. This is the constraint ratio, that is the number of constraints observed in a given law divided by the number of possible constraints. This ratio is then weighted by the delegation ratio and the resulting value is subtracted from the delegation ratio producing the following measure of discretion:

$$d_i = \frac{D_i}{M} - \left(\frac{C_i}{T_C} \times \frac{D_i}{M} \right) \qquad \text{for} \quad i = \text{c, n} \qquad (3.1)$$

where d_i is the executive discretion enjoyed by either the Commission (d_c) or the national administrations (d_n), M is the number of major provisions in an act, D_i is the number of provisions delegating authority either to the Commission (D_c) or to the national administrations (D_n), C_i is the number of constraints imposed either on the Commission (C_c) or on the national authorities (C_n) and T_C is the total number of possible constraints (twelve). D_i / M is the delegation ratio and C_i / T_C is the constraint ratio.

In summary, executive discretion is measured by the share of major provisions delegating powers in an act, weighted by the constraints imposed on executive action. For instance, seven out of forty-nine provisions delegate executive powers to the Commission in Regulation 2641/84 on the new commercial policy instrument (a delegation ratio of 14 percent). The Commission has the authority to open up and terminate an examination procedure, to carry out an investigation and to initiate a consultation or a dispute settlement procedure with third countries in response to illicit practices. However, the Commission is constrained by criteria defining injury and threat of injury, by the obligation to consult, at various stages, an advisory committee, to hold public hearings with interested parties and to present a report on its investigation. Further, the Council can revise a Commission's decision by qualified majority voting if, within a few days, it is referred by a member state to the Council. Finally, cases covered by existing commercial policy rules are exempted from the scope of the regulation. With six constraints and a constraint ratio of 43 percent, the executive discretion of the Commission in this act is 8 percent.

In Directive 79/279 coordinating the conditions for the admission of securities to the stock exchange, eighteen out of forty-five provisions delegate powers to member states and their competent authorities. At the general level, a member state may exempt some securities from the provisions of the directive and authorize derogations. More specifically, national competent authorities may refuse the listing of a security or decide on the suspension of a listing. Constraints are few. There are minimum requirements for the admission of securities and conditions for the derogations. The issuer had to be consulted prior to the diffusion of some information and member states must ensure the right to apply to the courts if a competent authority refuses the admission of a security to the stock exchange. National executive discretion is considerable. It is almost 32 percent. The Commission is only in charge of adjusting the minimum amount of market capitalization for the listing of securities. Further, a committee of national representatives oversees this

Table 3.1 *Descriptive statistics: delegation and constraint measures.*

Variable	Mean	Std dev.	Minimum	Maximum
Major provisions (*M*)	47.87	47.42	3	345
Delegation provisions	13.71	14.61	0	89
Constraints	3.2	2.24	0	9

Note: N = 158.

Table 3.2 *Descriptive statistics: summary for national administrations.*

Variable	Mean	Std dev.	Minimum	Maximum
	Delegation measures			
Delegation provisions – national Administrations (D_n)	9.46	13.2	0	83
	Constraint measures			
Rule-making requirements	0.72	0.45	0	1
Time limits	0.34	0.47	0	1
Reporting requirements	0.22	0.42	0	1
Consultation requirements	0.19	0.39	0	1
Appeals procedures	0.14	0.35	0	1
Executive action required	0.09	0.29	0	1
Executive action possible	0.06	0.23	0	1
Legislative action required	0.06	0.24	0	1
Spending limits	0.06	0.24	0	1
Exemptions	0.03	0.18	0	1
Legislative action possible	0.01	0.08	0	1
Public hearings	0.01	0.08	0	1
	Derived variables			
Delegation ratio (D_n/M)	20.09%	14.93%	0	55%
Constraints (C_n)	1.92	1.42	0	6
Constraint ratio (C_n/T_C)	16.03%	11.84%	0	50%
Discretion (d_n)	**16.23%**	**12.2%**	**0**	**48.99%**

Note: N = 158.

Commission power following an administrative procedure called "regulatory procedure". Hence, the Commission's executive discretion is very small, only 2 percent.

Delegation

Tables 3.1–3.3 provide a summary of the descriptive statistics for the main variables used. Although in about 40 percent of the acts the Commission and national authorities are both assigned some executive powers, a

Table 3.3 *Descriptive statistics: summary for the Commission.*

Variable	Mean	Std dev.	Minimum	Maximum
Delegation measures				
Delegation provisions – Commission (D_c)	3.82	6.88	0	29
Constraint measures				
Consultation requirements	0.32	0.47	0	1
Rule-making requirements	0.32	0.47	0	1
Reporting requirements	0.21	0.41	0	1
Executive action possible	0.18	0.38	0	1
Legislative action possible	0.18	0.39	0	1
Executive action required	0.14	0.35	0	1
Exemptions	0.13	0.34	0	1
Time limits	0.13	0.34	0	1
Public hearings	0.08	0.28	0	1
Legislative action required	0.04	0.19	0	1
Spending limits	0.04	0.21	0	1
Appeals procedures	0	0	0	0
Derived variables				
Delegation ratio (D_c/M)	6.93%	10.23%	0	45.45%
Constraints (C_c)	1.78	2.36	0	7
Constraint ratio (C_c/T_C)	14.82%	19.63%	0	58.33%
Discretion (d_c)	**4.4%**	**6.6%**	**0**	**34.09%**

Note: N = 158.

comparison between Table 3.2 and Table 3.3 clearly shows that EU legislators rely twice as much on national administrations as they do on the Commission. The mean delegation ratio for national administrations is three times that for the Commission. The standard deviation is also relatively higher in the case of Commission implementation, meaning that delegation to the Commission varies more widely across acts.

Table 3.4 illustrates the five acts with most and least delegation to national administrations and to the Commission, and Figure 3.3 shows the distribution of the delegation ratios with a normal curve overlaid. In the case of national execution, the top five are directives on the movement of persons, taxation and company law, while the most constraining ones are related to the common organization of agricultural markets, customs law and competition policy. Note also that there are a fair number of laws, almost 13 percent of the sample, where national authorities are completely excluded from implementation. This is illustrated by the spike at zero in panel *a* of Figure 3.3. The distribution of the national delegation ratios is mildly bimodal, with the highest frequencies at about 5–10

Table 3.4 *Acts and delegation.*

	Acts with no delegation		
	No. and percentage		No. and percentage
			87 55.06%
No delegation to national administrations	20 12.66%	No delegation to the Commission	
Delegation to national administrations	D_n	*Delegation to the Commission*	D_c
	Acts with highest delegation ratio		
Directive 74/561 Admission of road haulage operators in transport operations	55	Regulation 26/62 Competition rules applied to agriculture	45.45
Directive 77/388 VAT	54.97	Regulation 17/62 Competition rules	32.84
Directive 84/253 Approval of persons carrying out statutory audits	54	Regulation 19/62 Common organization of the market in cereals	31.71
Directive 80/390 Admission of securities to official stock exchange listing	53.45	Regulation 3975/87 Competition rules applied to air transport	31.58
Directive 78/855 Mergers of public limited liability companies	47.46	Regulation 2727/75 Common organization of the market in cereals	30.85
	Acts with lowest delegation ratio		
Regulation 1418/76 Common organization of the market in rice	1.09	Directive 89/440 Award of public works contracts	1.1
Regulation 805/68 Common organization of the market in beef and veal	1.2	Regulation 2137/85 European Economic Interest Grouping	1.15
Regulation 727/70 Common organization of the market in raw tobacco	1.47	Directive 89/391 Safety and health of workers at work	1.59
Regulation 1224/80 Valuation of goods for customs purposes	1.52	Directive 79/279 Admission of securities to stock exchange listing	2.22
Regulation 1017/68 Competition rules applied to transport	2.35	Directive 64/432 Animal health problems affecting trade	2.63

Note: Delegation ratios are percentages, acts with zero delegation are disregarded.

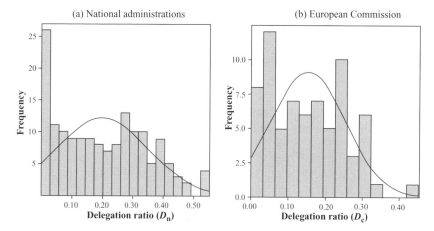

Figure 3.3 *Histograms of delegation ratios. Note:* The histogram in panel *b* excludes zero-delegation laws, with their inclusion the first bar would exceed 90.

and 25–30 percent. It appears that national authorities either play a minor role or are extensively involved in policy execution.

The most common example of delegation to national administrations is the transposition of the provisions of a directive giving member states a certain degree of flexibility. For example, Directive 77/249 aims to facilitate the provision of legal services across member states. However, governments may reserve some activities to prescribed categories of lawyers. Directive 67/227 requires member states to replace their turnover taxes by a common system of value added tax, without specifying the rates. Some requirements are very general, so they imply delegation and a degree of national flexibility. For instance, in Directive 88/378, governments should take all *appropriate* measures to prohibit or restrict the placing on the market of unsafe toys. The host member state should take *appropriate* measures to prevent a credit institution from initiating transactions if the institution has had its authorization to operate withdrawn (Directive 89/646). Other examples include the right to take measures, to designate authorities and institutions and to derogate from specific provisions. Member states may take protective measures to limit capital movement in the case of serious disturbances (Directive 88/361) and, in emergencies, they may take any precautionary measure with regard to credit institutions (Directive 89/646).[7] In Regulation 4/58, the first on social security

---

[7] These provisions are coupled with powers given to the Commission to either authorize or, *ex post*, decide on the amendment or annulment of national measures.

for migrant workers, the competent national authorities designate liaison bodies and give authorization for substantial benefits in kind for residents outside their jurisdiction. Member states may derogate from the provisions abolishing restrictions to the movement and residence of persons for reasons of public order, security and health (Directive 64/220).

The top five laws with most delegation to the Commission are in the areas of competition and agricultural policy (see Table 3.4). The delegation ratios of these acts are significantly lower than the delegation ratios of the acts with highest national delegation. The most constraining laws cover different issues from the internal market of public contracts, to company law and health and safety. A considerable number of laws, more than half of the sample, do not confer powers directly upon the Commission. The histogram in panel *b* of Figure 3.3 excludes zero delegation laws, that is those with the highest frequency. Nevertheless, the distribution of the Commission's delegation ratio is also bimodal, with the highest frequencies at about 5 and 25 percent. It appears that, as national authorities, the Commission either plays a minor role or is extensively involved in policy execution.

Typical examples of powers delegated to the Commission include those to grant exemptions, give clearance and sanction infringements, mostly in competition regulations. In commercial policy, the Commission can take surveillance measures of import (Regulation 288/82), make export subject to authorization (Regulation 2603/69) and negotiate with third countries (e.g. Directive 89/646). The granting, suspension and reduction of EU aid to, for instance, structural measures in agriculture and regional development projects are other typical powers delegated to the Commission (Directive 72/159 and Regulation 724/75). In the case of emergencies or serious market disturbances, the Commission may authorize member states or may, itself, take transitional or safeguard measures. For instance, the Commission decides the suspension of the mechanism for the clearance of job vacancies (Regulation 1612/68). In Directive 89/646, the Commission may decide that national authorities must amend or abolish precautionary measures they took in emergencies. In agricultural and fishery policy, there is a long list of prerogatives for the Commission, from the adoption of coefficients, the scale of premiums, derived prices and other implementing provisions to the fixing of refunds, levies and charges. In the single market directives on standards and in the environmental directives, the Commission adopts amendments to take into account technical progress (e.g. Directives 70/156 and 76/160). The Commission is asked to adjust the minimum amount of foreseeable market capitalization in Directive 79/279 on the admission of securities to the stock exchange. Other cases include the

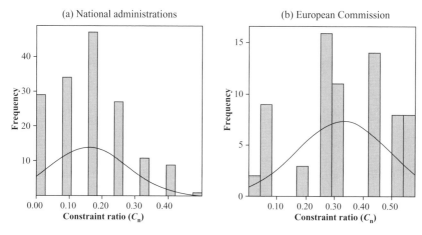

Figure 3.4 *Histograms of constraint ratios. Note:* The histogram in panel *b* excludes zero-delegation laws, with their inclusion the first bar would reach almost 90.

power to withdraw toy standards that do not satisfy EU safety require-ments (Directive 88/378) and to request a European standard (Directive 83/189). Finally, the Commission manages the machinery for clearance of job vacancies, the monetary compensatory amounts in agriculture and the statistical nomenclature of the common customs tariff (Regulations 1612/68, 974/71 and 2658/87).[8]

Statutory constraints

In contrast to the analysis of delegation, there appears to be not much dif-ference between national administrations and the Commission in terms of the number of constraints per act and constraint ratios (see Tables 3.2 and 3.3). Although the standard deviations are still relatively higher in the case of Commission implementation. Moreover, the distribution of the constraint ratios for both national administrations and the Commission seems to be normal as is shown in Figure 3.4. There are important dif-ferences however. The histogram in panel *b* of Figure 3.4 excludes zero delegation laws, which are those with the highest frequency. If we include them, the mode is zero because no delegation implies no constraints. If we exclude these laws, the mean of the Commission's constraint ratio reaches almost 33 percent, as can be seen in Figure 3.4*b*, while the mean national

---

[8] An extensive analysis of the powers delegated to the Commission is given in Franchino (2002).

constraint ratio increases only moderately to 18.4 percent. This means that, when powers are delegated to the Commission, this institution is, on average, almost twice as constrained as national administrations when they are in charge of implementation. The mean constraint ratio of the Commission in Table 3.2 is brought down by the very high incidence of laws that do not delegate powers to the Commission.

In this section, we review the twelve categories of statutory constraints used by EU legislators to delimit the execution of the common policies. Constraints are allocated as to whether they restrain the national administrations' or the Commission's executive action or both. They are listed in Tables 3.2 and 3.3 in decreasing order of incidence in the data sample. Below, I also refer to a set of administrative procedures, collectively called "comitology procedures", whereby, in some cases, representatives of member states oversee the Commission's measures within implementation committees.[9] Ten categories are adapted from the work of Epstein and O'Halloran (1999b: 276–84), the remaining two are more specific to the EU institutional setting. Further details are available in Appendix 3.1 and, for the case of national execution, in Franchino (2001).

Time limits.   Both national administrations and the Commission have had time limits imposed when delegated powers, though they are relatively more frequent when national authorities execute common policies. In the case of Commission implementation, EU legislators associate the authority delegated to it with limits to the amount of time that its decisions can affect the relevant parties. Time limits imposed on member states are mostly associated with provisions that facilitate the shift from the existing national policy to the European policy. In many cases, they are linked to the extension of national prerogatives that would have otherwise been transferred to the EU. In others, they are related to provisions on transitional measures or on the suspension or deferral of the application of the specific act. Only in a few instances have EU legislators set a time limit on the effects of specific measures taken by national administrations. The estimated time of common measures has not been coded as a constraint.

Spending limits.   Since distributive policies represent a small subset of the policy output of the EU, it should not come as a surprise that

---

[9] For details on the procedures see Institut für Europäische Politik (1989), Bradley (1992), Pedler and Schaefer (1996), Dogan (1997), Pollack (1997b, 2003a, 2003b), Vos (1997), Franchino (2000b: 69–71), and Ballmann, Epstein and O'Halloran (2002). I use the classification adopted by Council Decision 87/373 when referring to these procedures. The recent amendment in Council Decision 1999/468 has simplified this structure but, since it took place after 1993, it does not affect my analysis.

spending limits are not frequently used, both in the case of Commission and national execution. This constraint defines the maximum amount that administrators can allocate to specific activities. It is mostly employed in regional and agricultural policy. The majority of the structural measures include limits to national or EU expenditure. The estimated total contribution of common measures has not been coded as a constraint.

Reporting requirements. Reporting requirements are much more popular. They are the third most used constraint in the case of both Commission and national implementation. They include reporting to committees. Moreover, when member states have to communicate information for the Commission to draw up a report, this has been coded as a constraint on member states too. National authorities are frequently requested to produce a report on the implementation of social policy directives. Whereas the Commission must submit implementation reports to EU legislators in many policy areas. The constraint is also associated to important prerogatives of the Commission in the regulation of the internal market and the granting of funds.

Consultation requirements. This is one of the most frequently used constraints when powers are delegated to the Commission, but also national authorities are often required to consult with the Commission or other specified actors *prior* to taking some measures. Administrators do not need the approval of the consulted actors, while the simple notification of measures has not been coded as a constraint. This requirement is used when national administrations have to assist an EU-level policy and when member states want to (re)introduce market-distorting measures. Many measures of the Commission are subject to prior consultation of the Council or of a relevant member state. The category also includes a procedure, called the *advisory procedure*, whereby the Commission has to consult with a committee of representatives of member states.

Public hearings. The obligation to hold a public hearing before issuing decisions or regulations is among the least frequently used statutory constraints in the case of both national and Commission execution. It is used mostly in regulations of competition and commercial policy.

Rule-making requirements. The most common way for EU legislators to constrain the Commission, member states, their competent authorities or institutions is by setting detailed rules and procedures in the form of standards and criteria. Many of the rules that are imposed upon national administrations in laws on, for instance, workers and capital movement, structural aid and recognition of diplomas also delimitate the authority of the Commission. Almost all issue areas contain this type of constraint, from social security to capital movements, from freedom of establishment and service provision to credit, insurance and company law, from agriculture and fisheries to regional, competition and commercial policy.

Appeals procedures. Since national laws for judicial review of administrative decisions vary considerably across member states, in terms of obligations imposed on administrative action, access to courts and legal standing of private actors, it is relatively common for EU legislators to include into a law an explicit reference to appeals procedures. This is done with a view to imposing obligations on national administrative behavior or to specify legal standing. This category includes provisions whereby member states must ensure that their institutions state the grounds of decisions and specify the right of appeal and of other legal remedies. It is common in directives on gender equality, in some internal market and social security legislation. I have not found instances where this constraint is associated to prerogatives of the Commission, however it cannot be excluded a priori.

Exemptions. Exempting a group, product or a class of interests, temporarily or permanently, from the effects of an EU law is a constraint only in some circumstances. This category is used more frequently when the Commission is in charge of implementation. Here, exemptions are constraints on bureaucratic action because they specify where the Commission cannot exercise its powers. They can be found in competition, commercial policy, movements and internal market regulations. In the case of national implementation, a clause that allows member states to grant exemptions is a delegating provision, not a constraint, because it increases national executive discretion. Similarly, provisions limiting the scope of the specific act, so that national prerogatives with regard to the exempted group or class of interests are maintained, are not coded as a constraint on member states' powers. There are instead exemptions in the areas of workers' movements and structural aid that can be considered a constraint on national authorities.

The remaining four categories differ according to two principles: (i) the type of actor constraining executive action and (ii) the bias and timing of control. I shall refer to the Council only because it is the institution mostly involved in these procedures. In the first two categories, the Council limits the agent's policy authority. The difference between *legislative action required* and *legislative action possible* is that the former constraint is biased in favor of the revocation of an action while the latter is biased in favor of its maintenance. In the last two categories, it is a separate executive agent (i.e. the Commission, the member states or an implementation committee) that imposes constraints on the Commission or on national administrations. The difference between *executive action required* and *executive action possible* is the same as that of the *legislative action* constraints.

Legislative action required. This is a requirement of a Council's approval prior to a Commission's or a member state's measure becoming effective. It also includes cases whereby measures, when referred to the Council, are either suspended until Council action or, if immediately applicable, are revoked in the case of Council inaction after a set time period. It includes *variant b* of the *safeguard procedure*. This category of constraint is not frequently used but it is rather stringent. In the case of national implementation, it is associated with provisions allowing member states to defer or derogate from EU legal requirements. In areas such as taxation, spending and trade, Council approval is required for national measures that could have substantial trade-distorting effects. In the case of Commission execution, this constraint is used for measures related to trade, negotiations and decisions in competition policy.

Legislative action possible. This category includes procedures whereby actions of the Commission or a member state are referred to the Council prior to becoming effective or whereby these measures may be referred, by the Commission or another member state, to the Council (referral may suspend the effects of the measure). The default condition in the case of Council inaction, sometimes after a set time period, is the measure taken by the Commission or the relevant state. It also includes cases of Council direct action without a referral, but after the measures are already in force. It includes *variant a* of the *safeguard procedure*. It is used in acts approximating national laws when national measures may have a trade distorting effect. However, it is mostly used when powers are conferred upon the Commission to control state aid and to take protective and commercial policy measures.

Executive action required. This is a requirement that another executive agent must approve the agency's action prior to becoming effective. It includes the Commission's prior approval to member states' measures, and vice versa, and provisions asserting that the Commission can take a measure *only if* required by a member state. It also includes cases whereby the Commission needs the prior approval of member states' representatives of an implementation committee. This might be given by qualified majority voting (e.g. in both *variant a* and *b* of the *regulatory procedures*) or by a blocking minority (e.g. in *variant b* of the *management procedure*).[10] In the case of national execution, there are measures concerning deferral of implementation, aid, movement of workers and capital that require prior authorization from the Commission. In the case of Commission execution, it is used in commercial policy, EU funding and technical amendments of directives.

Executive action possible. In this category I have coded procedures whereby measures taken by member states may be overruled, within a set time limit, by actions taken by the Commission, and vice versa. The effects of the measure can be suspended during the set time frame. It includes *variant a* of the *management procedure* which is used to oversee the powers of the Commission in the areas of organization of agricultural markets and structural policy. This procedure differs from variant *b* in the fact that the committee acts after the Commission has taken its measure. Hence, prior approval is not required. National safeguard or precautionary measures and other decisions in the areas of commercial policy and recognition of diplomas are subject to this constraint.

The constraints index

Having established the categories of constraints that are most likely to be used in an EU law, we now need to construct an index that incorporates them. Two issues need to be dealt with. First, whether there is more than one dimension explaining the distribution of constraints and, second, whether the categories should be weighted equally for the construction of the index. The standard tool used to address these issues is factor analysis.

---

[10] These procedures differ in the degree of control exercised on the Commission. It is easier to block a Commission's measure under variant *b* of the regulatory procedure, while it is generally more difficult for a management committee. It can be argued that these procedures should be separated. However, the creation of other types of constraint violates a requirement for the factor analysis that will follow, namely that there should be more cases than variables. Gorsuch (1983) has also proposed a minimum of five cases per variable. There are only nine laws that use variant *a* of the regulatory procedure, two acts use variant *b* and three laws utilize variant *b* of the management procedure. Factor analysis would be unreliable with such small numbers. Furthermore, it is reasonable to conceive that these procedures collectively perform a similar function of *ex-ante* control by a separate executive agent.

Table 3.5 *Factor analysis and Pearson correlation coefficients.*

	Factor			Coefficient	
Category of constraint	1	2	3	D_c	D_n
Executive action possible	**0.876**	0.190	−0.026	0.581^a	−0.101
Legislative action possible	**0.827**	0.222	−0.165	0.554^a	−0.153
Spending limits	**0.748**	0.016	0.153	0.427^a	−0.009
Public hearings	−0.136	**0.749**	−0.066	0.374^a	−0.14
Legislative action required	0.221	**0.640**	0.222	0.318^a	0.156
Consultation requirements	**0.558**	**0.634**	0.093	0.55^a	0.071
Exemptions	−0.056	**0.592**	**0.467**	0.188^b	0.051
Time limits	0.280	**0.560**	−0.001	0.366^a	0.229^a
Executive action required	0.199	0.052	**0.721**	0.076	0.078
Rule-making requirements	−0.044	0.156	**0.565**	0.098	0.281^a
Reporting requirements	**0.408**	0.156	**0.519**	0.189^b	−0.055
Appeals procedures	−0.184	−0.022	**0.453**	$−0.187^b$	0.233^a

Note: Structure matrix, extraction method: principal component, rotation method: *oblimin* with Kaiser normalization. Results vary slightly with different extraction methods. Salient scores in **bold**. ^{a} $p < 0.01$; ^{b} $p < 0.05$.

A preliminary examination suggests that the distribution of these constraint categories can be significantly explained by three underlying dimensions or factors, with one dominating over the others.[11] Hence, Table 3.5 shows the results of an analysis restricted to three factors. Dimensions can be more easily distinguishable if their scores are salient (i.e. exceed 0.3) and unique (i.e. load on different constraint categories). In Table 3.5, salient loadings are given in bold and they are all positive. There are no factors that have only salient *and* unique loadings.

[11] The preliminary analysis reveals that four factors have an eigenvalue greater than one (3.044; 1.833; 1.385 and 1.188), but visual inspection of the scree plot shows a substantial drop after the first factor and a leveling off after the second factor. Moreover, the difference between the eigenvalues of the third and fourth factor is only 0.197, which is not greatly different from that between the eigenvalues of, say, the eighth and ninth factor (0.154). The distribution of statutory constraints seems to be characterized by a strong first dimension and a less important second dimension. The structure matrix, after an oblique rotation, shows that two factors have only one category of constraint with a unique and salient loading. Moreover, the coefficients of five constraints differ only marginally across factors. And extraction using maximum likelihood suggests that solutions using more than three factors should be interpreted with caution because at least one communality estimate is greater than one (the *oblimin* method with Kaiser normalization has been used for all the rotations). These results suggest that at least one dimension could be considered trivial and, therefore, we should restrict the analysis to three factors (see Gorsuch, 1983: 169–71). But not less than three however, as the χ^2 value comparing the model with three factors versus the model with two factors is 43.21 ($d_f = 10$), significant at the 1 percent level.

Consultation requirements load on both factors one and two, *exemptions* load on factors two and three, while *reporting requirements* load on factors one and three.

The first two factors group constraints that are used more frequently when policy authority is delegated to the Commission.[12] The fifth column in Table 3.5 shows that the Pearson correlation coefficients between these constraints and the Commission's delegation ratios for each law are positive and significant. The difference between the two factors can be explained by the correlation with the member states' delegation ratios in the sixth column. The constraints of the first factor tend to correlate negatively with these ratios, but coefficients are not significant. Most of the constraints of the second factor correlate positively with the member states' delegation ratios, but only the correlation coefficient for *time limits* is significant. Patterns of correlation with the independent variables developed for the empirical chapters confirm these results. The third factor groups categories of constraints that either do not correlate with any delegation ratio and independent variable or correlate positively and significantly with the member states' delegation ratios such as *rule-making requirements* and *appeals procedures*. Categories grouped under this factor do not seem to show a clear and unique relation with the Commission's delegation ratio. I have found no other empirical evidence distinguishing these factors. Frequency of usage is not an underlying dimension. This can be easily checked by comparing the factor analysis of Table 3.5 with the descriptive statistics in Tables 3.2 and 3.3. Also policy areas do not explain factor loadings. Constraints that are grouped into the same factor are used in a broad variety of policies as can be seen in the description of the previous section and in Appendix 3.1. Nor is there any clear relation with the independent variables that we will use.

The issue of weighting should be considered in two steps. First, we should assess whether the dimensions should be weighted differently. Clearly, the stringency of a constraint is independent from the executive actor. If EU legislators require their prior approval for a measure, it would be inappropriate to consider this constraint differently depending on whether the Commission or a member state takes the measure in question. Moreover, three categories load on two factors. This somewhat

---

[12] I follow Gorsuch (1983: 206–12) for the interpretation of factors. Correlation tests on factor scores and delegation ratios confirm the meanings given to the factors. It is important to point out that I refer to the *relative use* of the constraints. Since the Council is more likely to delegate powers to member states than to the Commission, there are, for instance, more laws imposing spending limits on member states than on the Commission. However, the typical law delegating policy authority to the Commission is more likely to contain a spending limit than the typical law delegating powers to governments.

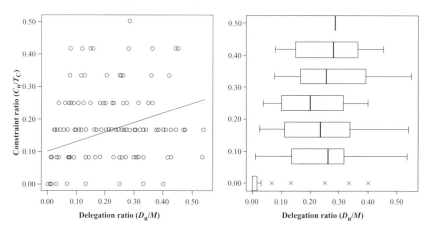

Figure 3.5 *Scatter plot and box plots: national administrations.*

blurs the difference across the three dimensions and makes the weighting highly problematic. Factors are therefore weighted equally. The second issue is to evaluate whether the categories of constraints within each factor should be weighted differently. The means of the salient factor scores of the three latent variables are 0.68, 0.64 and 0.55, the standard deviations are 0.196, 0.072 and 0.108. The categories cluster around similar values and the standard deviations of the second two factors are rather small. For these reasons, I opted for equal weighting of the categories too.

Delegation and constraints ratios

In their theory of delegation in the US Congress, McCubbins (1985: 737–41) and McCubbins and Page (1987: 416–9) suggest a positive relation between the regulatory scope, namely the domain of potential issues addressed by the administrators, and the stringency of the procedural requirements to which the administrators must abide. The delegation and constraint ratios can be interpreted as the scope of regulatory authority and the procedural stringency respectively. Epstein and O'Halloran (1999b: 106–7) confirms this expectation in the US case.

Figures 3.5 and 3.6 show the scatter and box plots of the delegation and constraint ratios for national and Commission implementation respectively. The scatter plots include a simple regression line of constraints on delegation. The box plots are with regard to the delegation ratios. The boxes represent the interquartile ranges which contain 50 percent of the values, the vertical lines across the boxes indicate the median values, while the whiskers are lines that extend from the box to

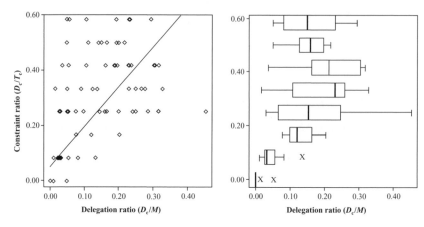

Figure 3.6 *Scatter plot and box plots: European Commission.*

the highest and lowest values. Outliers are cases with values more than 1.5 box lengths from either end of the box and are marked by a cross.

When the whole sample is considered there are no outliers for the delegation and constraint ratios of national administration. However, the small box at the bottom left end of the plot in Figure 3.5 indicates, first, the significant proportion of cases where member states are excluded from implementation, namely where both the delegation and constraint ratios are almost zero. Second, it highlights five outliers where the national administrations have some authority with no constraints.[13] In the case of Commission implementation, there are four univariate outliers with high values of the delegation ratio,[14] though there is none in the constraint ratio. Also the outliers in the bottom left of Figure 3.6 are a result of the significant number of cases where the Commission is excluded from execution and of three cases of some delegation with limited constraints.[15] No data points are simultaneous outliers on both dimensions for both national and Commission execution.

The two figures seem to confirm the expectations of McCubbins and Page. There is a significant relation between the two ratios for both

---

[13] These cases, which do not fall within the same issue area, are: Directive 72/156 on international capital flows, Directive 77/249 on lawyers' freedom to provide services, Directive 77/796 on diplomas of goods haulage operators, Directive 78/473 on co-insurance and Regulation 3181/78 on the European monetary system.

[14] These are: Regulation 26/62 on the competition rule in agriculture, Regulation 17/62 which was the first competition regulation, Regulation 19/62 on the market organization for cereals and Regulation 3975/87 on competition rules in the air transport sector.

[15] These are: Directive 89/665 on the award of public contracts, Regulation 2137/85 on the European Economic Interest Grouping and Directive 64/427 on self-employed persons in manufacturing and processing industries.

national and Commission implementation.[16] When EU legislators delegate greater authority, they also impose more constraints on executive action. But the difference between national and Commission implementation is staggering. The regression line in Figure 3.6 is much steeper. A 10 percent increase in the delegation ratio leads to a 2.9 percent increase in the constraint ratio for national administrations and a notable 14.5 percent in the Commission's constraint ratio. Legislators seem to be much more concerned to restrict the authority of the Commission than that of national administrations. Moreover, there is considerable variation around the regression line in the case of national execution. The bivariate correlation coefficient, though significant, is only 0.368. Local linear regressions show that the relation holds mostly for low values of both parameters. This reflects the fact that there are laws that delegate a considerable amount of authority attaching few constraints and other acts with less delegation and many constraints. This is clearly not the case for the Commission. The correlation coefficient is significant and very high at 0.753. Legislators seem to be much more careful in matching delegated authority with procedural constraints.

Discretion

Discretion is measured by the share of major provisions delegating powers in an act, weighted by the constraints imposed on executive action. A measure of discretion that results from the subtraction of the constraint ratio from the delegation ratio may produce negative values in acts that delegate limited authority and impose many constraints. To avoid this, equation (3.1) subtracts from the delegation ratio the product of the delegation ratio and the constraint ratio. This implies that constraints in high delegation acts have a greater policy impact than constraints in low delegation laws. Epstein and O'Halloran (1999b) lists three benefits for using this method: the avoidance of negative values, the translation of the delegation and constraint ratios into comparable common units, and a continuous measure of discretion bounded between zero and one.

Tables 3.2 and 3.3 show that the mean discretion ratio of the Commission is substantially lower (by almost a quarter) than the mean national discretion ratio. This results from the fact that (i) EU legislators rely twice as much on national administrations as they do on the Commission, so the mean national delegation ratio is three times the Commission's ratio,

---

[16] The OLS regressions are $C_n = 0.10 + 0.29 D_n$, with standard errors 0.02 and 0.06 respectively, and $C_c = 0.05 + 1.45 D_c$, with standard errors of 0.01 and 0.1 respectively. Coefficients are significant at 0.01 percent.

and (ii) when powers are delegated to the Commission, this institution is, on average, twice as constrained as national authorities when they are in charge of implementation. Table 3.6 illustrates the five acts with most and least discretion for national administrations and the Commission, and Figure 3.7 shows the distribution of the discretion ratios with a normal curve overlaid. The directives on company law that top the ranking of the national delegation ratio in Table 3.4 also feature as the acts with the highest discretion ratio. The two new entries are a directive on capital movement and one on the movement of persons, both characterized by high delegation and particularly low constraint ratios. The acts with the lowest national discretion are the same, they are on the organization of agricultural markets, customs law and competition policy. Apart from the zero delegation laws, the distribution of the national discretion ratio shows three spikes at about 5, 15 and 27 percent.

The top five laws in Table 3.6 with most discretion for the Commission are in the area of competition policy. Hence, the two regulations on agricultural policy in Table 3.4 with the highest delegation ratio have a comparatively greater number of constraints than the competition policy regulations. The discretion ratios of the acts in Table 3.6 are also significantly lower than the top national discretion ratios. There is not much difference instead with regard to the acts with the lowest discretion ratio which are still in the areas of public contracts, company law and health and safety. However, Regulation 1174/68 on tariff brackets in transport replaces Directive 64/432 on animal health. As the histogram in Figure 3.5b shows, the distribution of the Commission's discretion ratio, excluding zero delegation laws, is right-skewed with the highest frequencies at about 4–8 percent.

Delegation, constraints and discretion across time and the "new approach"

The relaunch of the single market in the mid 1980s was based on the "new approach' to law making, relying on principles such as "mutual recognition" and "reference to standards" (Commission of the EC, 1985b; Cockfield, 1992). It implied the production of less complex and prescriptive legislation, instead of the long and detailed "harmonization" directives. If this is what actually took place, it could be detected in two ways. First, quantitatively, we should see a trend toward shorter and more concise legislation, namely fewer provisions in each law. Second, qualitatively, we should see laws allowing greater discretion to member states and national authorities for the implementation of the measures at hand. These expectations are moderately confirmed.

Table 3.6 *Acts and discretion.*

Discretion of national administrations	d_n	Discretion of the Commission	d_c
		Acts with highest discretion ratio	
Directive 80/390 Admission of securities to official stock exchange listing	48.99	Regulation 26/62 Competition rules applied to agriculture	34.09
Directive 84/253 Approval of persons carrying out statutory audits	45	Regulation 3975/87 Competition rules applied to air transport	23.68
Directive 72/156 International capital flows	40	Regulation 17/62 Competition rules	21.89
Directive 78/855 Mergers of public limited liability companies	39.55	Regulation 19/65 Competition rules on agreements and practices	21.43
Directive 77/486 Education of the children of migrant workers	39.29	Regulation 2821/71 Competition rules on agreements and practices	18.75
		Acts with lowest discretion ratio	
Regulation 1418/76 Common organization of the market in rice	1.09	Directive 89/440 Award of public works contracts	1.01
Regulation 805/68 Common organization of the market in beef and veal	1.1	Directive 89/391 Safety and health of workers at work	1.06
Regulation 1224/80 Valuation of goods for customs purposes	1.39	Regulation 2137/85 European Economic Interest Grouping	1.15
Regulation 727/70 Common organization of the market in raw tobacco	1.47	Directive 79/279 Admission of securities to stock exchange listing	2.04
Regulation 1017/68 Competition rules applied to transport	1.96	Regulation 1174/68 System of bracket tariffs for carriage by road	2.08

Note: Discretion ratios are percentages, acts with zero discretion are disregarded.

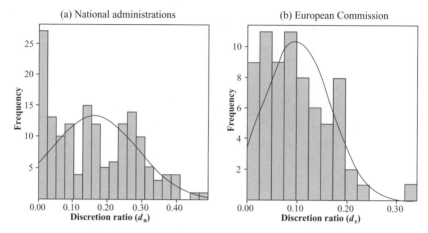

Figure 3.7 *Histograms of discretion ratios. Note:* The histogram in panel *b* excludes zero-delegation laws, with their inclusion the first bar would reach 90.

The trend line of the major provisions in Figure 3.8 is indeed negative. The one-year lagged values significantly explain the average number of provisions per year.[17] There are signs of a moderate shift toward shorter, more concise legislation taking place since the early 1980s, even before the adoption of the Single European Act (however, the acts adopted in the first half of the 1960s were also rather concise). Over the entire period, this means a reduction in the average length of legislation of 20 percent per year, equivalent to ten major provisions. Figure 3.9 shows the average levels of the national delegation, constraint and discretion ratios of the major laws across the twenty-five year period. As discussed above the three ratios are correlated, but, more importantly, the upward trend is clearly detectable, with the only exception being the year 1987. The one-year lagged values significantly explain the average discretion ratios, per year.[18] The ratio has increased by almost 1 percent a year. It means that the average law in the early 1990s was half as constraining for member states as the average law in the early 1960s. However, high discretion acts have been adopted in the 1970s too, showing more continuity than what the "new approach" thesis would suggest.

---

[17] The linear regression model is $Y_t = 54.958 - 0.216Y_{t-1} + u_t$, with a *t*-ratio of -1.8 for the lagged term, significant at the 10 percent level. Time series estimations have been carried with first-order autoregressive errors, AR(1). The estimation technique used for the parameters is the exact maximum-likelihood method, which is appropriate when the independent variable is the lagged dependent variable (Ostrom, 1990: 58–75).

[18] The result from the model is $Y_t = 0.049 + 0.703Y_{t-1} + u_t$, with a *t*-ratio of 5.22 for the lagged term, significant at the 1 percent level.

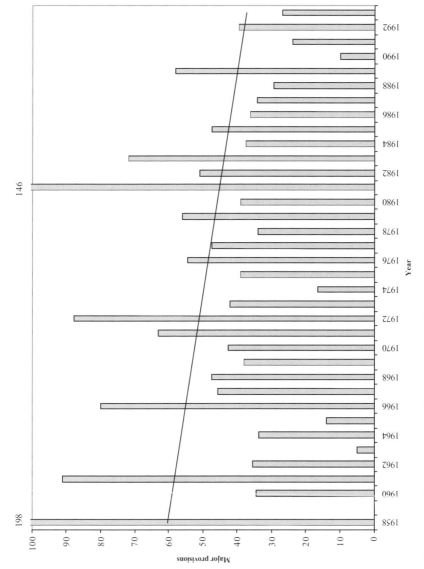

Figure 3.8 *Average yearly number of major provisions.*

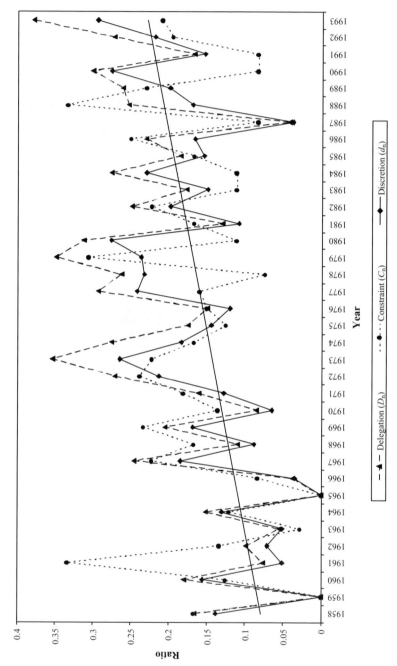

Figure 3.9 *Trends in national delegation, constraint and discretion ratios.*

As far as the role of the Commission is concerned, it could be argued that there are at least two periods in the history of the EU where the role of this institution in the implementation of common policies has been particularly salient. The first one was in the 1960s when the first core policies of the EU in the areas of agriculture, commerce and competition were established. The second period was in the 1980s with the relaunch of the integration process and the completion of the single market. Figure 3.10, illustrating the yearly averages of the Commission's ratios, confirms this view. The 1960s have been the period with the most extensive delegation of policy authority to the Commission, under the particularly strong leadership of its president, Hallstein. Powers have been conferred upon the Commission well beyond the 1965 empty chair crisis, which was precipitated by de Gaulle with the objective to forestall, among other things, the planned shift to qualified majority voting. Important powers, especially with regard to both the market organization and the structural features of the agricultural policy, commercial and competition policy and state aid, have been conferred up until the early 1970s under the two presumably weaker presidencies of Rey and Malfatti. Moravcsik (1998: 196) asserts that "it is striking how *little* of what de Gaulle sought he achieved and thus how little the crisis diverted the longer-term evolution of the EC". Our results confirm his conclusion.

The relaunch of the single market programme has clearly coincided with extensive delegation of policy authority to the Commission. On average, more powers have been conferred upon this institution during the nine years of the Delors presidency than under the previous three presidents.[19] Finally, no long-term trend in the delegation of policy authority to the Commission can be detected.[20]

In conclusion, it appears that, in line with Golub's (1999) conclusion, the relaunch of the integration process in the mid 1980s was not characterized by a comparatively higher legislative output, especially if we control for the significance of the laws adopted. It mostly represented a qualitative difference in the design of EU statutes which, on average, have relied much more on the Commission for policy implementation than the acts adopted in the previous decade. In this sense, EU policies have certainly become more supranational. However, we have also detected a long-term qualitative shift in the EU law-making process which runs counter to this assertion. Moderately in line with the expectations of the

---

[19] Interestingly, the worst performing presidency, in terms of conferral of powers, was under Jenkins, a president generally praised for his strong leadership.

[20] The result from the model is $Y_t = 0.037 + 0.15Y_{t-1} + u_t$, with a t-ratio of 0.86 for the lagged term. The coefficient of the lagged term is not significant and the trend line in Figure 3.10 is almost flat.

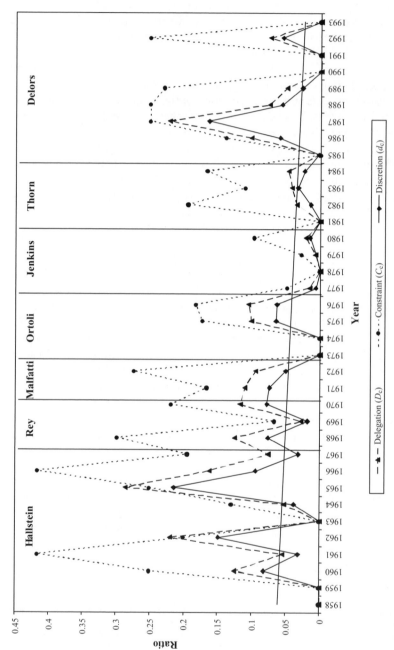

Figure 3.10 *Trends in Commission delegation, constraint and discretion ratios.*

"new approach" thesis, legislation has been not only less detailed but it has also allowed greater discretion to member states for the implementation of the specific measures at hand. From this perspective, the 1980s and early 1990s were *not* years of deeper integration.

Before proceeding on the quantitative test of our propositions in Chapter 5, the next chapter explains the measurement of the key variables that should explain the variance in delegation and discretion that we have illustrated here. These are decision rules, preferences of the members of the Council, preferences of the Commission and policy complexity.

Appendix 3.1 Additional information on the coding of discretion

The coding rules to compile my data set follow the guidelines of Appendix D in Epstein and O'Halloran (1999b). In this annex, I outline how I have adapted those rules to the EU legislation.

Counting major provisions: variable M

The number of major provisions in an act is counted following these rules:

(1) articles and numbered paragraphs count as separate provisions;

(2) subparagraphs and indents do not count if they merely elaborate on the previous paragraph, but they do count if they include new substantive authority;

(3) unnumbered paragraphs count as separate provisions only if they are substantively distinct;

(4) if a paragraph is followed by a colon and a list of elements, even if numbered, and if the elements of the lists merely elaborate on the main point of the paragraph, then the paragraph and accompanying list count as one provision;

(5) I count two provisions if, even in a single sentence or a paragraph, the Commission and the national administrations are delegated substantively different policy authority;

(6) I count only one provision if the Commission and the national administrations are delegated, in a sentence or a paragraph, policy authority on exactly the same issue (an example is where member states may take some measures but they need the Commission's authorization).

Counting major provisions delegating powers: variable D_i

The definition of delegation is any major provision that gives the member states or the Commission the authority to move the policy away from the status quo. Delegation to bureaus under the auspices of and with members appointed by the Commission is delegation to the Commission. Delegation to member states, national authorities and institutions is delegation to national administrations. I have only considered powers and constraints on executive action that are above and beyond those specified in the Treaty.[21] In addition to those listed by Epstein and O'Halloran (1999b: 276), I have regarded the following as examples of provisions delegating and not delegating powers.

Examples of what delegation to the Commission or to national administrations is:

- the right to issue implementing regulations or directives or to take decisions with some discretion;
- imposition of fines and penalties;
- carrying out negotiations with third countries;
- extension of discretionary authority to new issues or economic sectors;
- carrying out inspections or conducting investigations or inquiries (only if they complement other powers such as those to take decisions or to impose penalties);
- request of information (only if it complements powers to take decisions, to carry out investigations, to tax or to impose penalties);
- the authorization of or the right to take measures that may alter the policy;
- the right to grant derogations and exemptions;
- transposition of provisions of directives with some discretion;
- extension of policy authority that member states would have otherwise relinquished as a result of adopting the measure at hand;
- designation of authorities and institutions.

Examples of what delegation to the Commission or to national administrations is *not*:

- examination of member states' measures by the Commission but without the power to alter them or with only the faculty to issue recommendations or opinions;
- submission of proposals by the Commission (this is a legislative, not an executive, power);
- design and issuance of certificates, forms and documents;
- diffusing or exchanging information, setting rules for information exchange, notifying measures or ensuring professional secrecy;

---

[21] However, I have considered both the Treaty provisions delegating powers and the related constraints included in laws extending the scope of the Treaty. For instance, agriculture was initially exempted from the provisions on competition and state aid (Article 36 EC). But, where laws on the common market organizations extend articles 87–9 EC to the relevant agricultural market, the Commission's powers and constraints, as specified in the Treaty, have been taken into account.

- general calls to implement provisions;
- transposition of provisions of directives and obligation to take measures without discretion (these are constraints on member states);
- no prejudice provisions, that is provisions asserting that member states' existing prerogatives are unaffected (only if those prerogatives would have not otherwise been relinquished as a result of adopting the measure at hand);
- the execution, without discretion, by national authorities of measures taken by the Commission.

Most of the time, determining whether a provision delegates policy authority has been rather straightforward, especially when the delegatee was the Commission. Generally, provisions saying "Member States may" imply delegation with some discretion, those saying "Member States shall" imply obligation. However, general sentences such as "authorities shall ensure that controls are carried out" also imply delegation. In some cases, personal judgment was unavoidable but I tended to be conservative so that it was easier to reject the hypotheses.

Categories of procedural constraints

This section provides further details on the incidence of statutory constraints across polices and administrators.

Time limits. Many regulations on the common organization of agricultural and fishery markets allow member states to retain quantitative restrictions up to a specific date. During the transitional period, the Commission has been conferred powers to suspend or defer various provisions. Commercial policy regulations set a transitional period of a few months or years during which national prerogatives can still be exercised. Provisional anti-dumping duties and import surveillance measures decided by the Commission expire after a set time period (e.g. Regulation 459/68). This statutory constraint is also used for Commission decisions and regulations on competition policy (e.g. Regulation 1017/68).

In directives on VAT, company law and social policy, member states can adopt some transitional measures, normally for a period of a few years. Directives on banking and insurance allow some governments to retain national rules, to grant exemptions or to defer compliance for a specified time period. In Directive 89/646, the Commission may require national authorities to suspend for three months the granting of authorizations to exercise the activity of credit institutions. Some regulations, such as the 1968 system of bracket tariffs for the carriage of goods, contain sunset provisions. Finally, some powers of national authorities are constrained by time limits, for instance the prescription of the use of transport recording equipment with only national approval, the prohibition of the sale of hazardous vehicles and the prolongation of the posting and employment of some workers.

Spending limits.   Limits are imposed on aids to domestic producers of, say, cereals, milk and hops. In some cases, provisions assert that aid should be diminishing over time (e.g. German aid to milk producers in Regulation 804/68). Other provisions impose specific quantitative limits or specify that national aid should not exceed EU aid. If the Commission is involved in the programme of subsidization of agricultural products, such as oils and fats in Regulation 136/66, there are limits for the fixing of subsidies. When a regulation requires member states to establish organizations of producers, aid cannot exceed a percentage of the value of production and of the administrative costs. Similar constraints are imposed on compensation for market intervention and product disposal.

The Commission is normally in charge of granting financial support to structural measures of the EU agricultural and regional policy. Each regulation on this area imposes spending limits on the Commission's powers. For instance, the Commission can subsidize only 25 percent of the value of the projects under the guidance section of the European Agricultural Guidance and Guarantee Fund (EAGGF). Regulation 724/75 on the European Regional Development Fund (ERDF) specifies the distribution of funding resources across member states and limits on contributions to each project. The subsidization of the projects for the modernization of farms, the acquisition of occupational skills and the improvement of processing and marketing of agricultural products should generally not exceed 25 percent of national expenditure. In some cases, there are specific limits on the amounts of contributions. For instance, the Commission decides on granting of aid under Directive 72/159 on the modernization of farms, but the EU contribution should not exceed 150–250 units of account.

Reporting requirements.   In the case of national execution, EU legislators oversee implementation by requiring national authorities to submit periodic reports to them or to the Commission. It is frequently used in social policy directives. Member states have to report to the Commission on the implementation of the principle of equal treatment of the sexes and of the rules for collective redundancies. National authorities have to report every five years to the Commission on the execution of the directives on safety and health at work and on the organization of working time. National employment agencies must communicate results and problems related to the implementation of the system of vacancy clearance. While the European Coordination Bureau of the Commission must produce an annual report on this system and on other activities carried out in the labor market.

Reporting requirements can be considerably more specific as regards the information to be communicated. Directives 77/62 and 89/440 on public contracts demand national authorities to produce a yearly statement on the value and the number of contracts awarded, with an explanatory note on the rejection of low-priced tenders. Member states should communicate to the Commission the number and types of cases in which there has been a refusal for the taking up of the business of credit institutions. They should also forward to the Commission an explanatory text on the selection of the items comprising own funds of credit institutions.

The Commission is required to produce reports when it is involved in the granting of funds, mostly in agricultural and regional policy. Reporting is also a common requirement when the Commission exercises an important prerogative, such as carrying out anti-dumping investigations and taking other trade policy measures (e.g. Regulation 459/68). The Commission must also produce reports on the implementation of systems related to, for instance, the recognition of diplomas, the adoption of technical standards and various measures of environmental, social and competition policy. There are also more specific requests. In some laws, the Commission must draw up a report examining the treatment accorded to firms of the EU in third countries. In Regulation 1017/68 it must produce a report when it establishes that the transport section is in crisis. In Directive 89/646, the Commission must submit a report on cases of withdrawal of authorizations to exercise banking activities.

Consultation requirements. This constraint is used when national administrations have to assist an EU-level policy: for instance, when member states adopt measures supporting the EU competition policy, set penalties against discriminatory transport rates or implement rules on transport rest periods. Prior consultation of the Commission or, in some cases, of EU-level committees is especially important when member states want to (re)introduce market-distorting measures. These may range from import surveillance to quantitative or capital movement restrictions, export authorizations, exemptions and public service obligations. Directive 77/388 stipulates that prior consultation of the advisory committee on VAT is compulsory for any tax measure that may cause distortion. The banking advisory committee had to be consulted if member states wanted to defer the application of the banking Directive 77/780. In social security regulations, national competent institutions must consult an administrative commission if they decide to grant substantial benefits in kind to migrant workers. Some directives provide for mutual consultation among member states or their authorities prior to taking measures such the exchange of tax-related information between treasury ministries in Directive 77/799. Other laws provide for prior consultation with private parties. Regulation 1463/70 required the consultation of manufacturers when appointing fitters of recording equipment.

The Commission may have to consult the Council, the relevant member states or a committee composed of representatives of member states. Prior Council consultation was required before issuing regulations under Regulation 11/60 abolishing discriminatory transport rates. Decisions concerning investigations, imposition of penalties, modification of aid to agricultural and fishery products, amendment of precautionary measures, establishment of new intervention centers and the legality of agreements between companies require prior consultation of national authorities. There are many committees that must be consulted prior to taking specific measures. The most common ones are the advisory committee on restrictive practices, the EAGGF committee, the standing committee on agricultural structures, the advisory committee on anti-dumping duties and the ERDF committee. Other technical committees to be consulted are on the movement of workers, capital movements (the monetary committee), toy safety, public works contracts, and safety and health at work.

Public hearings. In Regulation 459/68 on anti-dumping, when taking transitional measures to protect a domestic industry, national authorities must hear explanations from the interested parties, if they have made a written request for a hearing. Moreover, parties shall also have an opportunity to meet so that opposing views may be presented and any rebuttal argument put forward.

Most of the regulations of competition and commercial policy, where the Commission can take decisions and issue regulations, contain the obligation to hold a public hearing. In Regulations 17/62 and 1017/68, the Commission must hear any interested parties before imposing sanctions. In Regulations 26/62 and 1017/68, it must do so before deciding if agreements between companies fulfill specific conditions. Decisions must be published and all interested parties are invited to submit comments within a set time period. In Regulation 4064/89 on merger control, the Commission must give companies the opportunity to present objections, at every stage of the procedure and before taking any decision. Before issuing regulations with regard to the validity of agreements and concerted practices, a power conferred in Regulations 19/65 and 2821/71, any legal person has the right to submit comments and the Commission must hear their concerns. In commercial policy, when the Commission carries out investigations with the view of imposing anti-dumping or countervailing duties, as established in Regulation 459/68, it must hear explanations from interested companies and give them the opportunity to meet. When the Commission is carrying out examinations of illicit commercial practices or that may lead to import surveillance, it must hold hearings. Finally, any action of the Commission concerning the abolition of discriminatory transport rates, following Regulation 11/60, must also be preceded by a hearing of the relevant companies.

Rule-making requirements.   In the case of national execution, regulations on social security, such as no. 3/58, specify detailed rules for when migrant workers and their relatives are entitled to benefits in a member state. They set criteria for computing contributions and reimbursements and procedures to obtain benefits. The directives on capital movements and on the freedom of establishment and to provide services have long and detailed lists of the types of capital free to move across Europe and of the restrictions to be abolished. Measures on workers movement specify criteria on the availability and employment of foreign workers and, for instance, rules on residence permits. Directive 77/780 on credit and insurance sets detailed conditions for granting authorizations to exercise those activities. Acts on company law specify rules for the layout of official documents. Structural measures in agriculture and fisheries impose detailed conditions governing aid to these sectors. Regulation 724/75 on regional policy has similar constraints, while Regulation 1191/69 sets criteria concerning the financial compensation of transport companies burdened by public sector obligations.

Many of the rules that are imposed on national administrations in laws on, for instance, workers and capital movement, structural aid and recognition of diplomas also delimit the authority of the Commission. Others are used specifically when this institution is involved in implementation. Competition regulations set limits to the penalties that the Commission can impose on violating companies and lists the practices that can be exempted. Regulations 4056/86 and 3975/87, for instance, list the cases when the Commission may revoke its decision. Regulation 4064/89 specifies detailed figures of aggregate turnover to determine the threshold for Commission action. Regulations on agricultural policy include detailed criteria on setting prices, levies, reimbursements and compensatory amounts. Measures on structural policies, such as Regulation 724/75, include rules on granting aid and eligibility. Commercial policy regulations detail criteria specifying a dumped product, goods wholly produced in one country, injury or threat of injury. They also include rules for setting duties, import surveillance and customs valuation.

Appeals procedures. All directives on the application of the principle of equality of treatment of the sexes are designed to ensure that national authorities and their policies are constrained by the possibility of judicial action by individual citizens. In Directive 76/207, for instance, member states must introduce measures to enable employees to pursue claims of unequal treatment and to protect them against dismissal in reaction to a complaint. The principle is applied to many issues ranging from working conditions to social security. In directives on insurance and banking, national authorities may refuse authorization to set up a business or may withdraw it. The legislation specifies the obligation to provide a reasoned opinion within a time period and to specify all legal remedies and time limits that private parties are entitled to. Similar requirements are imposed on many national measures. In Regulation 2137/85 on European Economic Interest Grouping, national authorities can oppose the transfer of assets and prohibit activities that contravene public interest. The regulation specifies that the judicial review of these decisions must be possible. In Directive 64/432, exporters have the right to obtain an opinion from a Commission's veterinary expert if import trade is blocked on the grounds of animal health problems. Directive 89/665 deals specifically with the application of review procedures to the award of public contracts. It provides for no discrimination between companies claiming injury and specifies the actors having a legal standing, such as, importantly, the Commission. Finally, social security regulations expedite the review process on benefit entitlement by allowing appeals against a national institution to be filed through a similar institution of another member state with the same time constraints.

Exemptions. The regulations on the freedom of movement of workers established a machinery of vacancy clearance. The central and regional employment agencies in charge of implementation could not extend the facility to some types of workers and employment contracts. Regulation 1174/68 introduced a system of bracket tariffs for the carriage of goods by road. Member states could not apply it to some types of transport. Finally, some measures in agriculture exclude certain activities. In Regulation 355/77, for instance, national authorities are authorized to use EU funds only for agricultural processing and marketing, but not for retailing.

With regard to the Commission's powers in competition policy, small and medium-size transport companies are exempted from Regulation 1017/68, while tramp vessel services are excluded from Regulation 4056/86. In commercial policy, Regulation 802/68 on the origin of goods does not apply to petroleum products and the common rules for imports of Regulation 288/82 do not apply to textile products. Workers operating in sectors such as coal, steel and nuclear energy are excluded from the regulations on the movement of workers. The general system for the recognition of diplomas does not apply to professions that are already subject to EU law. In internal market measures, annex I of Directive 88/378 on toy safety lists the products that are outside the scope of the act such as fireworks and air guns. Many institutions are excluded from the banking directives, such as the Belgian communal savings banks and the Irish credit unions. Armed forces and police are exempted from Directive 89/391 on safety at work.

Legislative action required. Member states could have prolonged the implementation of the first Regulation 19/62 on the common organization of the market for cereals, but only after unanimous approval of the Council. Approval was needed if member states wanted to postpone the compensation of public transport obligations. The deferral by more than eight years of the application of the first banking Directive 77/780 needed a similar approval. Finally, a member state could request an extension for complying with Directive 80/778 on the quality of water but, if the Commission disagreed, a Council decision was necessary. Council's approval is also required in important areas related to VAT and spending provisions. A member state setting up a particular simplification and anti-fraud measure that derogates from the VAT Directive 67/228 needs the Council's unanimous approval, if the measure is referred to it. Aids to agriculture and quantitative import restrictions are vetted in a similar way.

When the Commission decides, with immediate effect, that the export of a product should be subject to an authorization according to Regulation 2603/69, the measure is revoked if the Council does not approve it within six weeks. A similar safeguard procedure is used for import surveillance and the protective measures of Regulation 288/82. Negotiations with third countries to gain market access for credit institutions in Directive 89/646 or to assure comparable treatment to EU companies in competition issues require prior Council authorization. Finally, in Regulation 1017/68, the Council has to declare a state of crisis in the transport sector before the Commission gives its consent to restrictive practices.

Legislative action possible. In Directive 85/374 approximating national laws on the liability for defective products, if a member state wants to provide that a producer is liable even if the state of scientific knowledge was not such as to enable discovery of the defect at the time of production, it must notify the Commission and keep its measure in abeyance for a set time period. If a legislative proposal is tabled, the abeyance period is extended. The state can then put the measure into effect in the case of no proposal or inaction by the Council.

Many laws on the organization of agricultural and fishery markets extend the Treaty powers of the Commission in the field of control of state aid. A member state may refer to the Council a Commission's decision against the granting of aid. The Council must decide within a set time period and the default condition is the decision of the Commission. Structural measures in agriculture and Regulation 1107/70 on aid to the transport sector contain similar provisions. *Variant a* of the *safeguard procedure* is used when the Commission takes protective measures in the case of serious disturbances in the agricultural markets, provisional anti-dumping duties, decisions against illicit commercial practices and on the suspension of the system of vacancy clearance. In Directive 88/361, the decision of the Commission to authorize national authorities to take urgent protective measures in the capital markets can be revoked or amended by the Council. A similar procedure is used in Regulation 2603/69 if the Commission rejects a request for an export authorization.

Executive action required. In Regulation 15/61, Luxembourg could derogate from some provisions on the movement of workers only upon Commission authorization. The consent of the Commission was necessary for the deferral of the implementation of Regulation 802/68 on the origin of goods, in Directive 64/222 when a member state required proof of qualification of wholesale trade from a national of another member state, and, together with the approval of the committee on agricultural structures, for the eligibility of projects on farming modernization of Directive 72/159. Amendments to annexes of the first social security regulations needed the prior assent of an administrative commission. In Directive 73/239, if a national authority wants to verify the solvency of a subsidiary, it needs approval from its counterpart in the member state where the company was first established.

The Commission needs the approval of the relevant member state prior to funding a project under EAGGF Regulation 17/64. In the regulations on the movement of workers, the European co-ordination office needs the approval from specialist national services before operating the system of vacancy clearance. The regulatory procedure is used when the Commission adopts implementing provisions in commercial policy, as in Regulations 802–3/68, and technical changes to environmental, health and safety and company law directives. Decisions concerning the granting of ERDF assistance in Regulation 724/75 and amendments to the tariff nomenclature of Regulation 2658/87 and to the general system of diploma recognition of Directive 92/51 follow *variant b* of the *management procedure*.

Executive action possible. In the early commercial policy regulations, rejection of a dumping complaint by a member state can be objected by the Commission, and vice versa, leading to a union-wide investigation. Import or export authorizations issued by national administrations could be overruled by the Commission. In the system for diploma recognition, the Commission can object to a decision of a national authority to refuse the right to choose between an adaptation period and an aptitude test. In Directive 88/378, a national prohibition to market a toy, for safety reasons, is revoked if the Commission does not withdraw the relevant technical standard. The Commission may decide whether safeguard or precautionary measures adopted by national authorities during transitional periods of market organizations or in the case of emergencies in banking and capital movement directives should be maintained, modified or repealed.

All regulations on the organization of agricultural markets and many structural policy measures include the *variant a* of the *management procedure*. The prerogatives of the Commission that are subject to this constraint include the adoption of rules on imported products, supply contracts, granting aids and EAGFF payments, and the setting of commercialization centers, minimum quantities and qualities, the scale of premium, transitional measures, and derived and threshold prices.

Finally, provisions that would fall under the category of compensations in Epstein and O'Halloran (1999b) cannot be considered constraints on member states. In some cases, governments are free to determine whether to compensate private interests (see, for example, the monetary compensation amounts for farmers – Regulation 974/71). But, even when states are required to compensate social actors (e.g. fishermen organizations that have intervened in some markets – Regulation 100/76), member states' discretion is still considerable and is constrained mostly by time and (upper) spending limits. Both cases are coded as provisions delegating policy authority to governments. Equally, adaptation periods for companies cannot be considered constraints for member states (see, for example, Directive 79/267 on direct life assurance). Actually, it could be argued that national prerogatives are prolonged as a result of these periods. The only case of the sample that could be considered a constraint is in Regulation 1191/69 where member states are required to compensate transport companies for the imposition of public service obligations. Instead of creating a new category, I have included this constraint under *rule-making requirements* because the regulation specifies detailed rules to be followed.

4 Decision rules, preferences and policy complexity

The propositions derived in Chapter 2 have identified three factors explaining delegation to and discretion of the Commission and national administrations: decision rules, preferences of the members of the Council, preferences of the Commission and policy complexity. This chapter explains the operationalization of these key independent variables.

The analysis of the dimensions of conflict in EU politics and the related issue of measurement of preferences have been at the center of considerable scholarly attention. This is not surprising. Politics is as much about rules as it is about conflict. Three dominant cleavages have been identified. Political actors in the EU differentiate themselves along their attitudes towards European integration, along lines reflecting different views about substantive policy issues and along the left–right divide. I take these dimensions at face value without prejudging their relative saliency. But I suggest an advancement to the quantitative measurement of these preferences along these cleavages. I also develop a measure of conflict within the Council and use two different methods to operationalize the preferences of the Commission. Finally, I provide a longitudinal analysis of how the Commission's and the Council's preferences have evolved since 1958. An interesting finding from this exercise is with regard to the institutional sources of the pro-integration positions of the Commission. The median voter in the college of commissioners is significantly more supportive of European integration than the pivotal member in the Council under qualified majority voting, even when we consider commissioners as perfect agents of their national government or party.

As far as policy complexity is concerned, I first expand the proposition introduced in Chapter 2 and develop testable hypotheses that take into account how actor-related features inform choices of delegation. I then show how these features guide the measurement of complexity. Expectations will be tested qualitatively, using a classification of EU issue areas, and quantitatively, using three measures of policy complexity.

This and the previous chapter set the ground for the, largely quantitative, analysis of delegation in Chapter 5. Table 4.4 displays descriptive statistics of the independent variables. With the exception of decision rules, the quantitative measurement of these variables is not an easy exercise and can be subject to a number of criticisms. Therefore, Chapter 6 will present detailed qualitative evidence of the processes of delegation across four policy areas over a period of time. Certainly, also the case study method is not immune to critique, especially with regard to the generalization of the findings. However, if different methodologies corroborate our expectations, this would undoubtedly strengthen the robustness of our results.

Decision rules

I use for the regression analysis a dichotomous variable *Decision rule* taking the value of one for qualified majority voting and zero for unanimity. The variable also takes the value of one for the five laws on the movement of persons that have been adopted by simple majority voting.[1]

Preferences of the members of the Council

To my knowledge, there are no studies that have developed quantitative measures of the preferences of Council members across most EU policies since 1958. Works, of undoubtedly excellent quality, are limited to a small sample of policies and/or countries and/or time period. Moravcsik (1998) covers the whole 1955–91 period, but he limits the analysis to the preferences of only three member states on a subset of EU policies and he gives greater emphasis to Treaty negotiations than to secondary EU laws. Contributions to the volume edited by Bueno de Mesquita and Stokman (1994) compare the explanatory power of contending Council bargaining models. Their data set consists of twenty-two issues related to road and air transport and to banking, some of which were debated within the same piece of legislation. In assessing the influence of the European Parliament, König and Pöter (2001) map the preferences of Council members on a two-dimensional space but with regard to only four legislative proposals.[2] There is also a gargantuan literature comprising single case studies of most of the EU policy output. Given the qualitative, issue-specific and small sample nature of these studies, the methods used by these scholars to gauge Council preferences cannot be extended to our context.[3]

---

[1] These are Regulations 15/61, 38/64, 360/68, 1612/68 and Directive 77/486.
[2] Hubschmid and Moser (1997) carry out a similar exercise for legislation regarding car emission standards.
[3] For an insiders' account of negotiations in the EU see Meerts and Cede (2004).

The most impressive large sample work is the data set recently compiled by Thomson and Stokman as part of the Decision-Making in the European Union (DEU) project. These scholars have collected information on the policy positions of member states, the Commission, the Parliament and the status quo across 174 controversial issues raised by seventy proposals initiated by the Commission between 1996 and 2000. The data set has been the basis for a large body of work, recently collected in Thomson *et al.* (2006), on the dimensions of conflict within the Council (Selck, 2004; Thomson, Boerefijn and Stokman, 2004; Zimmer, Schneider and Dobbins, 2005), its bargaining dynamics (Arregui, Stokman and Thomson, 2004; Bailer, 2004) and the explanatory power of models of voting, bargaining and interest intermediation (Pajala and Widgrén, 2004; Schneider, Baltz and Finke, 2004; Schneider, Finke and Bailer, 2004; Selck, 2004; Selck and Steunenberg, 2004). Unfortunately, the data set cannot be used for our purposes given its limited time period. It would be rather arduous to transpose the highly provision-specific nature of the information collected on countries' policy positions to laws adopted twenty years earlier. The same applies for the large sample analyses of the 1994–2000 Council roll call votes carried out by Mattila and Lane (2001) and Mattila (2004). These votes are also likely to produce estimates of strategic, rather than sincere, preferences. Finally, in Franchino (2000c), I have used the results from a question in the Eurobarometer survey to develop a measure of preference convergence between the Council and the Commission. This measure, apart from yielding unsatisfactory results, disregards policy-specific preferences, does not produce a range and the position of the qualified majority pivot and assumes identity of citizens' and state officials' views.

In this section, I suggest a moderate advancement to the quantitative measurement of the policy positions of Council members.[4] I derive three measures of preferences from the work of Budge and his colleagues (2001) who have estimated the positions of parties from election manifestos across fifty-six substantive policy categories over the post-war period. This data set is certainly not flawless. The coding scheme could be considered rather coarse-grained. Moreover, the original motivation of the manifesto research group was to assess the salience of particular issues rather than the substantive positions on these issues. Hence, positive and negative attitudes towards specific issues at hand were not systematically

---

[4] König (2001) was the first to employ this approach. It has been used to measure conflict among member states and the bias of the Commission's proposals. Franchino and Rahming (2003) have used it to compare the preference profiles of Council formations.

recorded (Laver and Garry, 2000). However, these data provide the only means for a quantitative estimate of Council members' preferences over our time period. Expert surveys cover a shorter period and do not track changes in party positions over time. They also pre-structure the policy space into a fixed number of policy scales with predetermined meanings (Castles and Mair, 1984; Laver and Hunt, 1992; Huber and Inglehart, 1995; Laver, Benoit and Garry, 2003). As far as the new and promising computer-coding techniques, data sets that have sufficiently broad geographical and time coverage are not available yet (Laver and Garry, 2000; Laver, 2001; Laver, Benoit and Garry, 2003).

More promisingly, Gabel and Huber (2000) have recently derived from the manifesto data set rather accurate estimates of left–right policy positions, especially for governing parties (see also Pennings, 2002). Moreover, the limited evidence available suggests that manifesto promises make their way into government policy programs and that governing parties honor a non-negligible number of campaign pledges (Gallagher, Laver and Mair, 2001: 380–84).

The integration dimension.   My selection of preference measures is based on the EU literature.[5] The two classic theories of European integration, intergovernmentalism and neofunctionalism, implicitly assume that the dominant cleavage within the Council is the more–less integration dimension (Haas, 1958; Hoffmann, 1966; Moravcsik, 1998: 24–50). This dimension of conflict has, for instance, played an important role in the negotiation and ratification processes of the Amsterdam Treaty (Bräuninger, *et al.*, 2001; Hug and König, 2002). Some analyses of EU legislative procedures are also based on the more–less integration cleavage (Garrett, 1995; Garrett and Tsebelis, 1996; Tsebelis and Kreppel, 1998; Schulz and König, 2000). And, in his analysis of 180 roll call votes held by the Council between 1995 and 2000, Mattila (2004) shows that this dimension may inform voting behavior. A member state which, for policy reasons, would otherwise be inclined to abstain or vote against the majority of the Council is less likely to do so if it holds pro-integration preferences. Finally, Selck (2004) and Thomson, Boerefijn and Stokman (2004) use the DEU data set to map the positions of the member states, the Commission and the Parliament. They both show that there are significant differences between the preferences of the Commission and the Parliament on the one side and those of the governments on the other. This could represent a more–less integration cleavage, although these

---

[5] The cleavages in EU politics have been comprehensively analyzed in a recent work by Marks and Steenbergen (2004).

scholars do not endorse this interpretation as this dimension does not appear to be particularly relevant *within* the Council. In Budge *et al.* (2001: 166) there are two categories that gauge parties' position on the EU. Category 108 records favorable while category 110 records hostile mentions of the EU.[6] The first measure of preference, *Integration*, is the difference between the values coded for the favorable and the hostile category. Higher values imply a more pro-integration position.

The policy dimension. Other EU scholars take issue with the view that the dominant dimension of EU politics is more–less integration. Most in-depth case studies of Council bargaining strongly emphasize that the main dimension is the divergence on substantive policy issues. Disagreement emerges with regard to trade liberalization, exchange-rate stabilization, market and social regulation and environmental protection (e.g. Garrett, 1992; Bueno de Mesquita and Stokman, 1994; Héritier, 1995; Scharpf, 1996; Patterson, 1997; Moravcsik, 1998; Sandholtz and Stone Sweet, 1998; Héritier, *et al.*, 2001; Eising, 2002).[7] Some formal modelers have used a single dimension that reflects policy-specific or left–right divide (Steunenberg, 1994; Crombez, 1996, 1997a; Steunenberg, 1997; Tsebelis and Garrett, 2000). At least one cleavage reflecting substantive policy positions has been detected in all the works based on the DEU data set. The interpretation of the results diverges slightly among scholars because of the different methodologies employed. For Thomson, Boerefijn and Stokman (2004), a clearly significant dimension represents diverging views on market regulation and deregulation. Selck (2004) and Zimmer, Schneider and Dobbins (2005) put greater emphasis on the issue of subsidies and the conflict between contributors and beneficiaries of EU funds, but they also identify a divide between regulatory–protectionist and deregulatory–liberal views.[8]

---

[6] Favorable mentions include the desirability of expanding the EU, increasing its competence and/or remaining a member, hostile mentions include opposition to these issues and/or to specific EU policies (Budge *et al.*, 2001: 223). This is certainly an approximate measure but it is the only one available for the whole period under study. Alternative data sets start from 1984 (see Ray, 1999; Marks and Steenbergen, 2004).

[7] Most of the policy chapters in the well-known textbook on *Policy-Making in the European Union* of Wallace and Wallace (2000) emphasize the saliency of the substantive policy dimension, so do textbooks on the Council (Hayes-Renshaw and Wallace, 1997; Westlake, 1999).

[8] With the exception of Ireland, these divisions tend to correlate with the geographical location of member states, hence some scholars label this dimension as a north–south divide. Also Mattila and Lane's (2001) analysis of Council roll call decisions between 1994 and 1998 has identified a north–south cleavage in voting patterns. Elgström *et al.* (2001) have interviewed Swedish participants in EU negotiations and argue that coalitions form on the basis of substantive policy interests and cultural affinity (see also Beyers and Dierickx, 1998).

The second measure of preferences is then derived from matching the underlying policy dimension of each law with the substantive policy categories of Budge *et al.* (2001). Table 4.1 maps forty-one policy categories into which I have classified the sampled laws with the categories of Budge *et al.* (2001). This is what I consider the best match between the substantive policy content underlying the sampled EU laws and the manifesto coding scheme. The section below on policy complexity provides further details about this classification, Appendix 4.1 includes details on the matching of the policy categories given in Table 4.1, while Appendix 4.2 suggests two alternatives that will be used in the next chapters to assess the robustness of the results.

The majority of the EU policy categories reflect underlying support for or opposition to the establishment of a market economy. The category of market economy in Budge *et al.* (2001) includes favorable mentions of enterprise capitalism and economic orthodoxy. I subtract from these estimates the values for the category of planned economy which includes favorable references to market regulation, social market economy, economic planning and state intervention. The directive on education of the children of migrant workers reflects underlying views about the expansion of educational provisions, while opinions with regard to social justice, equality, fair treatment and the expansion of welfare provisions is the substantive policy dimension for the measures on equal treatment, rights and social security. Laws on environmental policy reflect views about environmental protection. Finally, support for specific social groups is the underlying dimension for the last two groups of measures: agriculture and farmers in the case of the fisheries and agricultural policy, middle class professionals for the establishment and provision of services and for qualifications and professions. The second measure of preferences, *Policy*, records party positions on the relevant substantive policy as matched in the first two columns of Table 4.1.

The left–right dimension. The third measure, *Left–right*, is the left–right position of parties estimated using the "vanilla" approach advocated by Gabel and Huber (2000). The method consists in performing a factor analysis on all the policy categories of the manifesto research group data for the entire post-war period and converting the resulting factor scores to an eleven-point left–right scale (Gabel and Huber, 2000: 97–6).[9] Higher values imply more left-wing positions. These scholars have demonstrated how their approach consistently produces the best estimates of

---

[9] Gabel and Huber (2000:98) shows that this method is superior to alternatives that pool data by country or by time periods.

Table 4.1 *Policy categories from the Manifestos Research Group and EU policy categories.*

Substantive policy category, Budge et al. (2001)	EU policy category	Direction of shift
Agriculture and Farmers (703)	Agriculture: financial provisions, organization of markets, structural policy; fishing: organization of markets, structural policy; monetary compensation amounts (30)	More support for agriculture Rightward
Education: Expansion – Limitation (506–507)	Education: children of migrant workers (1)	Expansion of education Leftward
Environmental Protection (501)	Environment (3)	More environmental protection Leftward
Market Economy – Planned Economy: Free Enterprise + Economic Orthodoxy – Market Regulation – Economic Planning – Controlled Economy (401 + 414 – 403 – 404 – 412)	Adoption of the ECU; company law: accounts, safeguards, stock exchange listing; commercial policy; competition: exemptions and limitation periods, rules for undertakings; cooperation among tax authorities; credit and banking; European economic interest grouping; industrial and commercial property; insurance; merger control; movement of capital; movement of persons: vacancy clearance; payments for services: liberalization; public contracts: procedure; taxation; technical standards; transport: market conditions (62)	More market economy Rightward
	Consumer protection; competition: exemptions and limitation periods†; international capital flows: regulation; organization of working time; regional policy; safety and health at work; social policy; transport: regulation (19)	*More planned economy Leftward*
Middle Class and Professional Groups (704)	Establishment and services: movement of workers; qualifications and professions: specific and general system (26)	More support for middle class Rightward
Welfare: Social Justice + Welfare State Expansion – Welfare State Limitation (503 + 504 – 505)	Equal treatment for men and women; movement of persons: rights and derogations; social security of migrant workers (17)	Expansion of welfare Leftward

Notes: In the first column, the number of the policy categories of Budge *et al.* (2001) is indicated in the parentheses. In the second column, the total number of sampled EU laws is given in parentheses.† The shift of one law on competition (exemptions and limitation periods) and three laws on commercial policy is toward a planned economy and leftward.

party positions, compared to the alternatives, and is accurate especially for governing parties. The latter point is particularly relevant because members of the Council are ministers of the national governments.

Nevertheless, the left–right dimension has traditionally been given very limited emphasis in studies on EU politics and, especially, on Council bargaining. Formal modelers have paid lip service to the issue by labeling their one-dimensional models accordingly (Crombez, 1996, 1997a; Steunenberg, 1997). In some case studies, there are references, mostly *en passant*, to the ideological profile of Council negotiators, and this is generally seen as secondary to the substantive policy views (e.g. Garrett, 1992; Scharpf, 1996; Patterson, 1997; Moravcsik, 1998). Scholars have only recently started to pay greater attention to the left–right dimension. Hix (1999; see also Hix and Lord, 1997; Hix, 2005) contends that it is as salient as the integration dimension. Comprehensive works on European elections and on the legislative behavior in the European Parliament reveal that they are either both relevant or that the left–right divide is the most prominent one (Thomassen and Schmitt, 1999; Hix, 2001; Gabel and Hix, 2002; Hix, Noury and Roland, 2002; Noury, 2002). Some scholars have recently shown that the issue of European integration is assimilated into the pre-existing left–right ideology of parties (Marks and Wilson, 2000; Aspinwall, 2002; Hooghe, Marks and Wilson, 2002; Marks, Wilson and Ray, 2002).

Results from studies of the Council are less clear cut however. On the one hand, Mattila (2004) shows that left-wing governments are less likely to vote against the Council majority than right-wing ones. On the other hand, both Thomson, Boerefijn and Stokman (2004) and Zimmer, Schneider and Dobbins (2005) find that the left–right cleavage is not particularly salient. If anything, it is subsumed within the conflict on more prominent substantive policy issues. Since these works refer to a relatively recent time period and have been, until very recently, mostly focused on the Parliament, the inclusion of the left–right dimension in this study allows us to assess its relevance over a longer time period and with respect to the Council.

For each of the preference measures, I have produced an estimate for each governing party as explained, using the data from the manifestos for the period when each sampled EU law has been adopted. The date of the document is normally incorporated in the title of the each law. I leave open the question of the relative relevance of these three measures. Moravcsik (1998) gives generally more importance to the substantive policy conflict than to the ideological or integration positions of actors. And evidence from the DEU data set reveals how this cleavage dominates over other dimensions of conflict (Selck, 2004; Thomson, Boerefijn and Stokman,

2004; Zimmer, Schneider and Dobbins, 2005). Formal models capture both the integration and the policy dimension (Tsebelis, 1994; Moser, 1997; Tsebelis, 1997; Crombez, 2001) and the empirical works testing these models recognize them, sometimes implicitly (Hubschmid and Moser, 1997; Tsebelis and Kalandrakis, 1999; Rittberger, 2000; König and Pöter, 2001). The integration dimension appears salient in studies on Treaty negotiations (Bräuninger, *et al.*, 2001; Hug and König, 2002), while the analysis of Council roll call votes shows that both the integration and the left–right cleavage are important (Mattila, 2004).

The next step is to produce a measure of governmental preferences. Budge *et al.* (2001: 166) contend that a valid one should incorporate information concerning (i) the relative share of power held by each of the governing parties and (ii) the positions of the governing parties. The formula is

$$\sum_{i=1}^{n} \text{preference}_i \times \frac{\text{no. posts}_i}{\text{total posts}} \qquad \text{for} \quad i = 1, \ldots, n.$$

The preference of a government is the sum of the preferences of each party *i* forming the government weighted by the share of cabinet ministerships held by the relevant party. For instance, the ideology of the eighteenth Irish cabinet (July 1989–February 1992) was composed of more than 80 percent Fianna Fáil and about 19 percent Progressive Democratic Party preferences. Fianna Fáil held thirteen cabinet posts, while the remaining three were allocated to the Democrats. The twentieth German cabinet that started the highly successful center-right governing coalition in October 1982 was composed of more than 72 percent Christian Democratic Union and about 28 percent Free Democratic Party preferences. Christian Democrats held thirteen and Free Democrats five of the eighteen cabinet posts. There is no weighting of course for the single-party governments that have occurred frequently in Denmark, Great Britain, Greece, Spain and Portugal. Data on portfolio allocation have been collected, for the period when each sampled EU law has been adopted, from Müller and Strøm (2000) and complemented with data from Woldendorp, Keman and Budge (1998, 2000).[10]

---

[10] I have counted the allocation of ministerial responsibilities or portfolios, not the number of ministers, because this is a more accurate reflection of the power share within a coalition. For instance, it is common for ministers in Belgian cabinets to hold more than one portfolio. Tindermans, the Prime Minister of the nineteenth cabinet, was also responsible for science policy, environmental policy and the civil service. I considered three portfolios allocated to the Flemish Christian Peoples Party. Ministers without portfolio have been considered, while nonpartisan ministers have been disregarded.

Council range

Once we have identified the preferences of the members of the Council at the time of the adoption of the sampled EU laws, as explained in the previous section, two variables are used for the statistical analysis. The first one is the *Range*, a measure of conflict within the Council. It is the difference between the maximum and the minimum preference values.[11] Since data are collected from different categories, the *Policy range* is standardized as follows:

$$Standardized\ policy\ range_{lc} = \frac{Policy\ range_{lc}}{max_c - |\ min_c\ |}$$

where *Policy range*$_{lc}$ is the difference between the maximum and minimum value for law *l* and category *c*, max_c is the maximum value of the policy category *c* throughout the whole period and min_c is its minimum value (it is always either negative or zero). *Standardized policy range* is then bounded between zero and one, where zero denotes low conflict within the Council and one denotes high conflict.

Figure 4.1 shows the development of the *Integration range* and the *Left–right range* throughout the relevant period. *Standardized policy range* is not shown in the figure because it does not provide relevant longitudinal information.

The range on the integration dimension has oscillated across the mean value of 5 up until 1986. In the late 1980s and early 1990s, conflict on the integration dimension has instead substantially increased as a result of strong pro-integration positions taken by the coalitions governing Germany, Denmark and Luxembourg[12] and the relatively euroskeptical views of the British conservative government. Interestingly, the enlargements do not seem to have increased conflict within the Council.

On the contrary, the *Left–right range* shows greater variance throughout the period and it appears to be particularly associated with the first two enlargements. At least up until 1972, the conflict within the Council on the left–right dimension has been relatively moderate, averaging 1.5 with most countries taking center-right positions. The mean has then risen to 2.5 for the post-1972 period. Britain has been the main reason for such an increase. It had the most left wing preferences in the 1970s, together with Ireland, and the most right wing preferences for most of the 1980s and

---

[11] Conflict within the Council also gauges the cost of national implementation. Other measures could be used, such as the index of polarization used by Schneider and Baltz (2005) and based on the model of Esteban and Ray (1999). I leave alternative operationalizations to further research.

[12] These were Free Democrats and Christian Democrats in Germany, Liberals and Conservatives in Denmark, Social Democrats and Christian Social Democrats in Luxembourg.

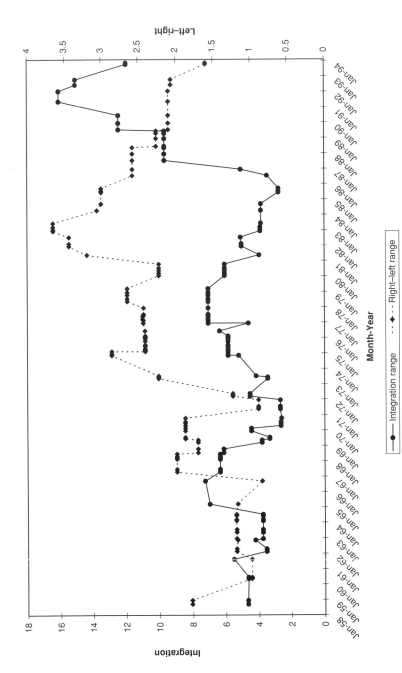

Figure 4.1 *Integration and left–right range.*

early 1990s. Denmark also contributed to an increase in the range under both liberal-conservative and social democratic governments, though for shorter periods. In the 1980s, the left-wing position of the Greek socialist government was an important factor in increasing the Council left–right range. Other important elements were the considerable swings occurring in France on the left–right spectrum from the communist–socialist governing coalition to the Gaullist–liberal one. Nevertheless, the 1980s and early 1990s saw a convergence of left–right positions in the Council. In 1993, the *Left–right range* was 1.6, less than half of the 1983 peak of 3.7. This was mostly due to left-wing governments and, in the accession states, Spanish socialists and Portuguese social democrats having relatively moderate views.

Council pivot

The second variable used for the statistical analysis is the preference of the Council member that is pivotal under either qualified majority voting or unanimity. This is the member whose positive vote would unblock legislation under the relevant decision rule. Its position varies depending on the direction of the shift along the one-dimensional space that the adoption of the new law generates. Consider, for instance, Directive 71/304 on the abolition of restrictions on freedom to provide services, adopted by qualified majority voting, and Directive 71/305 coordinating the procedures for the award of public works contracts, adopted by unanimity. It is plausible to assert that the adoption of these laws implies a shift toward more European integration. We can order the preferences of the member states on the day of adoption, 26 July 1971, along the less–more integration dimension as follows: Netherlands (1.08), Luxembourg (1.15), France (1.42), Belgium (1.79), Italy (3.65) and Germany (3.76). Since the legislation implied a shift toward more integration, the *Integration pivot* for Directive 71/305 was the Dutch minister, having the least integrationist position. For qualified majority voting, the voting weights were distributed as follows: France, Germany and Italy had four each, Belgium and the Netherlands two each and Luxembourg one. Six votes were necessary to block legislation. The French minister was the *Integration pivot* for Directive 71/304, being the pivotal member under majority voting. Belgium, Italy and Germany needed the French vote for a pro-integration shift in the policy or, conversely, Luxembourg and the Netherlands could not block this shift without French support.

If, instead, we consider that the underlying dimension for these laws is the attitude toward market intervention and that these laws imply a shift toward a market economy and away from a planned economy, the preferences of member states can be estimated from the categories of Budge *et al.* (2001) as shown in Table 4.1 and distributed along the planned-market economy dimension as follows: Belgium (-5.08), France (-4.97), Luxembourg (-3.24), Italy (-1.45), Netherlands (0.11) and Germany (0.65). In Directive 71/305, the *Policy pivot*, namely the pivotal Council member in the substantive policy dimension, was the Belgian minister because he was the least supportive member for a market economy. The *Policy pivot* for Directive 71/304 was also, in this circumstance, the French minister. As with *Policy range*, this variable is standardized as follows:

$$Standardized\ policy\ pivot_{lc} = \frac{Policy\ pivot_{lc} + |\min_c|}{\max_c - |\min_c|}$$

where the *Policy pivot$_{lc}$* is related to law *l* and category *c*, max$_c$ and min$_c$ are the same variables as those in *Standardized policy range*. *Standardized policy pivot* is also bounded between zero and one.

Finally, these laws can be considered a rightward shift along the left–right dimension. Gabel and Huber's (2000) left–right positions of member states are as follows: France (3.8), Belgium (3.11), Germany (3.09), Netherlands (3.08), Italy (3.01) and Luxembourg (2.91). The *Left–right pivots* were the French and Belgian ministers for Directives 71/305 and 71/304 respectively.

Since we have governmental preference measures and data on voting weights,[13] the key decision for the selection of the Council pivot consists in choosing the direction of the shift produced by the adoption of the each law. For the integration dimension this is not problematic as the adoption of an EU law can be reasonably conceived as a shift toward more integration. For the policy and left–right dimensions, the direction is shown in Table 4.1. There are no noticeable trends of the values of these pivots across the time period under analysis.

Preferences of the European Commission

When considering the integration dimension, formal scholars invariably position the European Commission at the integrationist end (Garrett, 1995; Garrett and Tsebelis, 1996; Tsebelis and Kreppel, 1998; Tsebelis

---

[13] After the first enlargement, the weights were: Britain France, Germany and Italy (10), Belgium and the Netherlands (5), Denmark and Ireland (3), and Luxembourg (2), with the blocking minority of 18 votes. Greece was allocated 5 voting weights when it joined the Community and the blocking minority increased to 19 votes. Spain and Portugal were allocated 8 and 5 voting weights respectively when they joined the Community and the blocking minority increased to 23 votes.

and Garrett, 2000). If having pro-integrationist preferences means supporting the pooling, centralization and delegation of policy competencies to the EU level, there is considerable agreement among scholars that the Commission holds these views. Moravcsik (1998) finds supporting evidence across the whole 1955–91 period and a substantial number of case studies reach this conclusion.[14] From a principal-agent perspective, Pollack (1994, 1997a, 1998) and Majone (1996: 65) contend that an important component of the Commission's utility function is the scope of its competencies. Expanding the policy competence of the EU does not necessarily imply an increase in the influence of the Commission on the policy process. However, when this expansion can only be pursued if the Commission's role is limited, there is evidence suggesting that the Commission is willing to accept this compromise (Kelemen, 2002: 100–1).

There are a few dissenting views however. Crombez (1997b) proposes a spatial model of Commission appointment and EU policy making, whereby the preferences of the Commission always belong to the set of preferences that all member states prefer to the status quo (see also Hug, 2003).[15] Even though Crombez considers only substantive policy dimensions, following his model, we should expect a Commission with preferences that are closer to the less integration end of the spectrum, if the status quo is less integration. In the most extensive study on the views of the Commission's top officials, Hooghe (1999a, 1999b, 2001) shows that they do not seem to be systematically orientated toward supranationalism.[16] Moreover, support for democratic decision-making and the prevalent view that bureaucrats should be responsive to national and functional interests cast doubt on the contention that the Commission takes systematically pro-integration positions. There is, however, no equivalent study on the college of commissioners, the political body at the top of the Commission's hierarchy, which is appointed by the member states and the Parliament and is in charge of directing its activities. Works have merely analyzed the backgrounds and careers of commissioners (Page and Wouters, 1994; Ross, 1995b; MacMullen, 1997; Page, 1997).

---

[14] See, for instance, Sandholtz and Zysman (1989), Cameron (1992), Cram (1993, 1994, 1997), Fuchs (1994), Mazey (1995), Esser and Noppe (1996), Smith (1996, 1998), Guay (1997), Schmidt (1998), Wendon (1998), Jabko (1999) and Nugent (2000).

[15] The Parliament's approval was also needed for the appointment of the Commission following the adoption of the Maastricht and Amsterdam Treaties.

[16] Depending on which items make up the intergovernmentalism–supranationalism dimension, officials may tend slightly toward intergovernmentalism (Hooghe, 1999b: 445) or supranationalism (Hooghe, 1999a: 356).

Instead, there are no general rules used in the literature on the substantive policy positions that the Commission may take. Formal modelers make no specific claims. For instance, Steunenberg (1994; see also Tsebelis and Garrett, 2000) produces comparative statics propositions based on different configurations of Commission preferences. Moravcsik (1998) shows that this institution had moderately pro-market views on areas such as internal market, trade and agriculture across the whole 1955–91 period. Under the second Delors presidency, it developed a strong position in favor of an encompassing social policy. Case studies reveal the idiosyncratic nature of the policy preferences of the Commission. It may support market liberalization (Sandholtz and Zysman, 1989; Cameron, 1992; Sandholtz, 1993b; Schmidt, 1998; Coleman and Tangermann, 1999; Thatcher, 2001; Eising, 2002), social policy regulation (Cram, 1993; Mazey, 1995) or environmental protection (Kelemen, 1995; Franchino and Rahming, 2003). Hug (2003) shows that the Commission's position varies systematically across the eight issue areas negotiated at the Amsterdam Intergovernmental Conference. Moreover, when policy objectives are mutually exclusive, there may be considerable internal disagreement (Cini, 1997; Hooghe, 1997; Harcourt, 1998; Behrens and Smyrl, 1999). However, interestingly, Hooghe (1999a, 2000, 2001) finds that top Commission officials share rather strong market regulation, rather than liberalization, preferences. In conclusion, the substantive policy positions of the Commission are dependent on the specific nature of the measure at hand and, following Crombez (1997b) and Hug (2003), they may represent the policy divisions that cut across member states.

Finally, left–right positions figure far less prominently in the works on the Commission. Consistent with his Commission appointment model, Crombez (1996, 1997a, see also Steunenberg, 1997) infers the Commission's position on the basis of the commissioners' party affiliation and locates it within the member states' left–right range. However, to the best of my knowledge, there are no studies that make specific claims of the Commission's left–right positions and possible implications for the EU policy output, even though scholars generally recognize the relevance of the partisan composition of this institution (Ross, 1995b; Hix and Lord, 1997; Page, 1997; MacMullen, 2000; Hix, 2005).

The preferences of commissioners and the median voter of the college of commissioners

I have measured the preferences of commissioners on the integration, policy and left–right dimensions using relatively simple rules. The monthly *Bulletin of the European Union* and the annual *General Report on the Activities of the European Union*[17] include brief biographies of the commissioners and information on the distribution of portfolio responsibilities. In some cases, the commissioner's party affiliation is mentioned explicitly, in other cases, there are references to the political positions that the commission has held, so the partisan affiliation can be easily derived. The integration, policy and left–right preferences of these commissioners are those of *their party at the time of their appointment*. Some commissioners have been academics, career diplomats, ambassadors or top-rank bureaucrats prior to the appointment. Their party affiliation cannot be easily inferred. For this set of commissioners, the preferences are those of *their national governments at the time of their appointment*.[18]

Figure 4.2 shows the composition of the college of commissioners with regard to the partisan affiliation of its members. The biographies of some commissioners in the first two commissions are not available and this partially accounts for the greater presence of nonpartisan commissioners. However, it is undoubtedly the case that commissioners with clear partisan affiliations have become increasingly dominant (see also MacMullen, 2000: 41). With the exception of the 1970 Malfatti and 1995 Santer Commission, partisan commissioners in each new commission made up a proportion of the college that was equal to or larger than that of the previous commission. Their share increased from 22 percent in the 1958 Hallstein Commission to 94 percent in the 1993 Delors Commission. It dropped marginally with the 1995 Santer and 1999 Prodi Commission. In five cases, a nonpartisan commissioner has been replaced by one with a clear partisan affiliation, while a partisan commissioner has never been replaced by a nonpartisan one.

I have used two measures of Commission preferences. According to the Rules of Procedure of the Commission, the college of commissioners decides by absolute majority.[19] The median voter in the college, at the time each law has been adopted, can be easily identified and is labeled *Commission integration median, Commission policy median* and *Commission left–right median* accordingly. Consider the example of Directive 71/305 that we have used for the Council. At that time, the college of the Malfatti

---

[17] The titles of these publications referred to the European Community up to June 1967 when the Merger Treaty came into force and to the European Communities up to December 1993 when the Maastricht Treaty entered into force. I have also used data from Olivi (1993), especially for individual replacements of commissioners.

[18] This rule also applies for the few commissioners in the first two commissions whose biographies were not available.

[19] See, for instance, article 8 of the latest edition of the Rules of Procedure, C(2000) 3614, *Official Journal of the European Communities* Series L 308/26.

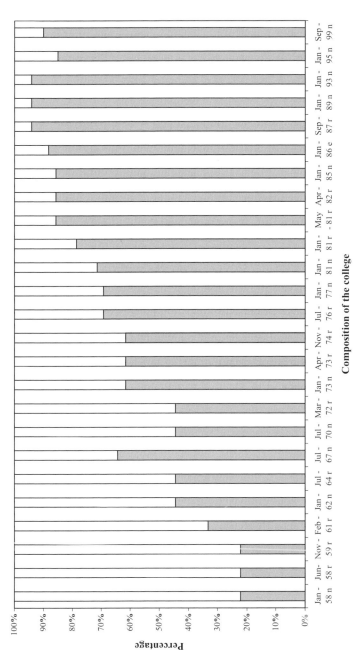

Figure 4.2 *Composition of the college of commissioners, 1958–99. Note:* For the X-axis: n = new Commission, r = replacement of commissioner(s), e = enlarged Commission.

Commission was composed of nine members. Hence, after ordering their preferences along the relevant dimension, the fifth member was the median voter. The *Commission integration median* was Sicco Mansholt from the Dutch Labour Party with a value of 1.8.[20] In order to find the *Commission policy median*, we need to order the members of the college along the planned economy–market economy dimension using the values estimated by Budge *et al.* (2001). In this case, the *Commission policy median* was the Belgian Socialist Albert Coppé with a value of −1.42.[21] Similarly to the other policy variables, this one is standardized as follows:

$$\textit{Standardized Commission policy median}_{lc}$$
$$= \frac{\textit{Commission policy median}_{lc} + |\min_c|}{\max_c - |\min_c|}$$

where the *Commission policy median*$_{lc}$ is related to law l and category c, $\max_c$ and $\min_c$ are the same variables as those in *Standardized policy range*.

Finally, the German Free Democrat Ralf Dahrendorf was the *Commission left–right median* with an estimate of 3.46.[22] In three instances, the Rey Commission (July 1967–June 1970), the Thorn Commission (January 1981–December 1984) and the Delors Commission from January 1984 up to the Iberian enlargement of January 1986, the number of commissioners has been even. So, the median voter depends on the direction of the policy shift shown in Table 4.1.

The second measure is the preference of the commissioner holding the portfolio under which and at the time the relevant law has been adopted.[23] For instance, Directive 71/305 was based on the Rome Treaty

---

[20] The less–more integration ordering was Borschette (Luxembourg, nonpartisan: 1.15), Barre and Deniau (France, nonpartisan: 1.42), Coppé (Belgium, PSC: 1.78), Mansholt (Netherlands, PvdA: 1.8), Dahrendorf (Germany, FDP: 2), Haferkamp (Germany, nonpartisan: 3.76), Spinelli (Italy, nonpartisan: 3.78) and Malfatti (Italy, DC: 5.6).

[21] The ordering on the planned–market economy dimension was Mansholt (−7), Barre and Deniau (−4.97), Borschette (−3.24), Coppé (−1.42), Spinelli (−0.96), Malfatti (−0.21), Dahrendorf (0) and Haferkamp (0.65).

[22] The right–left ordering was Malfatti (2.56), Borschette and Spinelli (2.91), Haferkamp (3.09), Dahrendorf (3.46), Coppé (3.76), Barre and Deniau (3.8) and Mansholt (5.32).

[23] The matching of the law with the relevant portfolio has been straightforward in most cases, though greater attention was necessary in some instances. Depending on the measures and the distribution of responsibilities, commercial policy laws fall within the external trade, external relations or customs union portfolios, consumer protection legislation shifted from the internal market portfolio to one on its own, movement of persons shifted from the internal market to the social affairs portfolio, responsibility for fisheries is separated from agriculture in some cases, movement of capital is under the economic and financial affairs portfolio, qualifications and professions and the movement of workers element of establishment and services is under the internal market portfolio, finally the transport portfolio includes laws on market regulation and qualifications. The reader can check the Commission's web site, http://www.europa.eu.int/comm/index_en.htm, to see how portfolios and policy areas are organized.

articles no. 57.2, 66 and 100 of the chapters on the right of establishment, freedom to provide services and approximation of laws respectively. Wilhelm Haferkamp was the commissioner in charge of the internal market and approximation of laws portfolio. His positions on European integration, market economy and left–right make up the three measures as follows: *Commissioner: integration* (3.76), *Commissioner: policy* (0.65) and *Commissioner: left–right* (3.09). The policy measure is standardized as follows:

$$Standardized\ commissioner:\ policy_{lc} = \frac{Commissioner:\ policy_{lc} + |min_c|}{max_c - |min_c|}.$$

Which of these two measures is the most appropriate? I have no knowledge of specific claims about the relative importance of the college of commissioners and individual commissioners in EU policy making. Most of the case studies cited refer to the Commission in general terms and many formal works explicitly refer to the college median voter when considering the preferences of the Commission. Moreover, since collective responsibility is a "cardinal principle *within* the college" (Peterson, 2001: 85), the college appears to be the center of Commission decision-making. Collective responsibility is also the underlying principle in the working of cabinets in parliamentary democracies (Gallagher, Laver and Mair, 2001: 55) and many scholars of comparative executive politics emphasize the importance of cabinet institutions and decision rules in determining policy outcomes (Huber, 1996; Huber and McCarty, 2001; Thies, 2001; Tsebelis, 2002:91–115).

Nevertheless, individual commissioners have the important prerogative of tabling legislative proposals that fall under their area of responsibility and are in charge of executing EU policies, even though, as we have seen in Chapter 3, implementation is frequently shared with national administrations. A few scholars contend that individual commissioners have played an important role in policy making (Smith, 2002), for instance in agricultural policy reform (Coleman and Tangermann, 1999), environmental legislation (Ross, 1995a: 162, 197; Sbragia, 1996: 244–6) and competition policy (McGowan and Wilks, 1995:151–2, 160–1; Allen, 1996b: 168, 178). Similarly, the distribution of ministerial portfolio responsibilities is also seen as an important determinant of governmental policy output in parliamentary democracies (Laver and Shepsle, 1996; Huber, 1998; Hallerberg and von Hagen, 1999; Heller, 2001). Since there is no clear agreement in the literature, I leave the question unanswered. The empirical analysis will show which of the two measures yields the most interesting results.

Finally, recall that the Commission is considered to have strong pro-integrationist preferences according to the large majority of EU scholars, with the notable exceptions of Crombez and Hooghe. It is possible to test this hypothesis with our data. The technique we have used to gauge the Commission's preferences is biased *against* this hypothesis because commissioners share either the preferences of their national parties or those of their national governments. In other words, they are perfect agents of their national government or party, exactly as in Crombez's (1997b) model. Therefore, we should not expect any systematic pro-integration bias in the Commission. Figure 4.3 compares the standardized positions of the Council qualified majority voting pivot, the Commission median and the portfolio commissioner across the integration dimension and the whole data set, regardless of whether the Council decision rules were unanimity or qualified majority voting.[24]

The results are striking. In almost 78 percent of the cases, the Commission median is more integrationist than the Council pivot. This percentage decreases to 72.5 for the laws adopted by qualified majority voting. The integration preferences of the Commission median have never exceed the maximum and minimum values of the Council members' integration preferences; however, they appear to be located systematically closer to the pro-integrationist end. The longest period where the Council pivot was more integrationist than the Commission median was between December 1987 and January 1992, though there have been a few shorter spells earlier on. In order to assess whether the Commission median is more integrationist than the Council pivot, the two data samples should not come from the same population and we should reject a Kolmogorov–Smirnov test on the equality of distribution. Moreover, the difference between the means of the Commission median and the Council pivot should be significantly greater than zero in a two-sample t test. Finally, since observations are taken in pairs for each law, a paired t-test on the difference between the Commission median and the Council pivot of each case should also be significantly greater than zero. Table 4.2 summarizes the results from these tests. We can reject the equality of distribution at a high level of significance. Moreover, the difference between the Commission median and the Council pivot, both for each case and

---

[24] The standardized variables are produced for each law as follows:

$$Standardized\ variable_l = (Variable_l + |min|)/(max + |min|)$$

where *variable_l* is the *Council integration pivot*, the *Commission integration median*, and the *Commissioner: integration* for law l, *min* (-17.2) and *max* (25.7) are, respectively, the minimum and maximum values for the integration category throughout the whole period.

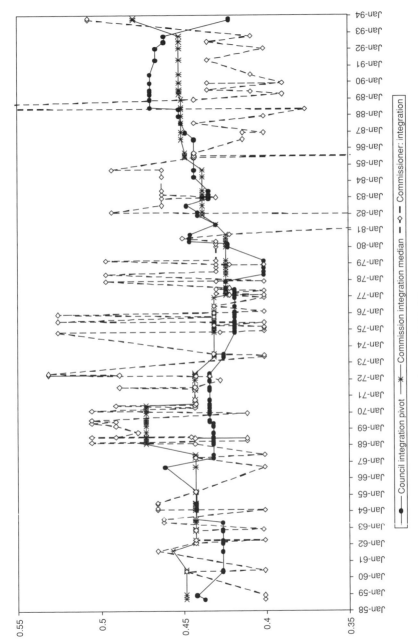

Figure 4.3 *Council and Commission integration preferences, 1958–93.*

Council integration pivot —— Commission integration median —*— Commissioner: integration —◇— ■—

Table 4.2 *Differences between the integration preferences of the Council pivot and the Commission.*

	Preference measure of the Commission			
	Commission integration median		*Commissioner: integration*	
	All laws	QMV laws	All laws	QMV laws
Kolmogorov–Smirnov D	0.380^a	0.425^a	0.253^a	0.313^b
Two-sample t	6.064^a	4.333^a	2.147^c	2.804^b
Paired t	7.999^a	4.942^a	2.144^c	2.788^b
N	158	80	158	80

Note: $^a\ p < 0.001$; $^b\ p < 0.01$; $^c\ p < 0.05$. The data sets of the two samples are not assumed to have equal variance for the t-tests.

for the sample means, is significantly greater than zero. Results are similar for the set of laws adopted by qualified majority.

The integration preferences of the relevant portfolio commissioners have much higher variance, though they are more integrationist than those of the Council pivot in slightly more than 60 percent of the sampled laws, increasing to 67.5 percent for the laws adopted under qualified majority voting. In a few circumstances in the 1960s and 1980s, the commissioner was less integrationist than the least integrationist Council member, while in a few cases in the 1970s and 1980s, s/he was more integrationist than the most integrationist Council member. Nevertheless, Table 4.2 shows that the two samples do not come from the same population and the difference between the commissioner and the Council pivot, both for each case and for the sample means, is greater than zero at a lower, but still high, level of significance. Levels of significance increase for the qualified majority laws.

Two conclusions can be drawn from these results. First, the college median voter appears to be relatively more accurate than the relevant portfolio commissioner in gauging the pro-integration preferences of the Commission. Second, the almost unanimous view in the literature about the pro-integration preferences of this institution does not need any assumption about a process of socialization at the EU level or of a self-selection mechanism of pro-integration commissioners. They may be simply institutional reasons. Even if we assume, following Crombez's (1997b) lead, that commissioners are perfect agents of their national government or party, it appears that the college median voter is systematically more in favor of European integration than the Council qualified majority voting pivot. However, I have no explanation for the pro-integration bias of the relevant portfolio commissioners.

Policy complexity

Recall that the proposition derived from the model in Chapter 2 simply asserts that the level of discretionary authority increases with the complexity of the issue area. The model does not produce propositions that distinguish between national administrations and the Commission on the basis of complexity. Here, I discuss how informational and actor-related features are likely to inform the choice between these two implementation paths when they generate similar distributive losses. I then show how these features guide our measurement of complexity.

In comparison with national administrations, the Commission is a small supranational bureaucracy made up predominantly of general administrators, lawyers, economists and other social scientists. The main recruitment mechanism, a competitive exam (the *concours*), is also normally biased in favor of generalist, legal or economic knowledge. Studies on the background and expertise of the Commission's personnel and the degree of interdepartmental mobility do not suggest a marked professional specialization (e.g. Spence, 1994: 65–8; Nugent, 2001:162–85; Stevens and Stevens, 2001: 122–5).

These administrative features are the indirect product of the decisions of EU legislators over time. Complexity in some areas may result from legislation that is designed to limit national authority, so a supranational bureaucracy is better suited to relieving legislators of their workload. It is plausible that one of the functions of the Commission's personnel is simply to make the decision-making more efficient since this delegation directly saves time and resources at the supranational level.[25] In summary, we should expect that the level of discretion of the Commission increases in issue areas that require general and managerial skills at the supranational level.

Delegation to national administrations is guided by the fact that they have far greater resources and technical expertise than the Commission. EU legislators can rely on national engineers to check the conformity of motor vehicles to the approved production types, on national biologists to ensure the safe disposal of industrial waste and on national accountants to oversee the listing of securities on the stock exchange. National

---

[25] Admittedly, delegation to the Commission might still use up some ministerial resources as the permanent representatives might be involved with the Commission in implementation through the so-called "comitology" procedures. Delegation, however, saves Council work for the individual minister.

bureaucracies also hold important politically relevant information on which the legislators may rely. They are likely to have a better idea of how the possibility of claiming various social security benefits outside of the competent member state may burden the system. They can better assess how the general system on the mutual recognition of diplomas may affect the movement of professionals and the domestic provision of professional services.

In comparison with the Commission, the situation resembles that facing Congress and the US administration (Epstein and O'Halloran, 1999b: 84–5). It is the intrinsic complexity of the policy (i.e. not resulting from the decisions of EU legislators) that should guide delegation in this case. National expertise is more valuable to the legislators than supranational generalist skills. Therefore, we should expect that the level of national discretion increases in issue areas that require specialized and technical knowledge.

Measuring complexity

How then can we measure policy complexity? Which indicators should we use to gauge these differences between the Commission and national administrations? I employ first a simple descriptive method to assess the impact of the complexity on discretion. Similar to the procedure used by Epstein and O'Halloran (1999b: 197–200), I have classified the major EU laws into the forty-one policy categories that are listed in the second column of Table 4.1. The bases of the Treaty provide the first level of classification but issue areas such as approximation of laws, economic policy, social provisions and freedom of establishment and to provide services are too general. Hence, I have adopted a more fine-grained classification and separated acts that are substantively different and show different levels of discretion. The general aim is to give the best possible visual representation of the pattern of delegation. The analysis in the next chapter will simply consist of a comparison between the average levels of discretion across these categories. For the quantitative test, the idea is to develop reasonable proxies for issue complexity that can be used across policies and time. Krehbiel (1991) uses the number of laws cited in a given act but, with more than 80 percent of the major EU laws not amending previous legislation, this measure cannot be used. In Franchino (2000b, 2000c), I use the length of legislation as a proxy of complexity. This measure is subject to the criticism that legislators facing high informational costs have actually lower incentives to write detailed provisions and may be more concise.

Although no measure is likely to be completely satisfactory, I suggest three proxies. One is related to delegation to the Commission, the remaining two are associated with delegation to national authorities.

The first proxy, *Detailed rules*, is the number of major provisions in an act that call for "detailed rules" to be adopted (*modalités d'application* in the French legislation). It is not unusual for the detailed implementation of the whole act or of a specific article to be subject to further proceedings. This is the case in about 40 percent of the acts in the sample. I suggest that the Council will make more frequent use of these provisions in more complex issue areas. But, more importantly, this postponement is a sign of the need of the Council to reduce its workload, especially where the policy complexity is a product of its own deliberations. Therefore, my contention is that the Council is likely to make greater use of the generalist and supranational personnel of the Commission in this case. In summary, the number of major provisions in an act calling for "detailed rules" to be adopted should be positively correlated with the Commission's executive discretion.

Epstein and O'Halloran (1999b: 211–6) use the number of committee hearings to gauge the information intensity of an issue area. This is because hearings are used as information gathering tools for legislators in the US Congress. Similarly, I relate the other two measures of complexity to the role of the Commission as the initiator of EU legislation and to the technical committees involved in the drafting of legislation.

The Commission is frequently prompted by member states, the Parliament or interest groups to make some proposals. On other occasions it acts on its own. In the most complex areas, it gathers the relevant information on the issue and drafts a report, normally called a *general* or *action programme*, containing a list of initiatives that could be taken. These reports are both a sign of information gathering and an instrument to induce the relevant political actors to signal support or voice opposition to the measures. The *General Programmes for the Abolition of Restrictions on Freedom to Provide Services and of Establishment*, drafted a few years after the Treaty of Rome, were used to assess the areas where early liberalization was possible. The *Action Programmes on the Environment* of 1973 and 1977 assessed the measures that could have been taken and led to the first directives in this area.

My contention is that programmes are produced in areas where there is a greater need to gather technical and political information relating to the measure at hand. Given the specialized nature and intrinsic complexity of the issues, we should expect that the Council would rely to a greater extent on the member states for implementation. A dichotomous variable *Programme* will take a value of one if provisions or recitals in the relevant act refer to general or action programmes and a value of zero otherwise.

Committees of member state representatives are another important means of information gathering. Some committees are established only for the implementation of a policy and they should be conceived as constraints on executive action. This is the case for committees that oversee, using various procedures, the measures taken by the Commission (Siedentopf and Ziller, 1988; Docksey and Williams, 1994; Dogan, 1997; Pollack, 1997b: 114–16; Franchino, 2000b: 76–7; Ballmann, Epstein and O'Halloran, 2002; Hix, 2005: 52–8). Other committees are instead set up to gather and exchange information, to carry out studies, to draw up reports and to support the Commission in the drafting of legislative proposals. Committees are generally established by the Council and are composed of experts seconded from national technical ministries. They can be senior officials responsible for public health, experts in agricultural or fisheries structures or in banking regulation. Some committees include representatives from trade unions and employers' associations, such as the *Advisory Committee on Social Security for Migrant Workers* and the *Advisory Committee* set up by the regulations on the movement of persons. Less frequently, the Commission establishes its own scientific advisory committee that provides relevant information for the drafting of proposals.

My contention is that the existence of these committees in an issue area is a sign of the need to gather technical and political information about specific measures. These committees deal with inherently complex and specialized issues. Therefore, we should expect that the Council would take advantage of national expertise and delegate greater executive discretion to the administrations of member states. A dichotomous variable *Committee* will take a value of one if a committee is involved in an issue area or a single act and zero otherwise. The programmes referred to in and the committees involved in the drafting of the sampled legislation are listed in Table 4.3.

Conclusion

Table 4.4 provides descriptive statistics for the variables that we have introduced in this chapter. The discretion of national administrations and of the Commission constitutes the core dependent variables for Chapters 5 and 6, while the following ones are the independent variables. Among these, the table also lists six indicators of *Conflict*, measuring the absolute distance between the preferences of the Commission and those of the pivotal member of the Council. Appendix 4.1 includes further details on the policy variables, while Appendix 4.2 introduces two matching alternatives for the policy measure.

An interesting finding that emerges from this chapter is with regard to the relative positions of the Commission and the Council on the

Table 4.3 *Programmes and committees in the sampled laws.*

Programmes	Committees
• Action programme (on commercial policy) • Action programme for the implementation of the Community Charter of the fundamental social rights of workers • Action programme on the promotion of equal opportunities for women • Action programmes on the environment (1973, 1977) • General programme for the abolition of restrictions on freedom of establishment • General programme for the abolition of restrictions on freedom to provide services • Programme concerning safety, hygiene and health at work • Programme for the opening up of the market for public works contracts • Second programme for a consumer protection and information policy • Social action programme	• Advisory committee on safety, hygiene and health protection at work • Administrative commission on social security of migrant workers • Advisory committee (movement of persons – vacancy clearance) • Advisory committee for public works contracts • Advisory committee of the competent authorities of the Member States of the European Economic Community (banking advisory committee) • Advisory committee on education and training in the field of architecture • Advisory committee on social security for migrant workers • Advisory committee on the training of midwives • Committee of senior officials on public health • Contact committees (company law – accounts and stock exchange listing; European economic interest grouping) • Coordinating group (qualifications and professions – general system) • EAGGF committee (agriculture – financial provisions) • Monetary committee • Scientific advisory committee for the evaluation of the toxicity and ecotoxicity of chemical compounds • Scientific and technical committee for fisheries • Standing committee (technical standards) • Standing committee for the fishing industry • Standing committee on agricultural structures

Table 4.4 *Independent variables: description and summary statistics.*

Variable	Description	Mean	Std. dev.	Min.	Max.
Decision rule	1 for qualified majority voting in the Council 0 for unanimity	0.506	0.502	0	1
Integration range	Difference between highest and lowest value in the Council on integration dimension	5.957	2.799	2.609	16.079
Standardized policy range	Standardized difference between highest and lowest value in the Council on policy dimension	0.2063	0.1253	0.0506	0.6201
Left–right range	Difference between highest and lowest value in the Council on left–right dimension	2.090	0.664	0.843	3.654
Integration pivot	Position of pivotal member in the Council on integration dimension	0.663	1.144	−1.070	2.941
Standardized policy pivot	Standardized position of pivotal member in the Council on policy dimension	0.382	0.279	0	0.780
Left–right pivot	Position of pivotal member in the Council on left–right dimension	3.183	0.905	1.243	4.716
Commission integration median	Position of median voter in the college on integration dimension	1.845	0.680	0.990	3.376
Standardized Commission policy median	Standardized position of median voter in the college on policy dimension	0.4206	0.2645	0	0.6912
Commission left–right median	Position of median voter in the college on left–right dimension	2.981	0.304	2.307	3.456
Commissioner: integration	Position of relevant portfolio commissioner on integration dimension	1.702	1.874	−4.6	10.989
Standardized commissioner: policy	Standardized position of relevant portfolio commissioner on policy dimension	0.4150	0.2978	0	0.8476

Commissioner: left–right	Position of relevant portfolio commissioner on left–right dimension	3.176	1.024	1.123	5.320
Conflict integration using Commission median	Absolute difference between *Integration pivot* and *Commission Integration median* using Commissioner	1.313	0.852	0	2.670
	Absolute difference between *Integration pivot* and *Commissioner: integration*	1.651	1.441	0	8.048
Conflict standardized policy using Commission median	Absolute difference between *Standardized policy pivot* and *Commission standardized policy median*	0.052	0.043	0	0.188
using Commissioner	Absolute difference between *Standardized policy pivot* and *Commissioner: standardized policy*	0.074	0.067	0	0.363
Conflict left–right using Commission median	Absolute difference between *Integration left–right* and *Commission left–right median*	0.708	0.532	0	1.918
using Commissioner	Absolute difference between *Left–right pivot* and *Commissioner: left–right*	1.134	0.848	0	3.214
Detailed rules	Number of major provisions calling for "detailed rules" to be adopted	1.006	2.545	0	13
Programme	1 if provisions or recitals refer to general or action programmes. 0 otherwise	0.203	0.403	0	1
Committee	1 if a committee is involved in an issue area or a single act 0 otherwise	0.342	0.476	0	1

integration dimension. We have found that, even under the assumption that commissioners are perfect agents of their national government or party, the median voter in the college of commissioners is systematically more pro-integration that the pivotal member of the Council under qualified majority voting (though it may still lie within the Pareto set of the member states, cf. Hug, 2003). Hence the pro-integration bias of the Commission may have simply institutional causes, and there is no need to rely on processes of socialization or self-selection.

The next two chapters test, both quantitatively and through case studies, the expectations derived from the model of Chapter 2.

Appendix 4.1 Additional information on the matching of policy categories

In this appendix I assess the plausibility of the matching between the forty-one policy categories that I have produced for this study with the categories of Budge *et al.* (2001). This matching is the basis for the *Policy* preference measure. I have considered the preferences of the states that were not founding members only since their accession to the EU. I also introduce two alternative matching strategies that will be used in the next chapters to assess the robustness of the results.

For the first three grouping of laws, there is substantial case study evidence that supports the distribution of preferences.

Market economy–planned economy

Categories: free enterprise (401) + economic orthodoxy (414) – market regulation (403) – economic planning (404) – controlled economy (412).

Throughout the 1960s and the early 1970s, Germany and the Netherlands were the countries most supportive of a market economy, while the remaining governments were decisively more supportive of a planned economy. In the 1970s, with the German Social Democrats, the British Labour and the Dutch Labour and Radical parties enjoying a long spell in government, the preferences of all the member states shifted in favor of a planned economy. The Irish governments, during the Labour–Fine Gael coalition of the mid 1970s, held particularly strong pro-planned economy views, while, at the opposite side of the spectrum, the French government coalitions, centered on the Gaullist and the Conservative parties, were relatively more supportive of a market economy. In the 1980s, the position of the French government oscillated between being a strong supporter for market economy reforms with the Gaullist–UDF governments to being an opponent to these measures, especially under the Communist–Socialist coalition in the early 1980s. Similar oscillations can be seen in Ireland and Greece. The British Conservative government had consistent and strong pro-market views throughout the whole period. The German and Danish governments were also consistently pro-market economy. The Socialist governments in Greece and Spain were instead the most supportive of a planned economy. Finally, there has been a trend in favor of the market economy starting from the late 1970s throughout the second half of the 1980s. This varied across states, leading to more conflict within the Council, although it has fizzled out since. There is good evidence that the relative and longitudinal positions of the member states are accurate (e.g. Pelkmans and Winters, 1988; Cameron, 1992; Garrett, 1992; Garrett and Weingast, 1993; Majone, 1993; Montanari, 1995; Gomà, 1996; Héritier, 1996; Pierson and Leibfried, 1996; Scharpf, 1996; Streeck, 1996; Moravcsik, 1998; Falkner, 1999).[26]

In the case of regional policy, namely Regulation 724/75 on the European Regional Development Fund in the sample, an important line of conflict divides contributing from recipient states (Mawson, Martins and Gibney, 1985; Armstrong, 1989; Marks, 1992; Hooghe and Keating, 1994; Pollack, 1995; Allen, 1996a; Hooghe, 1996). However, the relevant dimension on issues concerning delegation is the extent to which public authorities should intervene in the market through regulation, planning and control, and this is another debate underlying the politics of EU regional policy (Hooghe and Keating, 1994; Pollack, 1995; Hooghe, 1997; Behrens and Smyrl, 1999). In March 1975, the French, Italian and Danish governments were the most supportive of state intervention in the economy, while the Irish, British and Dutch governments were the least sympathetic.

Agriculture and farmers (703)

During the period up to the first enlargement, the founding member states showed a relatively high level of support for agriculture and farmers, in particular, Luxembourg, France and Germany. Support has stayed at lower, but stable, levels since. In the 1970s up to the second enlargement, Ireland joined France and Luxembourg in showing a relatively higher level of support for agriculture, while Denmark, under both Liberal and Social Democratic governments, was more lukewarm, together with the Netherlands and Belgium. The French Gaullist government was consistently more supportive than Social Democratic and Labour governments in Germany and Britain respectively. In the 1980s, the Socialist Spanish government had a relatively strong pro-farmers platform and the new coalition in Germany, based around the Christian Democrats, shifted

---

[26] Supporting evidence for the sections in this appendix can also be found in the relevant policy chapters of the various editions of Wallace and Wallace (2000).

toward greater support. The French position oscillated as a result of the partisan composition of the government. The Socialist-based coalitions were less supportive of agriculture than the Gaullist-based ones. Finally, the Italian governments joined the government of Denmark and the Netherlands in being relatively less supportive. Since the late 1970s, we can also see an increasing divergence in positions within the Council concerning agriculture. The relative and longitudinal positions of the member states appear to be relatively accurate, though more so with regard to the larger states (e.g. Swinbank, 1989; Tarditi, *et al.*, 1989; Rieger, 1995; Grant, 1997; Marsh, 1997; Moravcsik, 1998: 159–237).

Environmental protection (501)

The data set includes three environmental policy laws, a 1975 directive on waste and two directives on the quality of water adopted in 1975 and 1980. As far as the large member states are concerned, the German governments had relatively strong positions in favor of environmental protection, while the Italian governments were consistently less supportive. The French and British governments were somewhere in between, though the French position became more strongly pro-environment in 1980. Of the smaller states, the Benelux countries were relatively in favor of environmental protection, especially the Dutch governments. Denmark and, later on, Ireland were instead less supportive. With the exception of the Danish government, this distribution of preferences generally reflects the views of scholars of environmental policy, though most of their work covers the late 1980s and 1990s (e.g. Héritier, 1995; Kelemen, 1995; Weale, 1996; Weale *et al.*, 2003).

It is harder to find supporting evidence for the distribution of preferences of the next three groups because there is not enough research on these issues. Nevertheless, in my view, the preferences reflect relatively well the relative positions of European governments and parties on these issues (see, for example, Bartolini and Mair, 1984; Kirchner, 1988; Müller-Rommel, 1989; Padgett and Paterson, 1991; Kitschelt, 1994; Van Kersbergen, 1995; Kalyvas, 1996; Gorvin, 1998; Bartolini, 2000).

Welfare

Categories: social justice (503) + welfare state expansion (504) – welfare state limitation (505).

In the period up to the first enlargement, there was relative cohesiveness within the Council on issues regarding social justice and the expansion of welfare states. Germany, Luxembourg and the Netherlands, both under Social Democratic and Christian Democratic-based coalitions, had the governments holding the most welfarist positions. In the 1970s, the Danish and Irish governments joined this group, the latter only during the Labour–Fine Gael coalition. As a result of this and of the relatively less welfarist positions of the Christian Democratic governments in Italy and the Liberal–Christian Democratic coalitions in Belgium, divergence in the Council increased, but the mean preference increased only moderately and the position of the pivotal Council member did not. This was mostly due to the intermediate position of the French and British governments. Divergence in the Council remained relatively high also in the 1980s and early 1990s. The Socialist governments in Spain and Portugal and the Irish governments were those most emphasizing issues of social justice and the welfare state. The platforms of the Conservative British governments and the Danish Christian Democratic–Conservative coalitions were proposing welfare state retrenchment. A shift toward limitation took place in most of the other member states, most notably in the Netherlands, Luxembourg and Germany. The position of the Italian governments on the issue did not change much, while France was pro-social justice and welfare under the Socialist administration. As a result of this, the mean support for social justice and welfare decreased, but the position of the pivotal Council member did not. Some of these positions can be traced in studies on EU social policy (e.g. Majone, 1993; Mazey, 1995; Montanari, 1995; Gomà, 1996; Pierson and Leibfried, 1996; Scharpf, 1996; Streeck, 1996; Falkner, 1999).

Middle class and professional groups (704)

Luxembourg, Belgium and France had views that were consistently more favorable of these social groups than the other member states throughout the whole period. The remaining governments either did not reveal a specific opinion with regard to these groups or were moderately supportive. Nevertheless, differences within the Council have remained small, especially since the mid 1970s when the main laws on qualifications and professions were adopted.

Education

Categories: education: expansion (506) – education: limitation (507).

In July 1977, when Directive 77/486 on the education of children of migrant workers was adopted, the coalitions in Luxembourg and Germany, based around Social Democratic parties, and the Italian

Christian Democratic government were the most supportive of the expansion and improvement of educational provisions, while the British Labour government, the French and Belgian coalition governments, based around the Gaullist party and the Christian and Social Democratic parties respectively, were the least supportive. However, divergences within the Council were relatively low if we consider the entire period under study.

Appendix 4.2 Alternative matching of policy categories

The first alternative matching moves the three policy categories for which we have limited empirical evidence, *welfare*, *middle class, and professional groups* and *education*, into the *market economy–planned economy* grouping. The laws under *welfare* and *education* shift the status quo toward a more planned economy or leftward, those under *middle class and professional groups* shift it toward a more market economy or rightward.

The second alternative matching is shown in Table 4.A1. It adds two new categories, *protectionism* and *social justice*. Commercial policy reflects the policy positions with regard to free trade while views on equality, fair treatment and the end of discrimination, collected under the social justice category, are the basis of the measures on equal treatment and rights. Hence, only the social security regulations remain under *welfare*. It also unfolds the *market economy–planned economy* grouping, with the exception of regional policy regulation. Support of or opposition to *market economy*, measured as the sum of favorable mentions of enterprise capitalism and economic orthodoxy, is the underlying dimension of the majority of the EU policy categories. *Market regulation* instead includes measures of positive integration and reflects the views on market regulation and social market economy.

Table 4.A2 provides descriptive statistics for the two variables that we have introduced in this appendix. Standardization is carried out as explained in the main text of the chapter. The first variable represents a higher level of aggregation while the second represents a lower one. There are both strengths and weaknesses in this process. The lower level of aggregation of the second matching appears to be more precise in capturing the substantive areas of conflict. However, manifestos do not make reference to each category, so the party's policy positions may not be estimated. For instance, there may not be many references to protectionism and international trade, even though a party's support for market regulation and state intervention is likely to be correlated to a more protectionist stance. Social justice and welfarism are also likely to be correlated, though a manifesto may only reveal a party position with regard to welfare state

Table 4.A1 *Policy categories from the Manifestos Research Group and EU policy categories – alternative matching 2.*

Substantive policy category – Budge et al. (2001)	EU policy category	Direction of shift
Agriculture and Farmers (703)	Agriculture: financial provisions, organization of markets, structural policy; fishing: organization of markets, structural policy; monetary compensation amounts (30)	More support for agriculture Rightward
Education: Expansion – Limitation (506 – 507)	Education: children of migrant workers (1)	Expansion of education Leftward
Environmental Protection (501)	Environment (3)	More environmental protection Leftward
Market Economy – Planned Economy: Free Enterprise + Economic Orthodoxy – Market Regulation – Economic Planning – Controlled Economy (401 + 414 – 403 – 404 – 412)	Regional policy (1)	More planned economy Leftward
Market Economy: Free Enterprise + Economic Orthodoxy (401 + 414)	Adoption of the ECU; company law: accounts, safeguards, stock exchange listing; competition: exemptions and limitation periods, rules for undertakings; cooperation among tax authorities; credit and banking; European economic interest grouping; industrial and commercial property; insurance; merger control; movement of capital; movement of persons: vacancy clearance; payments for services: liberalization; public contracts: procedure; taxation; technical standards; transport: market conditions (56) *Competition: exemptions and limitation periods* (1)	More market economy Rightward *Less market economy*[†] *Leftward*
Market Regulation (403)	Consumer protection; international capital flows: regulation; organization of working time; safety and health at work; social policy; transport: regulation (14)	More market regulation Leftward

(cont.)

Table 4.A1 (cont.)

Substantive policy category – Budge et al. (2001)	EU policy category	Direction of shift
Middle Class and Professional Groups (704)	Establishment and services: movement of workers; Qualifications and professions: specific and general system (26)	More support for middle class Rightward
Protectionism: Protectionism: Positive –	Commercial policy (6)	Less protectionism Rightward
Protectionism: Negative (406 – 407)	*Commercial policy (3)*	*More protectionism* *Leftward*
Social Justice (503)	Equal treatment for men and women; movement of persons: rights and derogations (11)	More social justice Leftward
	Social security of migrant workers (6)	Expansion of welfare Leftward
Welfare: Social Justice + Welfare State Expansion – Welfare State Limitation (503 + 504 – 505)		

Notes: In the first column, the number of the policy categories of Budge *et al.* (2001) is indicated in the parentheses. In the second column, the total number of sampled EC laws is in the parentheses.[†] The shift of one law on competition (exemptions and limitation periods) is toward less market economy and leftward.[○] The shift of three laws on commercial policy is toward protectionism and leftward.

Table 4.A2 *Variables: description and summary statistics of the alternative policy matchings.*

Variable	Description	Mean	Std. dev.	Min.	Max.
Standardized policy range (1)	Standardized difference between highest and lowest value in the Council on the second policy dimension	0.1816	0.0909	0.0506	0.5498
Standardized policy pivot (1)	Standardized position of pivotal member in the Council on the second policy dimension	0.5285	0.2400	0	0.8694
Standardized Commission policy median (1)	Standardized position of median voter in the college on the second policy dimension	0.5499	0.2084	0.0236	0.6912
Standardized commissioner: policy (1)	Standardized position of relevant portfolio commissioner on the second policy dimension	0.5371	0.2543	0	0.8476
Conflict standardized policy (1) using Commission median (1)	Absolute difference between *Standardized policy pivot* and *Commission standardized policy median*	0.0564	0.0443	0	0.2297
using Commissioner (1)	Absolute difference between *Standardized policy pivot* and *Commissioner: standardized policy*	0.0726	0.0563	0	0.2312
Standardized policy range (2)	Standardized difference between highest and lowest value in the Council on the third policy dimension	0.2974	0.1621	0.0455	0.7105
Standardized policy pivot (2)	Standardized position of pivotal member in the Council on the third policy dimension	0.0774	0.1153	0	0.6768
Standardized Commission policy median (2)	Standardized position of median voter in the college on the third policy dimension	0.1279	0.1074	0	0.6397
Standardized commissioner: policy (2)	Standardized position of relevant portfolio commissioner on the third policy dimension	0.1435	0.1496	0	0.6499
Conflict standardized policy (2) using Commission median (2)	Absolute difference between *Standardized policy pivot* and *Commission standardized policy median*	0.0585	0.0489	0	0.2352
using Commissioner (2)	Absolute difference between *Standardized policy pivot* and *Commissioner: standardized policy*	0.0976	0.1007	0	0.5441

policies. Conversely, issues may not be correlated at the higher level of aggregation of the first alternative matching. Consider, for instance, the positions with regard to market regulation and welfarism or the market economy and support for the middle class. For these reasons, the main policy measure uses an intermediate level of aggregation.

Below I provide brief summaries and the relative and longitudinal trend of these additional variables. They change only moderately from the larger groupings and scholarly work provides similar empirical support.

Market economy

Categories: free enterprise (401) + economic orthodoxy (414).

The relative and longitudinal trends in this category are very similar to those explained in the section on *market economy–planned economy*.

Market regulation (403)

In the 1960s, Germany topped the list of countries, with France and Italy, supporting social market regulation. Benelux governments were less supportive. After the first enlargement, the Irish government joined the German one in supporting market regulation, similar shifts occurred in the Luxembourg and the Netherlands as the policy was supported by both Social Democratic and Christian Democratic governments. The British government was the least supportive and this position was shared, for some periods with the Italian and Danish governments. In the first half of the 1980s we see a convergence toward moderate support for market regulation across the majority of member states. The Socialist governments in France and Greece and the Irish Fianna Fáil governments were, however, pro-social market regulation outliers. Towards the end of the 1980s and beginning of the 1990s we see a significant shift in favor of market regulation in Italy, Portugal and even Britain. However, governments in Denmark, Spain and the Netherlands remained luke-warm, regardless of their ideological composition. Spain had a Socialist government, while coalitions in Denmark and the Netherlands included Conservative, Social and Christian Democratic parties. Finally, throughout the period, the governments in Ireland, Greece and Germany had, on average, the most pro-social market regulation views, while those in Spain, Denmark and Britain were the least supportive.

Protectionism

Categories: protectionism: positive (406) – protectionism: negative (407).

In the 1960s, there were not great differences across member states on trade related issues. Preferences tended to be moderately liberal.

Although, France and, to a lesser extent Belgium and Luxembourg, had more protectionist views, while the Dutch and, less so, the German governments were more liberal. A shift towards more protectionist views took place in the 1970s. Both the British and Irish governments had protectionist inclinations and even the German Socialist–Liberal coalition was relatively less supportive of free trade. In the 1980s, strong swings in favor of free trade took place in Britain and Italy. The Dutch government remained supportive of free trade, while the French, Irish and Belgian governments were relatively less supportive, joined, this time, by the Greek Socialist government. Portugal and Spain did not have strong views either way.

Throughout the period, the governments in Ireland, France and Greece had, on average, the most protectionist preferences, while those in Spain, Netherlands and Italy were the most liberal. Germany is the fourth most liberal state on average. This result seems surprising. This is because Spain and Italy have had neutral or moderately liberal views throughout the period, while Germany, and Britain especially, showed greater swings around the mean, depending on the governing parties.

Social justice (503)

The relative and longitudinal trends in this category are similar to those explained in the section on *welfare*. There are minor differences. France tops the list of the most pro-social justice governments in the 1960s up to the first enlargement and in the post second enlargement period. The period with greater conflict in the Council was in the 1970s.

5 Delegation in the European Union: quantitative analysis

Over the last ten years, the study of delegation in the EU has increasingly become a favored ground of scholarly examination. Meanwhile, warnings against centralization of powers and excessive bureaucratization in the EU are recurrent in many political circles across Europe. But our current understanding of these processes is both partial and biased. The most comprehensive analyses concentrate predominately on delegation to supranational institutions via the adoption of amendments to the Treaty establishing the EU (Moravcsik, 1998; Pollack, 2003b). However, as clearly illustrated in Chapter 3, delegation decisions abound not only in secondary legislation, EU legislators also extensively rely on national administrations for policy implementation. Hence, a series of questions arises. When are actors likely to prefer the national path of implementation? When are they likely to prefer the supranational one? Some secondary laws may require only a qualified majority in the Council, hence another crucial question, that is almost ignored in current studies, has to be considered: how do decision rules, mediating with policy complexity and with the preferences of member states and of the Commission, shape the choice of implementation path and the degree of discretionary authority conferred upon administrators?

Moravcsik (1998) and Pollack (2003b) emphasize the need to achieve policy credibility as the key rationale for delegating powers to supranational institutions. This view however neglects a strategic dynamics that is likely to occur in secondary legislation. Given that these scholars recognize that the Commission pursues its own objectives strategically, should we not expect this institution to exploit opportunities that arise with majority voting to shape delegation outcomes more to its liking and, importantly, above and beyond the mere need to ensure credibility?

In the pages that follow, I redress these biases in the literature and address these questions. I reformulate and group the first eight propositions derived from the model in Chapter 2 into eight testable hypotheses. Expectations are then tested using the dependent and independent variables developed in Chapters 3 and 4 respectively (see Table 2.1 mapping propositions onto hypotheses).

The main part of the chapter consists of three sections, one focusing on the national path of policy implementation, the second on the supranational path and the last assessing the relative reliance on the two paths. The first two sections are divided into three subheadings examining the following topics: (i) how decision rules affect the choice of implementation path; (ii) how decision rules, policy complexity and, in the case of delegation to the Commission, Council–Commission conflict shape the degree of discretion conferred upon administrators and (iii) limited to majority voting cases, how conflict within the Council shapes their degree of discretion. The chapter proceeds to the third section by extracting and testing two additional hypotheses about the level of discretion of national administrations *relative to* the discretion level of the Commission. I examine how relative discretion is shaped by the decision rules and, in qualified majority voting, by the intensity of conflict within the Council.

Before concluding, two additional topics are covered. First, I compare the explanatory power of the credibility-based explanation for delegation with that of my theory, based on preference-rule strategic interactions. What follows next is a brief comparison of the patterns of delegation in the EU with those in the United States.

The chapter is mostly based on regression analysis. Therefore, before we proceed, I outline in the next section the several diagnostics performed on the data and the methodological issues underpinning the results.

A note on methodology

Regression analysis is based on a set of assumptions that may be violated. Therefore, several diagnostics have been performed on the data and, where a violation has been detected, steps have been taken to correct the problem. Where models have revealed heteroscedasticity (using Cook and Weisberg, 1983), they were estimated using robust regressions.[1] With one exception discussed below, I have instead found no evidence of multicollinearity among the independent variables. Additionally, inspections of the (augmented) component-plus-residual plots and of the fitted-versus-residual plots do not reject the linear specification used for these models. In some circumstances, a Ramsey (1969) RESET test reveals that variables may be omitted (the coefficient of one fitted value is significantly different from zero). However, these problems disappear as

---

[1] I have used the statistical package Stata 7.0.

I gradually improve the specification of the models. Lastly, the measure of discretion for both national administrations and the Commission may be left censored at zero (see Figure 3.7). This could create two problems: the error term may not be normally distributed and estimators may be biased downward (e.g. Greene, 1997). Therefore, I have also estimated normal Tobit regressions, but I report the results only if the number of censored observations is large and, in the summary regressions, if results are significantly different.

I omit from the regressions the observations with Cook's distances greater than $4/n$, where n is the sample size (see Bollen and Jackman, 1990), because influential outliers may bias the estimations. The quantities of interest and the measures of uncertainty about their estimation, the 95 percent confidence limits, are calculated using the statistical simulation program of Tomz, Wittenberg and King (2003) as explained in King, Tomz and Wittenberg (2000).[2] Finally, the *ceteris paribus* clause is implied in the analysis of the impact of the independent variables.

The national path of policy implementation

Delegation to national administrations

We start out with the important choice of delegation. When are EU legislators likely to prefer the national path of implementation? The model unmistakably identifies an important circumstance when national implementation is preferred. The finding is summarized in Proposition 2.1 which can be easily translated into a testable hypothesis.

Hypothesis 5.1   *Delegation to national administrations and decision rules*
    Delegation to national administrations is more likely under unanimity than qualified majority voting.

We know from Chapter 3 that EU legislators extensively rely on national administrations. The question hence is whether this trend is more pronounced in laws adopted unanimously. Delegation refers to the likelihood of relying on a specific institution for the execution of EU policies. I use two measures of delegation. In the first model, I employ a dichotomous variable taking the value of one if at least one major provision in a law delegates executive authority to national administrations or, in other

---

[2] The program draws sets of simulated main and ancillary parameters from their asymptotic sampling distribution and converts these parameters into substantively relevant quantities, such as expected values, predicted values and first differences. The simulation procedure I employ produces 1000 sets, the default quantity for the program, and uses the mean values of the explanatory variables for the analysis of the quantities of interest.

Table 5.1 *Robust logistic regression of the effect of decision rules on delegation to national administrations.*

	Dependent variable: *Delegation*	
	Model I	Model II
Constant	2.317	2.037
	$(5.83)^a$	$(5.73)^a$
Decision rule	−0.677	−1.067
	(−1.35)	$(−2.45)^b$
Wald χ^2	1.83	6.01^b
Pseudo R^2	0.016	0.042
Log likelihood	−59.055	−74.948
% correctly classified	87.34%	80.38%
N	158	158

Note: Robust standard errors, z-statistics in parentheses. ^{a} $p < 0.01$; ^{b} $p < 0.05$.

words, if the delegation ratio introduced in Chapter 3 is greater than zero.[3] In the second model, delegation takes the value of one if this ratio is greater than 3.7 percent, the 20th percentile.[4] Since the dependent variable is dichotomous, the most appropriate statistical technique is a logistic regression. The results are shown in Table 5.1.

The coefficient of *Decision rule* in the first model is not significant. The reason for this result is due to the fact that less than 13 percent of the sampled laws do not delegate powers to national administrations, so the variance of the dependent variable is too low. However, as we marginally relax the cutoff point in model II, *Decision rule* significantly affects the likelihood of (substantial) delegation to national administrations. As expected, when a law is adopted by qualified majority voting, this probability diminishes by about 16 percent on average. However, there is a degree of uncertainty as this estimate may vary between 28 and 3 percent.

Discretion of national administrations

The choice of implementation path is the first, somewhat crude, decision EU legislators take. The second crucial issue concerns the degree of discretionary authority that, in this case, national administrations should

---

[3] Recall that the delegation ratio is the share of major provisions in a law that delegate substantive policy authority to national administrations.

[4] This value is lower than a standard deviation decrease from the sample mean, which equals 5.17 percent.

enjoy. This is at the core of the question of bureaucratization. We have seen that some EU laws are highly prescriptive and constraining while others leave ample room for maneuver to national authorities. Under which circumstances do ministers of the Council adopt more constraining legislation and, hence, tie each others' hands more tightly? Three propositions are directly related to national discretion. Proposition 2.2 states that discretion is higher under unanimity voting. Proposition 2.3 relates discretion to the level of conflict within the Council, but it qualifies this relation to only cases of majority voting and for specific preference configurations of the Commission. It will be analyzed separately in the next section. Finally, Proposition 2.8 summarizes the well-known positive impact of policy complexity on discretion. Recall, however, that the model does not identify the specific informational or actor-related features that prompt Council ministers to rely on national authorities. Hence, in the previous chapter, I have further elaborated on this issue suggesting that the considerable resources and technical expertise embedded into national administrations render them particularly attractive when ministers face highly specialized and technical issues. In summary, Proposition 2.2 and, the accordingly modified, Proposition 2.8 can be grouped together to produce the following hypothesis.

Hypothesis 5.2   *Discretion of national administrations, decision rules and policy complexity*
The discretion of national administrations increases under unanimity and in issue areas that require specialized and technical knowledge.

The expectation with regard to policy complexity is assessed first by comparing the average level of the discretion index of the national administrations across a list of mutually exclusive and exhaustive categories. This procedure has also been used by Epstein and O'Halloran (1999b: 197–200), further details on this classification have been provided in Chapter 4. Table 5.2 gives the first impression as to whether greater policy authority is delegated in more informationally intense issue areas. It lists the forty-one categories in ascending order of average national discretion.

The first result to highlight is that delegation to national authorities occurs across all categories, with the only exception being one competition category. EU legislators rely extensively on the technical expertise and resources of national authorities. If the Council wants to reap agency gains, domestic institutions are essential providers. A closer look at Table 5.2 provides some confirming and some evidence against the information intensity hypothesis. Competition rules (both general and specific to the transport sector), trade, regional policy, the system of vacancy clearance and the directives abolishing obstacles to payments

Table 5.2 *Average discretion of national administrations.*

Category	Number of laws	Average discretion
Competition – exemptions and limitation periods	2	0.00%
Merger control	1	2.91%
Competition – rules for undertakings	8	3.28%
Agriculture – financial provisions	3	3.39%
Agriculture – organization of markets	16	3.72%
Commercial policy	9	4.79%
Fishing – organization of markets	2	6.01%
Movement of persons – vacancy clearance	3	6.25%
Transport – market conditions	4	6.50%
Payments for services – liberalization	2	7.64%
Regional policy	1	7.98%
Fishing – structural policy	3	8.24%
Technical standards	2	8.97%
Transport – regulation	2	10.35%
Monetary compensation amounts	1	11.11%
Movement of capital	3	11.73%
Safety and health at work	2	11.92%
Adoption of the ECU	2	12.50%
Social security of migrant workers	6	12.90%
European Economic Interest Grouping	1	15.33%
Agriculture – structural policy	5	15.71%
Establishment and services – movement of workers	6	19.75%
Industrial and commercial property	2	20.14%
Public contracts – procedure	4	20.18%
Movement of persons – rights and derogations	6	20.88%
Consumer protection	5	21.23%
Credit and banking	3	21.42%
Insurance	3	21.90%
Qualifications and professions	18	22.69%
Equal treatment for men and women	5	22.70%
Social policy	3	25.58%
Cooperation among tax authorities	2	27.56%
Organization of working time	1	28.15%
Qualifications and professions – general system	2	28.64%
Taxation	6	29.29%
Environment	3	30.92%
Company law – safeguards	4	33.06%
Company law – accounts	3	37.57%
Education – children of migrant workers	1	39.29%
Company law – stock exchange listing	2	39.50%
International capital flows – regulation	1	40.00%

Table 5.3 *The effect of decision rules and information intensity on the discretion of national administrations: robust OLS regressions.*

| | Dependent variable: *Discretion of national administrations* | | | |
	Model 1	Model 2	Model 3	Model 4
Constant	17.560	17.292	15.837	13.566
	$(13.27)^a$	$(11.43)^a$	$(9.69)^a$	$(8.12)^a$
Decision rule	−6.119	−4.829	−5.601	−3.827
	$(-3.50)^a$	$(-2.64)^a$	$(-3.17)^a$	$(-2.17)^b$
Programme	8.085	–	6.623	–
	$(4.48)^a$		$(3.07)^a$	
Committee	–	2.436	3.876	–
		(1.33)	$(2.07)^b$	
Programme–	–	–	–	7.333
committee				$(4.18)^a$
F	16.04^a	4.53^b	8.72^a	13.69^a
Adjusted R^2	0.13	0.04	0.11	0.13
N	148	155	151	153

Note: Initial $n = 158$, observations with Cook distances greater than $4/n$ are subsequently omitted. *t*-statistics in parentheses, one-tailed test; $^a p \le 0.01$; $^b p \le 0.05$.

are relatively simple measures with limited discretion. Company law and environmental directives, tax provisions, the regulation of professions, the directives on credit and insurance and laws on consumer protection are generally complex and require specialized knowledge. They have higher average values of the discretion index. However, it would be inappropriate to consider the organization of agricultural and fishery markets of the EU as a simple area. We could also have expected greater delegation in the directives on technical standards and, especially, in the highly complex social security regulations. Equally, social policy legislation is not so complex as to justify considerable discretion. I will deal with some of these discrepancies below.

We get a clearer picture on delegation to national administrations if we analyze the results from regressing the discretion index on the two independent variables. The four models in Table 5.3 test the impact of decision rules and information intensity on the discretion of national administrations. The information variables have been considered first separately, then in an additive model. The combined *Programme– committee* variable in the fourth model takes the value of one if either legal provisions refer to action programmes *or* a committee is involved in an issue area.

The results are convincing. Most of the coefficients are significant at either the 1 or 5 percent level. The presence of a programme increases the discretion of national administrations by 6–8 percent. Substantively, this is an increase in discretion equivalent to that which national administrations enjoy from implementing equal gender treatment laws to that they have in executing environmental policy directives. An expert committee has a greater impact when we control for more variables. Here, its effect on the discretion of national administration is an increase of about 4 percent. This is equivalent to an increase in discretion that national administrations have in implementing directives liberalizing establishment and the provision of services to that they have in executing laws on qualifications and professions. The combined *Programme–committee* variable confirms these results. These figures are appreciable, considering that the average national discretion in the sample and the predicted value from the statistical simulation is around 16 percent, plus or minus about 2 percent. However, uncertainty with regard to these estimates is relatively high. The impact of *Programme* and *Programme–committee* can be as low as 4–5 percent and as high as 11–12 percent, while that of *Committee* oscillates between 1.2 and 6 percent.

Decision rule has a significant independent impact on the executive discretion of national administrations too. An act adopted under unanimity delegates between 4 and 6 percent more discretion to governments than one adopted under qualified majority voting. This result is consistent across all model specifications, though uncertainty remains relatively high. Values could swing between 1 and 8 percent. Separating the effect of decision rules from that of information intensity is not straightforward, but it is reasonable to assert that unanimity explains the greater discretion in tax-related legislation, in the regulation of international capital movements, in social policy and in the directives on the right of residence. Earlier acts on the organization of agricultural markets, adopted unanimously, also delegate more policy authority than later acts adopted by qualified majority voting (compare, for instance, Regulations 19/62 and 120/67 on the market organization for cereals).[5]

In summary, we have found confirming evidence for Hypothesis 5.2, although there is uncertainty about the precise value of the estimates. In

---

[5] In a personal communication, Joe Jupille has pointed out the apparent contradiction between this result and the trend toward more national discretion shown in Figure 3.9, since we know that qualified majority voting has been extended to new policy areas in the 1987 Single European Act. However, it should be noted that there are both low discretion post-1987 measures and high discretion pre-1987 measures in Figure 3.9. Moreover, the results show that, even in the case of a trend toward more national discretion, the impact of decision rules persists over time.

the following sections, I report only results with the *Programme–committee* variable because it is the model with the highest correlation coefficient.

Discretion of national administrations and conflict within the Council

When governments do not share similar policy objectives, national implementation is likely to diverge more across member states. My theory reveals that states with moderate preferences are likely to prefer more constraining legislation in these circumstances. However, whether the final act will be more prescriptive depends on two factors. First, the Commission should support a more constraining law. Second, the act has to be adopted by majority voting because, in unanimity, states with more extreme preferences have veto power and may prefer greater national room for maneuver as conflict within the Council intensifies. This finding was summarized in Proposition 2.3. It can be reworded as the following hypothesis.

Hypothesis 5.3   *Discretion of national administrations and conflict within the Council*
In the case of qualified majority voting and a Commission more in favor of the underlying shift of the measure than the Council pivotal member, the discretion of national administrations decreases as conflict within the Council increases.

The second condition translates the meaning of a supranational Commission used in the formal model. For instance, it would refer to a Commission that is more supportive of farmers than the Council pivot in the regulations of the common agricultural policy or that it is less liberal than the pivot when a protectionist commercial policy instrument is adopted.
    However, I first test this hypothesis including all acts adopted by qualified majority voting. In other words, I assume that the second condition is always realized, as it is the Commission that initiates the legislative process. I then restrict the data set further and rerun the regressions.
    Table 5.4 includes all the acts adopted by qualified majority voting. The expectation is corroborated with regard to the substantive policy dimension. A standard deviation increase in *Standardized policy range* causes a 2–3 percent decrease in national discretion, plus or minus 1.5 percent.[6]

---

[6] The values of standard deviation that I use in the analysis of the regression results are those reported in Table 4.4 for the whole sample, hence they are not the standard deviations of the sample included in the regression. Using the same values allows a more intuitive comparison across the different models.

Table 5.4 *The effect of conflict in the Council on the discretion of national administrations: robust OLS regressions. Qualified majority laws.*

	Dependent variable: *Discretion of national administrations*				
	Model 1	Model 2	Model 3	Model 4	Model 5
Constant	2.203	8.953	−2.869	6.924	2.112
	(1.29)	(5.03)^a	(−0.93)	(2.96)^a	(0.59)
Integration	0.581	–	–	0.356	0.105
range	(2.08)^b			(1.32)	(0.37)
Standardized	–	−16.350	–	−16.213	−26.309
policy range		(−2.87)^a		(−2.79)^a	(−3.72)^a
Left–right	–	–	4.195	–	4.496
range			(2.92)^a		(3.10)^a
Programme–	14.581	15.898	15.323	15.768	14.594
committee	(6.77)^a	(8.22)^a	(7.86)^a	(7.64)^a	(7.27)^a
N	75	73	75	72	73
F	39.49^a	38.26^a	35.72^a	30.23^a	23.56^a
Adjusted R^2	0.43	0.50	0.48	0.51	0.52

Note: Subset of laws adopted by qualified majority voting. Initial $n = 80$, observations with Cook distances greater than $4/n$ are subsequently omitted; t-statistics in parentheses, one-tailed test; ^{a} $p \leq 0.01$; ^{b} $p \leq 0.05$.

The Council is likely to adopt legislation that is more constraining for the national administrations when there is greater divergence of policy preferences (and, therefore, the risk of biased national implementation is higher). However, the other two measures of preference do not corroborate our expectations. *Integration range* has the wrong sign and becomes insignificant as we include more control variables, while a standard deviation increase in *Left–right range* leads to about a 3 percent *increase* in national discretion, plus or minus less than 2 percent. This is the opposite of what we expected. Increased conflict along the left–right dimension leads to more national discretion.

A more direct test is to include only the laws where the Commission is more in favor of the underlying shift of the adopted law than the Council pivotal member. For instance, for measures establishing the internal market, which shifted the status quo towards a market economy, the regression should only include laws where a Commission has preferences closer to the market end of the planned–market economy dimension than the Council pivot.

Table 5.5 includes only the cases that satisfy this additional condition. For instance, in model 1, they would only include the laws where the Commission is more integrationist than the Council pivot. The models

Table 5.5 *The effect of conflict in the Council on the discretion of national administrations: robust OLS regressions. Qualified majority laws, smaller data set.*

	Dependent variable: Discretion of national administrations					
	Measure of Commission's preferences					
	Commission median			Commissioner		
	Model 1	Model 2	Model 3	Model 1	Model 2	Model 3
Constant	−0.044 (−0.02)	8.452 (4.59)[a]	4.895 (0.93)	1.129 (0.37)	11.500[a] (3.82)	0.530 (0.14)
Integration range	0.901 (1.62)	—	—	0.760 (1.26)	—	—
Standardized policy range	—	−14.388 (−2.51)[b]	—	—	−9.376 (−1.00)	—
Left–right range	—	—	0.711 (0.31)	—	—	2.557 (1.65)
Programme–committee	15.947 (6.48)[a]	14.918 (7.08)[a]	15.425 (6.02)[a]	14.630 (5.13)[a]	13.264 (3.76)[a]	16.412 (6.52)[a]
N	54	63	47	50	44	47
F	23.04[a]	26.89[a]	18.36[a]	16.97[a]	7.08[a]	21.38[a]
Adjusted R^2	0.45	0.47	0.42	0.40	0.22	0.48

Note: Subset of laws adopted by qualified majority voting selected using different measures of Commission preferences. Observations with Cook distances greater than $4/n$ are omitted; t-statistics in parentheses; one-tailed test; [a] $p \leq 0.01$; [b] $p \leq 0.05$.

use first *Commission median*, then *Commissioner* as the measure of the Commission's preferences employed to select the cases to include. The table does not include regressions with more than one preference dimensions because, in these circumstances, the selection rule should apply across all the dimensions and the number of selected cases drops substantially below fifty, making any interpretation of the results inadvisable. In the case of *Commission median*, the results confirm the statistical and substantive significance of *Standardized policy range* in affecting the degree of national execution discretion. The integration and left–right variables instead do not reach the nominal level of significance.

In conclusion, in line with Hypothesis 5.3, the most robust result of the statistical analysis is that an increase in policy conflict within the Council diminishes the national discretionary boundaries for the execution of EU policies. Since more intense conflict in the Council increases the likelihood of divergent implementation, ministers opt for tying their own hands more tightly. However, contrary to expectations, there is also some evidence that greater divergence on the left–right dimension may lead to more latitude in national implementation. Nevertheless, I do not draw any definitive conclusion from this result because *Left–right range* is not significant in Table 5.5, nor it is significant in the summary regression that is presented in the next section.

Finally, how does conflict affect national discretion in the other circumstances, namely in unanimity or in majority voting, when the Commission favors the policy shift *less* than the Council pivot? The predictions from the model are ambiguous because the key actors may prefer either lower or greater discretion in these cases. Nevertheless, results regressing national discretion on conflict do not differ much from those reported in Tables 5.4 and 5.5. More intense conflict within the Council on the policy dimension has the same effect on discretion. National discretionary boundaries narrow. Conversely, national administrations are likely to have more room for maneuver if there is considerable divergence among member states with regard to the more general issue of European integration. Conflict on the left–right dimension does not produce robust results.

Summary regression and discussion

Since the preference variables have similar effects, regardless of the voting rule used in the Council, all the observations can be included in a single regression as shown in Table 5.6. Policy complexity and decision rules have the largest substantive impact on national executive discretion. The estimated effect, an increase in discretion of 6.5 percent if there is a committee or a programme and a decrease of 5.6 percent in the case of majority voting, plus or minus 3.4 percent in both cases, is similar to

Table 5.6 *Summary regression: the impact of decision rules, policy complexity and conflict in the Council on the discretion of national administrations.*

	Dependent variable: Discretion of national administrations	
	Robust OLS estimates	Tobit estimates
Constant	9.709	7.862
	$(2.81)^a$	$(1.83)^c$
Programme–committee	6.510	7.877
	$(3.86)^a$	$(3.97)^a$
Decision rule	−5.562	−4.242
	$(-3.23)^a$	$(-2.12)^b$
Integration range	0.855	0.768
	$(3.55)^a$	$(2.14)^b$
Standardized policy range	−20.754	−18.047
	$(-3.41)^a$	$(-2.24)^b$
Left–right range	2.108	2.284
	$(1.70)^c$	(1.50)
N	149	158
F	14.84^a	–
χ^2	–	35.12^a
Adjusted or pseudo R^2	0.26	0.03

Note: t-statistics in parentheses, one-tailed test; $^a\, p \leq 0.01$; $^b\, p \leq 0.05$; $^c\, p \leq 0.1$. OLS regression omits observations with Cook distances greater than $4/n$.

that of Table 5.3. Of the conflict variables, *Standardized policy range* has the largest substantive impact on national discretion. The discretionary authority of national administrations diminishes by 2.6 percent, plus or minus 1.4 percent, as a result of a standard deviation increase in conflict along the policy dimension. On the other hand, a similar increase in the *Integration range* augments national discretion by 2.4 percent, plus or minus 1.2 percent. *Left–right range* reaches, barely, statistical significance only in the ordinary least-squares (OLS) regression and its substantive impact is small.

The empirical analysis provides strong evidence that delegation to national administrations is more likely in the case of unanimity and that the discretion of national administrations increases:

(a) when unanimity is required in the Council;

(b) in issue areas that demand specialized and technical knowledge;

(c) as conflict decreases within the Council along the policy dimension;

(d) as conflict increases within the Council along the integration dimension, but only in the case of unanimity.

The hypotheses considered in this section are then mostly corroborated. I conclude with four remarks. First, the formal model deals specifically with the implementation of EU policies, so it should not come as a surprise that it is particularly powerful when we use substantive policy preferences. Moreover, as case studies and mapping exercises of Council members' preferences have shown, positions with regard to specific policy issues are dominant dividing lines. Second, the integration dimension reflects the more general ideological attitude toward the EU, which may be detached from specific policy positions. The fact that this variable is significant in the case of unanimity is coherent with the work of Moravcsik (1998). Moravcsik focuses mostly on Treaty amendments or policies that require unanimity and, although he concludes that policy preferences are key in determining outcomes across issue areas, he acknowledges that institutional design can also be explained by the general ideological positions of member states on European integration. Third, although Gabel and Huber's measure is based on the conception of left–right ideology as a constraint on policy positions (Gabel and Huber, 2000: 95), the level of generality, in terms of policy content, that left–right positions represent, probably explains the unsatisfactory performance. Finally, divergence among governments with regard to policy objectives raises concerns about the faithful national implementation of a measure and, hence, the credibility in the attainment of such objectives. Had the empirical results revealed that conflict in the Council (i.e. *Standardized policy range*) decreases national discretion under qualified majority voting *and* increases it under unanimity, we would have found empirical support for the conjecture that majority voting enhances policy credibility by facilitating the adoption of more constraining legislation.[7] Unfortunately, since *Standardized policy range* has a similar impact across the two decision rules in this sample, we do not find supportive evidence. The case studies in Chapter 6 will shed further light on this issue.

The supranational path of policy implementation

Delegation to the European Commission

We move on now to a second important topic. When do EU legislators prefer the supranational path of implementation? In other words, when do

---

[7] For further elaboration on this issue, see Franchino (2005).

Table 5.7 *Robust logistic regression of the effect of decision rules on delegation to the European Commission.*

	Dependent variable: *Delegation*
Constant	−0.934
	(−3.70)[a]
Decision rule	1.392
	(4.07)[a]
Wald χ^2	16.60[a]
Pseudo R^2	0.08
Log likelihood	−99.810
% correctly classified	66.46%
N	158

Note: Robust standard errors, z-statistics in parentheses. [a] $p \leq 0.01$.

they centralize powers? A clear-cut result of the model is summarized in Proposition 2.4 which leads to the following similarly worded hypothesis.

Hypothesis 5.4   *Delegation to the Commission and decision rules*
    Delegation to the Commission is more likely under qualified majority than unanimity voting.

The Commission is used much more sparingly by EU legislators, but is the likelihood of relying on this institution a function of the decision rules used to adopt the measure at hand? To test this, I employ a dichotomous dependent variable taking the value of one if the Commission delegation ratio is greater than zero, namely if at least one major provision in a law grants executive authority to this institution. The results from the logistic regression are shown in Table 5.7.

Decision rule significantly affects the likelihood of delegation to the Commission. When a law is adopted by qualified majority voting, this probability increases by a notable 32.7 percent on average, though this estimate may vary between 46 and 17 percent. The evidence corroborates this expectation rather strongly.

Discretion of the European Commission

The decision to centralize powers at the supranational level does not imply necessarily that the Commission enjoys considerable discretion for policy implementation. Only a few well-defined powers could be transferred to the supranational level. This is actually what has occurred in the EU.

In Chapter 3, we have seen not only that delegation to the Commission occurs only half as much as delegation to national administrations does, but also that the discretionary authority of this institution is lower and varies more widely across laws. What explains this variance? When do Council ministers confer broader powers to the Commission? My theory has identified four factors, summarized in corresponding propositions. Proposition 2.5 states that its discretion is higher under qualified majority voting. Proposition 2.6 asserts that discretion increases if the preferences of the Commission and of the pivotal government converge. Proposition 2.7 links discretion to conflict within the Council, but the relation is limited to majority voting. I deal with this expectation in the next section. Finally, as with the national case, Proposition 2.8 relates discretion to policy complexity. As argued in Chapter 4, the limited resources of this supranational bureaucracy and the less specialist nature of its personnel make the Commission an attractive locus of delegation only in policies that require general and managerial skills at the supranational level. In summary, Propositions 2.5, 2.6 and (accordingly modified) 2.8 can be grouped in a single hypothesis as follows.

Hypothesis 5.5   *Discretion of the Commission, decision rules, policy conflict and complexity*
The discretion of the Commission increases under qualified majority voting, as the preferences of the Commission and those of the pivotal government converge and in issue areas that require general and managerial skills at the supranational level.

Table 5.8 lists the categories, which were used in Table 5.2 for national administrations, where powers are delegated to the Commission, in ascending order of average discretion of this institution. It provides the first impression as to whether greater policy authority is delegated in issue areas requiring general and managerial skills.

Undoubtedly, the Commission plays a secondary role in policy execution. It has no executive discretion in seventeen categories, including social security, taxation, social policy, gender equality and categories that include some legislation on the movement of persons and on company law. The Council is less likely to rely on the less specialized and resourceful Commission and, as we already know, this institution is more constrained on average than national administrations. Areas of extensive discretion of national authorities show limited or no discretion for the Commission. This is true for most of the categories with no delegation and for those at the top of the table, where the Commission reduces the Council's workload by adopting minor amendments of the specific act.

Table 5.8 *Average discretion of the European Commission.*

Category	Number of laws	Average discretion
Credit and banking	3	0.79%
Company law – stock exchange listing	2	1.02%
Qualifications and professions	18	1.10%
European Economic Interest Grouping	1	1.15%
Consumer protection	5	1.25%
Public contracts – procedure	4	1.50%
Environment	3	2.13%
Fishing – structural policy	3	2.42%
Movement of persons – vacancy clearance	3	2.61%
Safety and health at work	2	2.61%
Technical standards	2	2.88%
Cooperation among tax authorities	2	3.21%
Movement of capital	3	4.20%
Qualifications and professions – general system	2	4.28%
Regional policy	1	6.21%
Agriculture – structural policy	5	6.33%
Transport – market conditions	4	6.51%
Agriculture – financial provisions	3	6.90%
Commercial policy	9	7.37%
Merger control	1	9.71%
Fishing – organization of markets	2	10.61%
Agriculture – organization of markets	16	14.74%
Monetary compensation amounts	1	15.00%
Competition – rules for undertakings	8	20.67%

Note: There is no delegation of policy authority in the remaining seventeen categories.

Delegation in agriculture and fishery is now explained. Here, the Council relies mostly on the Commission. The management of these markets is very complex and, importantly, is an outcome of Council decisions which, generally, tend to restrict national authority. As predicted, the Commission serves the Council's need for general managerial skills at the supranational level. Finally, information intensity cannot explain delegation of executive authority in competition, trade and regional policy.

The results from the regression analysis in Table 5.9 provide a clearer picture. The regressions employ as a measure of convergence the absolute distance between the preferences of the Commission and those of the Council member that is pivotal under the relevant procedure. This variable, *Conflict*, takes different values when we use *Commission median* or *Commissioner* as the measure of Commission preferences (see Table 4.4 for descriptive statistics). It should have a negative impact on the dependent variable. Table 5.9 also includes the estimates from Tobit regressions

Table 5.9 *The effect of policy complexity, decision rules and conflict on the discretion of the European Commission.*

	Dependent variable: Discretion of the Commission									
	Measure of Commission's preferences: *Commission median*					Measure of Commission's preferences: *Commissioner*				
	Robust OLS estimates				Tobit estimates	Robust OLS estimates				Tobit estimates
	Model 1a	Model 2a	Model 3a	Model 4a	Model 4a	Model 1b	Model 2b	Model 3b	Model 4b	Model 4b
Constant	-0.085	1.253	2.933	0.176	-3.560	1.942	1.260	1.123	1.898	-4.022
	(-0.09)	(2.09)[b]	(3.44)[a]	(0.15)	(-0.86)	(3.64)[a]	(2.05)[b]	(1.94)[c]	(2.48)[b]	(-1.41)
Detailed rules	1.578	1.524	1.553	1.457	1.628	1.625	1.626	1.605	1.574	1.566
	(9.95)[a]	(9.02)[a]	(9.38)[a]	(9.08)[a]	(4.44)[a]	(9.88)[a]	(9.51)[a]	(9.99)[a]	(10.04)[a]	(4.32)[a]
Decision rule	2.285	1.726	0.584	2.211	4.111	1.633	1.643	1.390	1.604	5.750
	(2.63)[a]	(2.14)[b]	(0.73)	(2.35)[b]	(1.31)	(2.48)[b]	(2.11)[b]	(2.04)[b]	(2.21)[b]	(2.61)[a]
Conflict integration	0.692			1.132	1.295	-0.434			-0.441	-0.873
	(1.31)			(1.80)[c]	(0.84)	(-2.33)[b]			(-2.22)[b]	(-1.30)
Conflict standardized policy		5.340		4.467	22.217		1.117		-2.614	6.598
		(0.77)		(0.74)	(0.86)		(0.24)		(-0.59)	(0.39)
Conflict left–right			-1.445	-1.085	-5.583			0.180	0.220	-0.378
			(-2.25)[b]	(-1.76)[c]	(-2.30)[b]			(0.56)	(0.62)	(-0.30)
N	145	149	147	146	158	146	148	146	145	158
F	45.34[a]	44.86[a]	41.93[a]	27.10[a]		48.12[a]	42.13[a]	44.56[a]	34.56[a]	
χ^2					4.41[a]					40.40[a]
Adjusted or pseudo R^2	0.29	0.22	0.24	0.24	0.07	0.24	0.22	0.22	0.23	0.06

Note: The variable *Conflict* has been generated using different measures of Commission's preferences. Initial $n = 158$, observations with Cook distances greater than $4/n$ are subsequently omitted; 87 left-censored observations in the Tobit regressions. t-statistics in parentheses, one-tailed test; [a] $p \leq 0.01$; [b] $p \leq 0.05$; [c] $p \leq 0.1$.

since the discretion index is left-censored at zero in more than half of the sample (see Chapter 3).[8]

The discretion of the Commission increases significantly in issue areas that require general and managerial skills at the supranational level. A standard deviation increase in *Detailed rules* leads to a 4 percent increase in discretion, plus or minus less than 1 percent. This is a significant impact, given the 4.4 per cent average discretion. It is equivalent to the different role the Commission plays in implementing the directives on technical standards compared to that it has in managing the financial provisions of the agricultural policy. Its powers originate mostly from the organizational and structural aspects of the agricultural and fishery policies. But, policy authority has been delegated also for the management of monetary compensations in agriculture, the system of vacancy clearance and a 1968 system of bracket tariffs for the carriage of goods by road.

The discretion of the Commission in acts adopted under qualified majority voting is, on average, more than 1.5 per cent higher than that in laws adopted by unanimous voting, plus or minus about 1 percent. This is a significant increase. Only in model 3a, is *Decision rules* not significant because of the strong correlation with *Conflict left–right*,[9] which creates problems of collinearity. The impact of majority voting is notable especially in the legislation on competition policy, state aid to the transport sector and in some commercial policy instruments. This decision rule also explains some Commission powers related to structural measures in the agricultural sector and in earlier acts on professional qualifications and on the movement of persons. Interestingly, the extension of majority voting to new areas, as a result of Treaty amendments, has led to moderate increases of the Commission's executive discretion in the subsequent acts. After this extension to the legislation on public contracts, the Commission has been conferred powers to invoke, prior to the conclusion of a contract, a review procedure if infringements are manifest (Directive 89/665, for more details see the case study in Chapter 6). Similarly, the Commission

---

[8] Since both variables are derived from reading statutes, it could be argued that the disturbance term of *Discretion* is correlated with the cause of *Detailed rules*, hence, there is a risk of violating the nonrecursivity assumption of OLS. Ideally, two-stage least-squares regressions could be used to deal with this problem, but we do not have a theory that would guide us in the selection of appropriate instruments. I have instead substituted *Detailed rules* with a dummy variable *Regulation*, taking the value of 1 if the measure is a regulation and rerun the regressions. This procedure is based on the, probably debatable, conjecture that the choice of legislative instruments, namely regulations, may reveal specific informational requirements at the supranational level. Results are confirmed throughout the analysis and *Regulation* is positively, significantly and systematically related to *Discretion of the Commission* (and negatively to *Relative discretion*).

[9] The Spearman's correlation coefficient is -0.65 ($p < 0.001$).

has been given additional powers to authorize and revoke protective measures in the new capital movement Directive 88/361. Examples can be found in the legislation on the recognition of diplomas, on credit and banking and, arguably, on consumer protection.[10]

The results from the *Conflict* variables are less convincing. Divergence on the left–right dimension consistently reaches statistical significance, but only if *Commission median* is used as the measure of the Commission's preferences. As expected, a standard deviation increase in *Conflict left–right* diminishes the Commission's discretion by 0.75 percent, plus or minus 0.7 percent. *Conflict integration* is significant if *Commissioner* is used as the preference measure. A standard deviation increase in this variable diminishes discretion by 0.6 percent (plus or minus 0.5 percent). However, its coefficient has the wrong sign in model 4a, though it is only weakly significant. *Conflict standardized policy* is instead not significant. In conclusion, although the substantive impact of *Conflict* is not trivial in these two circumstances and its direction is as expected, results are not very robust across the different measures of Commission's preferences.

The Tobit regressions confirm these conclusions. The estimate of *Decision rules* loses significance in model 4a, but it remains significant if we exclude influential outliers.[11] On the other hand, *Conflict left–right* becomes more significant, but only if these outliers are included. Finally, the estimate for *Conflict integration* becomes insignificant in the Tobit regression of model 4b. In summary, the expectations with regard to issue complexity and decision rules are corroborated and relatively robust, while we find supportive, but not very robust, evidence of the negative impact of preference divergence.

Discretion of the European Commission and conflict within the Council

More conflict within the Council is likely to generate more divergent national implementation. Consequently, the national path becomes less attractive, relative to the supranational one, for moderately placed governments. In these circumstances, these states prefer delegating powers to the Commission rather than relying on national authorities and a discretion-maximizing Commission is likely to exploit this opportunity. However, it

[10] The shift from unanimity to majority voting has led to greater discretion, compared to prior legislation in the same area, in Directives 89/48 and 92/51 on the general system for the recognition of diplomas, in the second banking Directive 89/646 and, probably, in Directive 88/378 on the safety of toys.

[11] In this case, the coefficient and t-statistics are 5.962 and 2.18 ($p < 0.05$).

Table 5.10 *The effect of conflict within the Council on the discretion of the European Commission in laws adopted by qualified majority voting.*

	Dependent variable: *Discretion of the Commission*				
	Robust OLS estimates				Tobit estimates
	Model 1	Model 2	Model 3	Model 4	Model 4
Constant	3.378	1.093	3.311	2.178	4.089
	$(3.06)^a$	(1.10)	$(2.18)^b$	(0.93)	(0.94)
Detailed rules	1.519	1.259	1.567	0.853	1.347
	$(8.61)^a$	$(7.31)^a$	$(9.15)^a$	$(4.75)^a$	$(4.14)^a$
Range integration	−0.004	–	–	0.002	0.228
	(−0.03)			(0.02)	(0.65)
Range standardized policy	–	13.444	–	16.582	2.775
		$(2.91)^a$		$(3.16)^a$	(0.33)
Range left–right	–	–	−0.132	−0.797	−2.397
			(−0.20)	(−1.17)	(−1.48)
N	74	71	73	73	80
F	37.94^a	40.19^a	41.96^a	15.25^a	–
χ^2	–	–	–	–	20.30^a
Adjusted or pseudo R^2	0.36	0.40	0.43	0.42	0.05

Note: Initial $n = 80$, observations with Cook distances greater than $4/n$ are subsequently omitted; 31 left-censored observations in the Tobit regression; *t*-statistics in parentheses, one-tailed test; ^{a} $p \leq 0.01$; ^{b} $p \leq 0.05$.

can only do so in majority voting where states with extreme preferences cannot veto decisions. This result was summarized in Proposition 2.7 which can be formulated as follows.

Hypothesis 5.6   *Discretion of the Commission and conflict within the Council*
In the case of qualified majority voting, the discretion of the Commission increases as conflict within the Council increases.

Table 5.10 shows the results from regressing the Commission discretion on conflict within the Council (i.e. *Range*) in qualified majority laws. Only positions along the policy dimension significantly affect discretion. A standard deviation increase in *Range standardized policy* leads to an increase of approximately 2 percent in Commission discretion, plus or minus 1 percent. This is equivalent to the greater role that this institution has in the structural pillar of the agricultural policy compared to that it has in the general system of diploma recognition.

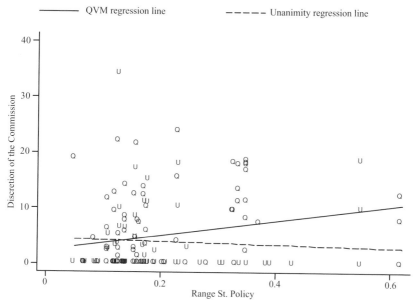

Figure 5.1 *Discretion of the European Commission by conflict within the Council along the policy dimension. Note:* Observation with Cook's distances greater than 4/*n* are omitted from the regressions. Regression lines use the mean value of *Detailed rules* = 1.006; unanimity cases are coded as U, while qualified majority cases are coded as QM. *Commission discretion* = 1.71 + 2.788 *Detailed rules* – 2.655 *Range standardized policy* (unanimity cases, *n* = 74). *Commission discretion* = 1.093 + 1.259 *Detailed rules* + 13.444 *Range standardized policy* (QMV cases, *n* = 71).

Moreover, the positive relation between conflict and discretion holds only in laws enacted under this decision rule. Figure 5.1 maps the relation between these two variables, separating the laws adopted by unanimity from those passed by qualified majority voting. In majority voting, the regression line is upward sloping, hence the relation is positive, strong and significant. In the case of unanimity, the line is moderately downward sloping, indicating a weakly negative relation between conflict and discretion. The coefficient of *Range standardized policy* is marginally significant ($p = 0.109$).

In conclusion, the expectation that, in majority voting, more conflict in the Council leads to more discretion of the Commission is corroborated only with regard to the policy preference dimension. It remains valid when we introduce more control variables, but it does not do so in the Tobit regression.[12] Interestingly, there is some evidence that greater policy conflict within the Council leads to less Commission discretion in the case of unanimity. This is likely to result from the fact that the government wanting to minimize the executive role of the Commission has veto power in this circumstance.

Summary and discussion

The empirical analysis provides strong evidence that delegation to the Commission is more likely in the case of qualified majority voting and that the discretion of this institution increases

(a) when qualified majority is required in the Council;

(b) in issue areas that require general and managerial skills at the supra-national level.

It also provides relatively strong evidence that, for laws adopted by qualified majority voting, the discretion of the Commission increases with greater conflict within the Council along the policy dimension. There is also some evidence that the relation is the opposite to this in laws adopted unanimously.

We have found empirical support for most of the hypotheses considered in this section. Two issues need a few additional comments. First, although the *Conflict* variables behave as expected in some cases, hence corroborating the well-known expectation that preference divergence between the principal (i.e. the Council pivot) and the agent (the Commission) decreases the latter's discretion (Tallberg, 2002a; Hug, 2003; Pollack, 2003a, 2003b). Results are not robust. There may be different explanations for this outcome. An obvious one is the reliability of the measures. A future challenge would be to develop more sophisticated techniques to measure the preferences of this institution. However, there may be other causes. For most of the history of the EU, members of the Commission have been appointed by the governments only.[13] Although we have found a systematic bias in favor of integration, the preferences of this institution are likely to reflect in a relatively faithful way the positions of the member states (Crombez, 1997b; Hug, 2003). Moreover, any EU law provides for specific aims and objectives that, if executive powers are delegated to the Commission, become an integral part of the implementation mandate for this institution, therefore *shaping* its preferences.

---

[12] But it remains significant if we exclude influential outliers. The coefficient and t-statistics for model 4 are 22.14 and 2.83 ($p < 0.01$).

[13] The Parliament is playing an increasingly relevant role in the appointment of the President of the Commission. The relation between the Parliament and the Commission is discussed in greater detail in Chapter 7.

Even if we reject this sociological interpretation, it is very likely that there are self-selection mechanisms operating both within the college of the Commission, at the stage of portfolio allocation, and within the Commission administration. Commissioners and bureaucrats are likely to navigate toward those policy areas the objectives of which they share the most. For instance, commissioners more concerned with environmental issues are more likely to lead the Directorate General Environment. Since these policy aims are inserted in the EU laws by the Council, this selection process would minimize Council–Commission conflict.

Second, at least with regard to the policy dimension, the empirical results have revealed that more intensive conflict in the Council increases Commission discretion under qualified majority voting *and* (weakly) decreases it under unanimity. Hence, we have unveiled an important mechanism through which qualified majority voting enhances the credibility of commitment to the relevant policy objectives. This decision rule facilitates reliance on the Commission when member states' views about the objectives of the measure at hand are likely to diverge and, consequently, national implementation lacks credibility. The case studies in Chapter 6 will shed further light on this issue.

Implementation paths and relative discretion

From the hypotheses tested in the previous two sections, we can derive additional expectations with regard to the importance of national administrations in the implementation of each law *relative* to that of the Commission. In more than 60 percent of the sample laws, the Council chooses a single implementation path, but, in the remaining acts, some executive powers are delegated to national administrations while others are conferred, in the same measure, upon the Commission. To ensure tractability, the model presented in Chapter 2 does not contemplate this possibility. Nevertheless, supplementary predictions can be generated through simple and logical deductions from the previous hypotheses.

The dependent variable is relative discretion. It results from subtracting the discretion of the Commission from the discretion of national administrations for each act.[14] An increase in relative discretion means that the Council is relying relatively more on national authorities than on the Commission for implementation.

If we combine Hypotheses 5.2 and 5.5, acts adopted by qualified majority voting should grant less discretion to national administrations and

---

[14] The mean of relative discretion is 11.82 percent, the standard deviation is 16.56 percent, the minimum is −21.43 percent while the maximum is 48.99 percent.

more discretionary authority to the Commission. Hence, relative discretion should clearly decrease. For policy complexity, the expectations are less straightforward. A highly technical issue area should increase national executive discretion, but the same act might also require generalist skills at the supranational level, hence increasing the Commission's discretion. The impact on the relative discretion is unclear. Equally, more conflict between the Commission and the pivotal government should diminish the room for maneuver of the supranational bureaucracy, according to Hypothesis 5.5. However, since we do not have expectations with regard to national discretion, we cannot formulate a precise prediction. Therefore, the new hypothesis is the following.

Hypothesis 5.7   *Relative discretion and decision rules*
Relative discretion decreases under qualified majority voting.

Table 5.11 shows the results from regressing relative discretion on *Decision rule* using *Range* and *Conflict* as control variables. They support this hypothesis. The discretion of national administrations diminishes by more than 5 percent, plus or minus 4.5 percent, relative to the discretion of the Commission when an act is adopted by qualified majority voting. Depending on the measure of *Conflict* used, the magnitude of the effect either decreases or increases. Nevertheless, this is not a trivial impact given that the mean of the relative discretion is about 12 percent.

Although we did not produce specific predictions with regard to policy complexity, the evidence strongly indicates that the same act rarely requires both specialized and technical knowledge and, at the same time, generalist skills at the supranational level. The presence of a programme or a committee increases national discretion relative to the Commission's discretion by a notable 10.7 percent, plus or minus 4.6 percent. It presumably leads to an increase in national discretion while keeping the Commission's discretion constant. The opposite occurs in the case of *Detailed rules*. A standard deviation increase in *Detailed rules* generates a decrease in the relative discretion by more than 3 percent, plus or minus 1.7 percent. I do not have an explanation for this outcome. EU legislators probably adopt distinct acts when the underlying informational requirements are different. Finally, although some of the other control variables show consistently high levels of statistical significance, I will not elaborate on these results because we do no have unambiguous expectations.

If we combine Hypotheses 5.3 and 5.6, an increase in conflict within the Council should lead to a decrease in relative discretion in the case of qualified majority voting. This is because the discretionary authority of national administrations should diminish whilst the discretion of the

Table 5.11 *The impact of decision rules on relative discretion.*

	Dependent variable: *Relative discretion*		
		Measure of Commission's preferences	
		Commission median	Commissioner
Constant	0.016	6.683	−4.658
	(0.00)	(1.17)	(−0.95)
Decision rule	−5.264	−11.953	−4.386
	(−2.27)[b]	(−3.18)[a]	(−1.72)[c]
Programme–committee	10.671	8.271	10.114
	(4.62)[a]	(3.54)[a]	(4.24)[a]
Detailed rules	−1.290	−1.291	−1.360
	(−3.58)[a]	(−3.48)[a]	(−3.66)[a]
Range integration	0.608	0.899	0.647
	(1.74)[c]	(2.47)[b]	(1.79)[c]
Range standardized policy	−19.091	−10.473	−12.675
	(−2.67)[a]	(−1.02)	(−1.49)
Range left–right	4.906	6.361	4.509
	(3.13)[a]	(3.37)[a]	(2.87)[a]
Conflict integration	–	−3.529	2.399
		(−1.85)[c]	(3.01)[a]
Conflict standardized policy	–	−42.617	13.705
		(−1.15)	(0.81)
Conflict left–right	–	−2.324	−0.805
		(−0.75)	(−0.58)
N	152	150	149
F	25.99[a]	18.92[a]	17.45[a]
Adjusted R^2	0.36	0.30	0.29

Note: Robust regressions, t-statistics in parentheses, one-tailed test; [a] $p \leq 0.01$; [b] $p \leq 0.05$; [c] $p \leq 0.1$. Observations with Cook distances greater than $4/n$ are omitted.

Commission should increase. The second new expectation is therefore the following.

Hypothesis 5.8   *Relative discretion and conflict within the Council*
In the case of qualified majority voting and a Commission more in favor of the underlying shift of the measure than the Council pivotal member, relative discretion decreases as conflict within the Council increases.

As with Hypothesis 5.3, I first test this expectation including all acts adopted by qualified majority voting or, in other words, I assume that the condition related to the Commission always holds. I then analyze the results briefly from a further restriction of the data set.

Table 5.12 *The impact of conflict within the Council on relative discretion in laws adopted by qualified majority voting.*

	Dependent variable: *Relative discretion*			
	Model 1	Model 2	Model 3	Model 4
Constant	−2.178	3.131	−14.035	−8.530
	(−0.65)	(1.02)	$(-2.91)^a$	(−1.47)
Range integration	0.300	–	–	−0.149
	(0.70)			(−0.33)
Range standardized policy	–	−28.328	–	−29.284
		$(-3.85)^a$		$(-3.17)^a$
Range left–right	–	–	6.065	6.797
			$(3.28)^a$	$(3.61)^a$
Programme–committee	19.131	21.614	21.153	21.081
	$(5.40)^a$	$(6.65)^a$	$(6.73)^a$	$(6.25)^a$
Detailed rules	−1.092	−0.570	−0.878	−0.592
	$(-2.83)^a$	(−1.65)	$(-2.36)^b$	(−1.63)
N	78	76	76	76
F	34.81^a	38.94^a	40.66^a	27.82^a
Adjusted R^2	0.44	0.50	0.54	0.54

Note: Robust regressions, *t*-statistics in parentheses, one-tailed test; ^{a} $p \leq 0.01$; ^{b} $p \leq 0.05$. OLS regression omits observations with Cook distances greater than $4/n$.

Table 5.12 shows the results from regressing relative discretion on conflict within the Council, controlling for policy complexity. They are somewhat contradictory. As expected, a standard deviation increase in *Range standardized policy* leads to a decrease by 3.6 percent in the relative discretion, plus or minus 2 percent. Greater policy divergence among governments raises the risk of incomplete compliance if EU policies are executed only by national authorities. In this circumstance, the Council tends to diminish reliance on national authorities and to confer more executive powers to the Commission to ensure a more correct implementation. The lower threshold to adopt a measure by majority voting facilitates this outcome. If I include in the regression only the cases satisfying the Commission-related condition, *Range standardized policy* is still significant when *Commission median* is used as measure of the Commission's preferences. It is not so when I use *Commissioner*. Table 5.12 also reveals that, contrary to our expectations, more conflict within the Council along the left–right dimension leads to an *increase* in the relative discretion. But this result is weakened in the smaller data set. *Range left–right* is not significant when *Commission median* is used to select cases, it is significant at the 5 percent level (rather than 1) when *Commissioner* is used.

In conclusion, our findings indicate that the Council relies relatively more on the Commission than on national administrations when acts are adopted by qualified majority voting. This outcome also occurs, in the case of majority voting, as Council conflict along the policy dimension increases. Hence, there seems to be supportive evidence of how majority voting operates as a commitment technology. It facilitates reliance on the Commission, especially as policy conflict within the Council intensifies. However, we should be cautious with regard to the latter result as I have found evidence that questions the impact of left–right conflict on relative discretion. A final observation is that the informational requirements seem to differ significantly among legislative acts.

The problem of commitment: an alternative explanation?

There is an important alternative explanation for the delegation of powers to the Commission. It was originally put forward by Gatsios and Seabright (1989: 49–50) and Majone (1992, 1994, 1996: 61–79, 2001). Delegation is motivated by the need for legislators to enhance the credibility of their substantive policy commitments. A mismatch between long- and short-term incentives, turnover in political personnel (i.e. the lack of political property rights) and *ex-post* incentives for unilateral noncompliance may substantially undermine policy objectives and the value of legislation. The severity of the commitment problem is particularly acute in policy areas that generate benefits for large, diffuse groups that face high costs of ongoing political participation whilst concentrate costs on small and well-resourced groups that are able to sustain participation. Legislators can protect the durability of the deal by reducing the scope of delegated authority or by delegating that authority to an independent agent (Horn, 1995:16–9; Majone, 1996: 71–8; Moravcsik, 1998; Pollack, 2003b: 29–31). In the most systematic attempt at applying agency theory to the EU, Pollack (2003b: 103–7) concludes that there is strong evidence in support of the commitment hypothesis with regard to both Treaty-based horizontal powers (i.e. cross-policy enforcement and agenda-setting) and issue-specific executive powers of the Commission. The focus of these works is predominantly on Treaty-based delegation where there is no variance in terms of decision rules. In this section, I disentangle the impact on discretion of the commitment problem from the impact of decision rules in issue-specific secondary legislation of the EU.

In a narrow sense, decision rules can be treated as indicators of underlying commitment problems. For instance, Moravcsik (1998: 73) sees both pooling, namely the adoption of qualified majority voting, and delegation to supranational institutions as strategies designed to precommit governments to a stream of future decisions. They are functionally equivalent. More specifically,

"unanimity, pooling and delegation [strike] different balances between the efficiency of common decisions and the desire of individual countries to reduce political risks by retaining a veto. As compared to unanimity voting, . . . QMV and *to an even greater extent* delegation reduce the bargaining power of potential opponents." (Moravcsik, 1998: 75, emphasis added)

In other words, as the severity of the commitment problem increases, one should see first pooling and then delegation of policy authority.[15] In addition to functional equivalence, empirical results so far also suggest complementarity. Qualified majority voting works as an indirect commitment technology by facilitating the adoption of legislation that increases the discretion of the Commission.

There are two problems with this interpretation. First, majority voting is extended to entire policy areas but, within them, each issue, or even each policy-specific act, has both informational and distributive components that vary in relevance and are difficult to separate (Epstein and O'Halloran, 1999b: 216–9).[16] Decision rules are imperfect indicators of the problem of commitment, which has only a distributive nature. Second, and more importantly, the strategic interactions that result from different decision rules and preference configurations suggest that rules gauge something that is qualitatively and theoretically different from the problem of commitment. A discretion-maximizing Commission should be systematically able to exploit conflict within the Council to garner more powers in qualified majority voting compared to unanimity, regardless of the legislators' need to precommit to specific policy objectives. Similarly, a Commission that wants to minimize national discretion should also be more likely to succeed in the case of majority voting when the Council is internally divided. Thus, decision rules capture both the severity of the commitment problem (imperfectly) and the strategic dynamic of EU decision-making.

However, this conclusion is also controversial. Powers are delegated to the Commission for credibility reasons under unanimity, as Majone (1996), Moravcsik (1998) and Pollack (2003b) clearly show in their analysis of Treaty provisions. Delegation and majority voting could be

---

[15] Moravcsik does not elaborate this point further. He later suggests that pooling is more likely where there is a need to facilitate future legislation, while delegation is more likely where the concern is to ensure implementation and compliance (Moravcsik, 1998: 76).

[16] For an analysis of these components, with regard to delegation to the Commission, see Franchino (2002).

functional substitutes. Hence, decision rules are not only an imperfect but also a partial indicator of the problem of commitment.

We have hence two *non-nested* theories of delegation, the first based on the problem of commitment and the second on decision rules. The first theory cannot be expressed as a restriction of the second one by setting the coefficient of *Decision rule* to zero because, following Moravcsik (1998) and considering the discretion outcomes that are more likely to result from qualified majority voting, this decision rule is, at least, a partial indicator of the problem of commitment facing legislators.[17] The partiality is due to the fact that (i) powers are also delegated by unanimous vote, (ii) the distributive component is only one of, at least, two components of a specific measure at hand and (iii) the strategic dynamic in majority voting produces outcomes that cannot be simply explained by the need to bolster credibility. Nevertheless, one model may *encompass* the other. In other words, one theory may not add significant additional information to the other.

In order to test this, I develop a variable *Commitment* that takes the value of one when the law at hand imposes concentrated costs in return for diffuse benefits. This operationalization is not as straightforward as it seems. According to Majone (1996: 77), social and environmental regulation has these features.[18] Competition, transport (state aid), commercial policy (anti-dumping and illicit practices)[19] and consumer protection should also fall within this category. On the other hand, policy areas were benefits are certainly concentrated are agriculture, fisheries, regional policy and some competition (exemptions), taxation and transport measures. Since most single-market legislation favors intra-EU export-oriented industries at the expense of import-competing ones, benefits (and costs) are concentrated, even though there are substantial gains for consumers too.[20] The same can be said for some liberalizing commercial policy measures

---

[17] Pollack (2003b: 103) makes a similar argument, though more implicitly. For an extensive test of non-nested theories of public debt see Franzese (2002: 126–95).

[18] In my classification they include safety and health, equal treatment, social policy, organization of working time and environment and transport regulation (which includes social and health and safety provisions).

[19] State aid and commercial policy measures should be interpreted as imposing costs on powerful groups because they limit the benefits they may gain at the expense of consumers and taxpayers. Note that these choices can all be criticized. Competition policy provides concentrated benefits to companies that are disadvantaged from restrictive practices and abuses of dominant positions. Even though an anti-dumping duty benefits extra-EU import-competing industries, it may also burden powerful importers. Companies competing with state aid beneficiaries are also burdened.

[20] The areas are payments for services, technical standards, movement of capital, the European Economic Interest Grouping, industrial and commercial property, credit and banking, insurance, public contracts, company law and transport (market conditions).

(common rules and customs). For the remaining policies, it is harder the assess the distributive impact though both costs and benefits appear (relatively) diffuse.[21]

Commitment has a mean of 0.215 and a standard deviation of 0.412. Interestingly, it is uncorrelated with *Decision rule* (the correlation coefficient is –0.068). I use Davidson and MacKinnon's (1981) J-tests to compare the two models $Y = f(X)$ and $Y = f(Z)$. The procedure consists of estimating the first (alternative) model $Y = f(X)$ and save the predictions $\hat{Y}$. The (null) second model is then estimated as $Y = f(Z, \hat{Y})$, adding the first model prediction. If the coefficient of $\hat{Y}$ is significant, $Y = f(X)$ rejects $Y = f(Z)$. The procedure continues by reversing the order of two models, treating $Y = f(X)$ as the null model. The aim of the exercise is to see whether a null model encompasses the alternative. A significant coefficient of $\hat{Y}$ means that the alternative model contains empirical information that is not entirely covered by the null model. The results are conclusive only if $Y = f(X)$ rejects $Y = f(Z)$ and is not rejected by $Y = f(Z)$, or vice versa. If the models reject each other, each adds significant additional information to the other. In the case of failure to reject in both directions, neither model is uniquely informative.

Table 5.13 illustrates the models that will be subject to the J-tests. They mirror the analysis carried out so far. There is no disagreement in the literature on the impact of policy complexity on delegation. Hence, this variable is included in all the models. In most cases, preferences (*Range* and *Conflict*) are also included as control variables because the *Commitment* hypothesis acknowledges their relevance, though not necessarily in the same direction. Pollack (2003b: 26–34) and Moravcsik (1998: 488) contend that intense conflict with the Commission should produce low discretion for this institution. However, for Majone (2001: 109–112), it is the presence of such conflict that ensures credibility. Moravcsik (1998: 75) and Pollack (2003b: 26–34) also suggest that, in the case of unanimity voting, the Commission's discretion should decrease with more intense conflict within the Council (i.e. greater *Range*).

Table 5.14 lists the t-statistics and significance levels of the coefficient of the alternative model predicted values. As explained above, it has been generated by adding these values to the regression of the null model. The results are quite interesting.

In the case of delegation to national administrations, the data show that the decision rule model clearly encompasses the commitment model

---

[21] They are adoption of ECU, qualifications and professions, establishment and services (movement of workers), international capital flows and taxation (VAT measures mostly). It is more arguable for movement of persons, social security and education where costs may be concentrated on national administrations.

Table 5.13 *The models for the J-tests.*

Model	Dependent variable	Control variables
(1) National Discretion: Information	*Discretion of national administrations*	*Programme–committee*
(2) National Discretion: Information and Range	*Discretion of national administrations*	*Programme–committee, Range*
(3) Commission Discretion: Information and Conflict I	*Discretion of Commission*	*Detailed rules, Conflict (Commission median)*
(4) Commission Discretion: Information and Conflict II	*Discretion of Commission*	*Detailed rules, Conflict (Commissioner)*
(5) Relative Discretion: Range and Information	*Relative discretion*	*Programme–committee, Detailed rules, Range*
(6) Relative Discretion: Range, Information and Conflict I	*Relative discretion*	*Programme–committee, Detailed rules, Range, Conflict (Commission median)*
(7) Relative Discretion: Range, Information and Conflict II	*Relative discretion*	*Programme–committee, Detailed rules, Range, Conflict (Commissioner)*

Note: All the three dimensions (*Integration, Standardized policy, Left–right*) are included in the model when *Range* and *Conflict* variables are used.

Table 5.14 *J-tests for the* Commitment *and* Decision Rule *models.*

Model	Null: *Commitment* Alternative: *Decision rule*		Null: *Decision rule* Alternative: *Commitment*	
	t-statistics of $\hat{Y}$	*p*-levels	*t*-statistics of $\hat{Y}$	*p*-levels
(1) National Discretion: Information	2.17	0.032	1.00	0.318
(2) National Discretion: Information and Range	3.24	0.002	1.13	0.260
(3) Commission Discretion: Information and Conflict I	2.08	0.039	1.43	0.156
(4) Commission Discretion: Information and Conflict II	2.19	0.030	1.92	0.057
(5) Relative Discretion: Information and Range	2.35	0.020	2.37	0.019
(6) Relative Discretion: Range, Information and Conflict I	3.03	0.003	2.10	0.038
(7) Relative Discretion: Range, Information and Conflict II	1.56	0.121	3.29	0.001

Note: Robust regressions. Initial $n = 158$, observations with Cook distances greater than $4/n$ are omitted.

(i.e. the null hypothesis is rejected), while the converse is rejected. In other words, the decision rule model adds significant new information to the commitment model, while the commitment model does *not* add much unique information to the decision rule model. With regard to delegation to the Commission, results vary depending on which measure of Commission preferences is used. The decision rule model incorporates the commitment model for any measure of preference. While the commitment model weakly encompasses the decision rule model only when I use *Commissioner*. However, these results need to be interpreted with caution. They are somewhat the opposite if I run Tobit regressions for the J-tests. The commitment model subsumes the decision rule model for both measures of preference, while it is encompassed by the decision rule model only when I use *Commissioner*.[22] Hence, it is likely that neither model strongly incorporates the other and that each is uniquely informative. The same is true for relative discretion, with the exception of the last test where the decision rule model does not add unique information to the commitment model.

These results allow us to clarify the added value of this work. The theory presented in these chapters appears to outperform the commitment model if we want to explain the scope of national executive discretion. A theory based on the interaction between preferences and decision rules yields more convincing results and encompasses one based solely on the problem of commitment. This does not mean that achieving credibility is irrelevant. It means that the decision rule variable captures this problem *and* additional significant strategic interactions. If our focus is on relative or Commission discretion, my theory adds, in most cases, significant new information to the already powerful theory based on the credibility of commitments. In secondary legislation, the preference-rule interactions produce delegation outcomes that cannot be explained only by the need to bolster credibility.

Cross-policy comparison with the United States

This section highlights similarities and systematic differences from the results of Epstein and O'Halloran (1999b). Although we should be cautious in comparing these results with those of the American system because of the different categorization of laws used, the pattern of

---

[22] When the null is *Commitment*, the t-statistics (*p*-level) for models 3 and 4 are 1.23 (0.221) and 2.47 (0.015) respectively. When the null is *Decision rule*, they are 3.53 (0.001) and 3.60 (0.000) respectively.

discretion of national administrations in Table 5.2 is similar for some social legislation, education, environment and consumer protection while areas, such as taxation, social security, trade and agriculture, differ markedly (though not with regard to Commission discretion) from Epstein and O'Halloran (1999b: 199–203).

Taxation and social security are key areas for ministers seeking re-election who use them to deliver benefits to highly mobilized constituents, mostly at the expense of taxpayers. This objective is attained by constraining the executive in the American political system, whilst, it is achieved by granting considerable discretion for the national authorities in the EU. Unanimity ensures the virtual exclusion of the Commission and constraints on national administrations that do not exceed what is strictly necessary. If anything, social security regulations appear relatively constraining, even though they require an ad hoc administrative commission and an advisory committee for the drafting of legislation and are adopted unanimously. There may be a need to ensure that these measures deliver benefits to the large and politically weak group of migrant workers across Europe and burden the effort-minimizing bureaucrats in the national social security departments.

Trade is notorious for trapping legislators into logrolls, producing outcomes which are detrimental to everyone. In the American political system, a way to solve this problem is delegation to the president who has an incentive to limit logrolling because of its national constituency (Epstein and O'Halloran, 1999b: 222–7). In the EU, majority voting provides a check over logrolling by facilitating the restriction of the national administrative powers and the reliance on a supranational bureaucracy which is more independent from short-term political pressures than Council ministers and has a European-wide constituency.

Many US agricultural bills feature a policy logroll that includes urban interests and, in exchange for greater executive discretion, presidential support (Epstein and O'Halloran, 1999b: 219–22). The European story is different. As aptly explained by Moravcsik (1998: 235–6), the overly constraining agricultural policy, designed mostly for the benefit of French farmers, was the result of De Gaulle's attempt to ensure implementation by a German government pressed by farmers strongly opposed to the policy. Majority voting ensured the durability of this outcome.

Conclusion

The quantitative evidence broadly corroborates our expectations. Results can be summarized under the four headings of the independent variables.

Decision rules (Hypotheses 5.1, 5.2, 5.4, 5.5 and 5.7). Delegation to national administrations is more likely in the case of unanimity, while the Commission is more likely to be delegated powers in the case of qualified majority voting. The discretion of national administrations increases when Council's decision rule is unanimity. In the case of majority voting, both the discretion of the Commission and the discretion of this institution *relative* to that of national authorities increase.

Policy complexity (Hypotheses 5.2 and 5.5). EU legislators tend to confer more discretion upon the administrators in the case of high policy complexity. The different institutional features and bureaucratic capabilities of the Commission and of national administrators guide this choice. National authorities have greater discretionary authority in issue areas that demand specialized and technical knowledge while the Commission has greater discretionary authority in issue areas that require general and managerial skills at the supranational level.

Preferences of the Commission (Hypotheses 5.3, 5.5 and 5.8). The preferences of the Commission come into the frame as a criteria to select the sample in Hypotheses 5.3 and 5.8. In these circumstances, it has simply helped to test the robustness of the results. In Hypothesis 5.5 instead, increased divergence between the position of the Commission and the pivotal government should decrease the discretion of the supranational bureaucracy. The evidence tends to corroborate this expectation in the case of the integration and the left–right dimension. However, results are not robust across the various regressions and the two measures of Commission preferences. The next chapter will explore this issue further.

Conflict within the Council (Hypotheses 5.3, 5.6 and 5.8). Conflict within the Council is another strong determinant of the choices of delegation in laws adopted by qualified majority voting. However, we have found confirmatory results only when conflict is measured along the policy dimension (see Appendix 5.1 for additional robustness tests). Both the discretion of the Commission and the discretion of this institution *relative* to that of national authorities increase with the severity of conflict. The discretion of national administrations decreases as conflict intensifies. Results are however contradictory when preferences are measured along the left–right dimension. Increased conflict leads to *greater* national and relative discretion. Conflict on the integration dimension does not yield noteworthy results. The case studies of the next chapter will pay particular attention to this variable.

Finally, more intense conflict in the Council increases Commission discretion under qualified majority voting *and* (weakly) decreases it under unanimity. We have unveiled the mechanism through which qualified majority voting enhances policy commitment, though limited to the policy dimension. This decision rule ensures credible implementation by facilitating increases in the Commission's discretion as conflict within the Council intensifies, making national implementation hardly credible.

The theory presented here adds significant new information to a theory of delegation based solely on the problem of commitment. Decision rules already capture some elements of this problem as argued by Moravcsik (1998). With regard to the scope of national executive discretion, my theory encompasses the commitment hypothesis, meaning that it includes information on both the credibility problem and the preference-rule interactions on which my theory is based. With regard to relative and Commission discretion, the theory adds unique new information to the already powerful credibility hypothesis.

The next chapter will employ four case studies to investigate some of these results further.

Appendix 5.1 Tests with alternative measures of policy preferences

The appendix uses alternative measures of policy preferences to assess the robustness of the main results. Recall from Appendix 4.2 that one alternative measure aggregates the laws into fewer policy categories, while the second one aggregates them into more categories. Both have strengths and weaknesses. In the latter case, a higher level of aggregation may overlook differences in policy positions across laws, while positions may be less precisely estimated at a lower level of aggregation because election manifestos do not refer to each policy category.

Discretion of national administrations

Table 5.A1 lists the results from regressing the discretion of national administrations on policy complexity, decision rules and conflict within the Council. It is the analog of the summary regression in Table 5.6. The substantive and statistical significance of *Programme–committee* and *Decision rule* is quite similar. National discretion increases by 6.2 percent if there is a committee or a programme and by 3.6 percent in the case of unanimity, plus or minus about 3.4 percent both. Only *Standardized policy range (1)*, the measure using a higher level of aggregation, is significant.

Table 5.A1 *The impact of decision rules, policy complexity and conflict in the Council on the discretion of national administrations. Alternative measures of policy preferences.*

| | Dependent variable: Discretion of national administrations | | | |
| | Robust OLS estimates | | Tobit estimates | |
	Model 1	Model 2	Model 1	Model 2
Constant	20.517	16.160	19.900	15.008
	$(8.65)^a$	$(6.86)^a$	$(7.14)^a$	$(5.79)^a$
Programme–committee	6.228	7.051	7.157	7.964
	$(3.53)^a$	$(4.05)^a$	$(3.54)^a$	$(3.87)^a$
Decision rule	−3.652	−5.216	−4.325	−4.532
	$(-2.12)^b$	$(-3.03)^a$	$(-2.16)^b$	$(-2.19)^b$
Standardized policy range (1)	−35.391	–	−33.087	–
	$(-4.93)^a$		$(-2.91)^a$	
Standardized policy range (2)	–	−5.923	–	−4.815
		(−1.12)		(−0.75)
N	153	149	158	158
F	23.22^a	12.88^a	–	–
χ^2	–	–	28.93^a	21.18^a
Adjusted or pseudo R^2	0.18	0.16	0.03	0.02

Note: t-statistics in parentheses, one tailed test; ^{a} $p \leq 0.01$; ^{b} $p \leq 0.05$. OLS regression omits observations with Cook distances greater than $4/n$.

Its substantive impact is stronger than in Table 5.6. The discretionary authority of national administrations diminishes by 3.2 percent, plus or minus 1.3 percent, as a result of standard deviation increase in *Standardized policy range (1)*.

Discretion of the European Commission

The results from testing Hypothesis 5.5 are the same as those shown in Table 5.9. The two alternative measures of *Conflict standardized policy* do not reach significance while the coefficients and t-statistics for *Detailed rules* and *Decision rule* are very similar. Table 5.A2 illustrates the results from regressing the Commission's discretion on policy complexity and conflict within the Council, including only qualified majority laws (Hypothesis 5.6). As far as policy complexity is concerned, results are similar to those shown in Table 5.10. *Standardized policy range (1)* is

Table 5.A2 *The effect of conflict within the Council on the discretion of the European Commission in qualified majority voting laws. Alternative measures of policy preferences.*

| | Dependent variable: *Discretion of the Commission* | | | |
| | Robust OLS estimates | | Tobit estimates | |
	Model 1	Model 2	Model 1	Model 2
Constant	1.049	3.107	−2.034	0.534
	(0.77)	(2.61)[b]	(−0.77)	(0.20)
Detailed rules	1.111	1.476	1.049	1.368
	(4.81)[a]	(8.24)[a]	(2.86)[a]	(4.35)[a]
Range standardized policy (1)	13.983	–	20.596	–
	(1.66)[c]		(1.49)	
Range standardized policy (2)	–	1.716	–	2.313
		(0.53)		(0.32)
N	74	75	80	80
F	30.22[a]	33.92[a]	–	–
χ^2	–	–	20.02[a]	17.93[a]
Adjusted or pseudo R^2	0.39	0.31	0.05	0.04

Note: Initial $n = 80$, observations with Cook distances greater than $4/n$ are subsequently omitted; 31 left-censored observations in the Tobit regression; t-statistics in parentheses, one-tailed test; [a] $p \leq 0.01$; [b] $p \leq 0.05$; [c] $p \leq 0.1$.

weakly significant. A standard deviation increase in *Standardized policy range (1)* leads an increase of 1.3 percent in the Commission's discretion. However, the Tobit estimate does not confirm this result.

Relative discretion

Table 5.A3 tests Hypothesis 5.8. It shows the results from regressing relative discretion on conflict within the Council for qualified majority laws and controlling for policy complexity. Results are similar to those in Table 5.12, but only for the first alternative measure of conflict.

A standard deviation increase in *Range standardized policy (1)* leads to a 4 percent decrease in relative discretion, plus or minus 3 percent. Moreover, the significance of *Programme–committee* and *Detailed rules* reinforces the conclusion that the same act rarely requires both specialized and technical knowledge and, at the same time, generalist skills at the supranational level.

Table 5.A3 *The impact of conflict within the Council on relative discretion in qualified majority voting laws. Alternative measures of policy preferences.*

	Dependent variable: *Relative discretion*	
	Model 1	Model 2
Constant	8.992	3.250
	(2.08)[c]	(0.81)
Range standardized policy (1)	−44.305	−
	(−2.75)[a]	
Range standardized policy (2)	−	−11.768
		(−1.42)
Programme–committee	16.900	19.077
	(4.89)[a]	(5.68)[a]
Detailed rules	−0.680	−1.125
	(−1.72)[c]	(−2.90)[a]
N	78	77
F	38.08[a]	35.89[a]
Adjusted R^2	0.44	0.44

Note: Robust regressions, t-statistics in parentheses, one-tailed test; [a] $p \leq 0.01$; [b] $p \leq 0.05$; [c] $p \leq 0.1$. OLS regression omits observations with Cook distances greater than $4/n$.

In conclusion, the findings are corroborated, especially with regard to national and relative discretion, when we use a policy preference variable of a higher level of aggregation than the one used in this chapter. The results using a lower level of aggregation do not reach the nominal level of significance, even though the signs of all the coefficients are as predicted.

6   Delegation in the European Union:
case studies

The analysis of the previous chapter has mostly confirmed the key arguments advanced by this book. Decision rules, policy complexity, conflict between the Commission and the pivotal government, and within
the Council are systematically related to the choices of delegation and
discretion taken by EU legislators. However, estimates and inferences
of quantitative models are only as good as our conceptualization, measurement, data sources and statistical estimation techniques. However
careful we could be, each of these steps could be fraught with problems
and implicit assumptions, and establishing association among variables
is not quite the same as establishing causality. Does majority voting facilitate delegation to and greater discretion of the Commission? Does it
lead to more constrained national implementation? Does intense conflict
within the Council, mediating with majority voting, also generate these
outcomes? Do the bureaucratic capabilities of the Commission and of
national administrators guide these decisions? Does the Council confer
less authority to a Commission with divergent preferences?

This chapter seeks to address these questions. It relies on case-oriented
qualitative evidence to unveil causal mechanisms and to provide analytical depth to the quantitative analysis of Chapter 5. The chapter includes
a detailed examination of the processes of delegation over a period of
time across four policy areas: public procurement, fisheries, internal
market and taxation. Respectively, the cases cover in detail the legislation
regulating the procedures for the award of public contracts, the measures
for the management and conservation of fisheries resources, the acts liberalizing and regulating the market for telecommunication services and
a directive on the taxation of savings income.

In the next section, I apply the model's expectations to these policy
areas and specify the research design and the case selection criteria to
test them empirically. I then explain the operationalization and measurement of the dependent and independent variables and briefly discuss the
added value of the case study method to my inquiry. The subsequent
four sections trace delegation, discretion and causal mechanisms across

the policy areas. I conclude illustrating how these findings strengthen the results reported in Chapter 5.

Research design, measurement and the case study method

Hypotheses and case selection

Of the four key features that are relevant to our study, I will concentrate the analysis predominantly on two: decision rules and conflict within the Council. I will also assess, though, the impact of the other two important factors: preferences of the Commission and policy complexity.

According to Gerring (2004: 342), a case study is "an intensive study of a single unit for the purpose of understanding a larger class of (similar) units." A unit for my purposes is a policy comprising a set of laws (cases) which have been adopted across a specific time period. For instance, the cases of the public procurement study comprise all the laws regulating the procedures for the award of public contracts adopted between 1971 and 2000. Hence, the empirical evidence I rely on varies both spatially (i.e. I examine the laws adopted at a specific time) and temporally (i.e. I examine how laws are amended over time). This research design allows for moderately high N in three case studies, while, for taxation policy, $N = 2$ as I investigate only one legislative proposal diachronically.

Central to my line of inquiry is understanding how these laws have been designed and amended. Measures within each policy share similar legal, political and public policy attributes which therefore are eliminated as potentially confounding factors to explain delegation and discretion. This allows me to concentrate the attention on conflict within the Council (and the related costs of national implementation) and decision rules to ascertain their impact on the dependent variables.[1]

Each policy area has been selected for the purpose of testing some expectations of the model. They are archetypal examples of the situations EU legislators encounter when they decide to delegate executive powers. Table 6.1 lists the case studies, the independent variables and summarizes the expectations from Hypotheses 5.1–5.8. I have not produced predictions with regard to information intensity as the policies appear to be similarly complex but, as we shall see, the requirements for supranational managerial skills are clearly higher in the fisheries policy.

---

[1] At least within each policy, this scheme is akin to the "most-similar-systems" comparative case study design (see Przeworski and Teune, 1970; Lijphart, 1975; Meckstroth, 1975).

Table 6.1 *Case studies and hypotheses.*

| Policy area | Decision rules | Independent variables | | Expectations from Hypotheses 5.1–5.8 |
		Severity of conflict within the Council	Preferences of the Commission	
Public procurement: procedures 1971–2000	1971–1986 Unanimity since 1987 QMV	High	Liberal	Increasing restriction of national executive discretion and reliance on the Commission but only after shift to QMV
Fisheries: management and conservation of resources 1983–2002	QMV	High	Conservationist	Increasing restriction of national executive discretion and reliance on the Commission
Internal market: telecommunications 1990–2002	QMV	Moderate to low	Liberal	Moderate restriction of national executive discretion and reliance on the Commission. No changes over time
Taxation: non-residents' savings income 1998–2003	Unanimity	High	Preserving national fiscal revenues, eliminating market distortions	Moderate to low restriction of national executive discretion and reliance on the Commission.

Public procurement has always been an area fraught with conflict and imperfect implementation which has experienced a change in decision rules. It is an ideal quasi-experiment for analyzing delegation and discretion before and after the rule change which, here, represents the "experimental stimulus." Fisheries and telecommunications policies have instead operated under the same majority voting procedure but reveal radically different intensity of conflict and national implementation costs. We should expect different dynamics of delegation. Member states have also been deeply divided on the taxation of savings income, but the requirement of unanimous voting leads to different expectations.

Measurement of discretion, decision rules and preferences

Each case study is divided into two main sections. First, I analyze the dependent variables, that is, the changes in executive discretion of national authorities and of the Commission over a period of time in the relevant policy area. Each case study starts with the description of the baseline measures, namely the first laws (cases) adopted on the subject, and then it provides a provision-by-provision analysis of how these measures have been amended and complemented over the years. The exception is taxation policy where the comparison is between the Commission's initial proposal, which reflected the initial views of the majority of member states, and the final directive.

I examine whether provisions for national execution have been relaxed or tightened, whether the Commission has been conferred executive powers, and whether these powers have been further expanded or restricted. This analysis consists mostly of comparing legal texts and, generally, judging whether powers have been delegated or requirements tightened is not particularly difficult. Nevertheless, to support my analysis, I will also use the operationalization of discretion used in Chapter 5, relevant documents, academic articles and personal communications with policy experts. Where a policy has expanded considerably, I also provide data on changes in the word length of the measures. According to Huber and Shipan (2002: 77), this is an appropriate proxy for the extent to which the policy constrains (in these cases, national) implementation (see Chapter 7 for more details and an application to the European Parliament).

The second section analyzes the independent variables to evaluate how they covary with the developments in national and Commission discretion. Since each case study focuses on changes in discretion across time within the same policy area, complexity is controlled for and, hence, disregarded in the analysis. Chapter 5 has already provided systematic evidence of how information intensity affects delegation. I will nevertheless make a few observations on complexity and patterns of cross-policy delegation in the concluding section of the chapter.

Determining the decision rules used for the adoption of each measure is straightforward, evaluating preferences is more complicated. The policy positions of the Commission can be derived from its actions (i.e. recommendations, decisions and directives), summaries of debates, reports, academic articles and relevant documentary evidence. I will assess whether the impact of these preferences on delegation outcomes corroborates Hypotheses 5.3, 5.5 and 5.8 only in the last section of the chapter because the explanatory potential of this variable is more revealing through a cross-policy analysis.

I disregard the European Parliament as Chapter 7 provides a comprehensive qualitative and quantitative analysis of its preferences. For the member states, I use a broad set of indicators. Where relevant and available, I use introductory recitals included in the laws, summaries of Council debates and activities, conclusions of Council meetings, reports, internal Council documents and academic articles to assess the severity of conflict across governments. When the secrecy surrounding the Council's internal workings creates insurmountable obstacles, conflict can also be gauged using broader measures, such as delays and the quality of national transposition of directives, the number and severity of infringements and other policy-specific indicators of effective implementation (e.g. overfishing in fisheries policy, intra-EU trade in public procurement and price reductions in telecommunications services).

The rationale for choosing these broader factors relies on the fact that, where it is hard to assess preferences at the Council negotiating table, conflict may also emerge down the line in the process of implementation. Note that, in the formal model of Chapter 2, the governments' utility function in the case of national implementation (and, hence, the relative value of the national and supranational paths) comprises the actions taken by each national administration in the *execution* of a policy. Once measures with a baseline level of national and Commission discretion have been adopted, conflict could emerge at the implementation stage and the distributional costs of national execution could be higher than initially anticipated by member states. This should lead to changes in discretion under the conditions and in the direction hypothesized by the model.

The use of these indicators of conflict is based on the premise that member states may not be entirely sure about the severity of national implementation bias at the stage of adoption of a law. This could be due to lack of information or strategic preference revelation at the negotiating table. Indicators of incorrect implementation should then reveal a more accurate level of conflict. Note moreover that, even if a member state has been sincere or simply unable to anticipate problems of national compliance, the expectations of the models still hold because its results are driven by the distributive losses originating from national implementation.

There is however an important caveat to this line of reasoning. Applying to the EU an important strand of the international relations literature that studies compliance with international law (e.g. Chayes and Chayes, 1993, 1995; Mitchell, 1994), Tallberg (2002b) argues that incorrect national implementation can result from rule ambiguity or limited administrative capacity rather than intentional noncompliance. It is then necessary in the analysis below to disentangle the two reasons for noncompliance since only the latter reason should produce changes in statutory control.[2]

The case study method

I have selected policy areas that represent the typical scenarios surrounding the processes of delegation that I aim to explain in this book. In Lijphart's (1971) words, mine are theory-confirming or theory-disconfirming case studies which, in my view, are necessary to put my results on firmer foundations, given the paucity of theoretical development in this field.

Case studies provide a greater depth of analysis, cases (laws) are more easily comparable and causal mechanisms can be more clearly elucidated through process tracing and pattern matching. The method certainly suffers from the inability to support broad and well-bounded propositions. A single policy cannot be considered representative of all EU policies and causal effects and probabilistic causal relations cannot be estimated (George and Bennett, 2004; Gerring, 2004).[3] However, the use of four case studies allows me to produce some cross-policy analysis which addresses, marginally, the first two problematic features. Moreover, the study of delegation in the EU is at such an early stage that it would be unwise to restrict our investigation to a quantitative analysis only. The core added value of the case study method is its potential to complement

---

[2] The literature on EU compliance is extensive, a nonexhaustive list includes, Krislov, Ehlerman and Weiler (1986), Siedentopf and Ziller (1988), Mendrinou (1996), Haas (1998), Börzel (2000, 2001) and Mbaye (2001).

[3] Well-known analyses of the case study method are by Ragin (1987), Ragin and Becker (1992), and McKeown (1999). King, Keohane and Verba (1994), Dion (1998) and Morton (1999) present more critical accounts. See Pahre (2005) for a discussion on the benefits of combining case studies and formal theory, with special reference to the EU literature.

and "triangulate" the evidence produced in Chapter 5, bring to light causal mechanisms and deal with issues which have produced less than satisfactory results.

Public procurement: procedures

The case study in brief

The first two measures regulating the procedures for the award of public contracts have been adopted in 1971 and 1977 under unanimity voting. They were moderately constraining for national administrations and did not confer specific policy powers to the Commission. These directives were transposed late and, in some cases, incorrectly. Application by national authorities was patchy at best, indicating considerable attrition against the policy across member states and severe distributive costs for more law-abiding states. In a 1985 review, the Commission concluded that implementation was "minimal" (Commission of the EC, 1985a: 23). Despite this dismal state of affairs, no new measure has been adopted in the entire period that required unanimous voting. With the entry into force of the Single European Act (SEA) in July 1987, new acts needed only qualified majority voting. As expected, in the succeeding six years, the combination of a lower threshold for decision-making and intense distributive losses from national implementation led to the adoption of nine new directives that systematically tightened the room for maneuver for national authorities and moderately expanded the executive role of the Commission. By the early 1990s, an entirely new legislative framework for EU public procurement law was in place. And, by the second half of the 1990s, there were clear signs that the market for public procurement was opening to intra-EU competition (although problems of national implementation did not disappear). As expected, the measures of this later period simply extended and consolidated the existing regulatory framework.

Delegation and discretion in public procurement policy

The market for public procurement accounts for a significant share of the EU's gross domestic product. Depending on the methodology used, estimates vary between 9 and 16 percent of the EU's GDP, amounting to 1500 billion euro in 2002 (OECD, 2001; Commission of the EC, 2004). The importance of this market and the consequences for the functioning of the internal market was recognized in the very early days of establishment of the then European Economic Community. The 1962 *General*

Programmes of the Abolition of Restrictions on Freedom of Establishment and to Provide Services referred to the need to adopt measures in this sector. However, it took more than six years of negotiations before the first important Directive 71/305 on the procedures for the award of public works contracts was finally adopted in July 1971. The extension to public supply contracts of Directive 77/62 took more than five years of negotiation. Until the late 1980s, these were the only two main measures on public procurement.[4]

The baseline measures. These directives were structured on three pillars. First, a set of provisions established the scope of the measures and listed the contracts that were excluded from their reach. They specified the types and the threshold values of contracts to which the directives applied. For instance, Directive 77/62 applied to contracts involving the purchase of products of an estimated pre-tax value of not less then ECU 200,000. However, contracts awarded by public utilities operating in the water, energy, transport and telecommunication sectors were excluded. Second, other provisions specified the award procedures that contracting authorities could choose. The choice was between an open procedure, where all interested suppliers could submit tenders, and a restricted procedure, where only contractors invited by the national authorities could submit tenders. Authorities could opt out from this choice for particular types of contracts (e.g. on research and development). Finally, the last pillar consisted of a set of common rules with regard to technical specifications and advertising of tenders, participation and selection of companies and award of contracts. For instance, notices of tender had to be made public through the *Official Journal of the European Communities*. Groups of companies could submit a tender without being required to assume a specific legal form.

These two directives were only moderately constraining for national administrations. Their executive discretion averaged almost 19 percent, higher than the mean of 16 percent of the sample selected in Chapter 3. Moreover, no substantive policy-specific powers were delegated to the Commission.

The post-SEA measures. We have to wait until the end of the 1980s for the first important changes to these laws. These were part

---

[4] Minor measures were Directive 72/277 stipulating the format of the notices to be published in the *Official Journal*, Directive 78/669 defining the European Unit of Account and Directive 80/767 adapting the legislation to the Agreement of the GATT Tokyo Round.

of the major drive of policy reform set in motion by the Commission's renowned white paper on *Completing the Internal Market* (Commission of the EC, 1985a). Directives 88/295 and 89/440 consisted of a comprehensive tightening of the provisions. All three main pillars were modified. First, the scope was more precisely defined. Public supply contracts now included lease, rental and hire purchase of products. Subsidized works and public works concessions were included in the scope of Directive 71/305 and a more exhaustive list of entities subject to EU public procurement law was introduced. Exemptions were clarified to avoid divergent interpretations. Second, the open procedure was made the rule for the award of supply contracts, while authorities had to justify in a written report the use of the restricted and negotiated[5] procedures. The rules for choosing the negotiated procedure, considered exceptional, were tightened. For instance, the circumstances invoked to justify extreme urgency, and hence to use this procedure, could not be attributable to the authorities and the length of recurrent supply contracts or contracts repeating similar works, awarded with this procedure, could not exceed three years. Third, the common rules were also tightened. In order to improve transparency, national authorities had to publicize in advance their yearly purchasing programmes exceeding 750,000 ECU and forthcoming public works projects. All relevant details of how public works contracts had been awarded should be also published, including details on subcontracting and conditions of employment. In public works, authorities were required to inform rejected candidates of the reasons for rejection and to draw up a report on the conduct of the proceedings. In order to improve participation, the time limits for the receipt of applications and tenders were extended and a minimum number of candidates invited to tender for public works was established. Rules for excluding abnormally low tenders for public works contracts were tightened. Finally, the Commission was given the power to amend, following the advisory procedure, the list of entities subject to Directive 71/305. This power was extended by Directive 93/4 to the rules on notices and statistical reports and to the nomenclature of economic activities.

An important supporting measure was Directive 89/665. It was designed to ensure compliance and effective application of the existing measures by providing firms with the same level of legal safeguards in respect of remedies across the EU. Three features needed emphasis. First, in terms of access, the directive sought to ensure that procedures

---

[5] Defined as procedures whereby authorities consult suppliers of their choice and negotiate the terms of contract with one or several of them (article 2 of Directive 88/295).

to review the decisions taken by national authorities were available to any potentially injured person having an interest in obtaining a given public contract. Second, in terms of speed and effectiveness, the powers of reviewing bodies had to include the possibility of taking interim measures, such as suspending the award procedure, setting aside of unlawful decisions and compensating injured parties. Lastly, the Commission could request, prior to awarding the contract, to correct clear and manifest infringements within 21 days. Noncompliance would lead to initiation of the Treaty infringement procedure and interim measures of the European Court of Justice (ECJ).

Extension and consolidation. The legislative framework of EU public procurement law was almost complete by the early 1990s. The subsequent measures were of three types. First, two new directives extended EU public procurement law to public service contracts (Directive 92/50) and utilities (Directive 90/531). Although there are some sector-specific differences, these measures are organized in the established three-pillared structure consisting of scope, choice of award procedure and common rules. The powers of national authorities and of the Commission do not differ substantially, with minor exceptions. For instance, the Commission can grant some activities exemption from the obligations of Directive 90/531. Second, an extended review directive was adopted in the case of utilities (Directive 92/13). In addition to provisions similar to those of Directive 89/665, this measure provides for the possibility of attestation by independent parties of compliance with EU law and establishes a conciliation procedure to settle disputes amicably. Third, two rounds of consolidation have taken place. The first one ended in June 1993 when three directives consolidated existing rules without introducing major changes.[6] At the time of writing the second round has not yet finished. According to the Commission, the aim of these proposals is to simplify existing measures and to introduce a few substantive changes without however, modifying the basic structure of this policy.[7]

In conclusion, the moderately constraining provisions of the 1970s have been systematically tightened and their scope expanded in the period from

---

[6] Directive 93/37 on public works contracts included minor changes to the advertisement rules, Directive 93/36 on public supply contracts aligned more closely the provisions in this sector to those of the other directives, while Directive 93/38 on utilities better clarified the scope of the measure. These laws were amended by Directives 97/52 and 98/4 following the conclusion of the Agreement of the GATT Uruguay Round.

[7] Proposal COD/2000/115 merges into a single text the measures on public works, service and supply contracts, introduces electronic purchasing mechanisms, some changes to the use of the negotiated procedure, award and selection criteria and thresholds. Proposal COD/2000/117 on utilities has similar objectives.

the late 1980s to early 1990s. The executive powers of the Commission were also moderately strengthened. A period of consolidation, simplification and minor changes then followed.

Decision rules, conflict and implementation of public procurement policy

The effect of decision rules. Do changes in decision rules and the behavior of key actors explain these patterns of delegation? The earlier measures were adopted under article 94 (ex art. 100) of the Treaty which required unanimity. All the subsequent measures that tightened control on national administrations or conferred powers to the Commission have been adopted after the entry into force of the SEA on 1 July 1987. This Treaty introduced article 95 (ex art. 100a) which required only qualified majority voting, in cooperation with the Parliament, for the adoption of new laws in this policy area. There is hence relatively strong evidence in support of the hypotheses. Majority voting facilitated the constraining of national authorities and reliance on the Commission.

Transposition and implementation. However, had the initial measures been implemented in time, correctly and the objectives achieved, we might have not seen major reforms. Instead, the policy was characterized by serious problems of implementation revealing conflict and substantial distributive losses from national execution. No member state transposed Directive 71/305 before the deadline of July 1972. Six months after this date, only Germany, Ireland and Britain had adopted the first measures of transposition, but this was only the beginning of the implementation process. For instance, Germany adopted the first regulation only three months after the deadline but it took almost three more years for the last ministerial circular to complete the transposition. In Ireland, the last *Circular Letter* transposing the directive was adopted in 1976.[8] And these were the best performers. Belgium adopted the first measure four years after the deadline.[9]

The transposition of Directive 77/62 did not fare particularly better, despite the fact that it was only an extension to supply contracts of the main principles of Directive 71/305. Only five member states transposed

---

[8] These measures are in Germany: *Anordnung* vom 30/10/1972 (*Bundesministeriums für Wirtschaft und Finanzen*), *Bekanntmachung* vom 11/08/1975 (*Bundesanzeiger Bundesministeriums für Wirtschaft* Nr. 152 vom 20/08/1975), in Ireland: The Circular Letter No. 13 of 1976 (Department of Local Government).
[9] *Loi du 14/07/1976 relative aux marchés publics de travaux, de fournitures et de services.*

the provisions before the deadline. Italy did it almost three years later, after an ECJ judgment of failure to fulfill its obligations.[10]

More importantly, correct transposition was problematic and implementation was patchy at best. Although Italy adopted the first measures implementing the directive relatively early, with a law of February 1973,[11] the content of these provisions differed substantially from the obligations arising from the directive. Procedures, other than by restricted invitation to tender, were excluded from the scope of the law and the "anonymous enveloped" procedure, a peculiarity of the Italian public procurement law, had not been abolished. There were no requirements to advertise notices in the *Official Journal of the Communities*, to set time limits, to comply with tender forms and to exclude certain companies from participation. Given the relative clarity of the provisions of Directive 71/305, it is very hard to sustain that rule ambiguity played any role in transposing them incorrectly. It was a deliberate attempt to deviate from the principles of the directive.

Italy was then subject to an infringement proceeding under article 226 (ex art. 169) and, although it did not contest these failures and sent the Commission an amending draft, a new law was adopted only in August 1977 after an ECJ judgment of noncompliance.[12] This saga continued when Italy amended the law in 1981 and was again taken to court for infringing many provisions of Directive 71/305. The ECJ ruled in favor of the Commission on most counts.[13]

As far as implementation is concerned, national administrations evaded the obligations of the directives by using narrow definitions of "contracting authorities"[14] and "public procurement contracts,"[15] interpreting the rules for use of the negotiated procedure broadly[16] and adding criteria that were incompatible with the directives.[17] In its 1985 white paper, the Commission stated that the application of the directives was "minimal"

---

[10] Case 133/80. Commission of the European Communities v Italian Republic. *European Court reports 1981*, p. 457.
[11] *Legge 2 Febbraio 1973 Procedure di aggiudicazione degli appalti di lavori pubblici.*
[12] Case 10/76. Commission of the European Communities v Italian Republic. *European Court reports 1976*, p. 1359.
[13] Case 274/83. Commission of the European Communities v Italian Republic. *European Court reports 1985*, p. 1077.
[14] Case 31/87 Gebroeders Beentjes BV v State of the Netherlands. *European Court reports 1988*, p. 4635.
[15] Case 3/88 Commission of the European Communities v Italian Republic. *European Court reports 1989*, p. 4035.
[16] Case 199/85. Commission of the European Communities v Italian Republic. *European Court reports 1987*, p. 1039.
[17] Case 76/81. Transporoute v Ministère des travaux publics. *European Court reports 1982*, p. 417; Case 243/89 Commission of the European Communities v Kingdom of Denmark. *European Court reports 1993*, p. 3353; Case 360/89 Commission of the

and only 25 percent of the public expenditure in the areas covered by the laws was advertised, let alone open to competition (Commission of the EC, 1985a: 23). In 1987, the total number of procurement notices was 12,000 and the share of imports for public contracts was only 5.4 percent (Commission of the EC, 1996a: 5).

It was clear that some governments and authorities were less than keen to implement the directives faithfully, at the expense of more law-abiding states. It should not come as a surprise that, as expected, intensive distributive losses from national implementation, combined with a lower threshold for decision-making, led, between 1989 and 1993, to the adoption of nine new directives designed to extend the scope of the measures, narrow the executive discretion of national authorities and to strengthen the Commission. These measures covered exactly those provisions (e.g. scope, use of procedures, rules and criteria) which were systematically violated by national authorities.

Towards an open market. A period of consolidation followed. In an EU of now fifteen member states, problems of correct transposition did not dissipate. On June 1996, national implementing measures had not yet been communicated, or only partially communicated, to the Commission in 15 percent of the cases. Infringement proceedings for noncompliance of at least one measure were under way against nine governments (Commission of the EC, 1996a: 51). However, other indicators were more promising. In the 1987–95 period, the total number of procurement notices rose from 12,000 to 95,000. In 1995–2002, the number of invitations to tender rose from 54,731 to 106,346 and the number of contract award notices from 28,551 to 58,513. There is a clear trend towards greater transparency in EU procurement markets, even considering the expansion of the policy into new areas and the diminishing real value of the thresholds. The share of public contracts that includes some cross-border activity has increased from 2 to 10 percent and about half of the firms of the EU procurement market now carry out some cross-border activity. Importantly, foreign firms bidding directly or through subsidiaries do not have lower rates of success and the purchases where EU procurement law does not apply are about 40 percent dearer. The share of imports for public contracts has increased from 5.4 to 10 percent in the 1987–95 period and intra-EU trade on typical public procurement goods has increased faster than extra-EU trade. Intra-EU export and

European Communities v Italian Republic. *European Court reports 1992*, p. 3401. A detailed analysis of irregularities in tender notices published between 1990 and 1993 has been produced by the Euro Info Centre Aarhus County (1996).

import prices of these goods have systematically converged in the 1988–2002 period (Commission of the EC, 1996a, 2004). These elements indicate that the reforms undertaken in the 1989–93 period are having a considerable impact in the EU procurement market. This is probably the reason why the new proposals introduced in 2000 mostly simplified and consolidated the existing measures.[18]

Fisheries policy: management and conservation of resources

The case study in brief

Three baseline regulations adopted, by majority voting, between 1980 and 1983 set the ground for this policy area. They provided for a system of yearly catch quotas, and for conservation and supervisory measures. The first two acts were relatively constraining for national authorities while the supervisory regulation allowed greater room for maneuver. The Commission enjoyed a nontrivial executive role, mostly related to the management of quotas. The policy operated smoothly in the early 1980s. Hence, although the regulations were frequently amended, no clear trend in term of patterns of delegation and discretion emerged. From the second half of the 1980s, the cumulative effects of the Council's methodical increase of quotas and of systematic misapplication by national authorities led to widespread overfishing and a severe conservation failure. As the extensive distributive losses from national implementation became clear, most of the measures adopted in the 1990s tightened, as expected, national discretion and reinforced the role of the Commission. There is now some evidence that these reforms are starting to work and, therefore, no major policy review is planned.

Delegation and discretion in the common fisheries policy

Fisheries and aquaculture account for approximately 1 percent of the EU gross domestic product and they are an important source of employment in regions, such as Brittany, Galicia and Scotland, with relatively few job opportunities.[19] The EU produces about eight million tons of fish annually, the third largest producer after China and Peru. The fishing fleet amounts to around 100,000 vessels.

---

[18] For a case study that illustrates the same dynamics of transposition, implementation and market opening presented in this section, but limited to Greece, see Dimitrakopoulos (2001).

[19] This section also relies on Franchino and Rahming (2003).

According to the Treaty, the common fisheries policy (CFP) is part of the agricultural policy, with which it shares many common features such as a structural policy for the modernization of equipment, facilities and production processes, backed by a financial instrument, a common organization of markets and a unified stance in international negotiations. However, the most important, distinguishing and arguably controversial aspect of the policy is a common approach to the conservation and sustainable management of fisheries resources. It is based on two main types of action: conservation measures, which include rules for the use and distribution of resources and special provisions for coastal fishing, and supervisory measures.[20]

The baseline measures. The debate on the establishment of a resource conservation policy started after the enlargement to countries with a strong fishing tradition (Britain, Ireland and Denmark). However, it took several years of negotiation to set up a framework of action. Regulation 170/83 established the most important conservation measure, namely a system of yearly setting of catch quotas (i.e. total allowable catch, TAC) for species which are exposed to intensive fishing in some regions. The system applies to vessels having minimum requirements and is based on the principle of relative stability to ensure that the fleet of each member state maintains entitlement to the same percentage of the TAC of each species over time. The regulation also included special provisions for coastal waters and a licensing system. Regulation 171/83 laid down technical measures for the conservation of fishery resources (e.g. on mesh sizes, by-catch rates and fish sizes) and special limitations of fishing. For instance, by-catches with small-meshed nets could not comprise more than 10 percent of certain species below given sizes. Finally, the Commission played a nontrivial executive role. It had to adopt many implementation rules, it could take urgent conservation measures and it had to approve national actions for strictly local stocks.

Supervisory measures were initially laid down by Regulation 753/80 on the rules for the recording and transmission of information concerning catches taken by EU fishing vessels. Three key features are worth highlighting. First, masters of vessels were required to keep a record of their operations and, at the time of landing, to submit a statement to the national authorities listing the quantities of fish landed and the location of catches. Second, member states were required to verify the accuracy of this statement, to ensure that all landings of species subject to TAC

---

[20] With its main aim of reduction in the EU fishing fleet, the structural policy of the CFP has strong conservationist implications but it will not be subject to analysis.

were recorded and to notify the Commission monthly. Once the quota was reached for a specific fish stock, national authorities had to prohibit fishing. Thirdly, the Commission had to adopt implementation rules, following the management procedure. More importantly, it could establish, on its own initiative and on the basis of the information received, the date on which catches were deemed to have exhausted the quota and, therefore, fishing should cease.

The extent to which these regulations were constraining for national authorities varied across the types of measures. The mean national discretion of the conservation measures was only 6.4 percent, considerably lower than the cross-policy average. However, the supervisory Regulation 753/80 allowed much greater room for maneuver. The national discretion index was more than 22 percent. The Commission enjoyed a nontrivial executive role across the board. The Commission's mean discretion index was above 9 percent, substantially higher than the sample average of 4.4 percent reported in Chapter 3. In order to understand the delegation trajectories of these laws in the succeeding twenty years, it is useful to distinguish two phases that are separated by the review of the TAC regulation in 1992.

The 1980–1991 period. The technical measure regulation was amended 17 times in this period and, half-way through, it was replaced by a new Regulation 3094/86 consolidating the previous amendments in a single text. The majority of these acts changed technical details, such as the mesh and fish sizes, and clarified provisions, such as on the definition of by-catch and methods of fish measurement. For our purposes, the most important amendment took place one year after the first measure was adopted. It implied a moderate loosening of the role of the Commission and greater national flexibility. Regulation 2178/84 specified that the decision to introduce a closed season for sprat and herring fishing in certain British waters could be taken by national authorities, after the Commission's approval, rather than directly by the Commission. The regulation also allowed greater flexibility for national authorities to adopt conservation measures applicable only to domestic fishermen.

The supervisory measure regulation has been amended four times and consolidated twice. Regulation 2057/82 repealed the first measure before the TAC regulation came into effect. It inserted provisions on inspection activities.[21] Member states were responsible for inspecting fishing vessels, taking appropriate action in the case of noncompliance,

---

[21] Provisions on the use of fishing gear were also inserted and small vessels were exempted from the obligation to record their operations.

and informing the Commission about these activities. The Commission had to adopt relevant implementation rules and, subject to conditions, could carry out on-the-spot inspections in liaison with national authorities. In the next six years, five new regulations specified the information to be recorded in greater detail, and the duties of national authorities and of the Commission. The inspection activity of national authorities was expanded to cover any fishing vessels and any activity whose inspection enabled verification of compliance. Greater emphasis was put on the obligation of national authorities to trace and verify the accuracy of the information on catches, to expedite the notification to the Commission, to inform the Commission on how they had dealt with irregularities and to provide the necessary support for the Commission's inspections. The last act, Regulation 3483/88, provided for additional control measures for noncomplying vessels. It also specified that, if a national authority had not taken action against a noncomplying vessel, the quantity of illegally caught fish could be counted against the quota of its state. On the other hand, provisions for reparation to member states were inserted if the Commission halted fishing before their quotas were exhausted. The Commission had to adopt various implementing rules and, more interestingly, could extend the monitoring of catches to additional stocks, subject to the management procedure.

In summary, in early 1980s, there was not a clear trend in terms of delegation and control. Some technical measures actually loosened control on national implementation but then, gradually and especially towards the end of the 1980s, measures tightened the provisions for national implementation and reinforced the executive role of the Commission.

The 1992–2003 period. The TAC regulation was replaced by Regulation 3760/92. This new act expanded the set of conservation measures that could be taken, established a system of fishing licenses and put greater emphasis on multi-annual, multi-species management objectives. For instance, new measures included restricting fishing effort and time spent at sea and promoting more selective fishing. A few years later, Regulation 847/96 allowed for the possibility, based on scientific evaluation, of changing the quotas during the fishing season and inserted a system of penalties whereby over-fishing would lead to a proportionally larger deduction of the following year's quota for the relevant member state.

The technical measure regulation was amended further 18 times and consolidated twice in this period. These amendments covered various aspects of fishing, from regulation of the use of driftnets to closure of fisheries. A comparison between the length of consolidating laws adopted in 1986 and 1998 provides an indication of how this legislation has become increasingly detailed (cf. Huber and Shipan, 2002: 77). Regulation 850/98 is about twice as long as Regulation 3094/86,[22] so there is strong evidence that fishing activities and the relevant national authorities have been increasingly subjected to more detailed regulation. The Commission has generally been delegated additional power to adopt implementation rules, such as in the latest Regulation 973/2001 on highly migratory species.

The most radical review of supervisory measures was introduced by Regulation 2847/93, which established a comprehensive control system of the implementation of the CFP. Existing features of the policy, such as the monitoring of fishing vessels, catches and the use of fishing gear, were strengthened. For instance, member states had to establish a computerized validation system based on cross-checks and verification of data. Sampling plans of national authorities and their results had to be communicated regularly to the Commission. In some cases, the Commission had to approve these plans and could carry out unannounced on-the-spot checks of the national inspection programmes. If a member state had not transmitted data in time, the Commission could set the dates when 70 and 100 percent of its quota would be exhausted. The Commission could also decide on deductions from a member state's quota in the case of overfishing, following the management procedure. An entirely new title was dedicated to the measures that needed to be taken in case of noncompliance, listing the sanctions and requiring national authorities to notify fines and infringements, and two other new titles extended the monitoring activity to the structural and market measures of the CFP.

Three of the eight amendments adopted in the succeeding ten years should be briefly examined. Regulation 2870/95 extended the monitoring and control measure to fishing effort.[23] Member states had to record their vessels' fishing effort and the Commission set the date on which the maximum fishing effort level of a member state would be reached. Regulation 686/97 established a satellite-based vessel monitoring system and required national authorities to operate fisheries monitoring centres. Regulation 2846/98 strengthened control on fishery products after landing, transshipment operations and third-country vessels. The Commission had been given the right of remote access to information, to conduct on-site observations of the measures taken by national authorities and to establish cross-state monitoring programmes. Finally, a related act is Regulation 1447/99, establishing the types of behavior that seriously

---

[22] The difference would be even greater if we include four regulations on fishing effort, adopted between 1995 and 1999, that have similar conservationist objectives.

[23] "Fishing effort" is the product of the capacity and the activity of a fishing vessel at sea.

infringe the CFP. It was designed to increase transparency of the actions taken by national authorities against noncompliant vessels.

In summary, this decade, and especially the years up to 1999, was clearly characterized by a qualitative leap in terms of greater tightening on the actions taken by national authorities and expansion of the Commission's executive role. To give an idea about the degree of change, the latest TAC Regulation 2371/2002, incorporating the changes of the decade, is almost three times as long as the 1992 regulation, which, in turn, is double the length of the 1983 regulation.

Conflict and implementation of the common fisheries policy

Since all CFP measures have been adopted by qualified majority voting, the question is whether these trends of delegation and discretion are related to substantial distributive losses originating from national execution. These losses should lead to a tightening of control on national authorities' actions and greater reliance on the Commission.

Failures of the Council. Before we proceed however, it must be pointed out that the conservation objectives of the policy have been seriously jeopardized by the tendency of the Council to increase the yearly TACs proposed by the Commission. From 1985 to 2000, more than 30 percent of the proposed TACs have been increased and these increases have averaged 30 percent. This is equivalent to 110,000 tons per year or to 80,000 tons per year, net of the quantities that the Council has reduced (Franchino and Rahming, 2003:24–25). Franchino and Rahming (2003) contend that the Fisheries Council, the council formation that sets the TACs, is likely to be composed of ministers that share the views of fishermen's organizations and overestimate the sustainability of fisheries. The policy output is a conservation failure. For instance, the quantities of mature demersal fish in the sea were about 90 percent greater in the early 1970s than in the late 1990s (Commission of the EC, 2001a: 7). North Sea cod and Northern hake stocks have been the subject of emergency measures in recent years by the Commission in an effort to undo some of the damage done by years of overexploitation. Both of these stocks are now considered by fisheries scientists to be in danger of collapse. As the Commission pointed out, "the annual pattern of decision-making has resulted *de facto* in a dilatory policy of stock management that has failed to safeguard or restore stocks" (Commission of the EC, 2000a: 3). The Advisory Committee for Fisheries Management[24] (ACFM) has

---

[24] This is a committee of the International Council for the Exploration of the Sea (ICES), an independent institution and a scientific advisory and research body.

estimated that the spawning stock biomass (SSB) and the fishing mortality (F) rates[25] for cod have been at critical levels for fourteen of the past eighteen years. The remaining four years' data show evidence of F rates above recommended levels and an SSB that was, at the beginning of 2000, too low to replenish stocks if fishing continued (ICES, 2000: 102). Hake stocks have also been below what the ACFM refers to as precautionary levels since 1978. In the last decade, except for 1989 and 1995, landings of hake in the North Sea have been significantly lower than the TAC. Mortality has regularly been higher than the maximum 28 percent recommended in order to ensure sustainability and SSB rates have only been above the B_{lim} rate (i.e. the rate estimated to lead to potential stock collapse) of 120,000 tons twice (ICES, 2001: 1–9). The Commission now has to organize recovery plans and the 2001 TAC for hake has been reduced to half that of the previous year, though, ironically, the Commission initially proposed a 74 percent reduction.

It is hence highly likely that the Council's failure to pursue one of the objectives of the CFP has led this institution to expand the conservation measures and to rely more on the Commission, a institution with a stronger conservationist bias (Lequesne, 2000; Franchino and Rahming, 2003). This is not too dissimilar from the tendency of the US Congress to delegate powers in international trade policy to a more liberal executive in order to avoid inefficient (protectionist) outcomes (Lohmann and O'Halloran, 1994; Epstein and O'Halloran, 1999b: 222–7).

Implementation problems.   In addition, serious problems of implementation emerged towards the end of the 1980s, revealing conflict and substantial distributive losses originating from national execution. Infringements were of three types. First, national authorities were conveniently slow in prohibiting fishing as the catches approximated the allocated quotas. The ECJ ruled that the Dutch authorities failed to comply with the regulations as they prohibited fishing "manifestly too late" (i.e. *after* catches exceeded their 1985–6 quotas!).[26] France was later found at fault, for similar reasons, for the 1988–92 quotas and Britain for the 1985–8 and 1990 quotas. They also failed to take action against overfishing and, Britain only, for misreporting landings.[27] Second, various

---

[25] Spawning stock biomass (SSB) estimates provide an indication of the size of the breeding stock available to replenish the resource, whereas fishing mortality (F) measures the pressure put on a specific stock in any given year.

[26] Cases 290/87 and C-52/91. Commission of the European Communities v Kingdom of the Netherlands. *European Court reports 1989*, p. 3083, *1993*, p. I–3069.

[27] Cases C-52/95 and C-333/99 Commission of the European Communities v French Republic. *European Court reports 1995* p. I–4443, *2001*, p. I–1025. Case C-454/99. Commission of the European Communities v United Kingdom of Great Britain and Northern Ireland. *European Court reports 2002*, p. I–10323.

arguments were used by national authorities to avoid recording catches, prohibiting fishing and taking action against infringements. France, for instance, argued that the simple possibility of exchanging quotas with another member state should free its authorities from the obligation of prohibiting fishing. Spain asserted that control measures should not apply to catches subject to a TAC and made outside the EU fishing zone. It is not easy to assess the extent to which this noncompliance is strategic or results from rule ambiguity, but the ECJ has systematically ruled against these arguments without calling for clarification by legislators.[28] Third, inspection activities of national authorities were, at best, deficient. After 73 inspections carried out in 26 ports from 1984 to 1987, the Commission decided to take France to court for failing to comply with the obligations to inspect and punish noncompliance. The ECJ ruled in its favor on all counts. French national standards on mesh and fish sizes were less strict than EU rules, inspectors did not even have the appropriate gauges to measure mesh sizes, no actions were taken against trawlers equipped with prohibited devices, excessive by-catches were not confiscated, infringements were not recorded and offenders were thus not charged.[29] The ECJ later ruled that France did not put in place the appropriate control measures also for the 1988–90 fishing years, and that Britain failed to do so for the years 1985–8 and 1990.[30]

Other indicators revealed problems of implementation. Evidence from court cases indicated that British fishermen have exceeded their allocated quotas by almost 30,000 tons in the years 1985–90 (see Figure 6.1). Considerable overfishing also took place in France in 1988 and 1990.[31] The amount of by-catch and discards are also important indicators of misapplication. When fishing takes place outside the fishing season, outside the assigned fishing areas or using inappropriate fishing gear, we are likely to see an increase in by-catch and discards. This leads to a further depletion of the stocks and seriously affects fellow fishermen who comply with the rules. It also seems that some practices tend to vary across

---

[28] Case C-62/89. Commission of the European Communities v French Republic. *European Court reports 1990*, p. I–925. Case C-258/89. Commission of the European Communities v Kingdom of Spain. *European Court reports 1991*, p. I–3977.

[29] Case C-64/88. Commission of the European Communities v French Republic. *European Court reports 1991*, p. I–2727.

[30] Case C-333/99. Commission of the European Communities v French Republic. *European Court reports 2001*, p. I–1025. Case C-454/99. Commission of the European Communities v United Kingdom of Great Britain and Northern Ireland. *European Court reports 2002*, p. I–10323.

[31] Cases C-333/99 and C-454/99. Lack of data availability prevents me from using other important indicators of misapplication such as illegal or black landings. The Commission considers them important causes of the CFP conservation failure (Commission of the EC, 2001a: 8).

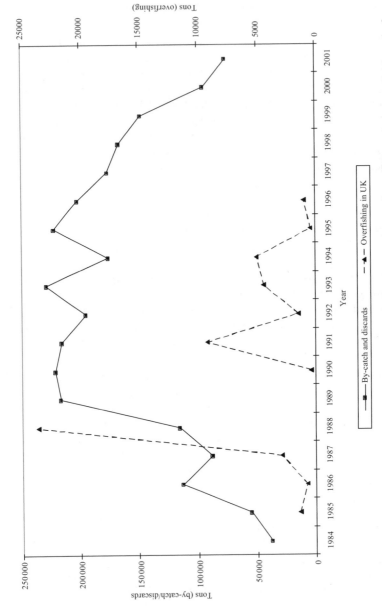

Figure 6.1 *By-catch, discards and overfishing. Note:* Pre-1989 data on by-catch and discards are available only for haddock, whiting, saithe and mackerel. *Source:* Franchino and Rahming, 2003, ICES Study Group on Discard and By-catch Information and court cases.

national lines, provoking inter-state conflict. Figure 6.1 illustrates the volume of by-catch and discards for the 1984–99 period. In the second half of the 1980s, it began to emerge, from rather incomplete data, that the by-catch and discards problem was of a sizeable nature. The amounts have increased by an average of 20 percent in the 1984–8 period from 37,000 to 115,000 tons. This last figure doubled once more accurate data covering a greater number of stocks became available in 1989.

By the early 1990s, there was enough evidence to suggest that the CFP regulations were misapplied by, especially some, national authorities, revealing underlying conflict across member states. The severity of the distributive losses of national implementation was aggravated by the progressive depletion of fish stocks due to overly generous TACs (Commission of the EC, 2000a). As expected, this decade saw a qualitative change in the pattern of delegation and control. Most of the amendments to the TAC regulation and to the technical and supervisory measures extended the scope of application, narrowed national executive discretion and strengthened the Commission. For instance, in Regulation 2847/93, the reinforced Commission prerogatives to inspect, sanction and set the dates of quota exhaustion and the new titles on infringements and monitoring were directly linked to previous patterns of noncompliance. Moreover, many introductory recitals referred to the need to "strengthen control of the application of the rules," in addition to that of clarifying provisions (hence rule ambiguity, especially in technical measures, affected implementation too).

The first half of 1990s was still characterized by belated closures of fisheries and failures to carry out inspections and to take action against infringements. French and British fishermen exceeded their allocated quotas eleven and thirty-one times respectively in the years 1991–6[32] and, as Figure 6.1 illustrates, the volume of by-catch and discards were still high. Consequently, penalties for over-fishing were inserted in the 1996 amendment of the TAC regulation and, in the 1995–9 period, the provisions on supervisory measures were changed on four occasions. As expected, amendments extended the scope of the measures, reinforced control on national inspection activities and strengthen the Commission (e.g. Regulations 2846/98 and 1447/99).

Signs of improvement. There is now some evidence that these measures are starting to work. The amount of by-catch and discards has

---

[32] Case C-140/00. Commission of the European Communities v United Kingdom of Great Britain and Northern Ireland. *European Court reports 2002*, p. I–10379. Joined cases C-418/00 and C-419/00. Commission of the European Communities v French Republic. *European Court reports 2002*, p. I–03969.

decreased, from its highest level of 223,000 tons in 1995, by an average of more than 15.6 percent in the six following years. The 2000–1 values approximate those of the late 1980s. Since 2000, no new action of infringement against member states has been initiated by the Commission. Consequently, the TAC regulation was merely consolidated in 2002 and no major review of the policy has been undertaken since.

Internal market: telecommunications

The case study in brief

Between 1990 and 1995, the Council adopted, by qualified majority voting and with the participation of the Parliament, three major measures that liberalized the telecommunications market. In 1997, three additional directives regulated authorizations, interconnection, universal service and privacy. Scholars have tended to agree that member states broadly shared, with minor exceptions, the substance, principles and direction of the policy. Therefore, as expected, these directives were only moderately constraining for national administrations, though they conferred some powers to the Commission. Evidence from transposition and implementation of these acts and their subsequent amendments also reveals a good record, with some scattered problems. The market opened up to new entrants, prices decreased and new technologies were introduced. In the 1998 and 2002 implementation reports, the Commission concluded that national measures were "very substantially compliant" with EU law (Commission of the EC, 1998, 2002: 6). As expected, the 2002 review of the regulatory framework did not introduce major changes to the nature of delegation and control in the policy.

Delegation and discretion in the regulation of telecommunications

In 2001, the turnover in telecommunication services was 3.5 percent of EU gross domestic product, equivalent to 312 billion euro. The sector employed 1.1 million persons, equivalent to 0.7 percent of total employment. The number of mobile phone subscribers in the EU reached 278 million and the density of mobile phones was 73 per 100 EU inhabitants. In 2002, there were 15 million Internet hosts (Lumio and Sinigaglia, 2003).

Over the last twenty years, the EU has played an important role in shaping the evolution from an industry originally dominated by state-owned monopolies to the current vibrant, competitive and contestable sector. Yet, in the 1950s, member states chose an alternative arena for international cooperation (the CEPT[33]) to set interconnection standards and tariff rules for cross-border traffic. However, since the early 1980s, a combination of technological innovations, unilateral liberalization, extensive consultations and the adoption of Commission Directives under Treaty article 86 (ex art. 90, with supportive ECJ rulings) led to a comprehensive regulatory framework.[34]

Deregulation. Three important measures deregulating the market were adopted between 1990 and 1995 while, just before the complete liberalization of telecommunications services and infrastructures, three reregulating directives were introduced in 1997. Directive 90/387 was the first major Council act of liberalization. It was a framework measure consisting of two pillars. First, it set out the broad principles governing access to the telecommunications infrastructure, the so-called open network provision (ONP). The conditions of access imposed by public operators had to be objective, transparent and nondiscriminatory. Second, it set out a work programme and a timetable for the application of these conditions to the different types of telecommunication services. The Commission had a moderate executive role. Apart from drawing up the work programme, it could adopt rules for the uniform application of these requirements and make the use of European standards compulsory, following the regulatory procedure.

As planned, Directives 92/44 and 95/62 applied the open network provision to leased lines and voice telephony respectively. These measures introduced rules and guarantees to users on information availability, offerings and contracts, conditions of access and use, tariff principles, billing and technical standards. They delineated the role of national regulatory authorities in the implementation of these rules and a national procedure to resolve disputes between users and operators. The Commission could adopt binding measures where convergence was inadequate, request standards and amend annexes, following the regulatory procedure. It granted derogations and could be involved if a dispute was unresolved.

These three directives were only moderately constraining for national administrations. Their executive discretion averaged 19 percent, higher than the mean of 16 percent of the sample selected in Chapter 3. The

---

[33] *Conférence Européenne des Administrations des Postes et des Télécommunications.*
[34] I will not treat these developments further as they are extensively debated by Schneider and Werle (1990), Sandholtz (1992, 1993b, 1998), Fuchs (1994), Schmidt (1996, 1998), Levi-Faur (1999) and Thatcher (2001). Moreover, I concentrate only on measures regulating the telecom market, leaving aside those on research and development, procurement procedures, type approval, standards and Commission Directives.

service-specific directives of 1992 and 1995 were even less constraining as they set only principles and minimum requirements and relied exclusively on national authorities for the regulation of the market. The role of the Commission however was not trivial. Its mean discretion index was 4.6 percent, close the sample average reported in Chapter 3.

Reregulation. Complete liberalization was set to take effect from 1 January 1998, so in 1997 three important reregulatory acts were adopted. Directive 97/13 regulated the national procedures for granting general authorizations and individual licences to provide telecommunications services. It established the principles governing these authorizations and the attached conditions. It also conferred to the Commission powers to unify and harmonize these procedures, following the management procedure, and to grant deferments. Directive 97/33 regulated interconnection of telecommunications networks to ensure interoperability and the provision of universal service. It established rights and obligations for interconnection, the principles for interconnection charges and for sharing the costs of universal service obligations.[35] The Commission had the usual standard role of requesting standards, amending annexes and granting deferments. Finally, Directive 97/66 harmonized national provisions on the processing of personal data and the protection of privacy. Issues covered security of data, confidentiality, traffic and billing data, calling features, and directories data. The Commission had to amend the annex.

In conclusion, even though these three measures were clearly of a different nature from the directives of the early 1990s, they did not differ radically in terms of national and Commission executive discretion. They were moderately constraining for member states, as they still relied extensively on the national regulatory authorities, and they conferred moderate executive powers to the Commission.

Amendments and review. By the end of 1997, the regulatory framework was complete. Subsequent amendments were of two types. Minor changes and complementary measures have been introduced in the following four years and a major review took place in 2002. Directives 97/51 and 98/10 adapted the ONP directives to the new competitive and liberalized market. The most important amendment introduced by Directive 97/51 was the requirement of a legal, functional and structural separation between national regulatory authorities and

---

[35] It also dealt with issues such as financial reporting, responsibilities of the national regulatory authorities, collocation and facility sharing, numbering, technical standards, information availability and a dispute resolution procedure.

telecommunications operators, since some member states still retained significant control over some companies. Additional guarantees for users had been added to the directive on leased lines and, where there was strong competition, tariff principles had been relaxed. Finally, clearer powers had been given to the Commission to withdraw references to nonconforming standards. Directive 98/10 simply incorporated the provisions on universal service and authorizations into the ONP directive on voice telephony. Minor changes consisted of the extension of certain provisions to mobile telephone services (e.g. on directory services and contracts) and the introduction of a national mechanism for consultation with interested parties. Two additional liberalizing measures were Directive 98/61 that required national authorities to encourage number portability and carrier preselection in order to guarantee equal access to numbering resources, and Regulation 2887/2000 requiring operators to offer unbundled access to their local loops and facilities.

A comprehensive review of the regulatory framework was undertaken in 2002.[36] It consisted of a new framework directive and four specific directives on authorization, access and interconnection, users' rights (i.e. universal service) and data protection. The framework Directive 2002/21, which repealed six directives and two Council decisions, covered all electronic communications networks and services, in order to account for the convergence resulting from market liberalization. It laid down the structure and tasks of national regulatory authorities and specified their operating and appeal procedures to ensure EU-wide harmonized implementation. Most of these features, such as independence, impartiality, transparency and appeal procedure, were already included in an ad hoc fashion in the earlier legislation. The same applies, even if somewhat more indirectly, to the tasks of these authorities, such as the promotion of competition, internal market and interests of EU citizens. Other tasks regarded the management of scarce resources such as radio spectrum and numbering. The most original provisions consisted of a procedure to determine whether operators have significant market power. With regard to the Commission, on the one hand, references to this institution in the case of unresolved national disputes have been deleted, on the other hand, the Commission can request national regulatory authorities to withdraw draft measures that are considered market barriers or incompatible with EU law. It can define transnational markets and harmonize national numbering resources, following the regulatory procedure.

---

[36] The analysis of the new framework has benefited from personal communications with David Coen and Mark Thatcher. On utility reform in Europe see also the special issue edited by Coen and Thatcher (2000).

Directive 2002/19 established rights and obligations of operators with regard to access to and interconnection of networks and, more extensively, the functions of national regulatory authorities in guaranteeing rights and imposing obligations. In a nutshell, this law reorganized the ONP directives to take into account the new competitive environment (e.g. defining the obligations for operators with significant market power), and the central role of national authorities in regulating the market. Any obligation, imposed by a national authority, which is beyond those specified in this measure, must be authorized by the Commission. Finally, three specific directives reorganized the 1997 laws on authorizations, universal service and data protection. Directive 2002/20 simplified and further harmonized national authorization rules in order to minimize regulatory barriers to market entry. Minor changes were included in Directive 2002/58 on privacy while Directive 2002/22 updated the universal service obligations. Apart from various minor amendments, it specified the rules to designate operators with these obligations, a procedure to review their scope, and additional powers of national regulatory authorities (e.g. control on retail services).

In conclusion, there is no clear indication that the amending laws adopted since 1997 and the 2002 comprehensive review radically modified the existing regulatory framework. Measures have been consolidated, updated and moderately changed but, as far as delegation is concerned, there is not a clear trend toward more or less control on national authorities or more or less delegation to the Commission. Actually, if we use word length of the whole framework regulating the telecommunication sector as a rough indicator of control on national authorities, evidence appears to indicate a loosening of control. In aggregate, the five 2002 directives were 15 percent shorter that the nine directives that were repealed.[37]

Conflict and implementation of the telecommunications directives

The measures regulating telecommunications have been adopted first in cooperation then, since 1994, in codecision with the Parliament. They required a qualified majority in the Council for adoption. Following our expectations, the trends in delegation and discretion that we have analyzed should be related to moderate to low conflict between member states and moderate to low distributive losses originating from national implementation.

---

[37] Thatcher (2001) shares the view that these measures, including the 2002 reform (personal communication), grant ample national discretion of implementation.

Conflict in the Council. A *prima facie* reading of the literature may suggest the opposite. Many works emphasize the entrepreneurship of the Commission in this policy area. This institution relied on ECJ precedents to adopt liberalizing measures under Treaty article 86 and it mobilized support from private actors against a background of divided and reluctant member states (Sandholtz, 1993b, 1998; Fuchs, 1994; Esser and Noppe, 1996; Schmidt, 1996, 1998). Sandholtz (1998: 153–4), for instance, argues that "the Commission clearly acted autonomously to push telecommunications liberalization faster than the member-states were prepared to go." The Commission relied on its Treaty-based powers because "member-states were dragging their feet on implementing even the liberalization measures to which they agreed." Thus, Council's measures were "agreed in the shadow of the Commission's legal powers."

Although the important role played by the Commission is undeniable,[38] divergence across member states on the substantive issue of liberalization is probably overplayed. Schmidt (1996: 253) sees a division between liberal Northern (Britain, Germany and the Netherlands) and pro-regulation Mediterranean countries, but no "manifest" conflict. Later, she states that liberalization drew considerable support from governments (Schmidt, 1998: 176). Thatcher (2001: 564) also sees a similar division in the Council, but he repeatedly sustains that the substance, principles and direction of the policy were widely accepted among governments.

The only notable substantive divergence was on the scope of the universal service obligations and the related functions of the national regulatory authorities. But, even on this latter issue, there was considerable agreement about their, relatively broad, powers (Thatcher, 2001: 572–3). Equally, governments agreed on the executive functions to be performed at the supranational level. The Commission floated the idea of establishing a European Regulatory Authority (Commission of the EC, 1994a) and, with the Parliament's support, was then given a mandate to investigate its feasibility in 1997. However, it dropped the plan in the 1999 policy review and noted that no government supported its establishment (Commission of the EC, 1999a: 9, 2000b: 2). Where other conflicts emerged, they were on procedural issues (e.g. the scope of the Commission's powers under Treaty article 86) and the timing of liberalization (Thatcher, 2001).

Transposition and implementation. Conflict could also be detected by late or incorrect transposition of the regulatory framework, but

---

[38] Schmidt (2000) neatly analyzes how the Commission used its Treaty-based powers to change the bargaining dynamics within the Council.

evidence is mixed. Full liberalization was due to take place from 1 January 1998 and by that date four ONP measures and two harmonization measures[39] were supposed to be transposed. In two implementation reports produced before and after this date, the Commission concluded that "transposed measured are very largely in place in most member states" (Commission of the EC, 1997, 1998: 12). This was a slightly optimistic assessment as, in October 1998, there were still five countries that had not notified transposition measures of at least one act. Nevertheless, the process was under way in the majority of member states and the 1999 implementation report shows only one case of nontransposition (i.e. Directive 97/51 in Italy[40]) (Commission of the EC, 1999b).

As far as the quality of transposition was concerned, there are no ECJ rulings on the liberalization directives while a few issues emerged with regard to completeness and correctness of the transposed reregulatory measures. The ECJ ruled that transposition in Luxembourg of Directive 97/13 and in Belgium of Directive 97/33 was either incomplete or incorrect.[41] But the relevant corrective measures on four of the five complaints raised by the Commission were already either adopted or drafted before the ECJ's final judgment. Later on the ECJ ruled that Belgium and France were not implementing some provisions of Directive 97/33 correctly.[42] The Belgian case was related to the powers of national regulatory authorities and the publication of information on the national numbering plan, while the French case was on the financing of universal service obligations. Nevertheless, it is rather difficult to detect whether misapplication was intentional or due to rule ambiguity. The French case for instance referred to highly technical accounting rules, but it was also rather clear that national provisions were favoring *France Télécom* at the expense of new market entrants.

This pattern of moderately good transposition with scattered problems continued. By October 1999, Directive 98/61 was mostly transposed. Italy was the only country that did not transpose, even partially, the new voice telephony Directive 98/10.[43] France was late and subject to an

[39] The ONP Directives were nos 90/387, 92/44, 95/62 and 97/51, and the harmonization measures were Directives 97/13 and 97/33.

[40] Duly subject to an adverse ECJ ruling, see case C-422/99 Commission of the European Communities v Italian Republic. *European Court reports 2000*, p. I–10651.

[41] Case C-448/99 Commission of the European Communities v Grand Duchy of Luxemburg. *European Court reports 2001*, p. I–00607. Cases C-384/99 Commission of the European Communities v Kingdom of Belgium. *European Court reports 2000*, p. I–10633.

[42] Case C-146/00 Commission of the European Communities v French Republic. *European Court reports 2001*, p. I–09767. Case C-221/01, Commission of the European Communities v Kingdom of Belgium. *European Court reports 2002*, p. I–07835.

[43] And was duly subject to an adverse ECJ ruling, see case C-423/99 Commission of the European Communities v Italian Republic. *European Court reports 2000*, p. I–11167.

infringement proceeding, but most of the measures were adopted by the time the ECJ ruled.[44] On the other hand, three countries did not even begin transposition of Directive 97/66 on privacy and, later on, the ECJ ruled against France and Luxembourg for this failing[45] (Commission of the EC, 1999b). Nevertheless, progress in implementing the directives continued at a steady pace. After an uneasy start and vigorous action by the Commission against nine governments, the implementation of Regulation 2887/2000 on the local loop also took off. The Commission developed a series of indicators of effective compliance (e.g. staffing of national regulatory authorities, number of licences issued, interconnection charges) and, in 2002, it could conclude that "after four and a half years of liberalization of telecoms services, the regulation put in place at national level is very substantially compliant with the EU framework" (Commission of the EC, 2002: 6).

An open market. As additional indicators that the policy was correctly implemented, the market opened up to new entrants, prices decreased and new technologies were introduced. By August 1998, there were 218 operators with authorization to provide national public voice telephony, 284 international public voice telephony licences and 77 national mobile licences. There were 526, 189 and 256 operators authorized to offer local, national and international network services respectively. By 2001, all EU customers could choose between more than five operators for long distance and international calls. For local calls, the same choice was open to customers of six member states. Over the 1997–2002 period, residential and business tariffs for international calls reduced by an average of more than 50 and 41 percent respectively. Tariffs for national and long-distance calls decreased by 50 and 45 percent respectively. Over the 2000–2 period only, consumer charges for mobile calls decreased by 23 percent. Between 1998 and 2001, incumbent operators' market shares by retail revenues have fallen on average by 10, 20 and 30 percent for local, long-distance and international calls respectively. In 2001, the market share of leading mobile operators was below 50 percent in ten member states. New services developed fast. Between 1995 and 2002, the average yearly growth of numbers of Internet hosts has been 35 percent. The average penetration rate of mobile telephony increased from 18 to 81 percent over the 1998–2003 period. In

---

[44] Case C-286/01. Commission of the European Communities v French Republic. *European Court reports 2002*, p. I–05463.

[45] Case C-151/00. Commission of the European Communities v French Republic. *European Court reports 2001*, p. I–00625. Case C-211/02 Commission of the European Communities v Grand Duchy of Luxembourg. *European Court reports 2003*, p. I–02429.

aggregate terms, between 1995 and 2001, the average yearly growth of turnover and employment in the telecommunications sector was 14.7 and 2.4 percent respectively, indicating considerable efficiency gains (Commission of the EC, 1998, 1999b, 2001b, 2002, 2003; Lumio and Sinigaglia, 2003).

In conclusion, convergence of policy objectives among member states had been translated into relatively unproblematic national implementation, substantial economic gains and limited, if any, distributive losses. As expected, the new 2002 regulatory framework did not introduce major changes to the nature of delegation and control in the policy.

Taxation policy: non-residents' savings income

The case study in brief

After the liberalization of capital movements in the late 1980s and with the elimination of exchange rate risk in the eurozone, concerns about opportunities for tax evasion and avoidance were raised by some member states. Therefore, in December 1997, the Council instructed the Commission to propose a directive on the taxation of savings which was tabled in May 1998. After protracted and difficult negotiations which extended over a period of five years and required several Council meetings and a second proposal by the Commission, the directive was finally adopted in June 2003. Tax provisions must be adopted in the Council by unanimity and, according to my theory, the veto player in this circumstance is the state that wants to minimize the Commission's role and may prefer ample national discretion. Empirical results from Chapter 5 also suggest greater national discretion in the case of intense conflict. As expected, both the Commission's proposal and the final directive extensively relied on national authorities and conferred no powers to the Commission. Delegation to the Commission was not even discussed during the negotiations and it could be argued that divisions in the Council led to a measure that is somewhat looser than the initial proposal.

Delegation and discretion in the taxation of non-residents'
savings income

The EU taxation measures cover three main areas. Indirect taxation includes the value-added tax (VAT) directives and various measures on excise duties and exemptions. Direct taxation covers company and individual taxation. The third area includes measures on administrative cooperation and training of national officials.

Tax competition and the 1998 proposal. In the late 1980s, an important measure of the single-market programme was the complete liberalization of capital movements, including direct investment. From 1 July 1990, it was then possible for EU citizens to avoid, due to lack of coordination of national taxation systems, any form of taxation on interest they received in a member state where they did not reside. Hence, as part of the liberalization package, the Commission was instructed to submit proposals aimed at reducing tax evasion and avoidance. In February 1989, the Commission proposed a 15 percent withholding tax on interest income from savings and bonds. But the measure did not generate enough support among the governments and was withdrawn only a few months after its introduction (Dehejia and Genschel, 1999; Genschel, 2002).

However, as the date of the launch of the single currency approached, some finance ministers, realizing that opportunities for tax avoidance would increase exponentially with the elimination of exchange rate risk, pressed for action. Hence, throughout 1996 and 1997, they restarted debating how best to tackle harmful tax competition. The Commission published a report on its risks (Commission of the EC, 1996b) and, in December 1997, was again invited by the Council to propose a directive on the taxation of savings, which was duly tabled in May 1998.

The proposed directive was based on a coexistence model whereby a member state would either operate a withholding tax rate of at least 20 percent or provide information on savings income to the member state of residence (or combine the two systems). An additional provision was designed to eliminate double taxation. Finally, the proposal set out the intention to negotiate with third countries similar systems of effective taxation in order to preserve the competitiveness of European financial markets. This proposal reflected faithfully the conclusions of the Economic and Financial (ECOFIN) Council meeting on December 1997. It provided for moderately high national executive discretion (about 25 percent), while the Commission had no executive powers.

The final act. Yet, it took five years of negotiation, several Council meetings and a second proposal by the Commission in 2001 before final adoption. Directive 2003/48 differed from the initial proposal in six important features. First, the directive included more detailed definitions of "beneficial owner" (i.e. the individual receiving an interest payment) and "paying agent" (i.e. the economic operator paying such interest). Second, by way of derogation, member states could exclude some types of income from the definition of "interest payment." Moreover, interest from negotiable debt securities approved or issued before 1 March 2001 was excluded for nine years (a grandfather clause for eurobonds). Third, the coexistence model was dropped in favor of a single model of automatic information exchange, with a somewhat more detailed list of the information to be exchanged. Fourth, during a transitional period, Belgium, Luxembourg and Austria have been exempted from exchanging information if they apply a withholding tax rate of 15 percent, increasing to 20 and 35 percent after three and six years respectively.[46] This period will last until several countries, including Switzerland, have signed agreements, unanimously approved by the Council, based on information exchange and a withholding tax, and until the Council agrees unanimously that the US is committed to exchange of information upon request. Fifth, member states are free to levy other types of withholding tax. Lastly, the final application of the directive will depend on a unanimous decision of the Council as to whether the third countries, with which agreements have been negotiated, and territories associated to member states have applied the relevant equivalent measures.

In conclusion, it is plausible to say that the final directive is somewhat looser than the initial Commission proposal[47] (the national discretion index changes only marginally though). The withholding tax model, which was dropped in the final act, is a blunter instrument than the information exchange model (though it may not be necessarily more effective in combating tax avoidance). Moreover, exemptions in the definition of interest payment, the setting of the transitional period and the application date as function of agreements with third countries, the grandfather clause and the provision to allow other types of withholding tax are likely to render the final law more lax than the initial proposal.

Decision rules and conflict in the taxation of non-residents' savings income

The effect of unanimity.   Tax provisions are adopted in the Council by unanimity, but can we argue that this decision rule led, as our hypotheses suggest, to extensive reliance on national authorities and limited delegation to the Commission? Undoubtedly, both the 1998 Commission proposal, which reflected rather faithfully the conclusions of the previous ECOFIN Council meetings, and the final directive of 2003 relied only on national authorities for policy implementation and conferred no powers to the Commission.[48] Additionally, delegation of powers to the

---

[46] Member states levying the tax retain 25 percent of the revenue.
[47] This view is shared by Claudio Radaelli (personal communication).
[48] The same applies to the withdrawn 1989 proposal and to new 2001 proposal which were not analyzed in the previous section.

supranational executive was never even discussed during the negotiations. Debates were only centered on issues that could be broadly construed as affecting national discretion and, on balance, the final agreement hinged toward greater room for maneuver. Empirical evidence seems to support our expectations.

Conflict and negotiations. We do not have unambiguous predictions of the impact of conflict within the Council on national discretion. Governments could agree to tie each others' hands more tightly at a moderate level of conflict (and even confer some powers to a moderate Commission). As disagreement intensifies, veto-holding states with extreme preferences are likely to press for greater national discretion and exclude the supranational executive. Indeed, the empirical results from Chapter 5 would suggest greater national discretion in the case of intense conflict.

Taxation is certainly a hotly debated issue in the EU. Dehejia and Genschel (1999) and Genschel (2002) argue that the difficulty in achieving cooperation in this field resides in the systematically divergent preferences of large and small member states. Large states prefer tax cooperation, whereas small states opt for tax competition. For instance, Dehejia and Genschel illustrate how the withdrawn 1989 proposal pitted Germany, France and Italy against Luxembourg, the Netherlands, Greece and Denmark (a reluctant Britain and a supportive Belgium were exceptions).

In this case, my impression is that there was broad agreement within the Council on the basic policy objectives, namely ensuring effective taxation of savings income and preventing market distortions. Although on various occasions Britain put greater emphasis on tackling tax fraud and Luxembourg on *minimum* effective taxation, fiscal sovereignty of governments and internal market principles were never questioned (Britain's change of heart from the 1989 proposal could be explained by its more pro-European Labour government). At a particularly delicate stage of the negotiations, the Helsinki European Council of December 1999 reaffirmed that "all citizens resident in a Member State of the European Union should pay the tax due on all their savings income" (Presidency Conclusions, point 34).

However, there was far less agreement on the details of the measure.[49] At the outset of the negotiation, there were many contentious

---

[49] I have derived member states' positions from the Conclusions of Council meetings and from 71 internal Council documents that are publicly available from the Documents section of the Council website at http://europa.eu.int/index_en.htm.

issues. Some member states, such as France and Italy, favored a broad and comprehensive definition of interest, covering, for instance, all transactions of bonds prior to the interest payment date, while others, such as Britain and the Netherlands, preferred a narrower one, presumably to limit practical application problems. Luxembourg was strongly opposed to the inclusion of income distributed by investment funds. A related, and ultimately crucial, issue was the British position for the exclusion of international bonds (i.e. eurobonds). This was considered unjustifiable for the majority of the member states. Hence, most governments reacted skeptically to two proposals for exclusion put forward by the British delegation in October 1999. Finally, there were divergences on less salient issues. For instance, Luxembourg wanted a stricter definition of beneficial owner, while Germany suggested including partnerships. Belgium, France, Greece and Italy preferred an identification procedure based on a residence certificate rather than on a modified address test proposed by Finland, Luxembourg and Britain. There were also divergent views on the provisions concerning the certificate needed to avoid the withholding tax and double taxation.

The turning point.   At the end of 1999, it was clear that no agreement was in sight but the Helsinki European Council of that December reiterated unanimously the need to ensure that taxes on savings income were duly paid. The British government was at the forefront of the opposition but it could not credibly reject the fundamental aim of the measure as it would have implied a direct challenge to fiscal sovereignty (and, presumably, to its new-found pro-European credentials). Under pressure to provide a solution, it slightly changed its position by supporting the inclusion of eurobonds if the coexistence model was dropped in favor of solely the principle of information exchange at international level. Belgium, Luxembourg and Austria vehemently rejected this proposal. Nevertheless, this idea gradually gathered support in the first months of 2000. By May of that year, France, Greece, Italy, the Netherlands, Portugal, Finland and Germany agreed to a review mechanism requiring the Council to take a decision, within a specified period, on whether to replace the coexistence model with the information exchange one (though, Britain stressed that the coexistence model would have to be replaced by information exchange within a finite transitional period). The change in approach was sealed at the June 2000 European Council in Santa Maria da Feira. The key elements (i.e. an exchange of information model, a transitional withholding tax model with revenue sharing, agreements with third countries and unanimous decision on the application date) formed the basis for the final directive.

Nevertheless, these and other issues were still highly controversial. They included the scope of the directive (e.g. the definition of interest and investment funds), the paying-agent method (e.g. the definition and identification of the beneficial owner), and the arrangements for the withholding tax (including the tax rate), information exchange and sharing of receipts. For the following year, these issues frequently pitted Luxembourg, Belgium, Austria and Greece, with ad hoc additions, against the other member states. These states supported a narrow scope with a broad grandfather clause for bonds, a nonautomatic exchange of a limited amount of information, a low, nontransitional withholding tax with revenue sharing and nonautomatic expiration of the transitional period. The debate strayed away from the original 1998 proposal so much that the Commission deemed it appropriate to withdraw the proposal and introduce a new one in July 2001 based on the Feira Council conclusions. Yet, member states still debated on fourteen of the twenty-one articles of this new proposal and reservations of substance or scrutiny were entered by all governments except Germany, Sweden, Finland and Denmark. Disagreement endured on the definition of interest, the identification of beneficial owners, the information to be exchanged, the grandfather clause, the transitional period and the conditions for the transposition of the directive. It took almost two years for the final adoption of Directive 2003/48.

In conclusion, the combination of unanimity and intensive conflict across member states led to a complex pattern of mutual concessions which however, as expected, never departed from the extensive reliance on national administrations and the exclusion of the Commission from implementation. It could be argue that it produced a moderate extension of national executive discretion from the initial proposal of the Commission to the final measure.

Conclusion

Case study evidence broadly corroborates our expectations. As in Chapter 5, results are summarized under the four headings of the independent variables. I start with those more central to the qualitative analysis of this chapter.

Decision rules (Hypotheses 5.1, 5.2, 5.4, 5.5 and 5.7). As expected, when measures are adopted by qualified majority voting rather than unanimity, delegation of powers to national authorities is less likely while reliance on the Commission is more probable. Moreover, national executive discretion is likely to be lower both in absolute terms and relative to the Commission's discretion. The Commission's discretion increases in the case of majority voting. These trends clearly emerge by comparing the patterns of delegation in the fisheries, telecommunications and (post-1987) public procurement policy with the delegation patterns in taxation and (pre-1987) public procurement. The change from unanimous to majority voting for public procurement measures is particularly significant because it facilitated the adoption of measures that restricted national executive discretion and conferred powers to the Commission in a policy plagued by severe distributive losses originating from national implementation.

Conflict within the Council (Hypotheses 5.3, 5.6 and 5.8). Case study evidence supports the expectation that, in majority voting, conflict among governments tends to produce measures than are increasingly restrictive for national authorities and reliant on the Commission for policy execution. Trends in discretion are as expected both in the fisheries and (post-1987) public procurement policies, where there was a high degree of inter-state conflict and distributional losses originating from national policy implementation, and in telecommunications policy, where conflict and losses were much less severe. Instead, intense conflict among member states in taxation and (pre-1987) public procurement policy had no clear impact on discretion because measures required unanimity in the Council. If anything, intense conflict led to *greater* national executive discretion in the case of taxation.

Policy complexity (Hypotheses 5.2 and 5.5). Assessing the differences in complexity across these policy areas is rather subjective, so I will not speculate on the implications of the evidence that I have produced. Nevertheless, it is clear that the nature and design of the fisheries policy require skills at the supranational level to manage the TACs regime. The extensive reliance on the Commission corroborates Hypothesis 5.5.

Preferences of the Commission (Hypotheses 5.3, 5.5 and 5.8). In the public procurement and telecommunications cases, the Commission is undoubtedly on the liberal end of the liberal–protectionist continuum that characterizes much of the conflict in these policy areas (Commission of the EC, 1985a; Sandholtz, 1993b, 1998; Schmidt, 1998; Thatcher, 2001). In the case of fisheries, it has a strong conservationist bias in a policy that must balance sustainability of fisheries and the fishing industry (Franchino and Rahming, 2003). It is harder to deduce the position of this institution in the taxation case but it is plausible to say that the Commission shares the measure's aim of eliminating market distortions and limiting the erosion of national fiscal revenues (Dehejia and Genschel, 1999; Genschel, 2002). Hence, the Commission has been in favor of the underlying shift of the measures (probably more than the pivotal state) and the conditions for Hypotheses 5.3 and 5.8 are fulfilled.

On the other hand, corroborating Hypothesis 5.5, according to which conflict between the Commission and the pivotal state diminishes the discretion of the supranational executive, is rather complicated. One could speculate that this conflict was more intense in taxation and (pre-1987) procurement policy than in the other cases because the pivotal state was, respectively, the least concerned about effective taxation and the most protectionist (and would oppose delegation to a pro-taxation and liberal Commission). But this difference correlates with the decision rules and the impact of the two variables is difficult to disentangle.[50] Moreover, this would not explain why reliance on the Commission has been much higher in fisheries and (post-1987) procurement policy than in telecommunications. What distinguishes the former two cases from the latter are (i) conflict and distributional losses originating from national implementation, which have undermined policy objectives (i.e. sustainable fisheries and a liberal public procurement market) *and* (ii) a Commission that shares those objectives.

The next chapter will analyze the revealed delegation and control preferences of the European Parliament, an institution that has become increasingly important in the EU.

---

[50] An ideal case study would be one where changes in the Commission's position are mapped, *ceteris paribus*, onto delegation outcomes. These situations are not common, though there is some supportive evidence. Pollack (1995), for instance, shows that the powers of the Commission in the 1993 reform of the regional policy have been moderately curtailed as a result of "excessive activism" of the Commission in implementing the Community Initiatives. See also the works of Hug (2003) and Jun (2003b), discussed in Chapters 1 and 7.

7　The delegation preferences of the European Parliament

The analysis of the previous two chapters is centered on the Council of Ministers and the Commission and the data set in Chapter 5 covered the period from the establishment of the then European Economic Community up to 1992. By serendipity, in November of the following year the Treaty of Maastricht came into force and a new major institution, the European Parliament (EP), entered the scene of EU legislative politics. Its powers were moderately expanded in July 1987 with the cooperation procedure of the Single European Act. However, it was the codecision procedure of the Maastricht Treaty, later amended by the Amsterdam Treaty, that granted this institution law-making powers on an equal footing with the Council.[1] How is the involvement of the Parliament likely to affect the choices of implementation path (centralization) and the level of discretion (bureaucratization)? How and when do the Parliament's discretion preferences differ from those of the Council? Should we expect greater centralization and bureaucratization?

This chapter addresses these important questions. In the next sections, after reviewing the current literature on the Parliament, I introduce the expectations about the differences between the discretion preferences of the Parliament and the Council, which have been derived from Propositions 2.9–2.11 of the model in Chapter 2. After a detailed description of codecision, I then proceed to test these expectations through both a quantitative and a content analysis of the amendments to 414 codecision proposals adopted by the Parliament. I conclude by evaluating the consequences of parliamentary involvement in the EU legislative process.

---

[1] Academics have debated whether the codecision procedure of the Maastricht Treaty had, in fact, enhanced the Parliament's powers. However, they now agree that its legislative role has increased as a result of the Amsterdam Treaty reform (Crombez, 1996, 1997a, 2001; Earnshaw and Judge, 1996; Garrett and Tsebelis, 1996; Scully, 1997a, 1997b; Tsebelis and Garrett, 1997, 2000; Tsebelis *et al.*, 2001).

Study of the European Parliament

Owing to its increasing legislative power, the Parliament has become the object of intense academic scrutiny over the last decade.[2] Empirical studies on legislative behavior have analyzed the pattern of coalition formation under different procedures (Kreppel and Tsebelis, 1999; Kreppel, 2000, 2002a; Hix, Kreppel and Noury, 2003; Kreppel and Hix, 2003) and the cohesion within the party groups of the Parliament (Attinà, 1990, 1992; Quanjel and Wolters, 1993; Brzinski, 1995; Bowler and Farrell, 1999; Carrubba and Gabel, 2002; Faas, 2003; Hix, 2004; Hix, Noury and Roland, 2005). Other works have focused on the factors shaping the voting behavior of its members and on the main underlying voting dimensions (Hix, 2001, 2002b; Noury, 2002; Hoyland, 2005; Whitaker, 2005).

An equally large body of work has concentrated on inter-institutional legislative relations, predominantly with the aim of assessing whether parliamentary amendments are incorporated into EU statutes. The first case studies provided evidence of parliamentary influence against a generally accepted view of a powerless institution (Earnshaw and Judge, 1993, 1997; Judge and Earnshaw, 1994; Judge, Earnshaw and Cowan, 1994). Case studies have become increasingly sophisticated and designed with the explicit purpose of testing propositions generated from theoretical models[3] (Hubschmid and Moser, 1997; Rittberger, 2000; König and Pöter, 2001). In large sample analyses, Tsebelis and Kalandrakis (1999) have found out not only that successful parliamentary amendments significantly change the content of EU law but also that official statistics tend to underestimate parliamentary influence. Factors that affect the success rate include the type of procedure, the opinion of the Commission (Tsebelis et al., 2001), the type of amendment, the degree of support within the Parliament and whether amendments are proposed at the first or the second reading (Kreppel, 1999, 2002b; see also Judge, Earnshaw and Cowan, 1994). Recently, Kasack (2004) has shown that the Parliament's influence under the Maastricht and Amsterdam Treaty variants of the codecision procedure is similar. While Selck and Steunenberg (2004) use the DEU data set to argue that the Parliament has been influential in the codecision procedure, even controlling for the similarity of parliamentary preference and final outcomes. None of these works, however,

[2] For a fifty-year perspective on the research into the EP see Hix, Raunio and Scully (2003). However, it is the last decade that saw truly outstanding growth.
[3] I will not review the extensive theoretical literature. The interested reader could start with the seminal works of Tsebelis (1994), Steunenberg (1994) and Crombez (1996).

analyzes the underlying reasons that induce the Parliament to propose specific changes to the legislative proposals.

This chapter looks at the role of the Parliament in the legislative politics of the EU from a different perspective. Instead of assessing the circumstances under which its amendments are successful, it concentrates on how the Parliament uses its legislative power to exercise control over the execution of EU statutes. In the well-known expression of McCubbins, Noll and Weingast (1987, 1989), my interest lies in understanding how the Parliament shapes the "structure and process" of EU policy implementation.

In the EU literature, a few scholars follow this theoretical tradition, though none systematically compares Parliament's preferences about national and Commission discretion with those of the Council. Jun's (2003b) work is probably the most extensive analysis to date. This scholar has recently coded the changes, in terms of Commission discretion, introduced by the Parliament in 549 first reading amendments to 148 legislative proposals. For our purposes, the most relevant finding, limited so far to the first year of the fifth parliamentary term (July 1999–June 2000), is that the Parliament attempts to constrain the Commission more tightly as the policy differences between these two institutions increase. Kelemen (2002) shows how, from 1995 onwards, the Parliament has used its budgetary powers to extend its control on the established European agencies and its legislative powers to shape the design of the new agencies, such as the European Food Safety Authority. Hix (2000) and Pollack (2003a, 2003b: 114–45) review the attempts by the Parliament to change the administrative procedures of the so-called comitology system for the execution of common policies. Their work builds on important earlier contributions from Bradley (1997) and Dogan (1997), which, however, have weaker theoretical underpinnings. The Parliament has generally held the view that the comitology system undermines its oversight role and sought to introduce more permissive procedures in the legislation. Its efforts were rewarded with a reform which repealed the most restrictive features of the system and enhanced its role in the policy process.[4]

The discretion preferences of the European Parliament

This chapter contributes to the literature by providing a theoretically grounded and large sample analysis of the revealed preferences of the

---

[4] See Council Decision 1999/468 repealing Decision 87/373. Whether the reform will have the intended effects is open to question though, see Ballmann, Epstein and O'Halloran (2002: 571–2). The comitology system is described in greater detail in the analytical section of the chapter.

Parliament with regard to the structure and the process of EU statutes. Three hypotheses (and two variants), derived from Propositions 2.9–2.11, will be subject to empirical test. Proposition 2.9 asserts that, in most circumstances, the Parliament should prefer lower discretion for national administrations than the Council. The following additional considerations suggest that this trend should apply beyond the circumstances set out in Proposition 2.9, which are only based on the configuration of the preferences of the Parliament and governments.

A well-established body of literature, predominantly studying the US Congress, has analyzed the mechanisms used by legislators to exert influence on the bureaucracy. This was in response to views that delegation of policy authority to the bureaucracy was the equivalent of abdication of legislative prerogatives. It is beyond the scope of this section to discuss these contributions in detail (see the review in Chapter 1). I will only focus on two control strategies: statutory control and ongoing nonstatutory oversight.[5] The former refers to the reliance on statutes to ensure faithful and correct execution by the bureaucracy. "Statutory control," as used in the literature by Bawn (1997) and Huber, Shipan and Pfahler (2001), is the mirror image of the term "discretion" adopted in the previous chapters and by Epstein and O'Halloran (1999b) and Huber and Shipan (2002). Hence, although they are related, it should not be confused with the constraints ratio developed in Chapter 3. Greater statutory control directly implies less discretion. "Ongoing oversight" refers instead to the other nonstatutory instruments available to legislators to ensure bureaucratic compliance.

What is relevant for our purposes is how discretion preferences are informed by the environment where the political actors operate. For instance, Bawn (1997) argues that US Congress legislators that do not sit on the committee in charge of overseeing implementation are more likely to insert control provisions into the statutes than members of such a committee. The cost of ongoing nonstatutory oversight is higher for these legislators, hence they prefer more statutory control. In her study on the adoption in the US Senate of two bills delegating powers to the Environmental Protection Agency, she shows that amendments sponsored by noncommittee members are significantly more likely to increase statutory control. Similarly, Huber and Shipan (2002) argue that the availability of a legislative veto, a nonstatutory control tool, reduces the need for statutory control. They show that, in the US states,

---

[5] When taking issue with the abdication thesis, these were the tools mostly referred to by McCubbins and Schwartz (1984), McCubbins, Noll and Weingast (1987, 1989) and Aberbach (1990) in their seminal work.

legislatures with a veto are less likely to rely on detailed Medicaid laws. The same underlying rationale operates in parliamentary systems. Huber and Shipan illustrate how, for labor legislation, the greater availability of ongoing control mechanisms in nonfederal, corporatist and civil law systems allows legislators to confer more discretion to the bureaucracy, without compromising a correct execution.

In the EU, since most policies are executed by national administrations, as we have seen in Chapter 3, members of the European Parliament (MEPs) have a systematic disadvantage vis-à-vis the ministers of the Council with regard to the ability to exert ongoing control. The only mechanisms available to them are standard tools that are common to legislators in most political systems, such as questions, inquiries and hearings (Corbett, Jacobs and Shackleton, 1995: 257; Raunio, 1996; Hix, 2005: 62–5). Instead, Council ministers, as heads of government departments and of their representations within the Council administration,[6] play an important role within national cabinets and legislatures in transposing and executing EU legislation. Although they may be constrained by cabinet institutions and decision rules, they enjoy a wide array of resources and instruments for shaping policy, such as setting legislative agendas, adopting decrees and regulations, changing budgetary priorities, appointing personnel and reorganizing staff. Unsurprisingly, scholars of executive politics consider the role of cabinet minister as one of the most sought after posts in any parliamentary democracy (Blondel and Müller-Rommel, 1988; Blondel and Thiebault, 1991; Laver and Shepsle, 1994) and the allocation of portfolio responsibilities is viewed by Laver and Shepsle (1996) as the defining moment of government formation.

In conclusion, because of the peculiar institutional setting of the EU, preferences with regard to discretion should systematically vary between the Parliament and the Council regardless of whether there is conflict between them. Paraphrasing Bawn (1997), MEPs face higher costs of ongoing nonstatutory oversight than Council ministers do, hence they should prefer lower-discretion statutes. An objection to this argument is that a Council minister in a specific member state is in the same position as the MEPs with regard to policy execution in another member state. The German environmental minister cannot oversee on an ongoing basis the implementation of an environmental directive in Spain. A minister will have to weight the costs for her own department of a low-discretion

---

[6] The Committee of Permanent Representatives is the main organ of the Council administration. It is mostly staffed by senior civil servants from national ministries. They are therefore under the control of the relevant minister. A small Council Secretariat performs administrative duties for the whole Council (Hayes-Renshaw and Wallace, 1997: 70–133).

statute with the benefits of a more controlled execution in the other states. The key difference is that the cost element that will be factored in is likely to be larger for the ministers than for the MEPs because ministers value policy autonomy for themselves and their departments much more than MEPs do. Hence, these considerations lead us to the first hypothesis.

Hypothesis 7.1   *European Parliament and discretion of national administrations*

The Parliament prefers less discretion for national administrations than the Council.

Instead, Proposition 2.10 can be simply formulated as follows.

Hypothesis 7.2   *European Parliament, discretion of national administrations and conflict*

The Parliament prefers less discretion for national administrations than the Council as conflict between the Parliament and the Council increases.

With regard to the Commission, it is harder to make the case that MEPs are systematically disadvantaged, compared to Council ministers, in the exercise of ongoing oversight. The Parliament can censure the whole Commission. Of course, this is a weakly credible threat because of the high decision threshold[7] and the impossibility of dismissing individual commissioners, but it is a measure which is not available to the Council. Moreover, the Parliament has been recently granted the power to veto the appointment of the Commission President in the Amsterdam Treaty while the Council appoints the whole college of commissioners. Finally, a panoply of other instruments, from budgetary measures to hearings and questions, are available to the MEPs as much as to Council ministers.

Instead, the formulation of a testable hypothesis from Proposition 2.11 is somewhat more straightforward. It suggests a negative relation between, on the one side, the Parliament's ideal level of discretion for the Commission *relative to* the Council's ideal level and, on the other side, Parliament–Commission conflict *relative to* Council–Commission conflict. In other words, the Parliament should prefer more discretion than the Council as the Commission's preferences move towards those of the Parliament and away from those of the Council. However, if we assume that the Commission is more likely to share policy positions with the Parliament than with the Council, the hypothesis can be formulated more straightforwardly as follows.

---

[7] The Parliament needs a two-thirds majority of votes cast, representing an absolute majority of MEPs (article 201 EC).

Hypothesis 7.3 *European Parliament and discretion of the Commission*
The Parliament prefers more discretion for the Commission than the
Council.

Parliament–Commission preference similarity could be open to question.[8] Moreover, observers have witnessed increased acrimony between
the two institutions during the fifth parliamentary term (June 1999–June
2004) because a center-right majority in the Parliament was confronting
a left-leaning Commission.[9] Where data permit, I shall differentiate the
analysis between the two periods of pre- and post-1999.

The codecision procedure

The EU institutions started to operate following the codecision procedure
when the Maastricht Treaty came into force on 1 November 1993. Here,
I briefly outline its main features. The procedure (codecision I) begins
with a proposal from the Commission submitted to the Parliament and
the Council. The Parliament may adopt amendments to the proposal by
simple majority in its first reading. The Council then adopts, by qualified majority voting, a common position confirming or amending the
proposal and incorporating or rejecting the Parliament's amendments. In
the second reading, the Parliament may approve the common position by
simple majority or may amend or reject it by absolute majority, namely a
majority of the Parliament's component members. After an opinion from
the Commission, if the Council accepts all the parliamentary amendments or in the case of no amendments, the Council definitely adopts
the act in question by qualified majority. If the Parliament fails to act
within three months, the Council adopts the act in accordance with its

---

[8] For many scholars, the Commission and Parliament are both "pro-integrationist" (Tsebelis, 1994, 1997; Garrett, 1995; Garrett and Tsebelis, 1996; Moravcsik, 1998: 24–50; Tsebelis and Kreppel, 1998). Some empirical studies reveal similar views on substantive policy positions (Tsebelis and Kalandrakis, 1999; König and Pöter, 2001) and works based on the DEU data set also show very similar positions (Selck, 2004; Thomson, Boerefijn and Stokman, 2004). But other works highlight differences (Judge, Earnshaw and Cowan, 1994; Hubschmid and Moser, 1997). The partisan composition varies across EU institutions and time, so positions along the left–right dimension may differ (Hix and Lord, 1997; Hix, 2005). Jun (2003a), for instance, shows that ideological differences between MEPs and the Commission guide, at least partially, the likelihood of granting of budgetary discharge to the Commission by the Parliament. Finally, the fact that between 30 and 50 percent of parliamentary amendments is rejected by the Commission reveals a degree of conflict, though this does not imply that it is more intense than Commission–Council conflict (Earnshaw and Judge, 1996: 96; Tsebelis and Garrett, 1997: 87; Tsebelis *et al.*, 2001: 580).

[9] I am indebted to Simon Hix (personal communication) for pointing out this conflict and Jun's (2003b) results appear to confirm this observation.

common position. Inaction however has never occurred. The Parliament has generally approved the common position in the form of a letter when there was no disagreement.

If there are still outstanding issues after the second reading, a conciliation committee, composed of members of the Council and of the Parliament in equal number, is convened to iron out the differences. If the committee agrees on a joint text, there is a third reading. To become law, the act must then be adopted by the Council by qualified majority and by the Parliament by simple majority. If no joint text is agreed upon, the Council may confirm its common position, possibly with parliamentary amendments, which could become law if the Parliament does not reject it by absolute majority.

The Treaty of Amsterdam came into force on 1 June 1999 and simplified this procedure as follows (codecision II). First, in the first reading, the proposal becomes law if the Council, acting by qualified majority, incorporates all the parliamentary amendments or if there are no amendments. There is no second reading in this case. Second, the act is deemed approved, without further action by the Council, in the case of inaction or approval of the common position by the Parliament in the second reading. However, the proposal fails in the case of rejection by an absolute majority of the Parliament. Third, the Council cannot reconfirm its common position in the third reading if the conciliation committee does not adopt a joint text. The proposal fails in this case.

Methodology and data set

The hypotheses will be tested using both content and statistical analysis of the amendments proposed by the Parliament. The content analysis will consider Parliament's amendments both to the Commission proposal in the first reading and to the Council common position in second reading. This methodology allows us to discriminate between different types of amendments and to get an idea of the Parliament's revealed preferences with regard to discretion. The statistical test in the first part of the chapter will concentrate, however, only on the second reading amendments. This stage of the procedure provides the best environment to test Hypotheses 7.1 and 7.2 for four reasons. First, since first reading amendments are to the Commission proposal they may not reveal clearly differences in preferences between the Council and the Parliament, even though the Parliament could anticipate the Council's view to a certain extent. Second, information is likely to be incomplete or asymmetrically distributed in the first reading. In complex policy areas, important issues may have been unintentionally disregarded in the initial proposal or the

Commission may have failed to read the positions of the Parliament and the Council clearly. In the second reading, much of the noise due to incomplete information is likely to have disappeared and amendments reveal more clearly the political conflict between the Council and the Parliament. Third, in the second reading the odds are heavily stacked against the rejection of the null hypotheses. The Council may have incorporated amendments in its common position anticipating that it has to concede to the Parliament's position eventually. Moreover, in order to have more disciplined MEPs, rule 80 of the Parliament's rules of procedure states that amendments to the common position are admissible only if they are germane to the first reading amendments, amend a text that differs from the Commission proposal or take account of a new fact that has arisen since the first reading. Even, as a concession to the Council, the Parliament may nevertheless decline to reintroduce an amendment. Finally, with regard to the third reading, it is more difficult to separate clearly the preferences of the Council from those of the Parliament because the output from this reading is likely to be the result of mutual concessions within the conciliation committee.

Online searches of the Parliament's legislative observatory[10] conducted between April and July 2003 have revealed that the Commission has initiated 414 proposals for directives or regulations under the codecision procedure.[11] The pie chart in Figure 7.1 provides a graphical illustration of the fate of these proposals after a first or second reading vote of the Parliament. A large majority, 300 of them, has become law, six were waiting for the second reading by the Council while 56 were waiting for the Council to adopt a common position. A significant percentage however (the remaining 52 proposals), lapsed or were withdrawn by the Commission. Of this group, the Parliament has rejected the joint text adopted by the conciliation committee in two cases, in other two instances the committee failed to reach an agreement,[12] while in the majority of

---

[10] The address of the web site of the observatory is http://www2.europarl.eu.int/oeil/. Searches have been conducted first for the adopted laws (29 April 2003), then for lapsed or withdrawn proposals and for those waiting for the Council second reading (16 June 2003), and finally for the proposals waiting for the Council common position (13 July 2003). Had the searches been conducted on a single day, there might have been minor changes for Figure 7.1 but it would have made no difference for the final data set because information on the latest proposals would not have been available anyway.

[11] This figure includes only proposals that have passed at least the first parliamentary reading. It includes 96 proposals that were originally proposed under a different procedure (91 under cooperation and five under consultation). These were subsequently either confirmed or rejected by the Parliament under the codecision procedure. These features and the focus on proposals for only directives and regulations explain why this data set is smaller than the one reported by Maurer (2003: 232).

[12] In one of these cases, the common position reconfirmed by the Council was rejected by the Parliament.

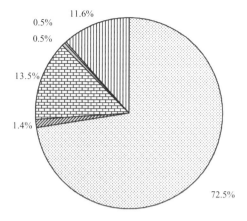

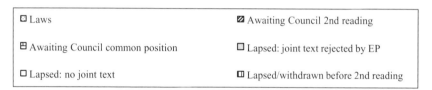

Figure 7.1 *The fate of 414 codecision proposals for directives or regulations after an EP vote, mid 2003.*

the cases (the remaining 48) the proposals did not even reach the second reading stage.

The initial data set for the statistical analysis includes the 310 proposals that became law or have been amended by the Parliament in the second reading. However, data on second reading amendments were available only up to the end of November 2002 at the time of writing. This brings the figure down to 270 observations and 1445 second reading amendments. Moreover, as we shall see, data availability problems with regard to some independent variables will reduce this number further.

Operationalization for the statistical test

Discretion of national administrations

Parliamentary amendments are not conducive to the type of operationalization of discretion that I have carried out in Chapter 3 because that method was designed for entire legislative acts. I will instead take the lead from the work of Huber, Shipan and Pfahler (2001) and Huber and Shipan (2002). These scholars argue that legislative statutes are blueprints for policy making and that policy-specific, rather than procedural, language plays a more important role in constraining implementation. Their key points are neatly summarized in the following statements.

"First . . . when comparing laws on the same topic, the length of a law serves as a useful, appropriate proxy for the extent to which it constraints agency policy making. Simply put, longer statutes provide more detailed instructions, and hence provide greater constraints on the actions of bureaucrats and other political actors. Longer statutes do not simply consist of general language, but instead provide instructions about specific policy areas. Second, while procedures do play a role in these statutes, it is clear that laws – especially longer laws – consist mostly of policy-specific language. When procedural language is put in place, it is often attached to specific policy instructions." (Huber and Shipan, 2002: 77)

I will argue that this reasoning applies also to the EU, especially when focusing on parliamentary amendments and national implementation.[13] Consider the following three cases of labor, internal market and environmental legislation. The objective of codecision proposal 2000/0142 was to improve the legislation on equal treatment for men and women at work, taking into account Treaty amendments and judgments of the European Court of Justice. It included additional definitions of discrimination, reinforced the protection system for victims, clarified the circumstances for the application of derogations, and acknowledged the rights for women to return to the same workplace after maternity leave and the rights of member states to adopt positive action measures. In the second reading the Parliament adopted fourteen amendments to the Council common position. Table 7.1 provides extracts from the most important ones.

A few amendments improved the clarify, coherence and precision of the definitions. Amendment four provides a more precise definition of *harassment* and *sexual harassment*. Similarly, amendment eight includes a more detailed definition of *positive measures*, namely the actions that member states may take to ensure equality in practice. Amendments five, six and seven make specific references to the actions that violate the directive such as harassment, general exclusions to work activities and unequal treatment related to pregnancy or maternity. Amendments seven and twelve strengthen the act by also giving women the right to return to their jobs in the case of adoption and by requiring member states to introduce measures to also protect from dismissal or adverse treatment those who support the victims, such as workers' representatives. The

---

[13] Golden (2003) makes the exact opposite argument but it appears to be limited to the system of widespread patronage and corruption of the Italian First Republic where highly detailed and verbose laws underpinned the provision of particular facilitation services by the politicians (see also Predieri, 1963).

Table 7.1 *Amendments in equal treatment legislation.*

Council common position	Amendments by Parliament

Amendment 4 (*definitions*)

Harassment *shall be deemed to be discrimination within the meaning of the first subparagraph when* an unwanted conduct related to the sex of a person *takes place* with the purpose or effect of violating the dignity of a person *and* of creating an intimidating, hostile, degrading, humiliating or offensive environment. Sexual harassment, *which manifests itself as unwanted* conduct of a sexual nature *expressed physically, verbally or non-verbally, constitutes a specific form of harassment.*

harassment: *the situation where* an unwanted conduct related to the sex of a person *occurs on the occasion of access to or at the place of employment, occupation or training* with the purpose or effect of violating the dignity of a person *or* of creating an intimidating, hostile, degrading, humiliating or offensive environment. sexual harassment: *the situation where any form of verbal, non-verbal or physical* conduct of a sexual nature *occurs, which the perpetrator knows, or is under a legal obligation to know, to have the purpose or effect of violating the dignity of a person or of creating an intimidating, hostile, degrading, humiliating or offensive environment.*

Amendment 6 (*actions violating the law*)

Any general exclusion of, or restriction on, one sex having access to any kind of professional activity or to the training required to gain access to such an activity shall constitute discrimination within the meaning of this Directive.

Amendment 10 (*sanctions*)

Member States shall introduce into their national legal systems such measures as are necessary to ensure *a real and effective* compensation or reparation *as the Member States so determine* for the loss and damage sustained by a person injured as a result of discrimination contrary to *Article 3, in a way which is dissuasive* and proportionate to the damage suffered.

Member States shall introduce into their national legal systems such measures as are necessary to ensure *effective, proportionate and dissuasive sanctions in case of breaches of the obligations under this Directive.* Compensation or reparation for the loss and damage sustained by a person injured as a result of *unequal treatment* contrary to *this Directive shall be real, effective* and proportionate to the damage suffered, *and may not be restricted by the fixing of a prior upper limit.*

(*cont.*)

Table 7.1 (*cont.*)

Council common position	Amendments by Parliament
Amendment 11 (*collective action*)	
Member States shall ensure that associations, organisations or other legal entities which have, *in accordance with the criteria laid down by their national law*, a legitimate interest in ensuring *that* the provisions of this Directive *are complied with*, may engage, either on behalf or in support of the complainants, with *his* or her approval, in any judicial and/or administrative procedure provided for the enforcement of obligations under this Directive.	Member States shall ensure that associations, organisations or other legal entities which have a legitimate interest in ensuring *compliance* with the provisions of this Directive: *(a)* may engage, either on behalf or in support of the complainant(s), with her, *his* or *their* approval, in any judicial and/or administrative procedure provided for the enforcement of obligations under this Directive, *(b) may, where national law so permits, bring a collective action, in any judicial and/or administrative procedure, on their own initiative and aside from the particular circumstances of an individual case, in order to determine whether or not the principle of equal treatment for men and women is applied.*
Amendment 14 (*information of employees*)	
	2a. Member States shall take all necessary measures to ensure that employers promote equal treatment for men and women in the workplace in a planned and systematic way. *2b. To this end, Member States shall encourage employers to provide annually appropriate information to workers and/or their representatives about equal treatment for men and women in the undertaking. Such information shall include statistics on proportions of men and women at different levels of the organisation and possible measures to improve the situation in cooperation with workers' representatives.*

remaining amendments are mostly aimed at reinforcing implementation. Sanctions should not have a upper limit, collective action (if provided for in national law) should be available to victims and national bodies in charge of execution should be properly funded and staffed. Member states should introduce measures to prevent harassment, encourage employers to inform employees about equal treatment and report to the Commission the outcomes of their implementation.[14]

Codecision proposal 2000/0183 was part of a package of four proposed directives with the aim of providing a regulatory framework to increase competition for electronic communication services (see the case study in Chapter 6). Specifically, this proposal covered the universal service provisions and users' rights. The main sections defined the scope of universal service, the process for reviewing it, the rights of users and the measures for compensating providers. Other important provisions specified the role and functions of the national regulatory authorities and supported industry's efforts to ensure interoperability of consumer digital television equipment. The Parliament introduced twenty-five amendments in the second reading, some are extracted in Table 7.2.

The amendments dealt mostly with three issues. A few strengthened the articles on the scope of universal service provisions. Accessibility to disabled users can justify the imposition of obligations. Six amendments specified in greater detail the functions of national regulatory authorities with regard to monitoring of retail tariffs, the use of accounting systems to compensate providers and the provision of information to users and consumers. Most amendments though, at least thirteen, were designed to strengthen consumers' rights by, for instance, specifying the particulars to be included into contracts and ensuring that national authorities consult all the parties in the exercise of their prerogatives and facilitate quality improvements. Moreover, member states were asked to avoid producing legislation that hampers dispute resolution.[15]

Proposal 1992/0436 introduced a harmonized approach to the management of packaging and packaging waste with the objective of reducing the overall volume of packaging and, therefore, preventing the creation of waste. The proposal set targets for the recovery and recycling of packaging and essential requirements for packaging. It stipulates measures to encourage reuse and recycling, and establishes a system of marking,

---

[14] Further details can be found in the recommendation for second reading by the EP Committee on Women's Rights and Equal Opportunities (Report no. A5–0358/2001) and in the Parliament's legislative resolution on the Council common position (*Official Journal of the European Communities*, 9.5.2002, Series C 112 Electronic Version, pp. 169–74). The final act is Directive 2002/73 on the implementation of the principle of equal treatment for men and women regarding access to employment, vocational training and promotion, and working conditions.

[15] Further details can be found in the recommendation for second reading by the EP Committee on Legal Affairs and the Internal Market (Report no. A5-0438/2001) and in the Parliament's legislative resolution on the Council common position (*Official Journal of the European Communities*, 27.2.2002, Series C 177 Electronic Version, pp. 157–64). The final act is Directive 2002/22 on universal service and users' rights relating to electronic communications networks and services.

Table 7.2 *Amendments in internal market legislation.*

Council common position	Amendments by Parliament
Amendment 10 (disabled users)	
Member States shall ensure that national regulatory authorities can impose obligations on undertakings in order to ensure that public pay telephones are provided to meet the reasonable needs of end-users in terms of the geographical coverage, the number of telephones and the quality of services.	Member States shall ensure that national regulatory authorities can impose obligations on undertakings in order to ensure that public pay telephones are provided to meet the reasonable needs of end-users in terms of the geographical coverage, the number of telephones, *the accessibility of such telephones to disabled users* and the quality of services.
Amendments 37, 16 and 22 (activities of national regulatory authorities)	
National regulatory authorities shall monitor the evolution of retail tariffs of the services . . .	National regulatory authorities shall monitor the evolution *and level* of retail tariffs of the services . . .
National regulatory authorities shall ensure that, where an undertaking is subject to retail tariff regulation, the necessary and appropriate cost accounting systems are implemented.	National regulatory authorities shall ensure that, where an undertaking is subject to retail tariff regulation *or other relevant retail controls*, the necessary and appropriate cost accounting systems are implemented.
	National regulatory authorities shall encourage the provision of information to enable end-users, as far as appropriate, and consumers to make an independent evaluation of the cost of alternative usage patterns, for instance by means of interactive guides.
Amendments 17–19, 27–28, and 30 (consumer protection)	
Member States shall ensure that *at least consumers* where subscribing to services providing connection and/or access to the public telephone network, shall have a right to a contract with an undertaking or undertakings providing such services. The contract shall specify at least: . . .(d) the means by which up-to-date information on all applicable tariffs and maintenance charges may be obtained;	Member States shall ensure that, where subscribing to services providing connection and/or access to the public telephone network, *consumers* have a right to a contract with an undertaking or undertakings providing such services. The contract shall specify at least: . . . (d) *particulars of prices and tariffs and* the means by which up-to-date information on all applicable tariffs and maintenance charges may be obtained; *Member States may extend these obligations to cover other end-users.*

Table 7.2 (*cont.*)

Council common position	Amendments by Parliament
Member States shall ensure as far as appropriate that national regulatory authorities take account of the views of end-users, manufacturers, undertakings that provide electronic communications networks and/or services on issues *which have a significant impact on the market* related to all end-user rights concerning publicly available electronic communications services.	*1.* Member States shall ensure as far as appropriate that national regulatory authorities take account of the views of end-users *and consumers (including, in particular, disabled users)*, manufacturers, undertakings that provide electronic communications networks and/or services on issues related to all end-user *and consumer* rights concerning publicly available electronic communications services, *in particular where they have a significant impact on the market.* *1a. Where appropriate, interested parties may, with the guidance of national regulatory authorities, develop mechanisms involving consumers, user groups and service providers to improve the general quality of service provision, inter alia by developing and monitoring codes of conduct and operating standards. Member States shall ensure that their legislation does not hamper the establishment of complaints offices and the provision of on-line services at the appropriate territorial level to facilitate access to dispute resolution by consumers and end-users.*

identification and information of packaging. The nineteen amendments adopted by the Parliament in the second reading dealt with four issues (see the extracts in Table 7.3).

Four amendments spelt out in greater detail and precision the definitions of *packaging, reuse, organic recycling* and *economic operators*. The term *packaging* includes nonreturnable items, that of *economic operators* includes public authorities and statutory organizations, while landfill is not considered a form of *organic recycling*. One amendment introduced the definition of *voluntary agreement*. Amendment twenty-nine and thirty call for harmonized databases on packaging and packaging waste and specify

Table 7.3 *Amendments in environmental legislation.*

Council common position	Amendments by Parliament
Amendments 40 and 19 (*definitions*)	
1) 'packaging' means all products made of any materials of any nature to be used for the containment, protection, handling, delivery and presentation of goods, from raw materials to processed goods, from the producer to the user or the consumer.	1) 'packaging' means all products made of any materials of any nature to be used for the containment, protection, handling, delivery and presentation of goods, from raw materials to processed goods, from the producer to the user or the consumer. *'Non-returnable' items used for the same purposes shall also be considered to constitute packaging.*
9) '*composting*' means the aerobic or anaerobic treatment of the *organic* parts of packaging waste, which produces stabilized organic residues;	9) '*organic recycling*' means the aerobic *(composting)* or anaerobic *(biomethanization)* treatment, *under controlled conditions and using micro-organisms,* of the *biodegradable* parts of packaging waste, which produces stabilized organic residues *or methane. Landfill shall not be considered a form of organic recycling*; 12a) '*voluntary agreement' means the formal agreement concluded between competent public authorities of the Member State and the economic sectors concerned, which has to be open to all partners who wish to meet the conditions of the agreement with a view to working towards the objectives of this Directive.*
Amendments 29 and 30 (*harmonised databases*)	
1. Member States shall take the necessary measures to ensure that databases on packaging and packaging waste are established, where not already in place, in order to contribute to enabling Member States and the Commission to monitor the implementation of the objectives set out in this Directive	1. Member States shall take the necessary measures to ensure that databases on packaging and packaging waste are established, where not already in place, *on an harmonized basis* in order to contribute to enabling Member States and the Commission to monitor the implementation of the objectives set out in this Directive
2. To this effect, the databases shall provide in particular information on the magnitude, characteristics and evolution of the packaging and packaging waste flows at the level of individual Member States.	2. To this effect, the databases shall provide in particular information on the magnitude, characteristics and evolution of the packaging and packaging waste flows *(including information on the toxicity or danger of packaging materials and components used for their manufacture)* at the level of individual Member States.

Table 7.3 (cont.)

Council common position	Amendments by Parliament
	5a. Member States shall require all economic operators to provide competent authorities with reliable data on their sector as required in this article.
Amendment 15 (*economic instruments*)	
Member State may adopt *economic instruments*, in accordance with the provisions of the Treaty, to promote the objectives of this Directive.	*The Council, on the basis of a request from the Commission, shall adopt economic instruments. In absence of Community measures,* Member State may adopt *measures*, in accordance with the provisions of the Treaty, to promote the objectives of this Directive. *Such economic instruments, adopted in accordance with the 'polluter pays' principle, shall not lead to distortion of competition, obstruct the free movement of goods or discriminate against imported goods.*

in greater detail the information to be included. Finally, two changes regard procedural instructions. Amendment twenty-four stipulates that the procedure to set targets should be repeated every five years, while amendment thirty-one requires the Council to adopt the instruments to promote the objective of the act. National measures may be taken only in the absence of Community measures and are subject to strict conditions of no discrimination and respect of the principle of "polluter pays."[16]

If we compare the columns on the left- and right-hand sides of Tables 7.1–7.3, it is clear that the language inserted by the Parliament is designed to provide more detailed instructions for policy execution. It reveals a desire to describe with greater accuracy and precision the scope and objectives of the relevant act and the specific policy measures that have to be taken. Therefore, it shows the need to exercise greater control on the actions of national administrations, the key actors in charge of EU policy

---

[16] Further details can be found in the recommendation for second reading by the EP Committee on the Environment, Public Health and Consumer Protection (Report no. A3-0237/94) and in the Parliament's legislative resolution on the Council common position (*Official Journal of the European Communities*, 25.7.1994, Series C 205, pp. 163–8). The final act is Directive 94/62 on packaging and packaging waste.

Table 7.4 *Descriptive statistics on second reading amendments.*

Amendments to	Number	Word changes (absolute values)	Percentage (proposals)
Recitals	327	11,486	36.30%
Articles	924	35,004	45.93%
Annexes	194	6,609	16.67%
Total	1,445	53,099	50.74%

implementation. Moreover, the changes put forward by the Parliament are related mostly to the policy-specific sections of the proposals. This is illustrated clearly in Table 7.4.

A straightforward method, applicable across policy areas, to separate general from specific language is to consider the three sections that make up any legislative proposal: introductory recitals, articles and, if any, annexes. Recitals are general statements of purpose, articles enumerate in detail specific legal requirements while annexes are used for a variety of reasons (e.g. for lists, tables, figures and additional guidelines). Articles are predominantly used for detailed policy instructions.[17] As Table 7.4 clearly shows, 64 percent of the amendments are to the policy-specific section of the proposals. A similar percentage of the changes in wording, in absolute terms, belong to this section. The last column shows that the Parliament has introduced amendments in the second reading to half of the proposed laws. In about 45 percent of the cases, at least one amendment relates to the articles, while more than 35 percent of the proposed laws has at least one amendment to the recital section. This implies that, whilst the likelihood of amending recitals and articles do not differ much, the changes proposed by the Parliament to the articles are considerably more substantial. Finally, as the content analysis that will follow shows, amendments to procedural language do play a role. However, especially in the second reading, they are considerably less frequent and generally attached to specific policy requirements.

In conclusion, the addition of words by the Parliament to the Council's common position tends to reflect a willingness to reduce the discretion of the national agents in charge of policy execution. A substantial part of the second reading amendments adopted by the Parliament are related to the

---

[17] This classification takes the lead from Kreppel (1999, 2002b). It does not mean, however, that recitals and annexes have less important policy implications. Jupille (2004), for instance, argues that the European Court of Justice may use recitals to solve disputes about the legal basis of proposals.

policy-specific section of the proposals. Changes to the general policy section are less frequent and procedural amendments are considerably less common. These considerations are similar to those of Huber and Shipan (2002). These scholars measure discretion as either the number of new words introduced by the legislature or the standardized page length of statutes (Huber and Shipan, 2002: 140–6, 176–83). I derive two measures of *Discretion* of national administrations from the changes in the word count to the article section of the proposal. This is arguably the most important part of a law and it is the same as used for the measurement of discretion in Chapters 3, 5 and 6. Recitals include mostly general language. Consequently, an increase in word count may not imply necessarily a desire to increase statutory control. Annexes vary widely. Some are lists of items, others are tables and even figures. Changes are harder to interpret and compare.

The two measurements of *Discretion* are the number of words added to or deducted from the Council common position (*Word count* Δ) and the percentage change in word count of the common position (*Percentage* Δ) as they result from parliamentary amendments. Positive values reveal a preference of the Parliament for less discretion. I employ the second measure to test the robustness of the results and to account for the fact that longer proposals may produce larger word count values.[18]

Conflict between the Council and the Parliament

I measure preferences along the three dimensions, *Integration, Policy* and *Left–right*, as I have explained in Chapter 4. In the case of the Council, I compute the preference of the member that is pivotal under qualified majority voting at the time of the adoption of the common position. Unfortunately, the data set of Budge *et al.* (2001) does not include information on the elections to the *Eduskunta*, the Finnish parliament, held on 21 March 1999. This means that we cannot compute the distribution of preferences of all Council members and the position of the pivot. Hence, where this variable is used, the number of observations will be reduced to 112 only.

With regard to the selection of the appropriate pivot, I consider, for the *Integration* dimension, the preference of the member that is pivotal for a shift toward more integration, while, for the other two dimensions, I follow the guidelines of Table 4.1. For the *Policy* dimension however,

---

[18] Indeed, the correlation coefficient between *Discretion* (*Word count* Δ) and the length of the common position (article section) is 0.352 (significant at the 5 percent level). *Discretion* (*Percentage* Δ) is instead uncorrelated. I am indebted to Andreas Warntjen for suggesting the use of the alternative measure.

about 90 percent of the laws reflect the underlying support for or opposition to the establishment of a market economy, that is the aggregate substantive policy category of Market Economy–Planned Economy proposed by Budge *et al.* (2001). We have less variety because the codecision procedure is not used for some important policy areas, such as agriculture and competition, and because the time frame is less than five and a half years long. I will hence use only this substantive policy category without further disaggregation. This will not affect the results.[19]

The methodology to measure the preferences of MEPs should produce values that are comparable to those of the Council and that generate a meaningful measure of conflict, our key independent variable. Our time frame spans from November 1993 to March 1999. Therefore, we need the positions of the 518 MEPs elected in June 1989 to the third legislative term, those of the 567 MEPs elected in June 1994 to the fourth term and, finally, the preferences of the additional 59 MEPs that entered the Parliament after the enlargement to include Sweden, Finland and Austria in January 1995.

I measure the positions of the MEPs at the level of national parties within the Parliament, such as the Dutch liberals or the Portuguese socialists, and use the data from the manifestos of the national election that is closest to the relevant European election and, for the three new member states, to January 1995. For instance, for the June 1994 elections, the preferences of the French national parties are derived from those of the parties competing at the national election in March 1993, while those of the Belgian delegations come from the May 1995 national elections.[20]

This choice of measurement can be defended on at least two grounds. First, European elections are second-order *national* contests (Reif and Schmitt, 1980; Reif, 1984, 1997; van der Eijk and Franklin, 1996; Marsh, 1998). They are primarily about national issues and the performance of national governments. Parties have strong incentives for using

---

[19] Four proposals (1991/0346, 1994/0299, 1994/0305 and 1996/0031) on the movement of workers for the provision of services were coded as a shift toward a more market economy. Eight proposals for environmental directives (1992/0425, 1992/0436, 1993/0458, 1994/0286, 1994/0312, 1995/0209, 1996/0164A and B) have been coded as a shift toward a more planned economy.

[20] Data on the national parties in the Parliament are taken from various issues of the *Bulletin on the Activities of the European Union*. If a party is not present in the nearest national election, I either use data from the next nearest one (this applies to a few Italian MEPs mostly) or derive their positions from their membership of the Parliament's party groups. For instance, in 1994 four members of the two Danish parties that competed only at the European elections joined the Independents for a Europe of Nations, a right-of-centre grouping. Their positions are those of right-wing Danish parties such as the Progress Party. Note that these problems are limited to very few MEPs, their misplacement is unlikely to affect the estimation of the Parliament's pivot or median voter.

European elections in this manner (Hix, 2005: 192–6). Their positioning and the space of political competition are unlikely to differ substantially from those in the national elections (voting behavior does change though). Party preferences estimated along the three dimensions from the nearest national election are hence a reasonable proxy for positions in the European elections. Second, most MEPs are also members of transnational party groups within the Parliament, such as the European People's Party, comprising most conservative and Christian democratic members, and the Party of European Socialists, grouping legislators from national socialist parties. Hix (2002b) shows that the positions of national parties are better predictors of MEP voting behavior than those of the Parliament party groups and, even, than the personal political preferences of each MEP. National parties are the most effective actors in disciplining voting behavior, hence using this level of aggregation seems appropriate.[21]

I have collected data on the positions of the Parliament's median voter along the three dimensions, *Integration, Policy* and *Left–right.* Since an absolute majority of the Parliament's members must approve the amendments to the Council common position, the median voter along a relevant dimension is the 260th (284th, 314th) legislator when the Parliament is composed of 518 (567, 626) members. In the case of an even number of members, the median voter is not the same legislator. It differs depending on the side of the dimension where the counting starts. However, it emerged that these two legislators shared the same preferences across all the dimensions, hence the identification of the median voter position has not been problematic.[22]

Absenteeism, however, creates problems in determining this position if MEPs supporting the proposal do not vote. Existing data on participation differ greatly. Scully (1997c: 237) reports a mean turnout of only 59 percent in 133 codecision votes between December 1993 and May 1995.

---

[21] An alternative data set is provided by Gabel and Hix (2002). These authors have coded the election manifestos of four transnational party federations, not the EP party groups, and they have used a modified coding methodology. These differences create problems of comparability with Council preferences. Moreover, as the authors admit, these documents are rarely used in the domestic area and may not reveal internal conflict (Gabel and Hix, 2002: 937, 954; Pennings (2002) takes a different view with regard to the 1999 elections). For the left–right position, I have also considered the first dimension NOMINATE scores produced by Hix, Noury and Roland (2002) for the MEPs who were elected at the start of each term. I have discarded them because, contrary to expectations, the median voter shifts to the left in the 1994 elections (see below for more details).

[22] This is because, when sorting the MEPs along, say, the left–right dimension, the two legislators (i.e. the two median voters for a rightward and a leftward shift) are next to each other. Hence, it is highly likely that they belong to the same national party and share the same preferences.

Kreppel (2002a: 155) randomly samples 100 codecision votes between 1993 and 1996, and reports a turnout of 65 percent. However, an unofficial web site[23] that records attendance to plenary sessions documents that turnout was 77 percent in 1999, 75 percent in 2000 and 84 percent in 2001–3, across all the procedures (these values should be even higher for codecision votes, both Scully (1997c) and Kreppel (2002a) report much higher attendance in this procedure). Two MEPs, Clegg and van Hulten (2003), write that turnout in plenary voting sessions reaches a maximum of 88 percent.

High absenteeism may not matter if the absent MEPs are against the proposal. Moreover, MEPs that are least likely to turn out could be those more likely to vote against. However, scholars argue that low participation affects the voting and coalitional behavior of MEPs (Kreppel, 2002a; Hix, Kreppel and Noury, 2003; Kreppel and Hix, 2003). Consequently, I determine for each proposal two additional positions of the Parliament with 75 and 85 percent turnout. I assume that at least half of the absent MEPs would have supported the measure (e.g. 47 MEPs in the case of 85 percent turnout and a Parliament of 626 members) and then compute the number of votes needed to approve the amendments (e.g. 361 votes). I finally determine the Parliament's pivotal member given the underlying direction of change to the measure at hand.

Finally, at least with regard to the left–right dimension, the data collected seem to reflect relatively well the actual outcome of the elections. The center-left party groups won an absolute majority of seats (265) in the 1989 elections. The left–right position of the median voter was 2.69. In 1994, although the Socialists remained the largest group, the centre-left parties managed to hold only a plurality of seats (268) because of the relatively stronger showing of centre-right parties.[24] The median voter shifted to 2.54, moderately to the right.[25]

In conclusion, the explanatory variable *Conflict* is the absolute difference between the position of the member of the Council that is pivotal

---

[23] http://www.europarliament.net

[24] Recall that, according to Gabel and Huber's (2000) left–right scale, higher values imply more left-wing positions. In 1989, centre-left groups included the European United Left (28 MEPs), Socialists (180), Coalition of the European Left (14), Greens (30) and Rainbow Group (13), representing 51.2 percent of the votes. In 1994, they included the European United Left (28 MEPs), Socialists (198), Greens (23) and the European Radical Alliance (19), representing 47.3 percent of the votes (left–right positions are derived from Hix and Lord (1997: 50), data on group membership are taken from the *Bulletin*).

[25] A rightward shift of the median voter is not a certain outcome if the liberals and the Christian democrats moved to the left in the 1994 elections. However, Gabel and Hix (2002: 950) shows the exact opposite. Those elections were more polarized along the economic left–right dimension than the 1989 elections.

under qualified majority voting (at the time of adoption of the common position) and that of the Parliament's median or pivotal voter (at the time of the second reading vote) across the three dimensions and the three levels of turnout. Our expectation is that the regression coefficients should be significantly greater than zero.

Control variable

I include one dummy variable, *Amending law*, that takes the value of one if the proposal amends previous legislation. In these circumstances, the status quo is not the collection of national measures but an EU policy. Consider, for instance, the case whereby the Council common position waters down the existing provisions set in EU law. If the Parliament disagrees, it may adopt an amendment that either deletes or changes, as we have seen in Tables 7.1–7.3, the relevant provisions of the common position. The underlying motivations of the Parliament are the same but our operationalization of discretion would capture only the latter type of amendment. We need therefore a variable that controls for this eventuality. We should expect that the tendency to add words to the common position is stronger in the case of acts related to new policy areas. The coefficient of *Amending law* should be negative.

Table 7.5 provides descriptive statistics for the dependent, independent and control variables.

Analysis of results: discretion of national administrations

According to Hypothesis 7.1, we should expect that the second reading amendments of the Parliament systematically add words, both in absolute and percentage terms, to the Council common position as a sign of the greater willingness of this institution to reduce discretion and to exercise statutory control.

I have performed two tests to assess the validity of this claim. One-sample t-tests reveal that the sample mean for both measures of discretion is greater than zero at a high level of significance, strongly supporting our expectations.[26] I have then added the conflict and the control variables and compute two sets of robust regressions. Results are displayed in Table 7.6

---

[26] One-sample t statistic is 5.763 for *Discretion (Word count Δ)* and 4.857 for *Discretion (Percentage Δ)*, both significant at the 1 percent level ($N = 270$). In the 43 cases where there has been no second reading I have entered a value of zero. This makes the rejection of the null hypothesis harder.

Table 7.5 *Description and summary statistics of the variables.*

Variable	Description	Mean	Std. dev.	Min.	Max.
	Dependent variables				
Discretion (Word count Δ)	Change in word count resulting from second reading parliamentary amendments to Council common position[a]	74.2297	211.6414	−511	1780
Discretion (Percentage Δ)	Percentage change in word count resulting from second reading parliamentary amendments to Council common position[a]	3.5916	12.1514	−17.974	106.9307
	Independent variables				
Conflict left–right	Absolute difference between the position of QMV pivotal member in the Council and that of Parliament's median voter on left–right dimension	0.2102	0.2154	0.0309	0.8638
	85 percent turnout	0.2491	0.1672	0.0631	0.6077
	75 percent turnout	0.2238	0.1523	0.0383	0.6681
Conflict policy	Absolute difference between the position of QMV pivotal member in the Council and that of Parliament's median voter on policy dimension	1.7491	2.292	0	8.8748
	85 percent turnout	1.6814	1.8253	0.0039	7.63
	75 percent turnout	2.2632	1.1774	0.6328	6.4195
Conflict integration	Absolute difference between the position of qmv pivotal member in the Council and that of Parliament's median voter on integration dimension	0.838	0.2188	0.522	1.4551
	85 percent turnout	0.7755	0.2253	0.5363	1.0011
	75 percent turnout	0.7494	0.2259	0.5134	1
	Control variable				
Amending law	1 if the proposal amends existing EC legislation, 0 otherwise	0.4519	0.4986	0	1

Notes: [a]Only article section of the proposal.

Table 7.6 *Council–Parliament conflict and second reading amendments: robust OLS regressions.*

	Dependent variable: *Discretion*					
	Word count Δ			*Percentage* Δ		
Constant	30.198	35.681	15.04	1.541	1.786	2.282
	$(2.25)^b$	$(2.92)^a$	(0.42)	$(2.09)^b$	$(2.58)^b$	(1.21)
Conflict left–right	86.320	–	–	5.822	–	–
	$(2.21)^b$			$(2.30)^b$		
Conflict policy	–	10.207	–	–	0.739	–
		$(2.28)^b$			$(2.31)^b$	
Conflict integration	–	–	35.925	–	–	0.215
			(0.88)			(0.11)
Amending law	−28.462	−35.116	−20.317	−0.728	−1.163	−0.018
	$(-1.93)^c$	$(-2.34)^b$	(−1.31)	(−0.70)	(−1.12)	(−0.02)
F	4.12^c	4.52^b	1.27	2.75^c	2.97^c	0.01
Adjusted R^2	0.06	0.08	0.01	0.04	0.07	−0.02
N	103	102	105	109	108	107

	Turnout 85 percent					
Constant	23.708	33.722	18.946	1.750	1.731	1.191
	$(1.67)^c$	$(2.74)^a$	(0.67)	$(1.77)^c$	$(2.44)^b$	(0.61)
Conflict left–right	93.378	–	–	4.257	–	–
	$(2.02)^b$			(1.44)		
Conflict policy	–	12.392	–	–	0.715	–
		$(2.42)^b$			$(1.99)^b$	
Conflict integration	–	–	33.886	–	–	1.973
			(1.03)			(0.83)
Amending law	−23.676	−37.435	−20.476	−0.807	−1.064	−0.237
	(−1.55)	$(-2.45)^b$	(−1.33)	(−0.77)	(−1.00)	(−0.21)
F	3.09^b	4.80^b	1.43	1.69	2.16	0.71
Adjusted R^2	0.04	0.07	0.01	0.00	0.04	−0.01
N	105	102	105	109	109	110

	Turnout 75 percent					
Constant	19.198	40.941	55.521	1.641	1.888	1.39
	(1.30)	$(2.31)^b$	$(1.80)^c$	(1.49)	(1.62)	(0.77)
Conflict left–right	125.384	–	–	3.674	–	–
	$(1.98)^b$			(0.88)		
Conflict policy	–	3.108	–	–	0.414	–
		(0.52)			(0.86)	
Conflict integration	–	–	−6.563	–	–	1.823
			(−0.19)			(0.76)
Amending law	−22.272	−22.752	−26.646	0.003	−0.878	−0.322
	(−1.45)	(−1.38)	$(-1.65)^c$	(0.00)	(−0.81)	(−0.28)
F	2.56^c	1.00	1.37	0.45	0.58	0.29
Adjusted R^2	0.05	0.00	0.01	−0.01	−0.01	−0.01
N	104	104	106	107	109	110

Note: Initial $n = 112$, observations with Cook distances greater than $4/n$ are subsequently omitted. *t*-statistics in parentheses, one-tailed test; ^{a} $p \leq 0.01$; ^{b} $p \leq 0.05$; ^{c} $p \leq 0.1$.

Hypothesis 7.1 is mostly corroborated also in this case because the intercepts or constants of the regressions are significantly greater than zero in ten out of eighteen regressions. Results are more convincing when conflict is measured along either the left–right or the policy dimension and at higher levels of turnout. The Parliament adds between thirty and forty words to each Council common position that reaches the second reading stage. This is equivalent to amendment six of Table 7.1 on equal treatment legislation. It increases the length of the common position by about 1.7 percent.

These changes do not lead to a radical revision of the common position. They tinker mostly with the margins of the legal requirements imposed on national authorities. Moreover, second reading amendments are less likely to be introduced in the final act (Kreppel, 1999, 2002b). However, the ongoing and relentless activity of specifying policy instructions in greater detail and precision, revealing the systematic desire of the Parliament to reduce discretion, may lead to substantial cumulative changes in the design of EU statutes over the long haul. Furthermore, second reading amendments are likely to be the tip of the iceberg of an activity that starts right after the Commission introduces a proposal.

A further look at descriptive statistics strongly reinforces the picture that has emerged so far. As shown in Table 7.4 (last column), half of the proposals reaching second reading are amended by the Parliament. Of these, words are added to the common position in more than 80 percent of the cases, without much difference across the three sections of the proposal. 72.8 percent of the amendments to the article section adds words to the common position. Of the absolute number of 35,004 word changes, 27,523 words, or 78.6 percent, are added to the common position. This proportion is similar across the three sections.[27] Only 19.6 percent of these amendments delete words.

In conclusion, the Parliament has adopted amendments that have added a net aggregate total of 20,042 words to the article sections of 227 proposals that have reached the second reading stage. This is higher than the sum of the net changes to the general policy language of the recital sections (8,144 net total) and to the annexes (4,013), indicating that amendments tend to concentrate on policy-specific instructions. This is not a trivial amount. It is almost equivalent to the sum of the word count (excluding annexes) of the final acts of the three proposals on labor, internal market and environmental policy that we have discussed in the previous section.

---

[27] 9,815 words are added to the recital section out of 11,486 absolute word changes and 5,311 words to the annex section out of 6,609.

In Table 7.6, we find support for Hypothesis 7.2 for the left–right and policy dimensions and at higher levels of participation. At 85 percent turnout, with a standard deviation increase in *Conflict policy*, the amendments of the Parliament increase the length of the article section of the Council common position by twenty-three words (this estimate oscillates between six and forty-two). This figure diminishes to sixteen words in the case of a similar increase in conflict along the left–right dimension. In percentage terms, a standard deviation increase in *Conflict policy* leads to a 1.3 percent increase in the length of the common position (the figure oscillates between 0.2 and 2.4 percent).

Figure 7.2 plots the values of *Conflict policy* at the three levels of participation on the word count measure of national discretion (in reverse order). At turnout levels above 85 percent, the downward sloping regression line neatly shows how more words are added to the Council common position (hence national discretion diminishes) as conflict intensifies. Moreover, the positive value of the intercept with the *Discretion* axis shows the systematic tendency to add words. However, this relation disappears with lower turnout, recommending caution in the interpretation of the results. Only the coefficient of *Conflict left–right* is significant at above the 5 percent level throughout the three levels of participation, but only when regressing *Discretion (Word count* Δ*)*.

There is then evidence than the Parliament wants to design EU law in greater detail (than the Council) if it confronts a Council pivot with different preferences. Historically, this meant that, in the first few years of the codecision procedure, parliamentary amendments increased the length of those acts that shifted the status quo to the left since a left-leaning Parliament was dealing with relatively right-leaning members of the Council who were pivotal for a leftward move (i.e. the Italian and French coalition governments). Instead, when an act implied a right-word move, the Parliament was less active as it shared the views of the Council pivot. Parliamentary activism waned over time as the positions of the two institutions converged. The Parliament's median voter shifted moderately to the right in the June 1994 elections. Whilst, both Council pivots gradually moved to the left when leftwing parties entered government in large member states (e.g. in Italy in 1995 and 1998, in Britain and France in 1997 and in Germany in 1998).

Admittedly, the substantive impact of these variables is not large. A twenty word increase is equivalent to amendment thirty in Table 7.3. Nevertheless, results are reassuring because the research design is heavily biased against the confirmation of the hypotheses. Data on preferences were available for just five and a half years instead of the whole nine and a half year period that the codecision procedure has been in operation.

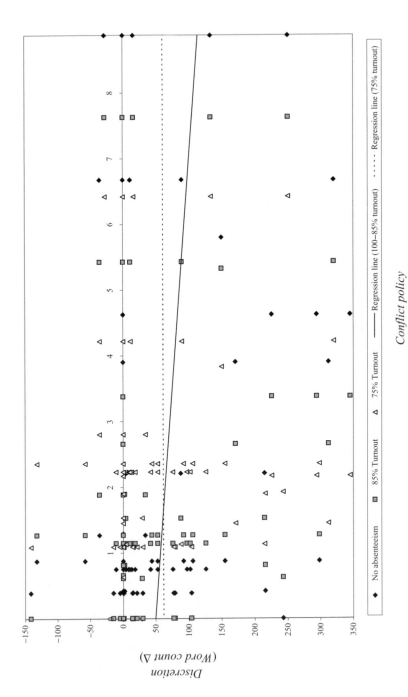

Figure 7.2 *Discretion of national administrations and Parliament–Council policy conflict.*

Once longer time series are available, a more comprehensive test could be carried out.

With regard to the control variable, the coefficient of *Amending law* is negative as expected but it reaches some level of significance only in four circumstances. Here, the Parliament adds about thirty-seven *fewer* words to the common position in the case of a proposal amending EU laws. This estimate varies between eight and sixty-seven. There is some evidence that the Parliament may be more likely to introduce policy instructions when there is not an EU policy and the status quo encompasses the collection of national measures. In the case of an EU policy already in force, the Parliament may prefer deleting the changes in the common position and reverting to the existing statute. This result is (weakly) confirmed in the analysis below. It is then worth investigating in future research how the status quo shapes the legislative behavior of the Parliament. Kreppel (2000), for instance, shows that the Socialist and the European People's Parties are less likely to coalesce in policy areas where the status quo appears to be in between the two parties' ideal policies.[28]

In conclusion, we have found support for the proposition that, since members of the Parliament face higher costs of ongoing oversight than those experienced by Council ministers, they systematically prefer lower-discretion statutes. Moreover, the Parliament prefers more detailed statutes as its preferences diverge from those of the Council qualified majority voting pivot, especially along the left–right and policy dimensions and as turnout increases. Whether these discretion preferences make their way into EU law depends on the bargaining taking place under codecision. This is not subject to analysis in this chapter but it would be surprising if that was not the case as it is widely acknowledged that parliamentary influence is not negligible in this procedure.

---

[28] A potential criticism to the regressions in Table 7.6 is that they fail to control for delegation to the Commission. Following Hypothesis 7.3, one could expect that the Parliament would be less likely to add words in policy areas where the executive role of the Commission is greater. The insertion of a policy area variable is problematic however because it would also gauge policy complexity whose inclusion would be theoretically unfounded (see the next section). I have then added to the regressions an additional variable *Directive* that takes the value of one if the codecision proposal is for a directive and zero if it is for a regulation. If we accept the, rather simplifying, view that regulations are adopted when the Commission is more involved in implementation, *Directive* would at least generate some control. Results reveal that the significance of the constant term drops across the board, *Conflict left–right* becomes less significant in one regression and more significant in another, *Conflict policy* becomes less significant in two regressions. At least with regard to the conflict variables, *Directive* does not change the results substantially. I have excluded it from Table 7.6 because there is no strong evidence that the dependent variable measures parliamentary preferences with regard to relative discretion.

Further analysis: discretion of the Commission and cross-policy patterns

I investigate cross-policy patterns as a first (indirect) attempt to assess the validity of Hypothesis 7.3. Before we proceed, I have already found some initial supporting evidence from the inclusion of a dummy variable *Directive* in the regressions of Table 7.6 (see footnote twenty-eight). The coefficients of this variable are significantly greater than zero in eleven out of eighteen regressions.[29] The Parliament is likely to add between twenty and thirty more words if the proposal is for a directive rather than a regulation. In other words, it is less likely to specify policy implementation in detail when the proposal is for a legal instrument that is more used where the Commission's executive role is greater.

In order to analyze this issue further, I have used the Parliament's four-tier classification[30] of policy areas and produced 36 dummy variables based on the second level of disaggregation. These categories are not mutually exclusive. For instance, codecision proposal 2000/0142 on equal treatment belongs to three areas: social policy (topic number 4.10), employment policy (4.15) and education policy (4.40). Proposal 2000/0183 on universal service provisions covers free movement of services (2.40) and information and communications (3.30).

Table 7.7 shows the results from regressing the two measures of discretion on the policy area variables, controlling for amending proposals. They will be analyzed with reference to Tables 5.2 and 5.8 which list the average levels of discretion delegated, across issue areas, by the Council to national authorities and the Commission respectively. The test of Hypothesis 7.3 is indirect because the dependent variable in Table 7.7 is the discretion of national administrations, rather than relative or Commission discretion. As clearly emerged in Chapter 5, the Commission has executive functions in a minority of EU laws and, even in these cases, only a few provisions delegate powers to it. It is the case also for these data sets.[31] Nevertheless, if the Parliament is less likely to

---

[29] The coefficient of *Directive* is significantly greater than zero at the 5 percent level in seven out of the nine regressions with *Discretion (Word count Δ)* (and at the 10 percent in the remaining two) and it is greater than zero at the 1 percent level in two regressions with *Discretion (Percentage Δ)*.

[30] The classification can be found at http://www2.europarl.eu.int/oeil/search.jsp.

[31] For instance, with regard to the data set used for Table 7.6, if we roughly assume that the relative executive role of the Commission is greater in regulations, only 8 percent of the proposals are for regulations and this percentage is considerably lower when we consider provisions referring to the Commission and amended in the second reading. The large majority of second reading amendments are related to national implementation. It is for these reasons that a measure of Council–Parliament–Commission conflict is not included. The dependent variables clearly do not measure the discretion of the Commission, either directly or relative to the discretion of national administrations.

Table 7.7 *The impact of European Parliament second reading amendments across policy areas: robust OLS regressions.*

	Dependent variable: *Discretion*	
	Word count Δ	*Percentage* Δ
Constant	103.306	5.154
	$(4.24)^a$	$(4.27)^a$
Amending law	−34.512	−2.028
	$(-1.71)^c$	$(-2.28)^b$
Citizen's rights	−137.639	−5.178
	$(-3.10)^a$	$(-5.11)^a$
Free movement of goods	−71.108	−3.326
	$(-3.22)^a$	$(-2.90)^a$
Free movement of services	−15.306	−2.575
	(-0.21)	(-1.19)
Free movement of capital	−70.062	−4.156
	$(-2.13)^b$	$(-2.95)^a$
Competition	•	3.445
		(1.05)
Taxation	•	0.676
		(1.03)
Agriculture	−76.975	−2.930
	$(-3.64)^a$	$(-1.85)^c$
Fisheries	0.390	−1.785
	(0.01)	(-1.38)
Transport	−103.696	−3.37
	$(-3.23)^a$	$(-2.47)^b$
Information and communications	60.001	−1.128
	(1.17)	(-0.69)
Industry	−11.37	−1.817
	(-0.36)	(-1.38)
Research and development	3.855	−1.681
	(0.06)	(-0.69)
Energy	−73.476	−3.887
	$(-1.73)^c$	$(-1.84)^c$
Environment	22.678	−0.31
	(0.82)	(-0.25)
Social policy	−68.794	−3.126
	$(-2.82)^a$	$(-2.40)^b$
Employment	4.862	0.848
	(0.14)	(0.45)
Public health	−77.307	−1.990
	$(-3.84)^a$	(-0.88)
Education	129.82	•
	$(1.79)^c$	
Culture	−73.964	−3.364
	$(-3.23)^a$	$(-2.76)^a$
		(cont.)

Table 7.7 (*cont.*)

Consumers	−6.312	0.638
	(−0.32)	(0.49)
Regional policy	−21.306	2.328
	(−0.87)	(1.93)[c]
Sustainable development	38.505	2.094
	(1.13)	(1.06)
Economic union	−80.298	−3.802
	(−3.27)[a]	(−2.84)[a]
Common foreign and security policy	−30.604	•
	(−1.64)	
Commercial policy	8.181	−0.196
	(0.67)	(−0.25)
Development cooperation	−72.702	−3.452
	(−3.38)[a]	(−3.23)[a]
External relations	−20.336	−1.454
	(−0.60)	(−1.20)
Humanitarian aid	−67.568	−3.328
	(−2.67)[a]	(−2.62)[a]
Judicial cooperation	211.269	•
	(7.58)[a]	
European statistical system	−64.794	−2.194
	(−2.64)[a]	(−1.48)
Union institutions	•	−1.123
		(−0.83)
Budget	−103.306	•
	(−4.24)[a]	
F	1.55[b]	1.20
Adjusted R^2	0.06	0.02
N	251	253

Note: Initial $n = 270$, observations with Cook distances greater than $4/n$ are subsequently omitted. t-statistics in parentheses, one-tailed test; [a] $p \leq 0.01$; [b] $p \leq 0.05$; [c] $p \leq 0.1$. • The variable has been dropped.

prefer low-discretion statutes in policy areas where the Commission is relatively more involved in execution (i.e. it adds *fewer* words), I consider this evidence as indirect support of Hypothesis 7.3. In other words, the coefficients of these areas should be negative.

I focus only on areas with at least five proposals[32] and results that are robust across both operationalizations of discretion. Second reading

[32] These are *Agriculture* (38 proposals), *Consumers* (42), *Development cooperation* (5), *Employment* (15), *Energy* (8), *Environment* (52), *Free movement of capital* (26), *Free movement of goods* (8), *Industry* (24), *Information and communications* (23), *Public health* (13), *Research and development* (8) and *Transport* (31).

amendments add between 69 and 104 *fewer* words to a Council common position on *transport, agriculture, energy, development cooperation, free movement of goods* and *free movement of capital.* These estimates oscillate between 237 and 11 words. They *shorten* the common positions by between 2.9 and 4.2 percent (oscillating between 0.1 and 9.7 percent). These areas appear to share either one or two features.

First, the involvement of the Commission in policy execution is comparatively greater. As Table 5.8 illustrates, the Commission enjoys relatively substantial executive powers in agriculture, transport (market conditions) and capital movement. To a lesser extent, this is also true for laws on the free movement of goods.[33] Development cooperation and energy are instead not present in Table 5.8. The first policy covers the relations between the EU and developing countries, and requires a non-trivial executive role of the Commission. The second is a traditional internal market policy, which also includes aid to trans-European networks, where the Commission enjoys some executive functions.

Results are even more revealing if I rerun the regressions separating the observations into two subsets depending on whether the second EP reading took place before or after 10 June 1999, to account for the more intense Commission–Parliament conflict in the fifth term. In the pre-June 1999 data set, the coefficients are significantly lower than zero in five of the above-mentioned six policy areas where the Commission exercises greater powers (goods and capital movement, agriculture, transport and energy). In the fifth term instead, only two areas (transport and development cooperation) remain significantly negative, suggesting a tendency by the Parliament to be stricter on the Commission. In summary, there is some evidence that Parliament may be less likely to increase statutory control in policies of greater executive involvement of the Commission, especially when the positions of these institutions do not diverge. Evidence indirectly supports Hypothesis 7.3. The content analysis in the next section, extended to first reading amendments, provides further evidence.

It could be argued that these policy areas share a second common feature. Their technical complexity is relatively high. During the 1990s, the legislative output in agriculture, transport and energy covered safety, risk management and technical standards. It included laws on animal nutrition, food and feeding stuff, transport safety (especially sea and road transport), dangerous substances, renewable energy and technical

[33] The Parliament's classification group customs union, public procurement and standards into the *Free movement of goods* category. Customs union laws are assigned to the commercial policy category in Table 5.8.

standards.[34] Moreover, according to the Parliament's classification, capital movement legislation covers company law, insurance, credit, banking and securities. As Table 5.2 shows, the Council has relied to a considerable extent on national authorities in these policies because of their complexity. The Parliament may have been more reluctant to increase statutory control in order to reap the benefits of bureaucratic expertise.

Nevertheless, there are both empirical and theoretical arguments against this conclusion. First, Table 5.2 reveals that national authorities also enjoy considerable discretion in environment and consumer protection legislation but their coefficients in Table 7.7 are not significantly negative. We should have also expected a significantly negative sign for *Research and development* since it includes intellectual and industrial property. Second, I do not control for policy complexity in Table 7.6 because such an inclusion is only justified on the expectation that MEPs have systematically less (or more) policy expertise than Council ministers. This proposition cannot be derived from the model in Chapter 2, which assumes that EU legislators in the two chambers have similar policy knowhow. The available evidence does not suggest that ministers are more specialized than MEPs. Policy expertise is one of many factors determining the allocation of cabinet portfolios in national governments (Browne and Franklin, 1973; Budge and Keman, 1990; Laver and Shepsle, 1996; Gallagher, Laver and Mair, 2001: 360–5) and there is ample evidence of policy specialization in the Parliament (Bowler and Farrell, 1995; Raunio, 1996; Mamadouh and Raunio, 2003). Nevertheless, this topic should be the subject of further research on the seniority and background of these important actors in EU politics.

Table 7.7 generates other findings worth mentioning. The constant terms are significantly greater than zero, corroborating the expectation of Hypothesis 7.1 for a larger data set. On average, the Parliament adds 103 words to or lengthens by 5.1 percent the Council common position. This is equivalent to the consumer protection amendments in Table 7.2 on internal market legislation. As in Table 7.6, the impact of *Amending law* is significantly negative (though only weakly in the first measure of discretion). The Parliament adds thirty-five *fewer* words or shortens by 2 percent the common position in the case of proposals amending EU laws.

In conclusion, the analysis of cross-policy patterns further corroborates Hypothesis 7.1 and, indirectly, Hypothesis 7.3. The impact of amending proposals is also as expected. Finally, there is evidence to suggest that the Parliament is willing to accept higher-discretion statutes in more complex

---

[34] The reader surely recalls the food scares and the disasters at sea that occurred in Europe during that period and prompted this legislation.

Table 7.8 *Components for the content analysis.*

Component	Content analysis
Scope	Is the scope of the law widened or narrowed?
Exemption/derogation	Is an exemption or derogation inserted/extended or deleted/tightened?
Consultation and public hearings requirements	Is a requirement for consultation or public hearing inserted/tightened or deleted/loosened?
Reporting requirements	Is a requirement for reporting inserted/tightened or deleted/loosened?
Appeal and dispute resolution procedures	Are appeal and dispute resolution procedures inserted/tightened or deleted/loosened?
Time limits and deadlines	Are time limits and deadlines inserted/shortened or deleted/extended?
Appointment rules	Has the composition of the committee/agency changed to strengthen or weaken the role of the Parliament?
Spending limits	Are spending limits inserted/tightened or deleted/loosened?
Inspection procedures	Are checks and inspection procedures inserted/tightened or deleted/loosened? Is the role of the Parliament strengthened or weakened? Is the dealing of the issue shifted from comitology to legislative procedures (reserve of law)?
Comitology	Are more or less issues dealt via the comitology procedures? Is the comitology procedure stricter or looser? Are criteria added to or deleted from the execution of implementing powers?

policy areas, but this conclusion is open to question on theoretical and empirical grounds. Further research is necessary.

Content analysis of parliamentary amendments

Word counts may be considered superficial measures of discretion. Hence, I have selected a set of components that are related to discretion and assessed how they are modified by the Parliament's amendments. Table 7.8 lists ten categories and the questions that have been used as the basis for the content analysis.

Eight components are directly linked to the constraint ratio used in Chapter 3 or to the categories of constraints used by Epstein and O'Halloran (1999b: 101). Scope is a measure of the degree to which an EU law encroaches upon national laws, imposes legislative requirements and, then, exercises control on the activities of national administrations. Inspection procedures have been singled out for their explicit control functions.

I test two hypotheses that are variants of Hypotheses 7.1 and 7.3. Although the process is not always straightforward, expectations are produced by allocating a category to the discretion of an executive actor. Four components are mostly linked to the discretion of national authorities (scope, exemptions and derogations, appeal procedures and time limits). Appointment rules and some aspects of comitology (i.e. the legislative–executive boundary and the role of the Parliament) are related to the relative importance of the Parliament vis-à-vis that of the Council in policy execution. Since the Council is the vehicle through which national authorities affect EU policy outcomes, I include two expectations about these categories in the variant of Hypothesis 7.1. Spending limits, inspection procedures and other aspects of comitology (i.e. the number of issues, procedures and criteria) relate mainly to the Commission and other EU-level institutions. Reporting and consultation requirements can be related to either national administrations, the Commission or both.

Component-specific expectations can then be derived from Hypotheses 7.1 and 7.3. The first one refers to components related to national execution.

Hypothesis 7.4 *European Parliament and discretion of national administrations (content variant)*

In the case of national implementation, the Parliament prefers a broader scope, fewer or stricter exemptions and derogations, more or stricter consultation requirements, reporting requirements and appeal procedures and more or shorter time limits. The Parliament prefers greater influence in the appointment of EU-level bodies and in the comitology procedures.

The second hypothesis refers to components related to the exercise of the policy functions of the Commission and EU-level bodies.

Hypothesis 7.5 *European Parliament and discretion of the Commission (content variant)*

In the case of supranational implementation, the Parliament prefers deleting or loosening consultation and reporting requirements, relaxing spending limits, inserting or strengthening inspection powers, expanding policy-specific powers and loosening the comitology procedures.

The data set includes 369 codecision proposals, 6,980 first and 1,445 second reading amendments. The analysis is extended to the first reading because the Parliament has adopted second reading amendments that are related to at least one of the components listed in Table 7.8 in only 99 proposals (fewer than ten proposals per component on average). The size of this data set is too small to conduct a comprehensive analysis. If we include all the amendments instead, 241 proposals include relevant amendments and the number of observations per component more than doubles.

However, first reading amendments create two problems for testing the hypothesis. First, strictly speaking, these amendments reveal the preferences of the Parliament vis-à-vis those of the Commission, not of the Council. They are a manifestation of Parliament–Council conflict only to the extent that they anticipate the Council common position. This degree of anticipation is almost impossible to measure.[35] Second, the degree of information asymmetry or incompleteness is greater at the early stages of the procedure. The Commission may have inadvertently omitted a provision in the initial proposal and an amendment may not necessarily reveal inter-institutional conflict. These qualifications need to be kept in mind in the empirical analysis below. On the positive side, since first reading amendments require a simple, rather an absolute, majority for adoption, they are easier to introduce and may reveal the preferences of the Parliament more comprehensively.

A note on methodology

I have triangulated three sets of documents to answer the questions in Table 7.8. The first, most important, set is the list of amendments adopted by the Parliament and published in Series C of the *Official Journal of the European Communities*. They are available online on the Parliament's legislative observatory for 1998 onwards. For the preceding years, I had to rely on the printed versions. The second is the summary of the debates and activities taking place within the Commission, Council and Parliament and of decisions and votes taken by these institutions at each stage of the codecision procedure. These summaries are available online on the legislative observatory for all the proposals. The third set of documents comprises, when available, the reports and recommendations tabled by the *rapporteur* of the parliamentary committee responsible for

---

[35] The Parliament could be expected to prefer more constraining provisions than the Commission in the case of national implementation, but not in the case of Commission execution. Therefore, Hypothesis 7.5 appears particularly implausible. However, assuming Parliament–Commission preference similarity, we should expect either very few first reading amendments or amendments anticipating the Council's position.

proposing amendments to either the Commission proposal or the Council common position. These reports frequently include opinions from other parliamentary committees and are also available on the legislative observatory for 1996 onwards.[36] However, it has to be noted that in the plenary session the Parliament may reject the proposed amendments and adopt new ones.

The content analysis has proceeded as follows. I selected English and French keywords for each of the component of the content analysis and ran word searches across the three sources (keywords are listed in Appendix 7.1). This has allowed me to identify whether a topic debated by the institutions or an amendment are related to one of these components. The questions listed in Table 7.8 are answered by triangulating the evidence extracted from the three sets of documents.[37] Appendix 7.2 provides additional details on coding and examples of amendments for each component.

Scope, exemptions and derogations

I analyze these three components together because they are normally interlinked in any given law. A provision that permanently exempts a specific social group or a product from the reach of the proposal at hand narrows the scope of the measure. A permanent derogation has the same effect. This is also evident when reading the parliamentary reports and the summaries of the inter-institutional debates. Nevertheless, I will proceed by steps. First, I analyze amendments that mention only the scope or field of application and make no references to exemptions or derogations. I then move onto exemptions and derogations and, finally, I consider the two components jointly.

The Parliament has adopted amendments that modify the scope of 112 codecision proposals. In 68 cases the aim of the Parliament has been to widen the scope of the measure at hand, while in 25 proposals, the Parliament has sought to narrow the field of application. In the remaining 19 proposals, there are amendments that both narrow and widen the scope. Table 7.9 shows the results of Z-tests on the equality of proportions. They examine whether the percentage of proposals where the Parliament has adopted scope-widening amendments is significantly

---

[36] I have downloaded 836 files from the legislative observatory (http://wwwdb.europarl. eu.int/dors/oeil/en/default.htm) comprising parliamentary committees' opinions, reports and recommendations and EP legislative resolutions on Commission proposals and Council common positions.

[37] Where only the printed versions of the *Official Journal* are available, I analyzed the content of the amendments guided by the result of the word searches of the available electronic documents which may have indicated that an amendment was related to one of the components in Table 7.8.

Table 7.9 *Content analysis: two-sample Z-tests on the equality of proportions.*

Components	Proportions	Z-test[a]	N	Z-test with N = 369
Scope	Widening – narrowing	5.831[b]	112	4.143[b]
Exemption/derogation	Tightening – loosening	1.700[c]	108	1.133
Scope and exemption/derogation	(Widening or tightening) – (Narrowing or loosening)	4.981[b]	161	3.398[b]
Consultation requirements:				
– Commission and *EU* bodies	Strengthening – loosening	8.695[b]	49	6.241[b]
– national administrations	Strengthening – loosening	5.735[b]	22	4.025[b]
– all	Strengthening – loosening	9.632[b]	63	6.966[b]
Reporting requirements:				
– Commission and *EU* bodies	Strengthening – loosening	14.432[b]	112	11.080[b]
– national administrations	Strengthening – loosening	11.775[b]	79	8.762[b]
– all	Strengthening – loosening	14.847[b]	120	11.434[b]
Appeal procedures	Strengthening – loosening	8.390[b]	39	5.946[b]
Time limits	Shortening – extending	6.803[b]	123	5.018[b]
Comitology				
– issues	More – less	3.354[b]	66	2.288[c]
– procedures	Looser – stricter	6.454[b]	35	4.676[b]
– procedures and criteria	Looser – stricter	2.006[c]	50	1.414[d]

Note: [a] One tailed Z-test on the difference of proportions. The hypothesis is that the difference is significantly greater than zero (e.g. proportion (widening) – proportion (narrowing) = diff > 0, the null hypothesis is diff = 0). [b] $p \leq 0.01$; [c] $p \leq 0.05$; [d] $p \leq 0.1$.

greater than the percentage where scope-narrowing amendments are introduced. The difference between these two proportions and its statistical significance depend on the choice of the sample size. Differences are smaller and the significance is likely to be lower if the sample size encompasses all the 369 proposals instead of only the proposals to which a scope-related amendment has been inserted (i.e. 112). On the other hand, expectations are more strongly validated if the Z-statistic is significant in both circumstances.

The second row in Table 7.9 clearly shows that the proportion of Commission codecision proposals where parliamentary amendments aim to widen the scope of the measure is significantly greater than the proportion of proposals where scope-narrowing amendments are introduced (regardless of the sample size used). In more than three out of four proposals, where at least one scope-related amendment is inserted, the aim is to expand the field of application of the legal act. There is hence strong evidence in support of Hypothesis 7.4.

Provisions related to exemptions and derogations are not easily separable. On the surface, exemptions may be permanent and derogations temporary. However, EU legislators do not adopt these definitions consistently and sometimes they use the two terms interchangeably. Hence, I group them together. Hereafter, for a clearer exposition, I will mostly use the term "exemption."

As argued above, exemptions are directly related of the field of application of a law. In this analysis, I include amendments that refer to scope only if the keywords for exemption are mentioned (see Table 7.A1 in Appendix 7.1) or if it is clear that the relevant amendment is more related to exemptions than to scope. I code as "tightening" cases where exemptions are deleted from a proposal or existing requirements (e.g. criteria, eligibility) are made stricter. "Loosening" is for cases where exemptions are inserted in a proposal or requirements are relaxed.

The Parliament has adopted amendments that modify the provisions on exemptions of 108 codecision proposals. In 45 cases, provisions have been tightened, in 33 cases they have been loosened, in the remaining 30 proposals some amendments have tightened and others loosened the relevant provisions. The Z-tests in Table 7.9 reveal that the proportion of Commission codecision proposals where parliamentary amendments tightened exemptions is significantly greater than the proportion of proposals where provisions are loosened. However, this only applies if we consider proposals including amendments that are related to this component of the content analysis (i.e. only the first Z-statistic, in the third column, is significant). In fewer than three out of four proposals, where there is at least one exemption-related amendment, the aim is to tighten the requirements or to delete the relevant provisions entirely. These results tend to corroborate, though less strongly, the expectations of Hypothesis 7.4. It has to be noted that exemptions are inserted or rules are eased in three out of five proposals.

We can now analyze scope and exemptions together. By grouping these two components, we can assess how the Parliament wishes to modify the broader boundaries of a proposal. The deletion of an exemption or the tightening of its requirements can be interpreted as the widening to the scope of an act. The outcomes of these decisions are, broadly, similar.

The Parliament has adopted amendments that modify the scope (intended in this broader sense) of 161 proposals. In 74 cases the aim of the Parliament has been to widen the scope, this institution has proposed to narrow the scope in 32 proposals, while the remaining 55 proposals include amendments that produce both outcomes. The results in Table 7.9 (fourth row) confirm the previous findings. The proportion of proposals with scope-widening amendments is significantly greater than the proportion with scope-narrowing ones. In 33 cases, the Parliament has tried to widen the scope of the measure *and* to tighten the exemptions, while it had attempted the opposite in 20 cases.

Consultation requirements

I include in this category amendments that insert, delete, reinforce or relax requirements for consultation of committees, public consultation and hearings. I include obligations for public statements and procedures to hold public hearings by agencies or committees. I code as "strengthening" cases where consultation requirements are inserted or reinforced and "loosening" where they are deleted or relaxed.

The evidence is strongly supportive of Hypothesis 7.4, but it is against Hypothesis 7.5. I have counted only three cases where requirements are deleted or relaxed (two cases of consultation by the Commission or by other EU-level agencies and one by national authorities). In fifty-seven out of sixty-three observations, requirements are either inserted or strengthened. Both types of amendments are present in the remaining three proposals. It is then not surprising that the results in Table 7.9 show that the proportion of proposals where amendments aim to strengthen the consultation requirements is significantly greater than the proportion of proposals where loosening amendments are introduced. The Parliament clearly does not differentiate between national authorities and the Commission.

Reporting requirements

I include in this category amendments that insert, delete, reinforce or relax reporting and reviewing requirements, such as cases where the content of the report is specified in greater or less detail and where the report must be addressed to additional institutions, such the Parliament and the Court of Auditors. "Strengthening" is for where reporting requirements are inserted or reinforced, and "loosening" is where they are deleted or relaxed.

I have found only two circumstances where reporting requirements are deleted from the proposal. In another case, requirements are relaxed in one provision but are inserted in another section of the proposal. The reporting provisions are strengthened in the remaining 117 proposals. The very large Z-test statistics in Table 7.9 result from the disproportionate presence of proposals with amendments strengthening the reporting requirements. There is no differentiation between national authorities and the Commission for this category. This is because the Commission is frequently also in charge of reporting on national implementation, hence additional requirements are imposed on this institution and, hence, indirectly on member states. In summary, in line with Hypothesis 7.4, there is very strong evidence that the Parliament prefers more or stricter reporting requirements than those proposed by either the Commission or the Council. However, contrary to Hypothesis 7.5, the Parliament does not show more leniency toward the Commission and other EU-level bodies.

Appeal procedures

Amendments that insert, reinforce, delete or relax provisions on appeal and dispute resolution procedures are considered in this category. It includes, for instance, measures that give standing to addition groups, expedite and facilitate the appeal or review process, or define a court jurisdiction. "Strengthening" is for where the procedures are inserted or reinforced, and "loosening" where they are deleted or relaxed.

I have not found a single case where appeal procedures are only loosened. In two cases where there are amendments that weaken somewhat the appeal or dispute resolution process, there are also some other changes that reinforce it. In the remaining thirty-seven proposals, the changes adopted by the Parliament either insert or reinforce the procedures. Hence, unsurprisingly, the Z-tests in Table 7.9 reveal that the proportion of proposals where amendments aim to strengthen the appeal procedures is significantly greater than the proportion of proposals where loosening amendments are introduced. Hypothesis 7.4 is strongly supported.

Time limits

This component includes amendments where a deadline or a time limit is inserted, shortened, deleted or extended. Frequent occurrences are changes to the deadline for the national implementation of directives. It includes sunset clauses and the establishment or deletion of transitional periods and of procedures that allow deferment. I denote as "shortening" cases where time limits are inserted or shortened, and "extending" where they are deleted or extended.

In 81 out of 123 observations, the Parliament has either inserted or shortened the time limit, in 28 proposals the deadline has been extended. In the remaining fourteen proposals, some amendments have shortened some time limits, other amendments have extended other limits. This evidence supports our expectations of Hypothesis 7.4. The results in

Table 7.9 confirm that the proportion of proposals with time-shortening amendments is significantly greater than that with time-extending ones.

Appointment rules

The Parliament has proposed amendments to the composition of committees or EU-level bodies in eight proposals. In three cases, it has demanded to be directly involved in the appointment of members of committees or agencies. In the five other cases, the Parliament changed the composition of committees to include independent experts and other representatives and, hence, to loosen the grip of national governments. These results support Hypothesis 7.4, although only superficially, given the small sample size.

Spending limits

The next three categories are primarily related to the Commission. Spending programmes are generally administered by the Commission or other EU-level agencies. However, two caveats need to be made explicit before we proceed. First, the room for changing budgetary allocations by the Parliament via the legislative procedure is limited. Since 1988, the Council has adopted multi-annual packages that fix the overall ceiling of the EU budget relative to the gross national product and sub-ceilings for broad categories of policies. The EU budget must also be balanced each year. The precise amount of revenue and expenditure is agreed by the Parliament and the Council in an annual budgetary cycle (Laffan and Shackleton, 2000; Nugent, 2002: 366–84; Hix, 2005: 275–81). Nevertheless, when spending programmes are attached to specific measures, the legislative stage could be considered as the initial battleground for the following years' budgetary allocations. Second, using the budget as an instrument to shape bureaucratic incentives is problematic. As Moe (1987: 487) points out, cutting budgets may have the unwanted consequence of undermining the financial foundations of policy programmes. This makes confirmation of Hypothesis 7.5 easier because, even if the Parliament may be tempted to reduce budgetary allocations to sanction the Commission, it may not proceed with this strategy in order to preserve an EU policy.

For this component of the content analysis, I focus only on requirements that are directly linked to spending programmes. I consider only amendments that change financial allocations, spending limits and criteria that have a direct impact on the allocated amounts. The procedures will be mostly covered in the section on comitology but they are considered here if there are changes proposed to the rules allocating projects to decision-making procedures.

The Parliament has proposed amendments to the spending limits of only nine proposals, making any statistical analysis and generalization unwise. Such a small figure is not surprising as most of the EU policy output is of a regulatory nature. Nevertheless, the Parliament's preference with regard to spending limits appears to be rather evident and to confirm Hypothesis 7.5. On the seven occasions where there were amendments to the spending amounts, the Parliament increased the financial allocation to the relevant programme. Moreover, the procedures for allocating funds have been relaxed in five out of six cases. In the other two circumstances, the Parliament has tried to increase the financial autonomy and transparency of EU agencies.

Inspection procedures

I include in this category amendments that insert, delete, reinforce or relax check and inspection procedures. There are nine proposals where the Parliament has modified the inspection procedures but only one instance of weakening. The inspection powers of the Commission and other EU bodies, such as the Court of Auditors and the European Anti-Fraud Office (OLAF), have been strengthened on two occasions. In another two circumstances, only the Commission's prerogatives have been reinforced. In the remaining four proposals, the Parliament has beefed up the powers of the Court of Auditors and of OLAF, especially with regard to the allocation of funding decided by EU agencies.

These provisional results appear to support Hypothesis 7.5 but, given the small sample size, any generalization is unwarranted. An additional qualification is necessary. In four cases, the institutions subject to inspection are other EU-level bodies. Hence, the Parliament's desire to strengthen the inspection procedures may not be due to preference similarity with other supranational institutions but, more likely, it reflects the well-known use of institutional checks (Kiewiet and McCubbins, 1991: 33–4). Agencies with conflicting interests are set up to facilitate efficient monitoring.

Administrative procedures (comitology)

Comitology is a system of procedures based on committees that are composed of representatives of the member states and chaired by the

Commission. Following a variety of rules, these committees assist and supervise the Commission in the exercise of the powers that have been delegated to it by EU legislators. The first advisory committee procedure was designed in the early 1960s with the first measures for the free movement of workers (e.g. Regulation 15/61) and on competition policy (e.g. Regulation 17/62). It simply required the Commission to consult the committee prior to taking the relevant measure. The more constraining management committee procedures were set up by the first regulations on the common agricultural markets (e.g. Regulation 19/62 on cereals). The committee could decide, by qualified majority, to refer the Commission's measure to the Council which could take a different decision. In 1968, the even more restrictive regulatory committee procedure was introduced (e.g. in Regulation 802/68 on the origin of goods). Only a QMV-blocking minority was necessary for referral to the Council. Finally, the anti-dumping Regulation 459/68 allowed member states to refer Commission decisions directly to the Council without the mediation of a committee. This was later termed the safeguard procedure.

The use of comitology increased considerably over the years and, to facilitate the implementation of the single market programme in the 1980s, Council Decision 87/373 codified these procedures and their variants. The Council did not recognize any parliamentary role in the comitology procedures even if the Commission was formally accountable to the Parliament and the Council moderately extended the legislative powers of the Parliament in the Single European Act. The Parliament has then tried to rectify this situation using legal, budgetary and legislative means. A series of inter-institutional agreements has culminated with a new Council Decision 1999/468 which removes variants and recognizes the Parliament's right to be informed and to signal its disapproval if it deems that the Commission is acting *ultra vires*.[38]

The results from the content analysis illustrate the Parliament's legislative battle on comitology in the codecision procedure. The Parliament has adopted comitology-related amendments to 119 proposals. In 59 cases, the aim has been to increase the role of the Parliament by asking to be informed or heard, to monitor, provide opinions or even vote on the implementing measures. These amendments also tried to increase transparency or simply referred to the inter-institutional agreements and decisions to make sure that the agreed procedures were used. In 26 cases, the

---

[38] For historical reviews on comitology, see Demmke *et al.* (1996), Vos (1997) and Haibach (2000). On the Parliament and comitology see Bradley (1997), Hix (2000) and Pollack (2003b: 114–25).

aim of amendments has been to reserve the specific issue at hand to the legislative process rather than the comitology procedures. A priority of the Parliament has always been a clear distinction between legislative acts and implementing measures (European Parliament, 1998). In practice, this has been translated into a systematic attempt to redress the balance in favor of the legislative process where the Parliament has a veto power. Unsurprisingly, I have found no amendments that tried to reduce the role of the Parliament or shifted an issue from the legislative procedure to the comitology process. Results support Hypothesis 7.4.

Comitology also allows us to analyze whether the Parliament tries to systematically strengthen or weaken the executive role of the Commission. The Commission is strengthened if additional powers to take policy-specific measures are conferred upon it (sometimes, simply by increasing the monetary thresholds for committee consultation) or if the procedures and criteria to exercise delegated powers are loosened.[39] In the content analysis, these circumstances are coded as "more" issues and "looser" procedures and criteria ("less" and "stricter" are used for the opposite type of amendment).

Strengthening appears to be the case, as Table 7.9 illustrates. In thirty-seven out of sixty-six proposals, the Parliament has asked the Commission to decide on additional policy issues, the Parliament has withdrawn policy prerogatives from the Commission in eighteen cases, while there are both types of amendments in the remaining eleven proposals. Thus, even though the Parliament has systematically tried to reconfigure the boundaries between legislation and implementation in favor of the former, hence shrinking back the Commission's powers, we still find that the proportion of proposals with issue-increasing amendments is significantly greater than that with issue-decreasing ones. This is in line with Hypothesis 7.5.

In thirty-one out of thirty-five proposals, the Parliament has adopted a looser comitology procedure. The Z-test of Table 7.9 confirms the significance of this preference ordering and this is line with other quantitative works (Dogan, 1997). However, it is also quite common for the Parliament to add further criteria to the comitology decision process or to shorter the period of applicability of the measures. This has happened in eighteen proposals and I have found only one circumstance where the decision-making criteria have been loosened. Nevertheless, the general picture remains unchanged. The last row in Table 7.9 still shows

---

[39] From the less strict to the stricter procedure, the ordering is: advisory committee, management committee, regulatory committee a, regulatory committee b (Steunenberg, Koboldt and Schmidtchen, 1996a, 1996b).

a significantly greater proportion of loosening (procedural or criteria-related) amendments. Hypothesis 7.5 is strongly confirmed.

Equally interesting, the number of readings with amendments loosening procedures and criteria has decreased from twenty-two to thirteen and those strengthening procedures and criteria have increased from seven to fifteen in the fifth parliamentary term, indicating greater willingness by the Parliament to exercise control on the Commission. Even the most demanding Z-tests on the equality of pre- and post-June 1999 proportions suggest that these changes are significant. With $N = 596$ (the number of readings), the proportion of post-1999 readings with loosening amendments is (weakly) significantly lower that the pre-1999 proportion ($z = -1.544, p < 0.06$) and the proportion with tightening amendments is significantly higher ($z = 1.722, p < 0.04$).

Conclusion

This chapter has analyzed the revealed preferences of the Parliament with regard to the discretion of national administrations and of the Commission. Overall, the involvement of this institution in the EU legislative process is likely to centralize powers. The Parliament has shown a preference for expanding and strengthening the policy prerogatives of the Commission. But this trend is counterbalanced by a tendency to tighten some procedural requirements, especially when the two supranational institutions do not share similar views. Additionally, EU law is likely to be more prescriptive as a result of the Parliament's inclination for increasing statutory control in the case of national implementation, and especially when the Council and the Parliament have different preferences. It must be noted, however, that these differences are not large and the final act will smooth them even further as it will be the product of mutual concessions between the Council and the Parliament.

These results are mostly in line with our expectations. They can be summarized in detail under three headings.

Implementation by national authorities (Hypotheses 7.1 and 7.4). In the case of national implementation, MEPs systematically prefer lower statutory discretion than Council ministers because they face higher costs of ongoing nonstatutory oversight. Procedurally, these preferences are translated into amendments that broaden the scope of the acts, tighten the provisions on exemptions, consultation and reporting requirements, appeal procedures and time limits, strengthen the role of the Parliament vis-à-vis the Council in the comitology procedures and in the appointment of EU-level bodies, and rearrange the proposed boundary between legislation and execution in favor of the former.

Parliament–Council conflict and implementation by national authorities (Hypothesis 7.2). The parliamentary preference for lower statutory discretion is heightened if conflict between the Parliament and the Council increases, especially along the left–right and policy dimensions and as turnout increases.

Implementation by the Commission (Hypotheses 7.3 and 7.5). In the case of Commission implementation, the Parliament is *less* likely to prefer low-discretion statutes in areas where this institution has a greater executive role. These preferences are translated into amendments that expand the Commission's comitology-specific powers and inspection prerogatives and that loosen spending limits, procedures and criteria.

However, against our expectations, the Parliament buttresses, rather than weakens, the consultation and reporting requirements imposed on the Commission. This may be due to the plausible fact that the Commission may propose looser requirements than those preferred by Parliament. But even this explanation cannot account for the desire of greater stringency than the Council. Instead, more likely, the premise on which these hypotheses are based (the similarity of preferences of supranational institutions) may not always hold. Evidence suggests that the Parliament has been keener on tightening statutory control on the Commission during the fifth term when the relations between the two institutions were less harmonious.

Appendix 7.1 Content analysis: keywords and sentences

Table 7.A1 lists the keywords that have been used for the first step of the content analysis. Where different from the English terms, French words are in italics. Some words are truncated at the root in order to include as many derived terms as possible. In some cases, I have used entire sentences.

Appendix 7.2 Content analysis: additional coding rules and examples of amendments

Scope. I disregard those amendments whose aim is clarification and where it is unclear whether the scope has been narrowed or widened. In Regulation 178/2002 on the general principles of food law,

Table 7.A1 *Keywords and sentences used for the content analysis.*

Component	Keywords and sentences
Scope	scope, field of application, *champ (d'application)*
Exemption/derogation	exempt, derog, *dérog*
Consultation and public hearings requirements	consult, hearing, heard, hear, statement, *séance, audience, déclaration, entend* review, report, study, revision, evaluation, *révision, rapport, étude, évalu*
Reporting requirements	the Commission shall submit a report the Commission shall submit an annual report the Commission shall inform the European Parliament and the Council of
Appeal and dispute resolution procedures	appeal, complaint, dispute, litigation, remedy, *appel, réclamation, litige, remède* deadline, transpos, time limit, timeframe, phasing out, transitional period, entry into force, date of implementation, defer, *délai, transpos, limite de temps, date limite, période de temps, suppression progressive, période de transition, entrée en vigueur, date de application, différer, mise en oeuvre*
Time limits and deadlines	Member States shall bring into force Member States shall adopt Member States shall apply this Regulation shall enter into force Regulation shall apply
Appointment rules	(as with comitology for the composition of committees, in addition I have analyzed the amendments to the composition of EU-level bodies) ECU, euro, euros, EUR, €, percent, appropriation, budget, fund,%, *pourcent, pour cent, fond*
Spending limits	financial framework for the implementation financial allocation for the implementation financial reference amount for the implementation
Inspection procedures	check, inspection, on the spot, on-the-spot, *contrôle, enrayer*
Comitology	comitology, comitology, committee, procedure, advisory, consultative, regulatory, management, modus vivendi, Decision 1999/469 of 18 June 1999, safeguard, *comitologie, comité, sauvegarde*

the Parliament sought to extend the scope of the proposal to the importation and exportation of foods and feed products. In Directive 2001/105 on rules for ship inspection and survey organizations, the Parliament widened the scope to also cover work related to classification certificates. The Parliament excluded historic vehicles and included spare parts to the field of application of the end-of-life vehicles Directive 2000/53.

Exemptions and derogations. I also consider procedures that provide for the possible adoption of exemptions and clear-cut provisions that do not refer to the keywords. In Directive 2002/73, the Parliament has sought to tighten up the possibilities to derogate from the principle of equal treatment for men and women. It deleted the exemption for military aviation activities in Directive 2002/49 on environmental noise. Insertion of exemptions is not uncommon. The Parliament introduced an exemption for certain machines, such as chainsaws, from Directive 2002/88 on measures against the emission of pollutants. In Regulation 2320/2002 on civil aviation security, it adopted an amendment allowing for derogations for implementing structural modifications to airports and terminals.

Consultation requirements. Consultation of and hearing by the Parliament are analyzed in the section on comitology, hence they are excluded here. Consultation requirements imposed on private actors are disregarded. Finally, I do not consider cases where an entirely new provision, and a consultation requirement attached to it, has been inserted, or an existing one is deleted with the related consultation procedure. In Directive 97/50 on the free movement of doctors, the Parliament required the Commission to consult the Standing Committee of European Doctors before submitting proposals for amendments. In proposal COD/1992/0437 on open network provisions, any interested party, rather than only a specified list, must be consulted by the Commission prior to taking specific decisions. In Directive 2002/19 on access to communications networks, the Parliament prescribed that national regulatory authorities had to consult interested parties before deciding on access obligations. In Directive 2000/34 on working time, member states could extend the reference period only after consultation with employers and employees.

Reporting requirements. I disregard cases where an entirely new provision, and a reporting requirement attached to it, has been inserted, or an existing one is deleted with the related requirement. I also disregard calls for the Commission to add legislative proposals to the reports as this is a Commission prerogative anyhow. The Parliament required from the Commission and indirectly from the member states, an implementation report of Directive 1999/44 on the sale of consumer goods and of Directive 2001/96 on rules for loading bulk carriers. The extension of specific programmes, such as those to aid uprooted people in Asia and Latin America (Regulation 1880/2000), is made dependent on the Commission submitting annual reports. The Parliament may also specify in greater detail the content of the report. In Directive 2001/81 on emission ceilings for atmospheric pollutants, the report had to cover, among other issues, the possibility for further emission reductions and the objective of controlling transport emissions.

Appeal procedures. In Directive 2000/31 on electronic commerce, the Parliament wanted to ensure rapid and effective court action and required that the law of member states also permits out-of-court settlements by electronic means. In proposal COD/1992/0437 on open network provisions for voice telephony, the Parliament specified that any party with an obvious interest has a right of appeal against decisions taken by the national regulatory authorities and procedures must be inexpensive. In the case of an unsolved dispute between providers of postal services (Directive 97/67), the matter may be referred to the Commission, which must arbitrate.

Time limits. I disregard cases where an entirely new provision, and the time limit attached to it, has been inserted, or an existing one is deleted with the related limit. I also do not consider situations where the extended deadline is only a sign of an unusually delayed legislative process and where the Parliament extends a deadline as a compromise with the Council in exchange for an early adoption of the proposal. These cases do not reflect a desire for longer deadlines. Typical examples are where deadlines for the implementation of directives are brought forward (e.g. Directive 2002/65 on distance marketing of financial services). The transitional period allowing exemption from rules on price indication of Directive 95/58 has been reduced by two years. In Directive 2001/95, the Parliament has set a one year deadline for the establishment of the European product safety network. There are, however, a nontrivial number of cases where time limits have been extended either with regard to transposition (e.g. Directive 1999/92 on safety and health at work) and specific provisions (e.g. reporting has been delayed by two years in Directive 2001/16 on the interoperability of the European rail system).

Appointment rules. The Parliament required a hearing of the candidates for the directorship of the European Food Safety Authority (Regulation 178/2002). In Directive 2002/98 on quality and safety standards for the treatment of human blood, the Parliament has changed the composition of the committee. In Regulation 258/97 on novel foods, three consumer representatives were added to the committee composition.

Spending limits. Amendments specifying *ex novo* authorizations or appropriations are excluded because I do not have the term of comparison, i.e. the figure proposed by either the Commission or the Council. I also disregard rules, such as those on eligibility, that are not directly linked to spending amounts. Examples include the financial framework for the implementation of the LIFE programme on the environment which has been increased from €613 to €850 million (Regulation 1655/2000). The amount allocated for development cooperation with South Africa (Regulation 1726/2000) was increased by €98 million. The threshold for granting funds without the approval of a management committee has been increased from €3 to €5 million in Regulation 2493/2000 on environmental measures in developing countries. The Parliament has tried to increase the financial autonomy and transparency of the European Food Safety Authority (Regulation 178/2002) and the European Aviation Safety Agency (Regulation 1592/2002).

Inspection procedures. Reinforcements of inspection powers must be above and beyond Treaty requirements. Examples include the Commission's inspections of airports which must be unannounced (Regulation 2320/2002 on civil aviation security). Powers of the Court of Auditors and of OLAF have been strengthened in Regulations 1592/2002 and 1406/2002, establishing the European aviation and maritime safety agencies respectively.

Administrative procedures (comitology). The Parliament required the right to vote in the regulatory committee procedure in the first reading of Directive 2001/18 on genetically modified organisms. It required to be consulted before initiating the advisory committee procedure of Regulation 1980/2000 on the eco-label award scheme. In terms of legislative–executive boundaries, the targets of recycling in Directive 94/62 on packaging waste were to be modified by law rather than via a comitology procedure. The same would apply for the main amendments to Directive 95/46 on the processing of personal data. As far as issues are concerned, the Parliament has required the Commission to regulate access to storage of billing data in Directive 97/66 on the processing of personal data. The Commission has been conferred a power to grant derogations to certain machinery in Directive 2002/88 on measures against the emission of pollutants. With regard to criteria, the Parliament has specified in greater detail the content of the guidelines, to be adopted by the Commission, for the financial instrument for the environment (Regulation 1655/2000).

8 Conclusion

In any political system, when adopting a law, legislators set the boundary between legislation and administration, and specify the administrative bodies in charge of policy execution and the latitude of bureaucratic prerogatives. EU legislators can choose between two types of bureaucratic actors: a supranational institution, the Commission and national administrations. The options, of course, are not mutually exclusive, both can be involved in policy implementation. Nevertheless, the relative reliance on the Commission and national administrations vary considerably.

The aim of this book has been to explain this variance. When do EU legislators decide to centralize executive powers at the supranational level? When do they insert into EU law tight procedures and detailed policy instructions? When instead do they allow for ample discretionary authority? I have presented a theory of EU delegation that captures the incentives and constraints facing legislators when delegating executive powers and that takes into account the institutional peculiarities of the EU. The theory suggests that there are four main variables that explain who does what: (a) decision rules operating in the Council, (b) policy complexity, (c) conflict within the Council and (d) conflict between the Council and the Commission. Furthermore, involvement of the Parliament systematically affects the distribution of powers, as does conflict between Parliament, the Council and the Commission.

It is plausible that, when confronted with a legislative proposal, ministers of the Council have a strong bias in favor of national implementation, ample discretion and limited or no involvement (beyond Treaty-based powers) of the Commission. In these circumstances, ministers can better control implementation, at least within their own country, and can rely on the extensive expertise of national bureaucrats. Moreover, they have no wish to tie their own hands too tightly. Evidence has clearly shown that no powers are delegated to the Commission in more than half of the major EU laws adopted since 1958, while national authorities are excluded from implementation in only one in ten measures. Overall, national administrations also enjoy considerable discretionary authority while, when involved, the Commission is tightly constrained.

When do ministers deviate from this course of action? A crucial factor is conflict within the Council. In other words, when there are strong suspicions that national implementation will undermine policy objectives and generate distributive losses across member states (or when evidence shows that this is the outcome of past delegation decisions), some ministers have the incentive to specify in greater detail the implementing measures, hence limiting national room for maneuver, and to rely on the Commission. Conflict is a necessary but not a sufficient condition. Achieving these objectives is harder if the decision rule in the Council is unanimity rather than qualified majority voting. In this case, the minister most likely to exercise their veto power is the one preferring ample national discretion, a minimal role for the Commission, and sometimes, even benefiting from loose application of the relevant policy. Majority voting instead provides the Commission with the opportunity to exploit the different opinions in the Council and to make a winning proposal that constrains national authorities and delegates powers to the supranational bureaucracy. Results illustrate that delegation to national administrations is less likely in the case of majority voting, while the Commission is more likely to be delegated powers. National administrations are also more tightly regulated while the Commission enjoys greater discretion. In majority voting, these latter outcomes are more likely to occur with more intense conflict within the Council and higher national implementation costs.

However, delegation to the Commission is not without risk. The Council's pivotal minister would be less inclined to rely on this institution and grant ample discretion if her policy preferences diverge from those of the Commission. Furthermore, the limited technical expertise of supranational bureaucrats, compared to that of national officials, advises against extensive reliance on the Commission in highly complex and technical policy areas. Greater discretionary authority is more likely when generalist skills for policy implementation at the supranational level are required.

Matters change when the Parliament enters the scene in the codecision procedure. How is its involvement likely to affect decisions over centralization and bureaucratization? Three factors need to be considered. First, MEPs face higher costs of ongoing control of national implementation than Council ministers do. Therefore, they systematically attempt to limit national executive discretion more than Council ministers. Second, this behavior is further intensified when the policy position of the national party pivot under absolute majority diverges from that of the Council's pivotal minister. This is because MEPs are confronted with implementation by national authorities headed by ministers with different positions from those of the majority of MEPs. Both factors suggest a preference for tighter control on national administrations and, therefore, greater bureaucratization. Third, in the case of Commission implementation, the Parliament prefers instead to increase the discretionary authority of this institution and, hence, supports greater centralization of powers. This behavior appears to be geared by the similarity of preferences between the two supranational institutions. The Parliament has been keener on limiting the Commission's discretion when the two institutions do not share the same policy objectives.

Although I eschew from assessing the success rate of parliamentary amendments, scholars agree that this rate is greater than zero. Accordingly, it is plausible to conclude that the involvement of the Parliament via the codecision procedure is likely to lead to more prescriptive legislation for national authorities (national executive discretion is likely to be lower) and, under some conditions, to more centralized powers (the Commission's discretion is likely to be higher).

This study and the literature on EU politics and European integration

Distinguishing features of this study

This study has distinguishing features and presents points of commonality and disagreement with existing works on delegation in the EU (Pollack, 1997b, 2003b; Moravcsik, 1998; Tsebelis and Garrett, 2001; Tsebelis, 2002; Kelemen, 2003; Kelemen, 2004). In terms of theory, with the exception of Kelemen and, more tangentially, Tallberg (2002b, 2003), none of the existing analyses has seriously taken into consideration the option of relying on national administrations for policy implementation as an alternative to the Commission. The dependent variable, delegation to and discretion of this institution, is a legitimate strategy if a researcher wants to limit her study to the supranational bureaucracy. However, the policy authority enjoyed by this institution is clearly dependent on the attractiveness of alternative delegation options available to EU legislators. The first implication of this choice is that most studies on EU delegation completely neglect the fact that EU laws rely extensively on, but also constrain, national administrations. The second implication is that these studies fail to fully appreciate the crucial importance of conflict within the Council as a factor mediating with decision rules and shaping delegation decisions. Moravcsik (1998: 75) and Pollack (2003b: 26–34) speculate that the Commission's discretion should decrease with more intense conflict within the Council without providing systematic supporting evidence.

Kelemen's (2004) study of the discretion of member states in the implementation of environmental, food and drug safety legislation is an exception. His argument that more fragmented federal polities produce lower discretion for their component states is in tune with the expectations of my theory. However, since Kelemen investigates how institutional variations across federal systems affect the discretion of states, his work has weaker microfoundations and glosses over institutional variations within federations. For instance, Kelemen does not appreciate precisely when EU legislators tighten national discretion or opt for supranational execution of a measure at hand. Tallberg (2002b, 2003), a second exception, recognizes the principal–agent relationship between EU institutions and national authorities in the national implementation of common policies, but he concentrates on the enforcement mechanisms rather than on the design of EU laws.

In terms of level of analysis, this study focuses on the daily operation of the EU where legislators adopt secondary measures, whereas both Moravcsik and Pollack center their analysis primarily on Treaty-level delegation and, hence, on the Intergovernmental Conferences where member states amend the Treaty. The important implication of shifting the level of analysis is that the Council operates with two different decision rules and, in some cases, the Parliament is fully involved. The inclusion of these new factors qualifies some of the conclusions in the literature (see below).

With regard to method, this study attempts to find supporting evidence from both large-N and case study research. Thus far, other scholars have relied exclusively on the case study method. Finally, in terms of substantive focus, this work presents, together with Jun's (2003b) study, one of the first analyses of the Parliament's role in shaping delegation outcomes.

Commonalties and differences in the results: challenging Tsebelis and Garrett

In line with previous scholarship, the results reported in this book clearly support the proposition that legislators rely to a greater extent on bureaucrats in more complex policy areas and that national administrations are the best equipped institutions that provide expert knowledge for the implementation of EU policies. They also support Moravcsik's (1998) and Pollack's (1997b, 2003b) view that delegation to supranational institutions is hardly motivated by the need to rely on expert knowledge. My conclusion is probably less dismissive than Moravcsik's charge against supranational expertise and more in line with Pollack's opinion that some supranational delegation reflects a demand for "speedy and efficient decision making" (Pollack, 2003b: 153). The informational role of the Commission is certainly secondary, but not entirely negligible. Finally, as far as the preferences of the Commission are concerned, findings are broadly consistent with the expectations of the extant literature, according to which delegation to this institution is less likely and its discretion diminishes as conflict between member states and the Commission intensifies.

It is on the consequences of decision rules and their relative importance vis-à-vis the problem of commitment where this study is more clearly set apart from existing work. Recall Tsebelis and Garrett's (2001: 383) claim that the executive discretion of the Commission is greater when new acts are adopted in the Council under unanimity rather than under qualified majority voting and, consequently, the move to majority voting reduces the discretionary authority of the Commission. Tsebelis (2002: 236) later refines his argument with two qualifications. First, he refers only to the *behavioral* independence (or discretion) of bureaucrats, namely to the set of policy-specific measures that a bureaucrat takes to implement a policy, such as the setting of interest rates by a central bank or approving a merger by a competition authority. *Behavioral* independence is distinct from the focus of this study, which is on *institutional* or *formal* independence as it is derived from reading statutes delegating executive powers. Second, Tsebelis clarifies that his argument applies if we keep legislation constant. In other words, it is valid for a given level of formal independence specified in the relevant legal act delegating powers.

Tsebelis and Garrett's contention still needs to be qualified though. A nontrivial degree of formal autonomy is a necessary condition for the Commission to exercise its behavioral independence. It is certainly harder to overrule a Commission decision when the Council has to act unanimously, but if the legal mandate on which the exercise of that power is clearly and very tightly constrained *ex ante*, a threat by a single member state of a referral to the Court of Justice for a *ultra vires* judgment is enough to limit behavioral autonomy. My results suggest that the exercise of executive powers in policy areas under unanimity is likely to be more constrained than in areas under qualified majority voting because of the fewer and more tightly defined statutory instruments at the disposal of the Commission. For this reason, a shift from unanimity to majority voting is unlikely to restrain the Commission further. As a result of the shift, however, new legislation may confer additional formal powers to the Commission, as the case study on public procurement clearly illustrates. Potentially, this could lead to more behavioral independence. The causal effect is the opposite of what Tsebelis and Garrett expect.

Consider the following example. In a law adopted unanimously by the Council, the Commission is given the power to inspect public tender procedures and to report to the Council the conclusion of those inspections. One could speculate on how broadly the Commission could interpret and exercise this prerogative, shielded by the Council's requirement of unanimity to overrule this interpretation. However, this is yet only a power to inspect, no more, no less. It is hardly ambiguous for judicial interpretation. A few years later, a Treaty amendment specifies that legislation in this policy area has to be adopted by majority voting. In line with Tsebelis and Garrett, this change should give the Council the opportunity to rein in bureaucratic drift of the Commission (presumably with new legislation). However, my results suggest that it is likely that new laws will delegate additional formal powers to the Commission (especially if national execution is deficient), for instance the power to suspend the tender procedure immediately in the case of severe infringement of EU law. Majority voting has made overruling Commission decisions easier, but it is also likely to expand the platform of formal powers on which the Commission could rely upon, hence potentially increasing the behavioral autonomy to shift the policy closer to its ideal.

In summary, with the proviso of keeping legislation constant, Tsebelis and Garrett's argument is *prima facie* flawless. However, it contains one substantive and one logical inconsistency. Substantively, deriving the Commission's discretion only from the rules of legislative override downplays the fact that the formal boundaries within which this institution can exercise its powers are set *ex ante*. Here, legislators are likely to anticipate its behavior and the degree of ex-post tinkering that a specific policy could be subject to. The formal executive latitude to shift the status quo becomes a crucial decision variable for them and decision rules important factors determining it. Formal autonomy is a necessary condition for behavioral autonomy. In order to explain the latter, the explanation of the former should not be exogenized. Otherwise, we could incur the following logical inconsistency: the shift to majority voting facilitates the sanctioning of bureaucratic drift, *but also* the delegation of additional formal powers. Both require new legislation and the net effect is not necessarily lower behavioral discretion. Once we fully endogenize the impact of different rules on *ex-ante* legislative design, Tsebelis and Garrett's argument may fall apart.

Pooling and supranational delegation: revisiting Moravcsik[1]

Moravcsik (1998) maintains that pooling (i.e. a shift from unanimity to qualified majority voting) enhances the credibility of Treaty objectives by reducing the bargaining power of recalcitrant member states once the Council fleshes out the details of the policy bargain in secondary legislation. Delegation to supranational institutions is motivated by a similar rationale. Pollack (2003b) shares this view. From the work of Moravcsik (1998: 75–6), it is not entirely clear whether the severity of the commitment problem leads first to pooling and then to delegation, or if pooling takes place where there is a need to facilitate future legislation, while delegation occurs where the need is to ensure implementation and compliance. In practice, this does not matter much as compliance and secondary legislation are both required to achieve the objectives of all but the simplest EU policies.

The works of Moravcsik and Pollack are predominantly centered on Treaty delegation where there is no variance in terms of decision rules. They neglect how decision rules interact with delegation decisions in the daily operation of the Council and how this interaction may or may not be conducive to achieving credibility. If we use the existing literature, some inconsistencies emerge in Moravcsik's interpretation.

Consider the following four policy scenarios. In the first scenario, secondary legislation is adopted by unanimity and the Commission has few policy powers. In line with Moravcsik's view, achieving policy objectives is hard because legislation can be vetoed by a single member state and the Commission has a limited number of policy instruments at its disposal. In the second scenario, legislation is adopted by majority voting. Achieving policy objectives is now easier because measures cannot be unilaterally blocked. Again, this is the standard view. In the third scenario, secondary legislation is adopted by unanimity and the Commission has extensive policy powers. Here, new laws could be easily blocked, so it is the Commission, with its measures, that ensures the achievement of policy objectives. The problem of commitment is solved by combining extensive supranational powers and unanimity which, following Tsebelis and Garrett, makes the Commission's decisions very hard to overrule. Notice that here unanimity, combined with supranational delegation, *ensures* credibility of Commission decisions (at the expense of future Council acts). This is the opposite of Moravcsik's view. In the last scenario, laws are adopted by majority voting and the Commission

---

[1] I thank Fabrizio Gilardi whose insightful comments have considerably improved this section.

enjoys extensive policy prerogatives. Here, new legal measures can be adopted against the wishes of a single member state, hence ensuring credible commitment, but the Commission's decisions can also be more easily overruled. Contradicting Moravcsik's interpretation, here majority voting, combined with supranational delegation, *reduces* the credibility of Commission measures (for the benefit of future Council acts). Hence, the net effect of the last two scenarios is ambiguous in terms of achieving overall credibility.

These examples illustrate the benefits of combining the analysis of the consequences of different institutional choices. Pooling *reduces* credibility if policy objectives are to be achieved via supranational delegation. It appears that there is not a single institutional set up that guarantees credibility for both future Council acts and Commission measures. This study suggests instead that there may be a way out if we use a theory that is based on preference-rule strategic interactions. The results show how majority voting facilitates the adoption of legislation that restrains national authorities (in coherence with Moravcsik's argument) and the delegation of powers to the Commission. Undeniably, overruling a Commission's decision is harder under unanimity (note that Chapter 5 shows that the theory based on credibility is also important in secondary legislation), but majority voting could give the Commission powers that would have not been conferred, were a unanimous vote required.[2]

Cleavages in EU politics

An important part of the literature investigates the dominant dimensions of conflict in EU politics. As I argued in Chapter 4, scholars recognize three such dimensions: a more–less integration, a policy-specific and a left–right cleavage. The measurement of preferences along the policy-specific dimension has produced the most convincing results across the three empirical chapters of this study. Variables have performed as expected with regard to the impact of conflict within the Council on national, Commission and relative discretion, both in the quantitative and the case study analysis, and of Council–Parliament conflict on parliamentary preferences about national executive discretion. However, results are less convincing when assessing the implications of Council–Commission conflict for the discretion of the Commission. The measurement of preferences along the left–right dimension has performed as expected when

---

[2] In view of the credibility thesis, this work suggests that delegation to the Commission is conditional upon the lack of credibility of national implementation. Conflict in the Council and transposition problems render national implementation less credible and may lead to greater reliance on the Commission.

testing hypotheses on parliamentary preferences. It also produced the expected results at least for one operationalization of the Commission's preferences, but the results of the impact of conflict within the Council on discretion are contradictory. Finally, measurement of preferences along the integration dimension has performed poorly. Results were insignificant, contradictory or weak. There could be many reasons for these outcomes. A plausible one is that the measurement of preferences that is derived from a larger number of Budge *et al.*'s (2001) policy categories produces more reliable estimates. This could explain the poor performance of the integration dimension.

However, this study invites two additional comments. First, although many recent contributions underscore the importance of the pro–anti-integration and left–right dimensions, it seems that policy-specific conflict is key to explain delegating decisions. This result is in line with the latest studies of Council bargaining which have (re)emphasized the saliency of this cleavage. Second, there is support, however, for the thesis that the left–right dimension, originally neglected in EU studies and, indeed, not performing well across the whole history of European integration, is coming to the forefront of EU politics, especially with regard to inter-institutional relations. The normative implications of this trend are discussed below.

National implementation of EU policies

This study also contributes to the flourishing literature on EU policy implementation. A review is beyond the scope of this section but, in a nutshell, scholars contend that variance in national compliance with EU laws could be explained by the divergence between existing national and new EU policies, constitutional provisions, administrative capacity and the number of veto points (Krislov, Ehlermann and Weiler, 1986; Knill, 1998; Knill and Lenschow, 1998; Haverland, 2000; Caporaso, Cowles and Risse, 2001; Giuliani, 2003). Expectations are tested quantitatively (Lampinen and Uusikylä, 1998; Mbaye, 2001; Giuliani, 2003) and with case studies of, predominantly, environmental directives (Knill, 1998; Knill and Lenschow, 1998; Börzel, 2000; Haverland, 2000). The results from this study suggest that these works should explicitly control for the degree of discretion that national institutions enjoy in the implementation of each specific measure, because this is a likely determinant of the final outcome. Moreover, in acts granting considerable latitude to member states, as in environmental policy, it is relatively arduous to pin down what exactly an EU policy entails and there might be a risk of mispecifying the dependent variable or the term of comparison.

Finally, recall Tallberg's (2002b, 2003) argument that rule ambiguity is likely to be an important cause of noncompliance. In these circumstances, violating EU law is not a state's intentional strategy, it is the unintended consequence of poor legislative design. The results presented in this book nevertheless emphasize how ambiguity and, hence, ample national discretion is a deliberate choice of EU legislators, therefore blurring somewhat the distinction between purposeful and accidental noncompliance.

Theories of European integration

Lastly, any book on EU politics has ultimately to confront the "grand theories" of European integration. Within the context of this study, the object of analysis – the operationalization of "integration" – is the delegation of executive powers through secondary legislation, and the key question is the extent to which this delegation reflects the preferences of member states and supranational institutions. Perhaps unsurprisingly and in line with an institutionalist interpretation of EU politics, the answer is not clear cut. Conceding to the intergovernmentalist view, members of the Council emerge as dominant actors. Outcomes are likely to reflect their views quite faithfully, especially when they are homogeneous and in the case of unanimity. Even in procedures where a single state does not hold veto power, such as in majority voting and codecision, it should be recognized that the position of the Council, collectively conceived, is the basis of most legislative agreements. On the other hand, there is also solid evidence of how conflict in the Council and majority voting offer the Commission the opportunity to shape outcomes to its liking. Equally, the Parliament may have different views about delegation from the Council, also because of its supranational nature. This institution therefore systematically attempts, and probably succeeds, to shape both the choice of implementation path and the levels of discretion.

This book has hence developed a formal institutionalist account of EU politics to move beyond the intergovernmentalist interpretation of the delegation of powers, but, in doing so, it has also challenged some existing institutionalist conjectures, more specifically the work of Tsebelis and Garrett (2001).

This study and the literature on legislative–bureaucratic relations

Distinguishing features of this study

This study is a distinctive contribution to the comparative literature on delegation. Substantively, existing works have either a US (e.g. Epstein and O'Halloran, 1999b; Volden, 2002a) or a comparative focus (Huber and Shipan, 2002). This is the first systematic application of the theory to the everyday operation of a supranational political system. Theoretically, this is the first work that has analyzed the impact of different decision rules, within the same legislature, on delegation outcomes. Another unique aspect is the explicit modeling of the choice between two types of administrators. This element props up in many studies. Recall Epstein and O'Halloran's (1999b: 154–5) and Volden's (2002a) result about independent agencies enjoying greater discretion under divided government. Volden's (2002b: 124) model also shows that, in a separation of powers system, a divergence of preferences between an agenda-setting legislature and an executive with veto power results in greater discretion of an independent agency (i.e. positioned between the executive and the legislature). My results echo this proposition. They reveal that, in majority voting, more conflict in the Council leads to greater discretion for the Commission, both in absolute terms and relative to national discretion. The underlying logic of my model is somewhat different though. It is based on a supranational bureaucracy with agenda-setting powers (the Commission) that exploits conflict within a legislature (the Council). Additionally, results from this work show that the choice between administrators is also guided by different informational logics and, most likely, by the level of governance where each administration operates. National administrators are undoubtedly the main suppliers of policy expertise in the EU, but the Commission provides some managerial skills that are in demand at the supranational level.

The study shares commonalties with and introduces novelties to existing works. Conflict and policy complexity are confirmed as key factors shaping decisions to delegate powers. As reviewed in Chapter 1, a recurrent empirical result is that the US Congress and state legislatures adopt more restrictive legislation during times of divided government. But they prefer looser statutes in more complex policy areas (Epstein and O'Halloran, 1999b; Huber and Shipan, 2002). In parliamentary systems, the legislative majority is more likely to constrain a minority or coalition majority government than a single-party majority government (Huber and Shipan, 2002). I have found some support for these propositions in the tendency to adopt lower discretion statutes when the preferences of the Commission diverge from those of (i) the pivotal minister in the Council and of (ii) the pivotal national party in the Parliament. With regard to national implementation, conflict within the Council can be interpreted as conflict between legislators (ministers) and bureaucrats (national administrators). The same applies to conflict between MEPs (legislators) and ministers (as actors in charge of national implementation). In this light, our results confirm the expectations that conflict between the authors and implementers of statutes limits executive discretion. Equally, EU legislators tend to confer more discretion upon administrators in the case of high policy complexity.

Finally, Chapter 7 provides important evidence in support of the view that discretion preferences are a function of the availability of nonstatutory control tools. Recall the results of Bawn (1997), who illustrates the systematically different positions of US senators that are members of a committee and those excluded from it, and the findings of Huber and Shipan (2002) who unearth lower levels of discretion when nonstatutory control mechanisms are unavailable. In line with these works, the results illustrate how MEPs systematically prefer lower national executive discretion than Council ministers because nonstatutory oversight of national implementation is costlier.

Bargaining environment: complementing and qualifying Huber and Shipan

The study invites a qualification to how the bargaining environment within the legislature affects delegation. Huber and Shipan (2002) show that, in a separation of powers system, the executive is less constrained when it is harder to reach an agreement within the legislature. If, for instance, only the upper chamber shares the executive's preferences (i.e. the legislature is divided), this chamber prefers higher executive discretion than the lower chamber and would use its veto power to impede any excessive limitation of authority. From one perspective, my results illustrate an aspect of this dynamics. For instance, I show the tendency of the Parliament to bias delegation in favor of the supranational bureaucracy with which the Parliament shares policy positions more than the Council. Similarly, bicameral conflict, namely the existence of divergent views between the Parliament and the Council, implies conflict between the Parliament and national authorities and explains the Parliament's attempt to constraint national discretion more than Council ministers.

On other grounds, Huber and Shipan's thesis should be qualified. In the EU Council, it is generally harder to take unanimous decisions than to take majority ones. My results therefore show that a more demanding bargaining environment (one requiring unanimity) leads to more discretion for national authorities, but – opposite to Huber and Shipan's argument – to *less* discretion for the Commission. This difference is related to the location of the status quo. Many laws analyzed in Chapters 3 and 6 are new acts where the status quo is extensive national discretion and no powers for the Commission and, therefore, is biased in favor of governments wanting to preserve national prerogatives and to constrain the Commission. In Huber and Shipan, the status quo encompasses the existing powers of the executive.[3] Hence, it is biased in favor of the legislative chamber that shares the preferences of the executive. If the other chamber were in this more beneficial position, it would have exercised its veto to impede any excessive delegation of authority and, therefore, the executive may not have obtained greater discretion.

Finally, another result seems to contradict Huber and Shipan's propositions. In majority voting, national discretion *lowers* as conflict within the Council intensifies (i.e. as the bargaining environment becomes more demanding). This difference, however, reflects the nature of policy implementation in the EU. Greater conflict within the Council is equivalent to more intense disagreement between the authors and implementers of statutes.

Veto players and bureaucratic autonomy: qualifying Tsebelis

The criticism of Tsebelis and Garrett (2001) in the previous section can be extended to the entire literature on veto players and bureaucratic autonomy. Recall that here the central proposition is that, keeping legislation constant, the behavioral discretion of a bureaucrat increases with policy stability (Tsebelis, 2002: 2–5, 236).

By analogy, this criticism is based on the need for a nontrivial degree of formal autonomy (discretion) as a necessary condition for bureaucracies to exercise their behavioral independence. Hence, a theory of formal or statutory independence should be fully included in a theory on behavioral independence. Otherwise, we could incur the inconsistency I described in the previous section, whereby a particular institutional setting may facilitate both the sanctioning of bureaucratic actions and the conferral of formal powers upon the administrators.

Most likely, in areas where informational and distributive concerns lead legislators to confer considerable formal independence on the administrators, the threat of legislative override, as results from the preferences of the current veto players, may determine the agent's behavior and its independence. In effect, Tsebelis (2002: 222–47) finds support for his argument in areas, such as adjudication and central banking, where executive actors have considerably more formal autonomy than in more traditional bureaucracies. If, instead, informational and distributive concerns

---

[3] *Discretion*, their dependent variable, is the number of new words inserted in an existing statute. This implies that the executive already has some policy prerogatives (Huber and Shipan, 2002: 143–6).

allow legislators to constrain administrators by adopting very restrictive statutes, the potential to be behaviorally independent is severely curtailed by the lack of formal powers and the preferences of veto players at the stage of legislative adoption should be more revealing of bureaucratic actions.

This study and the international relations literature

Two themes: delegation to international organizations and compliance with international law

This study contributes to one emerging and one established theme in the international relations literature. Scholars have recently employed the theory of delegation to explain the autonomy and behavior of international organizations (Thompson and Haftel, 2003). For instance, they have used it to examine institutional reforms and policies on conditionality and lending of the International Monetary Fund and the World Bank (Hawes and Broz, 2003; Martin 2003; Nielson and Tierney, 2003). At the core of the current research effort is the analysis of the circumstances under which member states delegate powers to international organizations and how member states reign in agency drift. My study invites scholars to consider how the choice available to member states of alternative implementation paths explains the broad institutional design of an international organization. It also illustrates how conflict among member states interacts with decision rules to determine specific delegation outcomes. To the extent that this conflict leads to noncompliance and distributional losses across states, as could be the case in environmental regimes or in the World Trade Organization, it should be a crucial determinant of the powers of international organizations, especially under majority-based decision rules.

State compliance with international law is instead a well-established field of inquiry in international relations. The literature has recently been divided into two camps. In a nutshell, the dividing line is whether noncompliance is intentional or inadvertent. For the enforcement school, the incentive structure is the predominant source of noncompliance, hence this view stresses the importance of appropriate mechanisms to monitor and sanction state behavior (Axelrod, 1984; Axelrod and Keohane, 1986; Downs, Rocke and Barsoom, 1996). For the management school, the primary causes are rule ambiguity, capacity limitations and uncontrollable social and economic changes. Consequently, the most suitable strategies to reduce noncompliance are capacity building, rule interpretation and transparency (Chayes and Chayes, 1993, 1995; Mitchell, 1994; Chayes,

Chayes and Mitchell, 1998). Tallberg (2002b, 2003) shows how both sources are at work in the EU.

This study undoubtedly underscores how purposeful noncompliance is in the mind of EU legislators. When distributive losses and conflict within the Council trigger fears of national misapplication, states opt for less ambiguous (more constraining) legislation and/or greater reliance on a supranational bureaucracy, with the facilitation of majority voting. The specificity of international law (hence, national executive discretion) results from the strategic interaction between states' preferences and decision rules. Or, in other words, *rule ambiguity reflects the overarching importance of deliberate noncompliance*. This consideration challenges at least one premise on which the management school relies. However, it should also be recognized that policy complexity remains a dominant source of delegation to national authorities. It is hard to negate the fact that the technical difficulty in translating policy instructions into written documents could lead to accidental misapplication.

The normative implications of this study

Democracy and the European Union

A frequently unchallenged assertion in European circles of policy makers and politicians concerns the deficient nature of EU democracy. A frequently ignored reply of (some) political scientists observes that the EU does not appear to have a deficit in democracy that is wider than what member states and other advanced democracies experience. I delve into this debate only with regard to how delegation of policy-making powers is related to our normative ideas of democracy.[4]

Representative democracy requires that bureaucrats should be accountable to politicians and implement policies that reflect the intent and preferences of their political masters. By holding politicians accountable to the electorate, we also ensure bureaucratic responsiveness to voters' preferences. (Note that this implies a convergence of politicians' and voters' preferences which is far from indisputable. The need for re-election could generate a severe mismatch between the short- and long-term objectives of voters and politicians.) Nevertheless, the insight of Tsebelis and Garrett (2001) is very troublesome from this normative perspective. The supposed deficit of democracy could widen considerably if commissioners and supranational bureaucrats could freely exploit

[4] For the latest review of this literature see Hix (2005:177–80).

conflict between EU legislators to implement the policy that they most prefer and, since it is so hard to replace them, get away with it. Moreover, the increased heterogeneity of preferences that is likely to emerge from EU enlargement could be seen as alarming.

The findings from this work suggest that worries about the lack of democratic accountability in the EU are misplaced because the executive latitude of supranational actors is extensively predetermined by the legislators. At least in this respect, the electoral connection of EU policies appears to be preserved.

On the other hand, in his defense of the democratic credentials of the EU, Crombez (2003) concedes that the accountability of the Commission is problematic because this institution involves at least three steps of delegation. This study, however, shows that the dominant role in EU policy implementation is played by national administrations, institutions that are closer to the citizens in the "democratic chain of delegation." Overall, the problem does not appear to be too serious because the Commission takes only a minority of implementation measures. Or, one could even argue that it is exactly because of the Commission's weak democratic accountability that this institution enjoys those powers. Indeed, this is what emerges from this study. Conflict within the Council generates a credible threat of national misapplication and distributional losses, because ministers are easily hostages to powerful domestic constituencies. Isolation from this pressure is what makes delegation to the Commission appealing in these circumstances. Calls for parlamentarization of this institution should heed these concerns and reforms should preserve this precious function (see Majone, 2000, 2002).

Finally, an additional sign that the EU is moving towards democratic normality is the increasing importance of the left–right dimension. This is not to say that the EU would be less democratic if other cleavages were to dominate EU politics, but it seems to me that the natural home for contesting the policy output of this political system is the left–right divide. Hence, I welcome this trend.

Centralization, subsidiarity and the Constitutional Treaty

Is the EU too centralized? Since the early 1990s, provisions guiding the distribution of powers in the EU were introduced to heed concerns about excessive centralization. And the draft Treaty establishing a constitution for Europe now considers subsidiarity, along with conferral and proportionality, a fundamental principle governing the competencies of the EU. Article I-9 states:

"Under the principle of subsidiarity, in areas which do not fall within its exclusive competence the Union shall act only if and insofar as the objectives of the intended action cannot be sufficiently achieved by the Member States, either at central level or at regional and local level, but can rather, by reason of the scale or effects of the proposed action, be better achieved at Union level."

The principle was initially introduced in the Maastricht Treaty. The Commission has since developed guidelines and it submits an annual report on its application. The Treaty of Amsterdam added a protocol on its application which has been further strengthened by the draft Constitutional Treaty. For instance, national parliaments can require a review of a Commission's proposals if one-third of them consider that such a proposal does not comply with subsidiarity.

Does this all matter? On a symbolic level, it does. The subsidiarity principle is used by political leaders to sell the Treaty to, especially, the most skeptical segments of their public. It is a signal and a reassurance against excessive centralization of powers. In practical terms, its relevance is more dubious. Two years after the Maastricht Treaty, two renowned legal scholars recognized that some changes have occurred as a result of the new principle but concluded:

"It is extremely difficult to see how judges can decide whether a measure complies with [the principle of subsidiarity] without second-guessing the political judgement of the Community institutions. It seems likely that the Court of Justice will confine itself to a form of procedural, rather than substantive review." (Weatherill and Beaumont, 1995: 15)

In other words, the assessment as to whether powers should be centralized is a predominantly political one, notwithstanding the legal principles. This study strongly reinforces this view and sheds light on some aspects of this debate. At least with regard to executive powers, the results dampen fears of excessive centralization. The conferral of policy prerogatives to the Commission is a second best option for Council ministers and it is mostly avoided. The primacy of the national path for implementation shows how policy powers are extensively decentralized in the EU.

Nevertheless, a judgment about centralization in the EU is a just reflection of our values. Even this limited role of the supranational bureaucracy could be excessive for some. What is more important is unveiling the imperatives and underlying trade-off facing decision makers in these circumstances. For each minister, the choice is between expert, somewhat more controlled but also more divergent national implementation (with the risk of jeopardizing policy objectives) and somewhat less expert and controlled but certainly more uniform supranational execution. When the risk and the costs of national implementation are high, there are no legal principles that impede the delegation of powers to the Commission (though, decision rules may). Illuminating is how frequently ministers' positions on individual cases dealt by the Council are in strident contrast with their general views on subsidiarity but in line with their concerns about national implementation (Commission of the EC, 1994b).

Bureaucratization and federalism

Is EU law excessively prescriptive and unnecessarily detailed? Kelemen (2004) argues that the EU, with its fragmented institutional design, shares many similarities with the American federal system and tend to adopt, as in the US, rather constraining statutes for the states in charge of implementing them. In an earlier work (Franchino, 2001), I argue that EU laws appear even more constraining (and with lower variance across the sample) than their American counterparts.[5]

EU law is rather prescriptive and detailed then. Kelemen (2004) illustrates well the rationale underpinning cross-national differences. But is EU law *too* constraining? Again, only our values form the basis for answering positively or negatively to such a question. But, to reiterate, what is important is understanding the underlying trade-off facing decision makers. For each minister, the choice is between keeping their hands loose and extensively relying of the expertise of national bureaucrats, but at the risk of allowing widely divergent national measures across the EU – which could jeopardize policy objectives – and tying their own hands more tightly to ensure more uniform implementation but at the cost of losing flexibility and reliance on national expertise.

Bureaucratic capacity and enlargement

This work shows that the Commission provides a secondary, but very valuable function in the implementation of EU policies. However, it still remains a small and understaffed bureaucracy. Limited resources to undertake implementation actions have been common features of the history of this institution, but the recent enlargement to ten new countries could put serious strains on its capacity to deliver on ministers' and MEPs' demands. Huber and McCarty (2004) have illustrated the consequences of this scenario. In addition to reducing the quality of bureaucratic outcomes, the low capacity reduces the incentives for bureaucrats to comply

---

[5] Considerable caution should be exercised here however. Differences in methodology, saliency of policy areas and institutional design can easily render these considerations untenable.

with legislative statutes. Consequently, EU legislators will have to design laws that allow the Commission more latitude to pursue its preferred policies rather than those of legislators. Not only would this decrease the incentives to adopt new measures (a low-capacity Commission is an impediment to policies which would otherwise receive support from Council ministers and MEPs) but, more worryingly, it would worsen the democratic accountability of this institution.

Huber and McCarty (2004) also argue that, in a low-capacity environment, politicians are caught in a trap whereby their incentives to reform the political system are actually lowest. It may be far fetched to say that the EU suffers from low capacity, but the risk of dangerously overstretching the resources of the Commission could have disastrous consequences on the quality of the EU democracy, policy output and future attempts at reform.

A research agenda

This study can be extended in different directions. I make a few suggestions in this section.

This work can be replicated using other approaches to estimate positions from the party manifestos data or other data sets on party preferences. Although Gabel and Huber's (2000) approach provides the best estimates of left–right positions, scholars could consider replicating the study using the expert surveys results reported by Castles and Mair (1984) and Huber and Inglehart (1995). Laver and Hunt (1992) provide data on other dimensions which could be used as an alternative to my estimates of policy positions and, recently, Marks and Steenbergen (2004) and Ray (1999) estimate post-1984 positions on the more–less integration dimension. Finally, the new computer-based estimation technique of Laver, Benoit and Garry (2003) could be used in future research.

A related issue is the measurement of the preferences of the Commission. The results from my study, although broadly corroborating the expectations and previous scholarship (Kelemen, 2002; Hug, 2003; Pollack, 2003b), are not very robust and do not perform well along the policy dimension. Alternative estimation techniques could be considered. Future research should also evaluate how best to balance the positions of the entire college of commissioners and of individual commissioners. My results do not provide a clear-cut answer. Using estimates of the college's median voter generates good results on the left–right dimension, while estimates of individual commissioners do well on the integration dimension.

With regard to theory, recent developments in formal modeling could be extended to the EU, especially given their emphasis on simultaneous discretion and policy decisions (Volden, 2002b), risk propensity, policy technology and multidimensionality (Bendor and Meirowitz, 2004), conflict among legislators (Epstein and O'Halloran, 2006), and bureaucratic capacity and compliance (Huber and Shipan, 2002; Huber and McCarty, 2004, 2006). More generally, theoretical advances should pay closer attention to how social actors influence the choices of delegation. Their actions are mostly neglected by scholars but may crucially shape policy outcomes and, consequently, bureaucratic design (Kydland and Prescott, 1977; Epstein and O'Halloran, 1995; Keefer and Stasavage, 2003).

Substantively, more attention should be paid to the choice between different bureaucratic actors. This study shows that the implementation of a policy measure may require different types of expertise that resides in different bureaucratic organizations. The choice of which level of governance should execute a measure deserves closer scrutiny, especially in federal systems where similar decisions are frequently taken. And the relation between delegation and bureaucratic capacity should also be investigated, especially in conjunction with enlargement. Bache (1998), for example, sustains that lack of capacity at the supranational level could have explained partial renationalization of the regional policy. In competition policy, the latest reform is based on private litigation within the national judiciary systems. This partial renationalization has been proposed by the Commission to address a potential "regulatory overload," namely the expected strain on its resources after enlargement[6] (Commission of the EC, 1999c; cf. Wilks, 2005).

The dynamics of delegation or, in other words, how past decisions of delegation condition new ones could also be studied. There are many works on how the Commission uses its existing powers to shape EU policy outcomes (Bulmer, 1994; Schmidt, 1996, 2000; Sandholtz, 1998), but they do not focus on the dependent variable of our interest, namely the distribution of power across EU institutions and levels of governance.

Once we have enough data to work with, a last interesting area of research is a detailed analysis of parliamentary decisions in the first and second reading and in the conciliation committee of the codecision procedure. Since the Amsterdam Treaty, a law can be adopted at each of these three stages and, since decisions rules differ across stages, it would be

---

[6] However, other important factors were the large body of existing case law and the convergence among states toward common policy principles which has progressively taken place since the mid 1980s.

interesting to analyze how laws, parliamentary amendments and choices of delegation vary accordingly (for a related and sophisticated study see Hoyland, 2005).

In conclusion, this book has offered a theoretically grounded empirical analysis of how implementation powers are distributed in the EU. It has used theories of legislative–bureaucratic relations and showed how its results contribute to the literature on comparative bureaucratic design, EU studies and international relations. More importantly, it has illustrated how positive political science provides valuable insights into our normative views on bureaucratic structures, distribution of powers and democracy in the European Union.

References

Aberbach, J. D. 1990. *Keeping a Watchful Eye: the Politics of Congressional Oversight.* Washington, DC: Brookings Institution.

Alesina, A. and Wacziarg, R. 1999. Is Europe going too far? *Carnegie–Rochester Conference Series on Public Policy* 51: 1–42.

Allen, D. 1996a. Cohesion and structural adjustment. In *Policy-Making in the European Union*, ed. H. Wallace and W. Wallace. Oxford: Oxford University Press, pp. 209–33.

1996b. Competition policy: policing the single market. In *Policy-Making in the European Union*, ed. H. Wallace and W. Wallace. Oxford: Oxford University Press, pp. 157–83.

Armstrong, H. W. 1989. Community regional policy. In *The European Community and the Challenge of the Future*, ed. J. Lodge. New York: St. Martin's Press.

Arregui, J., Stokman, F. and Thomson, R. 2004. Bargaining in the European Union and shifts in actors' policy positions. *European Union Politics* 5: 47–72.

Aspinwall, M. 2002. Preferring Europe: ideology and national preferences on European integration. *European Union Politics* 3: 81–111.

Aspinwall, M. D. and Schneider, G. 2000. Same menu, separate tables: the institutionalist turn in political science and the study of European integration. *European Journal of Political Research* 38: 1–36.

Attinà, F. 1990. The voting behaviour of the European Parliament members and the problem of the Europarties. *European Journal of Political Research* 18: 557–79.

1992. *Il Sistema Politico della Comunità Europea*. Milan: Giuffrè.

Axelrod, R. 1984. *The Evolution of Co-Operation*. London: Penguin.

Axelrod, R. and Keohane R. O. 1986. Achieving cooperation under anarchy: strategies and institutions. In *Cooperation under Anarchy*, ed. K. A. Oye. Princeton, NJ: Princeton University Press.

Bache, I. 1998. *Politics of European Union Regional Policy: Multi-level Governance or Flexible Gatekeeping?* London: Routledge.

Bailer, S. 2004. Bargaining success in the European Union: the impact of exogenous and endogenous power resources. *European Union Politics* 5: 99–123.

Balla, S. J. 1998. Administrative procedures and political control of the bureaucracy. *American Political Science Review* 92: 663–73.

Balla, S. J. and Wright, J. R. 2001. Interest groups, advisory committees, and congressional control of the bureaucracy. *American Journal of Political Science* 45: 799–812.

Ballmann, A., Epstein D. and O'Halloran, S. 2002. Delegation, comitology, and the separation of powers in the European Union. *International Organization* **56**: 551–74.

Banks, J. S. and Weingast, B. R. 1992. The political control of bureaucracies under asymmetric information. *American Journal of Political Science* **36**: 509–24.

Bartolini, S. 2000. *The Class Cleavage*. Cambridge: Cambridge University Press.

Bartolini, S. and Mair, P., eds. 1984. *Party Politics in Contemporary Western Europe*. London: Cass.

Bawn, K. 1995. Political control versus expertise: congressional choices about administrative procedures. *American Political Science Review* **89**: 62–73.

1997. Choosing strategies to control the bureaucracy: statutory constraints, oversight, and the committee system. *Journal of Law, Economics and Organization* **13**: 101–26.

1999. Money and majorities in the Federal Republic of Germany: evidence for a veto players model of government spending. *American Journal of Political Science* **43**: 707–36.

Bednar, J., Ferejohn, J. and Garrett, G. 1996. The politics of European federalism. *International Review of Law and Economics* **16**: 279–94.

Behrens, P. and Smyrl, M. 1999. A conflict of rationalities: EU regional policy and the single market. *Journal of European Public Policy* **6**: 419–35.

Bendor, J. and Meirowitz, A. 2004. Spatial models of delegation. *American Political Science Review* **98**: 293–310.

Bendor, J., Taylor, S. and Van Gaalen, R. 1987. Stacking the deck: bureaucratic missions and policy design. *American Political Science Review* **81**: 873–96.

Beyers, J. and Dierickx, G. 1998. The working groups of the Council of the European Union: supranational or intergovernmental negotiations? *Journal of Common Market Studies* **36**: 289–317.

Bignami, F. 1999. The administrative state in a separation of powers constitution: lessons for European Community rulemaking from the United States. *Jean Monnet Working Paper* 5/99. Cambridge, MA: Harvard Law School.

Blondel, J. and Müller-Rommel, F., eds. 1988. *Cabinets in Western Europe*. London: Macmillan.

Blondel, J. and Thiebault, J.-L., eds. 1991. *The Profession of Cabinet Minister in Western Europe*. London: Macmillan.

Bollen, K. and Jackman, R. 1990. Regression diagnostics: an expository treatment of outliers and influential cases. In *Modern Methods of Data Analysis*, ed. J. Fox and S. J. Long. Newbury Park, CA: Sage.

Börzel, T. A. 2000. Why there is no 'southern problem': on environmental leaders and laggards in the European Union. *Journal of European Public Policy* **7**: 141–62.

2001. Non-compliance in the European Union: pathology or statistical artefact? *Journal of European Public Policy* **8**: 803–24.

Bowler, S. and Farrell, D. M. 1995. The organizing of the European Parliament: committees, specialization and co-ordination. *British Journal of Political Science* **25**: 219–43.

1999. Parties and party discipline within the European Parliament: a norms-based approach. In *Party Discipline and Parliamentary Government*, ed. S. Bowler, D. M. Farrell and R. S. Katz. Columbus, OH: Ohio State University Press, pp. 208–22.

Bradley, K. StC. 1992. Comitology and the law: through a glass, darkly. *Common Market Law Review* **29**: 693–721.

1997. The European Parliament and comitology: on the road to nowhere? *European Law Journal* **3**: 230–54.

Bräuninger, T., Cornelius, T., König, T. and Schuster, T. 2001. The dynamics of European integration: a constitutional analysis of the Amsterdam Treaty. In *The Rules of Integration: Institutionalist Approaches to the Study of Europe*, ed. M. Aspinwall and G. Schneider. Manchester: Manchester University Press.

Browne, E. C. and M. Franklin. 1973. Aspects of coalition payoffs in European parliamentary democracies. *American Political Science Review* **67**: 453–69.

Brzinski, J. B. 1995. Political group cohesion in the European Parliament, 1989–1994. In *The State of the European Union. Building a European Polity?*, ed. C. Rhodes and S. Mazey. Harlow: Longman, pp. 135–58.

Budge, I., Hofferbert, R. I. and Klingemann, H.-D. 1994. *Parties, Policies, and Democracy*. Boulder, CO: Westview Press.

Budge, I. and Keman, H., eds. 1990. *How Party Government Works: Testing a Theory of Formation, Functioning and Termination in 20 Democracies*. Oxford: Oxford University Press.

Budge, I., Klingemann H.-D., Volkens, A., Bara, J. and Tanenbaum, E., eds. 2001. *Mapping Policy Preferences: Estimates for Parties, Electors, and Governments 1945–1998*. Oxford: Oxford University Press.

Bueno de Mesquita, B. and Stokman, F. N., eds. 1994. *European Community Decision Making: Models, Applications, and Comparisons*. New Haven, CT: Yale University Press.

Bulmer, S. 1994. Institutions and policy change in the European communities: the case of merger control. *Public Administration* **72**: 423–44.

Bursens, P. 2002. Why Denmark and Belgium have different implementation records: on transposition laggards and leaders in the EU. *Scandinavian Political Studies* **25**: 173–95.

Calvert, R. L., McCubbins, M. D. and Weingast, B. R. 1989. A theory of political control and agency discretion. *American Journal of Political Science* **33**: 588–611.

Cameron, D. R. 1992. The 1992 initiative: causes and consequences. In *Euro-Politics: Institutions and Policymaking in the "New" European Community*, ed. A. M. Sbragia. Washington, DC: The Brookings Institution, pp. 23–74.

Caporaso, J., Cowles, M. G. and Risse, T., eds. 2001. *Transforming Europe: Europeanization and Domestic Change*. Ithaca, NY: Cornell University Press.

Carrubba, C. and Gabel, M. 2002. Roll-call votes and party discipline in the European Parliament: reconsidering MEP voting behaviour. *EPRG Working Paper*.

Castles, F. and Mair, P. 1984. Left–right political scales: some expert judgments. *European Journal of Political Research* **12**: 73–88.

Chayes, A. and Handler Chayes, A. 1993. On compliance. *International Organization* **47**: 175–206.

1995. *The New Sovereignty: Compliance with International Regulatory Agreements.* Cambridge, MA: Harvard University Press.

Chayes, A., Handler Chayes, A. and Mitchell, R. B. 1998. Managing compliance: a comparative perspective. In *Engaging Countries: Strengthening Compliance with International Environmental Accords*, ed. E. Brown Weiss and H. K. Jacobson. Cambridge, MA: MIT University Press.

Christiansen, T. 1996. A maturing bureaucracy? The role of the Commission in the policy process. In *European Union. Power and Policy-Making*, ed. J. Richardson. London: Routledge, pp. 77–95.

1997. Tensions of European governance: politicized bureaucracy and multiple accountability in the European Commission. *Journal of European Public Policy* **4**: 73–90.

Christiansen, T. and Kirchner, E., eds. 2000. *Europe in Change – Committee Governance in the European Union.* Manchester: Manchester University Press.

Cini, M. 1996. *The European Commission: Leadership, Organization and Culture in the EU Administration.* Manchester: Manchester University Press.

1997. Administrative culture in the European Commission: the cases of competition and environment. In *At the Heart of the Union. Studies of the European Commission*, ed. N. Nugent. London: Macmillan, pp. 71–88.

Clegg, N. and van Hulten, M. 2003. *Reforming the European Parliament.* London: Foreign Policy Centre.

Lord Cockfield, A. 1992. The real significance of 1992. In *The Politics of 1992: Beyond the European Single Market*, ed. C. Crouch and D. Marquand. Oxford: Oxford University Press.

Coen, D. and Thatcher, M. 2000. Utility reform in Europe. *Current Politics and Economics of Europe* **9**, special issue.

Coleman, W. D. and Tangermann, S. 1999. The 1992 CAP reform, the Uruguay round and the Commission. *Journal of Common Market Studies* **37**: 385–405.

Commission of the EC. 1985a. *Completing the Internal Market.* Brussels: CEC.

1985b. *Technical Harmonization and Standards: a New Approach.* Brussels: CEC.

1994a. *Green Paper on the Liberalisation of Telecommunications Infrastructure and Cable Television Networks.* Brussels: CEC.

1994b. *Report to the European Council on the Application of the Subsidiarity Principle.* Brussels: CEC.

1996a. *Public Procurement in the European Union: Exploring the Way Forward.* Brussels: CEC.

1996b. *Taxation in the European Union – Report on the Development of Tax Systems.* Brussels: CEC.

1997. *Third Report on the Implementation of the Telecommunications Regulatory Package.* Brussels: CEC.

1998. *Fourth Report on the Implementation of the Telecommunications Regulatory Package.* Brussels: CEC.

1999a. *The 1999 Communications Review: Towards a New Framework for Electronic Communications Infrastructure and Associated Services.* Brussels: CEC.

1999b. *Fifth Report on the Implementation of the Telecommunications Regulatory Package.* Brussels: CEC.

1999c. *White Paper on Modernisation of the Rules Implementing Articles 85 and 86 of the EC Treaty.* Brussels: CEC.

2000a. *Communication from the Commission to the Council and the European Parliament: Application of the Precautionary Principle and Multiannual Arrangements for Setting TACS.* Brussels: CEC.

2000b. *The Results of the Public Consultation on the 1999 Communications Review and Orientations for the New Regulatory Framework.* Brussels: CEC.

2001a. *The Future of the Common Fisheries Policy.* Brussels: CEC.

2001b. *Seventh Report on the Implementation of the Telecommunications Regulatory Package.* Brussels: CEC.

2002. *Eighth Report on the Implementation of the Telecommunications Regulatory Package.* Brussels: CEC.

2003. *Ninth Report on the Implementation of the Telecommunications Regulatory Package.* Brussels: CEC.

2004. *A Report on the Functioning of Public Procurement Markets in the EU: Benefits from the Application of EU Directives and Challenges for the Future.* Brussels: CEC.

Cook, R. D. and Weisberg, S. 1983. Diagnostics for heteroscedasticity in regression. *Biometrika* **70**: 1–10.

Coombes, D. 1970. *Politics and Bureaucracy in the European Community – a Portrait of the European Commission.* London: George Allen and Unwin.

Corbett, R., Jacobs, F. and Shackleton, M. 1995. *The European Parliament.* Edinburgh: Catermill.

Cram, L. 1993. Calling the tune without paying the piper? Social policy regulation: the role of the Commission in European Community social policy. *Policy and Politics* **21**: 135–46.

1994. The European Commission as a multi-organization: social policy and it policy in the EU. *Journal of European Public Policy* **1**: 195–217.

1997. *Policy-Making in the EU: Conceptual Lenses and the Integration Process.* London: Routledge.

Crombez, C. 1996. Legislative procedures in the European Community. *British Journal of Political Science* **26**: 199–228.

1997a. The co-decision procedure in the European Union. *Legislative Studies Quarterly* **22**: 97–119.

1997b. Policy making and Commission appointment in the European Union. *Aussenwirtschaft* **52**: 63–82.

2001. The Treaty of Amsterdam and the codecision procedure. In *The Rules of Integration: Institutionalist Approaches to the Study of Europe*, ed. M. Aspinwall and G. Schneider. Manchester: Manchester University Press, pp. 101–22.

2003. The democratic deficit in the European Union: much ado about nothing? *European Union Politics* **4**: 101–20.

Crombez, C., Steunenberg, B. and Corbett, R. 2000. Understanding the EU legislative process: political scientists' and practitioners' perspectives. *European Union Politics* 1: 363–81.

Crozier, M., Huntington, S. P. and Watanuk, J. 1975. *The Crisis of Democracy*. New York: New York University Press.

Davidson, R. and MacKinnon, J. G. 1981. Several tests for model specification in the presence of alternative hypotheses. *Econometrica* 49: 781–93.

de Figueiredo, R. J. P., Jr, Spiller, P. T. and Urbiztondo, S. 1999. An informational perspective on administrative procedures. *Journal of Law, Economics, and Organization* 15: 283–305.

Dehejia, V. H. and Genschel, P. 1999. Tax competition in the European Union. *Politics and Society* 27: 403–30.

Dehousse, R. 2003. Comitology: who watches the watchmen? *Journal of European Public Policy* 10: 798–813.

Demmke, C., Eberharter, E., Schaefer, G. F. and Türk, A. 1996. The history of comitology. In *Shaping European Law and Policy: the Role of Committees and Comitology in the Political Process*, ed. R. H. Pedler and G. F. Schaefer. Maastricht: European Institute of Public Administration, pp. 61–82.

Dimitrakopoulos, D. 2001. Learning and steering: changing implementation patterns and the Greek central government. *Journal of European Public Policy* 8: 604–22.

Dimitrova, A. and Steunenberg, B. 2000. The search for convergence of national policies in the European Union. An impossible quest? *European Union Politics* 1: 201–26.

Dion, D. 1998. Evidence and inference in the comparative case study. *Comparative Politics* 30: 127–45.

Docksey, C. and Williams, K. 1994. The Commission and the execution of Community policy. In *The European Commission*, ed. G. Edwards and D. Spence. Harlow: Longman, pp. 117–45.

Dogan, R. 1997. Comitology: little procedures with big implications. *West European Politics* 20: 31–60.

Doleys, T. J. 2000. Member states and the European Commission: theoretical insights from the new economics of organizations. *Journal of European Public Policy* 7: 532–53.

Donnelly, M. 1993. The structure of the European Commission and the policy formation process. In *Lobbying in the European Community*, ed. S. Mazey and J. Richardson. Oxford: Oxford University Press, pp. 74–81.

Downs, G. W., Rocke, D. M. and Barsoom, P. N. 1996. Is the good news about compliance good news about cooperation? *International Organization* 50: 379–406.

Dunleavy, P. 1985. Bureaucrats, budgets and the growth of the state: reconstructing an instrumental model. *British Journal of Political Science* 15: 299–328.

Earnshaw, D. and Judge, D. 1993. The European Parliament and the sweetners directive: from footnote to inter-institutional conflict. *Journal of Common Market Studies* 31: 103–16.

1996. From co-operation to co-decision. The European Parliament's path to legislative power. In *European Union. Power and Policy-Making*, ed. J. Richardson. London: Routledge, pp. 96–126.

1997. The life and time of the co-operation procedure. *Journal of Common Market Studies* **35**: 543–64.

Edwards, G. and Spence, D., eds. 1994. *The European Commission*. Harlow: Longman.

Egan, M. 1998. Regulatory strategies, delegation and European market integration. *Journal of European Public Policy* **5**: 485–506.

Eichener, V. 1997. Effective European problem-solving: lessons from the regulation of occupational safety and environmental protection. *Journal of European Public Policy* **4**: 591–608.

Eising, R. 2002. Policy learning in embedded negotiations: explaining EU electricity liberalization. *International Organization* **56**: 85–120.

Elgström, O., Bjurulf, B., Johansson, J. and Sannerstedt, A. 2001. Coalitions in European Union negotiations. *Scandinavian Political Studies* **24**: 111–28.

Epstein, D. and O'Halloran, S. 1994. Administrative procedures, information, and agency discretion. *American Journal of Political Science* **38**: 697–722.

1995. A theory of strategic oversight: Congress, lobbyists, and the bureaucracy. *Journal of Law, Economics and Organization* **11**: 227–55.

1999a. Asymmetric information, delegation, and the structure of policy-making. *Journal of Theoretical Politics* **11**: 37–56.

1999b. *Delegating Powers: a Transaction Cost Politics Approach to Policy Making under Separate Powers*. Cambridge: Cambridge University Press.

2006. A theory of efficient delegation. In *Delegation in Contemporary Democracies*, ed. D. Braun and F. Gilardi. London: Routledge, pp. 77–98.

Esser, J. and Noppe, R. 1996. Private muddling through as a political programme? The role of the European Commission in the telecommunications sector in the 1980s. *West European Politics* **19**: 547–62.

Esteban, J. and Ray, D. 1999. Conflict and distribution. *Journal of Economic Theory* **87**: 379–415.

Euro Info Centre Aarhus County. 1996. *Analysis of Irregularities Occurring in Tender Notices Published in the Official Journal of the European Communities 1990–1993*. Aarhus.

European Parliament. 1998. *Report on the Proposal for a Council Decision Laying Down the Procedures for the Exercise of Implementing Powers Conferred Upon the Commission (Com(98)0380)*. Brussels: European Parliament.

Faas, T. 2003. To defect or not to defect? National, institutional and party group pressures on MEPs and their consequences for party group cohesion in the European Parliament. *European Journal of Political Research* **42**: 841–66.

Falkner, G. 1999. European social policy: towards multi-level and multi-actor governance. In *The Transformation of Governance in the European Union*, ed. B. Kohler-Koch and R. Eising. London: Routledge.

Fiorina, M. P. 1977. *Congress: the Keystone of the Washington Establishment*. New Haven, CT: Yale University Press.

1982. Legislative choice of regulatory forms: legal process or administrative process? *Public Choice* **39**: 33–71.

Franchino, F. 2000a. The Commission's executive discretion, information and comitology. *Journal of Theoretical Politics* **12**: 155–81.

2000b. Control of the Commission's executive functions: uncertainty, conflict and decision rules. *European Union Politics* **1**: 59–88.

2000c. Statutory discretion and procedural control of the European Commission's executive functions. *Journal of Legislative Studies* 6: 28–50.

2001. Delegation and constraints in the national execution of the EC policies: a longitudinal and qualitative analysis. *West European Politics* 24: 169–92.

2002. Efficiency or credibility? Testing the two logics of delegation to the European Commission. *Journal of European Public Policy* 9: 677–94.

2004. Delegating powers in the European Community. *British Journal of Political Science* 34: 449–76.

2005. A formal model of delegation in the European Union. *Journal of Theoretical Politics* 17: 217–47.

Franchino, F. and Rahming, A. J. 2003. Biased ministers, inefficiency, and control in distributive policies: an application to the EU fisheries policy. *European Union Politics* 4: 11–36.

Franzese, R. J., Jr. 2002. *Macroeconomic Policies in Developed Democracies.* Cambridge: Cambridge University Press.

Fuchs, G. 1994. Policy-making in a system of multi-level governance – the Commission of the European Community and the restructuring of the telecommunications sector. *Journal of European Public Policy* 1: 177–94.

Gabel, M. and Hix, S. 2002. Defining the EU political space: an empirical study of the European election manifestos, 1979–1999. *Comparative Political Studies* 35: 934–64.

Gabel, M. J. and Huber, J. D. 2000. Putting parties in their place: inferring party left–right ideological positions from party manifestos data. *American Journal of Political Science* 44: 94–103.

Gallagher, M. Laver, M. and Mair, P. 2001. *Representative Government in Modern Europe.* London: McGraw-Hill.

Garrett, G. 1992. International cooperation and institutional choice: the European Community's internal market. *International Organization* 46: 533–60.

1995. From the Luxembourg compromise to codecision: decision making in the European Union. *Electoral Studies* 14: 289–308.

Garrett, G. and Tsebelis, G. 1996. An institutional critique of intergovernmentalism. *International Organization* 50: 269–99.

Garrett, G. and Weingast, B. R. 1993. Ideas, interests, and institutions: constructing the European Community's internal market. In *Ideas and Foreign Policy. Beliefs, Institutions, and Political Change,* ed. J. Goldstein and R. O. Keohane. Ithaca: Cornell University Press, pp. 173–206.

Gatsios, K. and Seabright, P. 1989. Regulation in the European Community. *Oxford Review of Economic Policy* 5: 37–60.

Genschel, P. 2002. *Steuerharmonisierung und Steuerwettbewerb in der Europäischen Union.* Frankfurt: Campus.

George, A. L. and Bennett, A. 2004. *Case Studies and Theory Development.* Cambridge, MA: MIT Press.

Gerring, J. 2004. What is a case study and what is it good for? *American Political Science Review* 98: 341–54.

Gilligan, T. and Krehbiel, K. 1989. Asymmetric information and legislative rules with a heterogeneous committee. *American Journal of Political Science* 33: 459–90.

1990. Organization of informative committees by a rational legislature. *American Journal of Political Science* **34**: 531–64.

Gillingham, J. 2003. *European Integration, 1950–2003: Superstate or New Market Economy?* Cambridge: Cambridge University Press.

Giuliani, M. 2003. Europeanization in comparative perspective: institutional fit and national adaptation. In *The Politics of Europeanization*, ed. K. Featherstone and C. Radaelli. Oxford: Oxford University Press, pp. 134–55.

Golden, M. A. 2003. Electoral connections: the effects of the personal vote on political patronage, bureaucracy and legislation in postwar Italy. *British Journal of Political Science* **33**: 189–212.

Golub, J. 1999. In the shadow of the vote? Decision making in the European Community. *International Organization* **53**: 733–64.

2000. Institutional reform and decisionmaking in the European Union. *PSA Conference*, 10–13 April. London: London School of Economics.

Gomà, R. 1996. The social dimension of the European Union: a new type of welfare system? *Journal of European Public Policy* **3**: 209–30.

Gorsuch, R. L. 1983. *Factor Analysis*. Hillsdale, NJ: Lawrence Erlbaum.

Gorvin, B., ed. 1998. *The Transformation of Contemporary Conservatism*. Beverly Hills, CA: Sage.

Grant, W. 1997. *The Common Agricultural Policy*. London: Macmillan.

Greene, W. 1997. *Econometric Analysis*. New York: Macmillan.

Guay, T. R. 1997. The European Union, expansion of policy-making, and defense industrial policy. *Journal of European Public Policy* **4**: 404–21.

Haas, E. B. 1958. *The Uniting of Europe: Political, Social and Economic Forces, 1950–57*. London: Stevens & Sons.

1964. Technocracy, pluralism and the new Europe. In *A New Europe?*, ed. S. Richards Graubard. Boston, MA: Houghton Mifflin.

Haas, P. M. 1998. Compliance with EU directives: insights from international relations and comparative politics. *Journal of European Public Policy* **5**: 17–37.

Haibach, G. 2000. The history of comitology. In *Delegated Legislation and the Role of Committees in the EC*, ed. M. Andenas and A. Türk. Boston, MA: Kluwer Law International.

Hall, M. 1992. Behind the European Works Council Directive: the European Commission's legislative strategy. *British Journal of Industrial Relations* **30**: 547–66.

Hall, P. 1983. Policy innovation and the structure of the state: the politics–administration nexus in Britain and France. *Annals* **466**: 43–59.

Hallerberg, M. and von Hagen, J. 1999. Electoral institutions, cabinet negotiations, and budget deficits within the European Union. In *Fiscal Institutions and Fiscal Performance*, ed. J. Poterba and von Hagen, J., Chigaco, IL: Chicago University Press, pp. 209–32.

Hammond, T. H. and Knott, J. H. 1996. Who controls the bureaucracy?: presidential power, congressional dominance, legal constraints, and bureaucratic autonomy in a model of multi-institutional policy-making. *Journal of Law, Economics and Organization* **12**: 119–66.

Hammond, T., Hill, J. and Miller, G. 1986. Presidential appointment of bureau chiefs and the 'congressional control of administration' hypothesis. *Annual Meeting of the American Political Science Association*, Washington, DC.

Harcourt, A. J. 1998. EU media ownership regulation: conflict over the definitions of alternatives. *Journal of Common Market Studies* **36**: 369–89.

Haverland, M. 2000. National adaptation to European integration: the importance of institutional veto points. *Journal of Public Policy* **20**: 83–103.

Hawes, M. and Lawrence Broz, J. 2003. *Domestic Politics of International Monetary Fund Policy*. San Diego, CA: University of California.

Hayes-Renshaw, F. and Wallace, H. 1997. *The Council of Ministers*. London: Macmillan.

Heclo, H. 1974. *Modern Social Politics in Britain and Sweden*. New Haven, CT: Yale University Press.

Heller, W. B. 2001. Making policy stick: why the government gets what it wants in multiparty parliaments. *American Journal of Political Science* **45**: 780–98.

Héritier, A. 1995. "Leaders" and "laggards" in European clean air policy. In *Convergence or Diversity: Internationalization and Economic Policy Response*, ed. B. Unger and F. van Waarden. Aldershot: Avebury, pp. 278–306.

1996. The accommodation of diversity in European policy-making and its outcomes: regulatory policy as a patchwork. *Journal of European Public Policy* **3**: 149–67.

1997. Policy-making by subterfuge: interest accommodation, innovation and substitute democratic legitimation in Europe – perspectives from distinctive policy areas. *Journal of European Public Policy* **4**: 171–89.

1999. *Policy-making and Diversity in Europe: Escaping Deadlock*. New York: Cambridge University Press.

Héritier, A., Kerwer, D., Knill, C., *et al.*, eds. 2001. *Differential Europe: New Opportunities and Restrictions for Member-State Policies*. Lanham, MD: Rowman & Littlefield.

Hix, S. 1999. Dimensions and alignments in European Union politics: cognitive constraints and partisan responses. *European Journal of Political Research* **35**: 69–106.

2000. Parliamentary oversight of executive power: what role for the European Parliament in comitology? In *Europe in Change – Committee Governance in the European Union*, ed. T. Christiansen and E. Kirchner. Manchester: Manchester University Press.

2001. Legislative behaviour and party competition in the European Parliament: an application of nominate to the EU. *Journal of Common Market Studies* **39**: 663–88.

2002a. Constitutional agenda-setting through discretion in rule interpretation: why the European Parliament won at Amsterdam. *British Journal of Political Science* **32**: 259–80.

2002b. Parliamentary behavior with two principals: preferences, parties, and voting in the European Parliament. *American Journal of Political Science* **46**: 688–9.

2004. Electoral institutions and legislative behavior: explaining voting-defection in the European Parliament. *World Politics* **56**: 194–223.

2005. *The Political System of the European Union*. London: Macmillan.
Hix, S. and Gabel, M. 2002. The European parliament and executive politics in the EU: voting behaviour and the Commission president investiture procedure. In *Institutional Challenges in the European Union*, ed. M. Hosli, A. Van Deeman and M. Widgren. London: Routledge, pp. 22–47.
Hix, S. Kreppel, A. and Noury, A. 2003. The party system in the European Parliament: collusive or competitive? *Journal of Common Market Studies* 41: 309–31.
Hix, S. and Lord, C. 1995. The making of a president: the European Parliament and the confirmation of Jacques Santer as President of the Commission. *Government and Opposition* 31: 62–76.
1997. *Political Parties in the European Union*. London: Macmillan.
Hix, S., Noury, A. and Roland, G. 2002. A "normal" Parliament? Party cohesion and competition in the European Parliament, 1979–2001. *EPRG Working Paper* 39.
2005. Power to the parties: cohesion and competition in the European Parliament, 1979–2001. *British Journal of Political Science* 35: 209–34.
Hix, S., Raunio, T. and Scully, R. 2003. Fifty years on: research on the European Parliament. *Journal of Common Market Studies* 41: 191–202.
Hoffmann, S. 1966. Obstinate or obsolete? The fate of the nation-state and the case of Western Europe. *Daedalus* 95: 862–915.
Hooghe, L. 1997. A house with differing views: the European Commission and cohesion policy. In *At the Heart of the Union. Studies of the European Commission*, ed. N. Nugent. London: Macmillan, pp. 72–108.
1999a. Images of Europe: orientations to European integration among senior officials of the Commission. *British Journal of Political Science* 29: 345–67.
1999b. Supranational activists or intergovernmental agents? Explaining the orientations of senior Commission officials toward European integration. *Comparative Political Studies* 32: 435–63.
2000. Euro-socialists or Euro-marketeers? EU top officials on capitalism. *Journal of Politics* 62: 430–54.
2001. *The European Commission and the Integration of Europe*. Cambridge: Cambridge University Press.
ed. 1996. *Cohesion Policy and European Integration: Building Multi-Level Governance*. Oxford: Clarendon Press.
Hooghe, L. and Keating, M. 1994. The Politics of European Union Regional Policy. *Journal of European Public Policy* 1: 367–93.
Hooghe, L. and Marks, G. 2000. *European Integration and Multi-level Governance*. Boulder, CO: Rowman & Littlefield.
Hooghe, L., Marks, G. and Wilson, C. J. 2002. Does left/right structure party positions on European integration? *Comparative Political Studies* 35: 965–89.
Hopenhayn, H. and Lohmann, S. 1996. Fire-alarm signals and the political oversight of regulatory agencies. *Journal of Law, Economics and Organization* 12: 196–213.
Horn, M. J. 1995. *The Political Economy of Public Administration*. New York: Cambridge University Press.

Horn, M. J. and Shepsle, K. A. 1989. Administrative process and organizational form as legislative responses to agency costs. *Virginia Law Review* 75: 499–508.

Hoyland, B. K. 2005. Government and opposition in the European Union. London: London School of Economics and Political Science.

Huber, J. D. 1996. The vote of confidence in parliamentary democracies. *American Political Science Review* 90: 269–82.

   1998. How does cabinet instability affect political performance? Portfolio volatility and health care cost containment in parliamentary democracies. *American Political Science Review* 92: 577–91.

Huber, J. D. and Inglehart, R. 1995. Expert interpretations of party space and party locations in 42 societies. *Party Politics* 1: 73–111.

Huber, J. D. and Lupia, A. 2001. Cabinet instability and delegation in parliamentary democracies. *American Journal of Political Science* 45: 18–33.

Huber, J. D. and McCarty, N. 2001. Cabinet decision rules and political uncertainty in parliamentary bargaining. *American Political Science Review* 95: 345–60.

   2004. Bureaucratic capacity, delegation, and political reform. *American Political Science Review* 98: 481–94.

   2006. Bureaucratic capacity and legislative performance. In *The Macropolitics of Congress*, ed. E. S. Adler and J. Lapinski. Ithaca, NY: Cornell University Press, pp. 50–78.

Huber, J. D. and Shipan, C. R. 2002. *Deliberate Discretion? The Institutional Foundations of Bureaucratic Autonomy*. Cambridge: Cambridge University Press.

Huber, J. D., Shipan, C. R. and Pfahler, M. 2001. Legislatures and statutory control of bureaucracy. *American Journal of Political Science* 45: 330–45.

Hubschmid, C. and Moser, P. 1997. The co-operation procedure in the EU: why was the European Parliament influential in the decision on car emission standards? *Journal of Common Market Studies* 35: 225–42.

Hug, S. 2003. Endogenous preferences and delegation in the European Union. *Comparative Political Studies* 36: 41–74.

Hug, S. and König, T. 2002. In view of ratification: governmental preferences and domestic constraints at the Amsterdam Intergovernmental Conference. *International Organization* 56: 447–76.

ICES. 2000. *Report on the Assessment of Demersal Stocks in the North Sea and Skagerrak*. Copenhagen: ICES.

   2001. *Report of the Working Group on the Assessment of Southern Shelf Demersal Stocks*. Copenhagen: ICES.

Institut für Europäische Politik. 1989. *"Comitology": Characteristics, Performance, and Options*. Preliminary Final Report. Bonn: Institut für Europäische Politik.

Jabko, N. 1999. In the name of the market: how the European Commission paved the way for monetary union. *Journal of European Public Policy* 6: 475–95.

Jensen, M. C. and Meckling, W. H. 1976. Theory of the firm: managerial behavior, agency costs and ownership structure. *Journal of Financial Economics* 3: 303–60.

Joerges, C. and Neyer, J. 1997a. From intergovernmental bargaining to deliberative political process: the constitutionalisation of comitology. *European Law Journal* **3**: 273–99.

1997b. Transforming strategic interaction into deliberative problem-solving: European comitology in the foodstuffs sector. *Journal of European Public Policy* **4**: 609–25.

Judge, D. and Earnshaw, D. 1994. Weak European Parliament influence? A study of the environmental committee of the European Parliament. *Government and Opposition* **29**: 262–76.

Judge, D., Earnshaw, D. and Cowan, N. 1994. Ripples or waves: the European Parliament in the European Community policy process. *Journal of European Public Policy* **1**: 27–52.

Jun, Hae-Won. 2003a. Catching the runaway bureaucracy in Brussels. *European Union Politics* **4**: 421–45.

2003b. Initiatives and amendments: Euro-parliamentarians' preferences on the Commission's discretion. *Annual Meeting of the American Political Science Association*, August 21–31, Philadelphia, PA.

Jupille, J. 2004. *Procedural Politics: Issues, Interests, and Institutional Choice in the European Union*. Cambridge: Cambridge University Press.

Kalyvas, S. N. 1996. *The Rise of Christian Democracy in Europe*. Ithaca, NY: Cornell University Press.

Kasack, C. 2004. The legislative impact of the European Parliament under the revised co-decision procedure: environmental, public health and consumer protection policies. *European Union Politics* **5**: 241–60.

Kassim, H. and Menon, A. 2003. The principal-agent approach and the study of the European Union: promise unfulfilled? *Journal of European Public Policy* **10**: 121–39.

Kaufman, H. 1956. Emerging conflicts in the doctrines of public administration. *American Political Science Review* **50**: 1057–73.

Keefer, P. and Stasavage, D. 2003. The limits of delegation: veto players, central bank independence, and the credibility of monetary policy. *American Political Science Review* **97**: 407–23.

Kelemen, R. D. 1995. Environmental policy in the European Union: the struggle between Court, Commission and Council. In *Convergence or Diversity: Internationalization and Economic Policy Response*, ed. B. Unger and F. van Waarden. Aldershot: Avebury.

2002. The politics of "Eurocratic" structure and the new European agencies. *West European Politics* **25**: 93–118.

2003. The structure and dynamics of EU federalism. *Comparative Political Studies* **36**: 184–208.

2004. *The Rules of Federalism: Institutions and Regulatory Politics in the EU and Beyond*. Cambridge, MA: Harvard University Press.

Keohane, R. O. 1984. *After Hegemony: Cooperation and Discord in the World Political Economy*. Princeton, NJ: Princeton University Press.

Kiewiet, D. R. and McCubbins, M. D. 1991. *The Logic of Delegation. Congressional Parties and the Appropriations Process*. Chicago, IL: University of Chicago Press.

King, A. 1975. Overload: the problem of governing in the 1970s. *Political Studies* **23**: 284–96.

King, G., Keohane, R. O. and Verba, S. 1994. *Designing Social Inquiry: Scientific Inference in Qualitative Research*. Princeton, NJ: Princeton University Press.

King, G., Tomz, M. and Wittenberg, J. 2000. Making the most of statistical analyses: improving interpretation and presentation. *American Journal of Political Science* **44**: 341–55.

Kirchner, E. J., ed. 1988. *Liberal Parties in Western Europe*. Cambridge: Cambridge University Press.

Kitschelt, H. P. 1994. *The Transformation of European Social Democracy*. Cambridge University Press: Cambridge.

Knill, C. 1998. European policies: the impact of national administrative traditions. *Journal of Public Policy* **18**: 1–28.

2001. *The Europeanisation of National Administrations*. Cambridge: Cambridge University Press.

Knill, C. and Lenschow, A. 1998. Coping with Europe: the impact of British and German administrations on the implementation of EU environmental policy. *Journal of European Public Policy* **5**: 595–614.

Kohler-Koch, B. and Eising, R., eds. 1999. *The Transformation of Governance in the European Union*. London: Routledge.

König, T. 2001. Principals, agents and the process of European legislation. *ECPR Joint Sessions of Workshops*, Grenoble.

König, T. and Pöter, M. 2001. Examining the EU legislative process: the relative importance of agenda and veto power. *European Union Politics* **2**: 329–51.

Krehbiel, K. 1991. *Information and Legislative Organization*. Ann Arbor, MI: University of Michigan.

Kreppel, A. 1999. What affects the European Parliament's legislative influence? An analysis of the success of EP amendments. *Journal of Common Market Studies* **37**: 521–38.

2000. Rules, ideology and coalition formation in the European Parliament. *European Union Politics* **1**: 340–62.

2002a. *The European Parliament and Supranational Party System*. Cambridge: Cambridge University Press.

2002b. Moving beyond procedure: an empirical analysis of European Parliament legislative influence. *Comparative Political Studies* **35**: 784–813.

Kreppel, A. and Hix, S. 2003. From grand coalition to left–right confrontation: explaining the shifting structure of party competition in the European Parliament. *Comparative Political Studies* **36**: 75–96.

Kreppel, A. and Tsebelis, G. 1999. Coalition formation in the European Parliament. *Comparative Political Studies* **32**: 933–66.

Krislov, S., Ehlermann, C.-D. and Weiler, J. 1986. The political organs and the decision-making process in the United States and the European Community. In *Integration through Law*, ed. M. Cappelletti, M. Seccombe and J. Weiler. Berlin: De Gruyter, pp. 3–110.

Kydland, F. and Prescott, E. C. 1977. Rules rather than discretion: the inconsistency of optimal plans. *Journal of Political Economy* **85**: 137–60.

Laffan, B. and Shackleton, M. 2000. The budget. In *Policy-Making in the European Union*, ed. H. Wallace and W. Wallace. Oxford: Oxford University Press, pp. 211–41.

Laffont, J.-J., ed. 2003. *The Principal Agent Model: the Economic Theory of Incentives*. Cheltenham: Edward Elgar.

Laffont, J.-J. and Martimort, D. 2002. *The Theory of Incentives: the Principal-Agent Model*. Princeton, NJ: Princeton University Press.

Lampinen, R. and Uusikylä, P. 1998. Implementation deficit – why member states do not comply with EU directives. *Scandinavian Political Studies* 21: 231–51.

LaPalombara, J. 1958. Political party systems and crisis government: French and Italian comparisons. *Midwest Journal of Political Science* 2: 117–42.

Laver, M., ed. 2001. *Estimating the Policy Positions of Political Actors*. London: Routledge.

Laver, M., Benoit, K. and Garry, J. 2003. Extracting policy positions from political texts using words as data. *American Political Science Review* 97: 311–31.

Laver, M. and Garry, J. 2000. Estimating policy positions from political texts. *American Journal of Political Science* 44: 619–34.

Laver, M. and Hunt, W. B. 1992. *Policy and Party Competition*. London: Routledge.

Laver, M. and Shepsle, K. A., eds. 1994. *Cabinet Ministers and Parliamentary Government*. New York: Cambridge University Press.

eds. 1996. *Making and Breaking Governments: Cabinets and Legislatures in Parliamentary Democracies*. Cambridge: Cambridge University Press.

Lenaerts, K. 1991. Some reflections on the separation of powers in the European Community. *Common Market Law Review* 28: 11–35.

Lequesne, C. 2000. The common fisheries policy. Letting the little ones go? In *Policy-Making in the European Union*, ed. H. Wallace and W. Wallace. Oxford: Oxford University Press, pp. 345–72.

Levi-Faur, D. 1999. The governance of competition: the interplay of technology, economics, and politics in European Union electricity and telecom regimes. *Journal of Public Policy* 19: 175–207.

Lijphart, A. 1971. Comparative politics and the comparative method. *American Political Science Review* 65: 682–93.

1975. The comparable-cases strategy in comparative research. *Comparative Political Studies* 8: 158–77.

Lindberg, L. N. 1963. *The Political Dynamics of European Economic Integration*. Stanford: Stanford University Press.

Lohmann, S. and O'Halloran, S. 1994. Divided government and US trade policy: theory and evidence. *International Organization* 48: 595–632.

Lumio, M. and Sinigaglia, L. C. 2003. *Statistics in Focus: Telecommunications in Europe*. Brussels: Eurostat.

Lupia, A. and McCubbins, M. D. 1994a. Designing bureaucratic accountability. *Law and Contemporary Problems* 57: 91–126.

1994b. Learning from oversight: fire alarms and police patrols reconstructed. *Journal of Law, Economics and Organization* 10: 96–125.

MacMullen, A. 1997. European Commissioners, 1952–95: national routes to a European elite. In *At the Heart of the Union. Studies of the European Commission*, ed. N. Nugent. London: Macmillan, pp. 27–48.

2000. European Commissioners, 1952–99: national routes to a European elite. In *At the Heart of the Union. Studies of the European Commission*, ed. N. Nugent. London: Macmillan, pp. 27–48.

Majone, G. 1992. Market integration and regulation: Europe after 1992. *Metroeconomica* 43: 131–56.

1993. The European Community between social policy and social regulation. *Journal of Common Market Studies* 31: 153–70.

1994. The rise of the regulatory state in Europe. *West European Politics* 17: 77–101.

1996. *Regulating Europe*. London: Routledge.

2000. The credibility crisis of Community regulation. *Journal of Common Market Studies* 38: 273–302.

2001. Two logics of delegation: agency and fiduciary relations in EU governance. *European Union Politics* 2: 103–22.

2002. The European Commission: the limits of centralisation, the perils of parliamentarisation. *Governance* 15: 375–92.

Mamadouh, V. and Raunio, T. 2003. The committee system: powers, appointments and report allocation. *Journal of Common Market Studies* 41: 333–51.

Marks, G. 1992. Structural policy in the European Community. In *Euro-Politics: Institutions and Policymaking in the "New" European Community*, ed. A. M. Sbragia. Washington, DC: The Brookings Institution, pp. 191–224.

Marks, G. and Steenbergen, M. R., eds. 2004. *European Integration and Political Conflict*. Cambridge: Cambridge University Press.

Marks, G. and Wilson, C. J. 2000. The past in the present: a cleavage theory of party response to European integration. *British Journal of Political Science* 30: 433–59.

Marks, G., Wilson, C. J. and Ray, L. 2002. National political parties and European integration. *American Journal of Political Science* 46: 585–94.

Marsh, J. 1997. The common agricultural policy. In *New Challenges to the European Union: Policies and Policy-Making*, ed. S. Stavridis, E. Mossialos, R. Morgan and H. Machin. Aldershot: Darthmouth, pp. 401–37.

Marsh, M. 1998. Testing the second-order election model after four European elections. *British Journal of Political Science* 28: 591–607.

Martin, L. L. 2003. *Distribution, Information, and Delegation to International Organizations: the Case of IMF Conditionality*. Mimeo, Cambridge, MA: University of Harvard.

Mashaw, J. L. 1985. Prodelegation: why administrators should make political decisions. *Journal of Law, Economics and Organization* 1: 81–100.

Mastenbroek, E. 2003. Surviving the deadline: the transposition of EC directives in the Netherlands. *European Union Politics* 4: 371–95.

Mattila, M. 2004. Contested decisions: empirical analysis of voting in the European Union Council of Ministers. *European Journal of Political Research* 43: 29–50.

Mattila, M. and Lane, J.-E. 2001. Why unanimity in the Council? A roll call analysis of Council voting. *European Union Politics* 2: 31–53.

Maurer, A. 2003. The legislative powers and impact of the European Parliament. *Journal of Common Market Studies* 41: 227–47.

Mawson, J., Martins, M. R. and Gibney, J. T. 1985. The development of the European Community regional policy. In *Regions in the European Community*, ed. M. Keating and B. Jones. Oxford: Clarendon Press, pp. 20–59.

Mayhew, D. R. 1991. *Divided We Govern: Party Control, Lawmaking, and Investigations, 1946–1990*. New Haven, CT: Yale University Press.

Mazey, S. 1995. The development of EU equality policies: bureaucratic expansion on behalf of women?" *Public Administration* 73: 591–609.

Mbaye, H. A. D. 2001. Why national states comply with supranational law: explaining implementation infringements in the European Union. *European Union Politics* 2: 259–81.

McCormick, J. P. 2001. Machiavellian democracy: controlling elites with ferocious populism. *American Political Science Review* 95: 297–313.

McCubbins, M. D. 1985. The legislative design of regulatory structure. *American Journal of Political Science* 29: 721–48.

McCubbins, M. D., Noll, R. G. and Weingast, B. R. 1987. Administrative procedures as instruments of political control. *Journal of Law, Economics, and Organization* 3: 243–77.

1989. Structure and process, politics and policy: administrative arrangements and the political control of agencies. *Virginia Law Review* 75: 431–82.

McCubbins, M. D. and Page, T. 1987. A theory of congressional delegation. In *Congress: Structure and Policy*, ed. M. D. McCubbins and T. Sullivan. Cambridge: Cambridge University Press, pp. 409–25.

McCubbins, M. D. and Schwartz, T. 1984. Congressional oversight overlooked: police patrols versus fire alarms. *American Journal of Political Science* 28: 165–79.

McGowan, L. and Wilks, S. 1995. The first supranational policy in the European Union: competition policy. *European Journal of Political Research* 28: 141–69.

McKeown, T. 1999. Case studies and the statistical world view. *International Organization* 53: 161–90.

Meckstroth, T. W. 1975. "Most different systems" and "most similar systems": a study in the logic of comparative inquiry. *Comparative Political Studies* 8: 132–57.

Meerts, P. W. and Cede, F. 2004. *Negotiating European Union*. London: Palgrave.

Mendrinou, M. 1996. Non-compliance and the European Commission's role in integration. *Journal of European Public Policy* 3: 1–22.

Meunier, S. 2000. What single voice? European institutions and EU–US trade negotiations. *International Organization* 54: 103–35.

Meunier, S. and Nicolaïdis, K. 1999. Who speaks for Europe? The delegation of trade authority in the EU. *Journal of Common Market Studies* 37: 477–501.

Mitchell, R. B. 1994. *International Oil Pollution at Sea: Environmental Policy and Treaty Compliance*. Cambridge, MA: MIT Press.

Mitrany, D. 1966. *A Working Peace System: an Argument for the Functional Development of International Organization*. Chicago, IL: Quadrangle.

Moe, T. M. 1985. Control and feedback in economic regulation. *American Political Science Review* **79**: 1094–116.

1987. An assessment of the positive theory of congressional dominance. *Legislative Studies Quarterly* **12**: 475–520.

1989. The politics of bureaucratic structure. In *Can Government Govern?*, ed. J. Chubb and P. Peterson. Washington, DC: The Brookings Institutions, pp. 267–329.

1990a. Political institutions: the neglected side of the story. *Journal of Law, Economics and Organisation* **6**: 213–53.

1990b. The politics of structural choice: toward a theory of public bureaucracy. In *Organization Theory: From Chester Barnard to the Present and Beyond*, ed. O. E. Williamson. Oxford: Oxford University Press, pp. 11–153.

Montanari, I. J. 1995. Harmonization of social policies and social regulation in the European Community. *European Journal of Political Research* **27**: 21–45.

Moravcsik, A. 1991. Negotiating the single European act: national interests and conventional statecraft in the European community. *International Organization* **45**: 19–56.

1998. *The Choice for Europe: Social Purpose and State Power from Messina to Maastricht.* Ithaca, NY: Cornell University Press.

1999. A new statecraft? Supranational entrepreneurs and international cooperation. *International Organization* **53**: 267–306.

Morton, R. B. 1999. *Methods and Models: a Guide to the Empirical Analysis of Formal Models in Political Science.* Cambridge: Cambridge University Press.

Moser, P. 1997. A theory of the conditional influence of the European Parliament in the cooperation procedure. *Public Choice* **91**: 333–50.

Müller, W. C. and Strøm, K, eds. 2000. *Coalition Governments in Western Europe.* Oxford: Oxford University Press.

Müller-Rommel, F., ed. 1989. *New Politics in Western Europe: the Rise and Success of Green Parties.* Boulder, CO: Westview Press.

Nielson, D. L. and Tierney, M. J. 2003. Delegation to international organizations: agency theory and World Bank environmental reform. *International Organization* **57**: 241–76.

Niskanen, W. A. 1971. *Bureaucracy and Representative Government.* New York: Aldine-Atherton.

Noel, E. 1973. The Commission's power of initiative. *Common Market Law Review* **10**: 123–5.

Noury, A. G. 2002. Ideology, nationality, and Euro-parliamentarians. *European Union Politics* **3**: 33–58.

Nugent, N. 1995. The leadership capacity of the European Commission. *Journal of European Public Policy* **2**: 603–23.

ed. 2000. *At the Heart of the Union. Studies of the European Commission.* London: Macmillan.

2001. *The European Commission.* New York: Palgrave.

2002. *The Government and Politics of the European Union.* London: Macmillan.

OECD. Government procurement: a synthesis report. Paris: OECD, 2001.

Offe, C. 1972. Political authority and class structures: an analysis of late capitalist societies. *International Journal of Sociology* 2: 73–108.

Olivi, B. 1993. *L'europa Difficile: Storia Politica della Comunità Europea*. Bologna: Mulino.

Ostrom, C. W. J. R. 1990. *Time Series Analysis: Regression Techniques*. London: Sage.

Padgett, S. and Paterson, W. E. 1991. *A History of Social Democracy in Postwar Europe*. London: Longman.

Page, E. 1997. *People Who Run Europe*. Oxford: Oxford University Press.

Page, E. C. and Dimitrakopoulos, D. 1997. The dynamic of EU growth: a cross-time analysis. *Journal of Theoretical Politics* 9: 365–87.

Page, E. C. and Wouters, L. 1994. Bureaucratic politics and political leadership in Brussels. *Public Administration* 72: 445–59.

Pahre, R. 2005. Formal theory and case-study methods in EU studies. *European Union Politics* 6: 113–45.

Pajala, A. and Widgrén, M. 2004. A priori versus empirical voting power in the EU Council of Ministers. *European Union Politics* 5: 73–97.

Patterson, L. A. 1997. Agricultural policy reform in the European Community: a three-level game analysis. *International Organization* 51: 135–65.

Pedler, R. H. and Schaefer, G. F., eds. 1996. *Shaping European Law and Policy. The Role of Committees and Comitology in the Political Process*. Maastricht: European Institute of Public Administration.

Pelkmans, J. and Winters, L. A. 1988. *Europe's Domestic Market*. London: Royal Institute of International Affairs.

Pennings, P. 2002. The dimentionality of the EU policy space: the European elections of 1999. *European Union Politics* 3: 59–80.

Peterson, J. 2001. The college of commissioners. In *The Institutions of the European Union*, ed. J. Peterson and M. Shackleton. Oxford: Oxford University Press, pp. 71–94.

Peterson, J. and Shackleton, M., eds. 2001. *The Institutions of the European Union*. Oxford: Oxford University Press.

Pierson, P. and Leibfried, S. 1996. Multitiered institutions and the making of social policy. In *European Social Policy*, ed. S. Leibfried and P. Pierson. Washington, DC: Brookings.

Pollack, M. A. 1994. Creeping competence: the expanding agenda of the European Community. *Journal of Public Policy* 14: 95–145.

1995. Regional actors in an intergovernmental play: the making and implementation of EC structural policy. In *The State of the Union. Building a European Polity?*, ed. C. Rhodes and S. Mazey. Harlow, UK: Longman, pp. 361–90.

1997a. The Commission as an agent. In *At the Heart of the Union. Studies of the European Commission*, ed. N. Nugent. London: Macmillan, pp. 109–28.

1997b. Delegation, agency, and agenda setting in the European Community. *International Organization* 51: 99–134.

1998. The engines of integration? Supranational autonomy and influence in the European Union. In *European Integration and Supranational Governance*, ed. W. Sandholtz and A. Stone Sweet. New York: Oxford University Press, pp. 217–49.

2000. The end of creeping competence? EU policy-making since Maastricht. *Journal of Common Market Studies* **38**: 519–38.

2001. International relations theory and European integration. *Journal of Common Market Studies* **39**: 221–44.

2002. Learning from the Americanists (again): theory and method in the study of delegation. *West European Politics* **25**: 200–19.

2003a. Control mechanism or deliberative democracy?: two images of comitology. *Comparative Political Studies* **36**: 125–55.

2003b. *The Engines of European Integration: Delegation, Agency, and Agenda Setting in the EU*. Oxford: Oxford University Press.

Predieri, A. 1963. La produzione legislativa. In *Il Parlamento Italiano 1946–1963*, ed. S. Somogyi, L. Lotti, A. Predieri and G. Sartori. Naples: Edizioni Scientifiche Italiane, pp. 205–76.

Przeworski, A. and Teune, H. 1970. *The Logic of Comparative Social Inquiry*. Malabar, FL: Robert E. Krieger Publishing.

Puchala, D. J. 1999. Institutionalism, intergovernmentalism and European integration: a review article. *Journal of Common Market Studies* **37**: 317–31.

Putman, R. D. 1975. The political attitudes of senior civil servants in Britain, Germany and Italy. In *The Mandarins of Western Europe*, ed. M. Dogan. New York: Sage, pp. 87–127.

Quanjel, M. and Wolters, M. 1993. Growing cohesion in the European Parliament. *Joint Sessions of the European Consortium for Political Research*, Leiden.

Ragin, C. C. 1987. *The Comparative Method: Moving Beyond Qualitative and Quantitative Strategies*. Berkeley, CA: University of California.

Ragin, C. C. and Becker, S. H., eds. 1992. *What is a Case? Exploring the Foundations of Social Inquiry*. Cambridge: Cambridge University Press.

Ramsey, J. 1969. Tests for specification errors in classic linear least squares regression analysis. *Journal of the Royal Statistical Society* B **31**: 350–71.

Raunio, T. 1996. Parliamentary questions in the European Parliament: representation, information and control. *Journal of Legislative Studies* **2**: 356–82.

Ray, L. 1999. Measuring party orientations towards European integration: results from an expert survey. *European Journal of Political Research* **36**: 283–306.

Reif, K. 1984. National election cycles and European elections, 1979 and 1984. *Electoral Studies* **3**: 244–55.

1997. Reflections: European elections as member state second-order elections revisited. *European Journal of Political Research* **31**: 115–24.

Reif, K. and Schmitt, H. 1980. Nine second-order national elections – a conceptual framework for the analysis of European election results. *European Journal of Political Research* **8**: 3–44.

Rieger, E. 1995. Protective shelter or straitjacket: an institutional analysis of the common agricultural policy of the European Union. In *European Social Policy: Between Fragmentation and Integration*, ed. S. Leibfried and P. Pierson. Washington, DC: Brookings Institution, pp. 194–230.

Rittberger, B. 2000. Impatient legislators and new issue-dimensions: a critique of the Garrett–Tsebelis "standard version" of legislative politics. *Journal of European Public Policy* **7**: 554–75.

Ross, G. 1995a. Assessing the Delors era in social policy. In *European Social Policy: Between Fragmentation and Integration*, ed. S. Leibfried and P. Pierson. Washington, DC: Brookings Institution, pp. 357–88.

1995b. *Jacques Delors and European Integration*. Oxford: Oxford University Press.

Ross, S. 1973. The economic theory of agency: the principal's problem. *American Economic Review* **63**: 134–9.

Sandholtz, W. 1992. *High-Tech Europe: the Politics of International Cooperation*. Berkeley, CA: University of California Press.

1993a. Choosing union: monetary politics and Maastricht. *International Organization* **47**: 1–39.

1993b. Institutions and collective action: the new telecommunications in Western Europe. *World Politics* **45**: 242–70.

1998. The emergence of a supranational telecommunication regime. In *European Integration and Supranational Governance*, ed. W. Sandholtz and A. Stone Sweet. New York: Oxford University Press, pp. 134–63.

Sandholtz, W. and Stone Sweet, A., eds. 1998. *European Integration and Supranational Governance*. New York: Oxford University Press.

Sandholtz, W. and Zysman, J. 1989. 1992: recasting the European bargain. *World Politics* **42**: 95–128.

Sbragia, A. 1996. Environmental policy: the "push–pull" of policy making. In *Policy-Making in the European Union*, ed. H. Wallace and W. Wallace. Oxford: Oxford University Press, pp. 235–55.

Scharpf, F. W. 1996. Negative and positive integration in the political economy of European welfare states. In *Governance in the European Union*, ed. G. Marks, F. W. Scharpf, P. C. Schmitter and W. Streeck. London: Sage, pp. 15–39.

Scheinmann, L. 1966. Some preliminary notes on bureaucratic relationships in the European Economic Community. *International Organization* **20**: 750–73.

Schmidt, S. K. 1996. Sterile debates and dubious generalisations: European integration theory tested by telecommunications and electricity. *Journal of Public Policy* **16**: 233–71.

1998. Commission activism: subsuming telecommunications and electricity under competition law. *Journal of European Public Policy* **5**: 169–84.

2000. Only an agenda setter? The European Commission's power over the Council of Ministers. *European Union Politics* **1**: 37–61.

Schneider, G. and Baltz, K. 2005. Domesticated Eurocrats: bureaucratic discretion in the legislative pre-negotiations of the European Union. *Acta Politica* **40**: 1–27.

Schneider, G., Baltz, K. and Finke, D. 2004. Paying the piper, calling the tune: interest intermediation in the pre-negotiations of EU legislation. *Pan-European Conference on International Relations*, The Hague, The Netherlands, September 9–11.

Schneider, G. and Cederman, L.-E. 1994. The change of tide in political cooperation: a limited information model of European integration. *International Organization* **48**: 633–62.

Schneider, G., Finke, D. and Bailer, S. 2004. Bargaining power in the European Union: an evaluation of competing game-theoretic models. *International Studies Association*, Montreal, Canada, March 17–20.

Schneider, V. and Werle, R. 1990. International regime or corporate actor? The European Community in telecommunications policy. In *The Political Economy of Telecommunications*, ed. K. Dyson and P. Humphreys. London: Routledge.

Schulz, H. and König, T. 2000. Institutional reform and decision-making efficiency in the European Union. *American Journal of Political Science* 44: 653–66.

Scully, R. M. 1997a. The European Parliament and the co-decision procedure: a reassessment. *Journal of Legislative Studies* 3: 58–73.

1997b. The European Parliament and the co-decision procedure: a rejoinder to Tsebelis and Garrett. *Journal of Legislative Studies* 3: 93–103.

1997c. Policy influence and participation in the European Parliament. *Legislative Studies Quarterly* 22: 233–52.

Selck, T. J. 2004. On the dimensionality of European Union legislative decision-making. *Journal of Theoretical Politics* 16: 203.

Selck, T. J. and Steunenberg, B. 2004. Between power and luck: the European Parliament in the EU legislative process. *European Union Politics* 5: 25–46.

Shipan, C. R. 2004. Regulatory regimes, agency actions, and the conditional nature of congressional influence. *American Political Science Review* 98: 467–80.

Sidjanski, D. 1965. Some remarks on Siotis' article. *Journal of Common Market Studies* 3: 47–61.

Siedentop, L. 2000. *Democracy in Europe*. London: Allen Lane.

Siedentopf, H. and Ziller, J., eds. 1988. *Making European Policies Work: the Implementation of Community Legislation*. London: Sage.

Siotis, J. 1964. Some problems of European secretariats. *Journal of Common Market Studies* 2: 223–50.

Skinner, Q. 1981. *Past Masters: Machiavelli*. New York: Hill and Wang.

1993. The Republican ideal of political liberty. In *Machiavelli and Republicanism*, ed. G. Bock, Q. Skinner and M. Viroli. Cambridge: Cambridge University Press, pp. 293–309.

Smith, A. 2002. Why European commissioners matter. *Journal of Common Market Studies* 41: 37–55.

Smith, M. P. 1996. Integration in small steps: the European Commission and member-state aid to industry. *West European Politics* 19: 563–82.

1998. Autonomy by the rules: the European Commission and the development of state aid policy. *Journal of Common Market Studies* 36: 55–78.

Spence, A. M. and Zeckhauser, R. J. 1971. Insurance, information and individual action. *American Economic Review* 61: 380–7.

Spence, D. 1994. Staff and personnel policy in the Commission. In *The European Commission*, ed. G. Edwards and D. Spence. Harlow: Longman, pp. 62–94.

Spence, D. B. 1999a. Agency discretion and the dynamics of procedural reform. *Public Administration Review* 59: 425–42.

1999b. Managing delegation *ex ante*: using law to steer administrative agencies. *Journal of Legal Studies* 28: 413–59.

Spinelli, A. 1966. *The Eurocrats: Conflict and Crisis in the European Community.* Baltimore, MD: Johns Hopkins University Press.

1986. Federalism and the EUT. In *European Union: the European Community in Search of a Future,* ed. J. Lodge. New York: St. Martin's Press.

Stetter, S. 2000. Regulating migration: authority delegation in justice and home affairs. *Journal of European Public Policy* 7: 80–103.

Steunenberg, B. 1994. Decision making under different institutional arrangements: legislation by the European Community. *Journal of Institutional and Theoretical Economics* 150: 642–69.

1996. Agency discretion, regulatory policymaking, and different institutional arrangements. *Public Choice* 86: 309–39.

1997. Co-decision and its reform. In *Political Institutions and Public Policy. Perspectives on European Decision Making,* ed. B. Steunenberg and F. van Vught. Dordrecht: Kluwer, pp. 205–29.

Steunenberg, B., Koboldt, C. and Schmidtchen, D. 1996a. Beyond comitology: a comparative analysis of implementation procedures with parliamentary involvement. *Aussenwirtshaft* 52: 87–112.

1996b. Policymaking, comitology, and the balance of power in the European Union. *International Review of Law and Economics* 16: 329–44.

Stevens, A. and Stevens, H. 2001. *Brussels Bureaucrats?* New York: Palgrave.

Stone Sweet, A., Fligstein, N. and Sandholtz. W., eds. 2001. *The Institutionalization of Europe.* Oxford: Oxford University Press.

Strauss, E. 1961. *The Ruling Servants: Bureaucracy in Russia, France – and Britain?* London: Allen & Unwin.

Streeck, W. 1996. Neo-voluntarism: a new European social policy regime? In *Governance in the European Union,* ed. G. Marks, F. W. Scharpf, P. C. Schmitter and W. Streeck. London: Sage, pp. 64–94.

Swank, D. 2003. *Global Capital, Political Institutions, and Policy Change in Developed Welfare States.* Cambridge: Cambridge University Press.

Swinbank, A. 1989. The common agricultural policy and the politics of European decision making. *Journal of Common Market Studies* 27: 303–22.

Tallberg, J. 2002a. Delegation to supranational institutions: why, how and with what consequences? *West European Politics* 25: 23–46.

2002b. Paths to compliance: enforcement, management, and the European Union. *International Organization* 56: 609–43.

2003. *European Governance and Supranational Institutions: Making States Comply.* London: Routledge.

Tarditi, S., Thomson, K., Pierani, P. and Croci-Angelini, E., eds. 1989. *Agricultural Trade Liberalisation and the European Community.* Oxford: Clarendon Press.

Taylor, P. 1983. *The Limits of European Integration.* New York: Columbia University Press.

Thatcher, M. 2001. The Commission and national governments as partners: EC regulatory expansion in telecommunications 1979–2000. *Journal of European Public Policy* 8: 558–84.

Thies, M. F. 2001. Keeping tabs on partners: the logic of delegation in coalition governments. *American Journal of Political Science* 45: 580–98.

Thomassen, J. and Schmitt, H. 1999. Partisan structures in the European Parliament. In *The European Parliament, the National Parliaments and European Integration*, ed. R. S. Katz and B. Wessels. Oxford: Oxford University Press, pp. 129–48.

Thompson, A. and Haftel, Y. 2003. Theorizing and operationalizing IO independence. *Annual Convention of International Studies Association*, 25 February–March 1, Portland, OR.

Thomson, R., Boerefijn, J. and Stokman, F. 2004. Actor alignments in European Union decision making. *European Journal of Political Research* 43: 237–61.

Thomson, R., Stokman, F., Achen, C. and König, T., eds., 2006. *The European Union Decides*. Cambridge: Cambridge University Press.

Tomz, M., Wittenberg, J. and King, G. 2003. Clarify: Software for interpreting and presenting statistical results. Version 2.1. Stanford University, University of Wisconsin and Harvard University. Available at http://gking.harvard.edu/.

Tsebelis, G. 1994. The power of the European Parliament as a conditional agenda setter. *American Political Science Review* 88: 128–42.

1995. Decision making in political systems: veto players in presidentialism, parliamentarism, multicameralism and multipartyism. *British Journal of Political Science* 25: 289–325.

1997. Maastricht and the democratic deficit. *Aussenwirtshaft* 52: 29–56.

1999. Veto players and law production in parliamentary democracies: an empirical analysis. *American Political Science Review* 93: 591–608.

2002. *Veto Players: How Political Institutions Work*. Princeton, NJ: Princeton University Press.

Tsebelis, G. and Garrett, G. 1997. Agenda setting, vetoes and the European Union's co-decision procedure. *Journal of Legislative Studies* 3: 74–92.

2000. Legislative politics in the European Union. *European Union Politics* 1: 9–36.

2001. The institutional foundations of intergovernmentalism and supranationalism in the European Union. *International Organization* 55: 357–90.

Tsebelis, G., Jensen, C. B., Kalandrakis, A. and Kreppel, A. 2001. Legislative procedures in the European Union: an empirical analysis. *British Journal of Political Science* 31: 573–99.

Tsebelis, G. and Kalandrakis, A. 1999. The European Parliament and environmental legislation: the case of chemicals. *European Journal of Political Research* 36: 119–54.

Tsebelis, G. and Kreppel, A. 1998. The history of conditional agenda-setting in European institutions. *European Journal of Political Research* 33: 41–71.

van der Eijk, C. and Franklin, M., eds. 1996. *Choosing Europe? The European Electorate and National Politics in the Face of the Union*. Ann Arbor, MI: University of Michigan Press.

Van Kersbergen, K. 1995. *Social Capitalism*. London: Routledge.

Vaubel, R. 1994. The public choice analysis of European integration: a survey. *European Journal of Political Economy* 10: 227–49.

Volden, C. 2002a. Delegating powers to bureaucracies: evidence from the states. *Journal of Law, Economics and Organization* 18: 187–220.

2002b. A formal model of the politics of delegation in a separation of powers system. *American Journal of Political Science* **46**: 111–33.

Vos, E. 1997. The rise of committees. *European Law Journal* **3**: 210–29.

1999. *Institutional Frameworks of Community Health and Safety Legislation. Committees, Agencies and Private Bodies.* Oxford: Hart.

Wallace, H. and Wallace, W., eds. 2000. *Policy-making in the European Union.* Oxford: Oxford University Press.

Weale, A. 1996. Environmental rules and rule-making in the European Union. *Journal of European Public Policy* **3**: 594–611.

Weale, A., Pridham, G., Cini, M. *et al.* 2003. *Environmental Governance in Europe: an ever Closer Ecological Union?* Oxford: Oxford University Press.

Weatherill, S. and Beaumont, P. 1995. *EC Law. The Essential Guide to the Legal Workings of the European Community.* London: Penguin Books.

Weingast, B. R. and Moran, M. J. 1983. Bureaucratic discretion or congressional control? Regulatory policymaking by the Federal Trade Commission. *Journal of Political Economy* **91**: 756–800.

Wendon, B. 1998. The Commission as image-venue entrepreneur in EU social policy. *Journal of European Public Policy* **5**: 339–53.

Wessels, W. 1998. Comitology: fusion in action. Politico-administrative trends in the EU system. *Journal of European Public Policy* **5**: 209–34.

Westlake, M. 1999. *The Council of the European Union.* London: John Harper Publishing.

Whitaker, R. 2005. National parties in the European Parliament: an influence in the committee system? *European Union Politics* **6**: 5–28.

Wilks, S. 2005. Agency escape: decentralization or dominance of the European Commission in the modernization of competition policy? *Governance* **18**: 431–52.

Woldendorp, J., Keman, H. and Budge, I. 1998. Party government in 20 democracies: an update (1990–1995). *European Journal of Political Research* **33**: 125–64.

2000. *Party Government in 48 Democracies, 1945–1998.* London: Kluwer.

Wood, B. D. 1988. Principals, bureaucrats, and responsiveness in clear air enforcement. *American Political Science Review* **82**: 213–34.

Wood, B. D. and Waterman, R. W. 1991. The dynamics of political control of the bureaucracy. *American Political Science Review* **85**: 801–28.

Wright, V. 1978. *The Government and Politics of France.* London: Hutchinson.

Yondorf, W. 1965. Monnet and the action committee: the formative period of the European Communities. *International Organization* **19**: 885–912.

Zimmer, C., Schneider, G. and Dobbins, M. 2005. The contested Council: the conflict dimensions of an intergovernmental institution. *Political Studies* **53**: 403–22.

Index